SUPERVISION

A REDEFINITION

SIXTH EDITION

Thomas J. Sergiovanni
Trinity University

Robert J. Starratt
Boston College

McGraw
Hill

Boston, Massachusetts   Burr Ridge, Illinois   Dubuque, Iowa
Madison, Wisconsin   New York, New York   San Francisco, California
St. Louis, Missouri

MCGRAW-HILL
A DIVISION OF THE **MCGRAW-HILL** COMPANIES

SUPERVISION A REDEFINITION, SIXTH EDITION

This book is printed on acid-free paper.

2 3 4 5 6 7 8 9 0   DOC   DOC   9 0 9 8

ISBN 0-07-057891-5

Sponsoring editor: Beth Kaufman
Marketing manager: Dan Loch
Project manager: Marilyn M. Sulzer
Production supervisor: Sandy Ludovissy
Full service project supervision: The Total Book
Design manager: Joan O'Connor
Cover design: Carla Bauer
Compositor: ComCom
Typeface: 10/12 Palatino
Printer: R. R. Donnelley & Sons

Library of Congress Cataloging-in-Publication Data

Sergiovanni, Thomas J.
    Supervision : a redefinition / Thomas J. Sergiovanni, Robert J.
Starratt.—6th ed.
        p.   cm.
    Includes bibliographical references and index.
    ISBN 0-07-057891-5 (alk. paper)
    1. School supervision—United States. 2. School management and
organization—United States. 3. School personnel management—United
States. I. Starratt, Robert J. II. Title.
LB2806.4.S47 1998
371.2'03'0973—dc21   97-12511

www.mhhe.com

ABOUT
THE AUTHORS

THOMAS J. SERGIOVANNI is presently Lillian Radford Professor of Education and Senior Fellow, Center for Educational Leadership at Trinity University and founding director of the Trinity Principals' Center. He received his Masters degree from Teachers College, Columbia University and Ed.D. from the University of Rochester, in educational administration. An active teacher, writer, and editor, he brings to the text his extensive experience teaching and writing about educational administration and supervision. His recent books include: *Moral Leadership, The Principalship, Building Community in Schools,* and *Leadership for the Schoolhouse.*

ROBERT J. STARRATT is Professor and Program Director in Educational Administration at the School of Education of Boston College. He received his Masters degree in Philosophy from Boston College, his Masters degree in Education from Harvard University, and his Doctor of Education degree from the University of Illinois, specializing in administration and curriculum theory. He has written extensively about educational leadership and the process of change. His recent books include: *The Drama of Schooling/The Schooling of Drama, The Drama of Leadership, Building an Ethical School, and Transforming Educational Administration.*

CONTENTS

PREFACE

COMPLETING a book used to have a certain finality to it. One could place it in a prominent part of one's library and get on with other projects. If an author wished to change a position taken in that book in a subsequent publication, it was an easy matter of a footnote reference. This book, however, has refused to be finished.

Despite numerous changes as the book evolved over the first four editions, the underlying theory had remained the same. That was not the case with the fifth edition and this edition. Expectations and assumptions about schools have changed so significantly that schooling is now being reinvented. This reinvention includes new understandings about school structures, time frames, accountability, professionalism, teaching and learning, leadership, and sources of authority for what is done. In such a dramatically altered context, supervision itself has to be redefined. This redefinition includes not only new ways to do old things but a change in the theory itself which underlies supervisory thought and practice.

The first edition focused on "human perspectives in supervision, linking human concerns which emerged from research on organizational dynamics with human concerns as found in instructional and curriculum literature." In that first edition we asserted, "Humanizing education, with its focus on self-actualization of youngsters, can be achieved only in a humanizing organization which focuses on the self-actualization of teachers and other educational professionals." The second edition unfolded similarly, giving attention to the supervisor's human concerns in organizational leadership, educational leadership, and instructional leadership. The theme of human resource development, articulated in the second edition, was carried forward in more sophisticated and expansive treatments in the third and fourth editions. We introduced more of our own thinking in the fourth edition, adding analogies such as mindscapes, clockworks, and teaching as surfing to categories such as reflective practice. Likewise, we proposed our own theory of leadership and added a chapter on a relatively new concern, supervision as moral action.

The first edition appeared under the title, *Emerging Patterns of Supervision: Human Perspectives.* Editions two through four appeared as *Supervision: Human Perspectives.* The title for the fifth and sixth editions, *Supervision: A Redefinition,* signals a new emphasis. This redefinition includes the disconnection of supervision from hierarchical roles and a focus on community as the primary metaphor for schooling. Supervision is viewed here as a more democratic and professional process, involving multiple skills that are equally available to teachers and administrators who have the word "supervisor" in their title or job description. The new supervision embraces peer clinical supervision, mentoring, action research, collective work on teaching platforms, program evaluation, group discussions of specific translations of school mission statements, and other configurations of teachers as colleagues working together to increase their understanding of their practice. In a similar vein, staff development and supervision are now joined in such a way that they are often indistinguishable.

Earlier editions included bureaucratic authority, the personal authority of the supervisor, and technical-rational authority as equally legitimate grounds for what was done in schools. This edition places professional and moral authority as the driving force behind what teachers should do and how the process of supervision should unfold. Teachers and supervisors are not viewed primarily as independent decision makers who calculate individually the costs and benefits of their actions, but rather as members of an educating community who respond to shared norms and values. Both teachers and supervisors are seen as capable and willing to sacrifice self-interest for shared ideals; these ideals are viewed as intrinsic to the definition of teaching as a profession. Furthermore, commitments to these ideals become moral commitments; their neglect is a moral perversion of the profession. In the fifth and sixth editions professionalism itself is redefined from something that has to do primarily with enhanced competence and expert authority to something that has to do with virtue as well. The virtuous side of this equation is understood as a powerful source of authority for what teachers do and should do. Together, professional and moral authority hold a promise of promoting self-governing and self-managing teachers who in turn make traditional conceptions of supervision obsolete.

Supervision often is defined by criteria extrinsic to the moral qualities of teaching and learning. For us supervision takes its moral character from its close involvement with the intrinsic moral qualities of teaching and learning. That is to say, teaching by its very nature assumes a caring for the one taught and a respect for the integrity of what is being taught and its connection to the past, present, and future life of the community. Not to care for the person being taught, or to distort the meaning of what is being taught, violates the very idea of teaching. Supervision is an activity that involves another in supporting and furthering that caring for the learner and respect for the significance of what is taught. The moral authority of the supervisor is joined with the moral authority of the teacher.

In the fifth edition the metaphor for schooling itself was changed from organization to community as a way to express the new context for supervision. The sixth edition continues to explore and redefine this new context proposing that for supervision to count in today's schools its emphasis and meaning must continue to change. Though we continue to emphasize the skills and practical applications of such traditional supervisory processes as in-class supervision, enhancing reflection about teaching and learning, teacher evaluation, and staff development, these activities are recontextualized and substantially altered. In schools as learning communities rather than organizations, these activities are more than technical components of an efficient organization. They imply deeper, professional and moral concerns at work. In the new supervision, moreover, responsibility for these functions is no longer the exclusive domain of principals, supervisors, and others positioned within the school hierarchy. Instead, they embrace a common set of concepts and skills that are shared by everyone involved in the process of improving schooling. The supervisor's role remains important but is understood differently. She or he emerges as an advocate, developer, and linking pin in relationship to the teacher's efforts to improve the process of teaching and learning.

Finally, the new supervision is seen not as a separate function removed from the dynamics of institutional reinvention that is going on in schools, but as a necessary element of such dynamics. In earlier editions, we portrayed supervision as a relatively self-contained activity, dealing with the improvement of an individual teacher's instructional activities. Because of the importance of a supervision of what schools are supposed to be, those exercising supervisory responsibilities are in a unique position to nurture, develop, and articulate the community's vision of what a learning community can and should be. Hence, supervision is also redefined as an essential process within the complex and continuous dynamic of reinventing schools.

Thomas J. Sergiovanni
Robert J. Starratt

SUPERVISION
A REDEFINITION

PART ONE

PERSPECTIVES FOR SUPERVISION

CHAPTER 1

IMAGES OF SUPERVISION

INTRODUCTION: THE NATURE OF SUPERVISION

IN editions one and two published in the 1970s we characterized supervision in schools as being largely ritualistic. Supervisors continued to be hired and university courses continued to be offered in the subject, but much of what took place under the name of supervision seemed not to matter very much. A good deal of the supervisor's time was spent on administrative matters. Teacher-evaluation systems tended to be perfunctory. Overall a certain complacency characterized the role and function of supervision.

The third edition published in 1984 noted that a mild renaissance of interest in supervision and supervisory activities was in the making. At the national level the Association for Supervision and Curriculum Development had begun to place stronger emphasis on supervision. The literature in the field was expanding and improving in quality. For classroom supervision, clinical strategies and artistic strategies began to emerge and to compete successfully with more traditional checklist approaches to teacher evaluation. At least this was the case in the literature and at academic conferences if not in actual practice. Publications focusing on problems and issues in supervision increased in popularity, becoming among the most popular offered by the Association for Supervision and Curriculum Development. Supervisory topics were appearing more frequently on the programs of this organization's national conference and series of National Curriculum Study Institutes. The founding of the Conference of Professors of Instructional Supervision in 1976 was evidence that scholars studying problems of supervision were increasing in numbers, interested in identifying themselves and in establishing better communication networks and developing more systematic approaches to research and development.

As the fourth edition of this book appeared in 1988 supervision was becoming the "in thing" in American schooling. What previously was a mild renaissance had turned into a revolution. Supervision began to rank high on the agendas of both state policymakers and local school administrators. Many states, for example, began to mandate increases in supervision and evaluation of teachers. These mandates ranged from required "training" in the techniques of supervision and evaluation for principals and supervisors to the provision of comprehensive and standardized state systems of supervision and evaluation. Many of these systems were based on a body of research associated with the teaching effectiveness and school effectiveness movements. This research noted that "effective schools" were characterized by principals and other supervisors who exercised strong instructional leadership. It noted further that one best way to teach could be identified, provided for, and evaluated.

Instructional leadership became the hot topic in thousands of seminars and workshops provided for administrators and supervisors by states, professional associations, local school districts, and individual entrepreneurs. Some states even went so far as to mandate that all principals and supervisors go through state-approved and state-sponsored instructional leadership training programs as a condition of their continued employment and as part of a licensing system to certify them as teacher evaluators.

The academic side of the professional educational community experienced a similar flurry of interest in supervision. In 1985 the Association for Supervision and Curriculum Development established *the Journal of Curriculum and Supervision.* Scholarly articles on supervision and evaluation began to appear more frequently in such established publications as *Curriculum Inquiry* and *Educational Evaluation and Policy Analysis.* The *Journal of Personnel Evaluation in Education* was established in 1986. The prestigious American Educational Research Association established a special-interest group in instructional supervision in 1983. This marked the beginning of a concentrated and continuous appearance of sessions devoted to supervision at the annual meeting of this association.

Since the appearance of the fifth edition of this book in 1993 the emphasis in supervision has shifted from evaluating teachers to promoting teacher development and building professional community among teachers. Further, the characterization of principals and other supervisors as instructional leaders has given way to supervisors as developers and leaders of leaders. In this new configuration teachers assume more of the responsibility for providing instructional leadership.

All of this places supervision at a critical point in its evolution. It is clear that supervision is emerging as a key role and function in the operation of schools. At issue, however, is the form and substance of this new emergence and interest, how its influence will be felt by teachers, and what its effects will be on teaching and learning. Will this "new supervision," for example, provide support for teachers and enhance their roles as key professional decision makers in the practice of teaching and learning? Or will this new supervision result in increased regulation and control of teachers and teaching? If the latter, what are the consequences of supervision for teacher professionalism and for teaching and learning? Will attempts to share traditional supervisory roles, functions, and responsibilities with teachers, to advance teacher leadership, and to promote collegial patterns of supervision that emphasize reflective conversation and shared inquiry result in broad teacher empowerment that leads to professional community? Or will attempts to share traditional roles, supervisory functions, and responsibilities with teachers lead to the development of a new hierarchy that benefits some teachers but not most? The increased importance attributed to supervision then and now is attractive. But whether this new emphasis will develop into promises fulfilled or promises broken will depend, we believe, on the form that supervision takes.

THEORIES OF PRACTICE

Supervisors and teachers typically do not characterize their work as being informed by theory. Instead they talk about their practices in the classroom, their hunches about what succeeds, the principles that they can derive from these hunches, and the new insights and ideas that evolve from this very practical view of their work. What at first glance seems not to be theoretical turns out to be quite theoretical. In fact, it is very difficult to engage in teaching or supervisory practice without being theoretical. Much of the theory that guides professional practice, however, is implicit and informal.

Van Miller, one of the pioneers in administrative theory, often spoke of the practical art of using theory. He noted that it was difficult to administer and supervise in schools without using theory.[1] Practices typically do not lead to other practices without some help. When practice does lead to practice directly, the relationship can be depicted as follows:

$$practices \rightarrow practice$$

This is a monkey see, monkey do operation. Practices are rooted in custom. When something new is proposed, teachers and supervisors ask, Where else is it being done? and How does one do it?

Very few practices evolve simply from other practices. Instead professionals think about what they are doing and form hunches. The relationship between hunch and practice can be depicted as follows:

$$practices \rightarrow hunch \rightarrow practices$$

---

[1]This discussion of practices, hunches, theories, and principles follows closely Van Miller, "The Practical Art of Using Theory," *The School Executive,* vol. 70, no. 1 (1958), pp. 60–63.

Hunches, however, do not just appear. They are shaped by insights derived from one's broader experience with events and activities similar to the problem under consideration as well as one's assumptions and beliefs. Insights, assumptions, and beliefs comprise informal and implicit theories. As supervisors and teachers work, they think about their practice and develop hunches that guide subsequent practices. With experience, hunches become more established and codified into formal and informal operating procedures. Practice based on operating principles is more advanced than practice based on hunches.

The relationship among hunches, principles, and practice can be depicted as follows:

$$\text{practices} \rightarrow \text{hunches} \rightarrow \text{principles} \rightarrow \text{practices}$$

Here experience is used to select the most appropriate hunch. This use represents a degree of codification that results in the development of operating principles to guide subsequent professional practice.

Operating principles stand and fall on the basis of trial and error. Furthermore principles become more elegant as hunches become more refined. Readings, interactions with other professionals, and practical experience in assessing operating principles provide the basis for the development of theories of practice. When theories of practice emerge to connect hunches and principles, professional behavior is more deliberate. Supervisors and teachers are more conscious of the theoretical basis of their practice, can articulate this basis, and can continuously revise this theory of practice as a result of their actual practice. How theory fits into this chain of events is depicted as follows:

$$\text{practices} \rightarrow \text{hunches} \rightarrow \text{theories of practice} \rightarrow \text{principles} \rightarrow \text{practices}$$

With theory, the professional can reach a new step in professional decision making and practice. Theory can provide the professional with a surer view of the situation, serve as a guide to the selection of principles, and provide a basis for evolving improved practices in light of improvements in one's theoretical outlook.

In sum, rarely does teaching or supervisory practice emerge from other practices. Instead, hunches are at play and operating principles emerge as theories of practice that provide a more rational basis for what one does. Typically, hunches and operating principles are implicit, and when they are explicit they are not thought about systematically. The question for most supervisors and teachers, then, is not whether they are being theoretical but what are the theories (the implicit hunches and operating principles) that help shape the way they see their professional worlds and provide the basis for professional decisions and practice.

IMAGES OF SUPERVISION

Different theories of supervision and teaching compete with each other for the attention of professionals. Present supervisory practices in schools, for example, are largely based on one or a combination of four general views. Which of the four theories best matches the hunches and operating principles that govern the way you think about teaching and supervision and are likely to provide the basis for your behavior as a supervisor?

One way in which these implicit theories can be made explicit is by evaluating the decisions that you make or the ways in which you size up supervisory situations. For example, place yourself in the role of school supervisor in Metro City. A year ago another school in Metro City was selected by the superintendent and central office staff to become a model school. This school was to incorporate a new educational system featuring explicit goals and teaching objectives across grade levels and a highly structured and tightly paced curriculum linked to the objectives. The curriculum included new textbooks and workbooks for all the major subject areas as well as carefully thought out assignments and activities designed to provide students with needed practice. Daily and weekly lesson plans were provided to make things easier for teachers and to ensure that students received the same instruction and assignments. Criterion-referenced weekly, 6-week, and semester tests were included in the package. The system provided as well for test scores to be evaluated by grade level and by each class within grade level every 6 weeks to monitor student progress. Teachers were formed into quality-control committees or quality circles to discuss the scores and in instances of low scores to come up with ways in which the system might be better implemented. The administration was particularly proud of this quality-circle concept, for it wanted teacher participation.

The administration felt that teachers needed only to become familiar with the materials and that by following directions carefully and relying on their own ingenuity in presenting instruction they would teach successfully. An incentive system was also introduced. Teachers were trained in methods of teaching that reflected the then popular teaching effectiveness research. An evaluation system employing observation checklists that were based on this research was used to evaluate their performance. Teachers scoring the highest received cash bonuses.

To help things along, the principal received extensive training in the new curriculum and in staff supervision and evaluation. Further, a new supervisor who had a thorough understanding of the new curriculum, the testing procedures, the daily and weekly lesson plans, the needed teaching to make things work, and the evaluation system was assigned to the school. Both principal and supervisor provided instructional leadership by monitoring teaching carefully to ensure compliance with the new system and by providing help to teachers who were having difficulty in complying.

Prior to the beginning of the school year teachers were provided with a carefully planned and implemented weeklong training program, receiving a week's salary for their participation. Schools ran on a half-day schedule for the first week, thus allowing additional training and debugging. The training seemed to be successful, for by the end of September teachers appeared to develop an acceptable level of understanding and competence in using the system. The central office had high hopes for the success of this new initiative and saw it as a model for export to other schools in the district.

Before the introduction of the new educational system the teachers and principal of this school enjoyed a reputation for being a closely knit faculty with high morale. This situation began to change shortly after the new system was introduced. Teachers begin to complain. They did not like the new curriculum, feeling that frequently it did not fit what they thought was important to teach. They complained of pressure from the tests. They found themselves teaching lessons and adopting teaching strategies that they did not like. They expressed displeasure too with the overall climate in the school, describing it as increasingly impersonal with respect to students and competitive with respect to colleagues. Discontent among teachers grew as the semester continued. Things really began to sour when it became apparent that student performance did not measure up to the high expectations of the administration. The administration was puzzled as to why such a well thought out and carefully implemented educational system was not working in this school. Shortly after the spring break the principal became disillusioned enough to request a transfer. The supervisor was equally discouraged.

With the departure of the principal imminent, the superintendent has asked you and three other supervisors to review matters at the school in an effort to determine the source of the supervision problems and to arrive at a solution to these problems. Each has been asked to work independently to develop solutions and to bring ideas to the meeting that is to take place shortly. Below are descriptions of how the four supervisors size up the problems at this school and the solutions that they propose. Each of the supervisors is working from an implicit theory of how the world of schooling, and perhaps even the world itself, works. Which of the four descriptions best matches your own view of the situation and your opinion as to how the situation might be remedied?

Supervisor A

You feel that the present problems in the redesigned school are obviously attributable to the people who work there. If the teachers have not yet adapted to the new curriculum and its procedures, they probably are incapable of functioning in a school committed to school improvement. It is also possible that the principal and the new supervisor are not the experts they were assumed to be and are therefore to blame for inadequate monitoring of the system and for their inability to provide the teachers with the proper help and supervision needed so that they might use the system better.

If you had had your way from the beginning, you would have staffed the school with new teachers. A systemwide search would have been conducted to find the kinds of teachers who would best fit such a system: those who would carefully follow the pattern of teaching and working that the system requires. In introducing the new system at the school, you believe that too much emphasis was placed on helping existing teachers to develop a conceptual understanding of the new procedures. This resulted in too many questions, too much confusion, doubts, and other problems. All teachers needed to know was how they fit into the system, what their jobs were, and what outcomes were expected. Clearer directions and expectations combined with better training and close monitoring would have provided the needed controls to make the system work.

You believe that the curriculum, lesson plans, materials, tests, the teaching design, and the evaluation system introduced into the school are the best available. Although you know that it is possible for snafus to occur and that no educational system can be designed perfectly, you attribute the failure in this case to the unwillingness and inability of the teachers to do what they're supposed to do. Therefore, during the upcoming meeting you plan to make it clear that the problem is not the new educational system but the teachers who are using it. The answer is not to change the system but to train teachers better and to more closely supervise the teachers or to find teachers who are willing to use the system in the way in which it is intended.

Supervisor B

You are convinced that the source of the problems at the redesigned school is the lack of emphasis on human relations. Throughout the year the teachers and other employees have been complaining. As you suspected from the outset, the teachers were not consulted about the type of curriculum or the procedures that should be used, just as they were excluded from the decision-making process that led to the development of this model of the school of the future. You believe that teachers want to feel that they have a say in the matters that influence them. They want to be remembered and noticed, to be considered important. The formula for success is simple and straightforward. When these conditions do not exist, morale sinks. When teachers are satisfied and morale is high, on the other hand, they are more cooperative, more willing to comply, and their performance improves.

The teachers state that the new curriculum and teaching procedures were too cumbersome and rigid and thus made it impossible for them to work comfortably. As you have always said, when the school fulfills its responsibility to teachers' needs, everything else falls into place and school goals are met automatically. After all, the teachers were happy before the redesigning process and student performance was higher then than it is now. Under the new system teachers have to cope not only with a reduction in the amount of teamwork that previously had promoted morale and satisfaction but also with new supervisors who were hired or trained because of their technical skills instead of their human skills.

During the upcoming meeting you plan to discuss top management's error in judgment. You intend to point out that teachers must be noted and appreciated, that the evaluation system is competitive and thus disruptive to group harmony, and that providing a little attention and lots of cheerleading can go a long way toward making things work. Fix up the human relationship and teachers will gladly cooperate with the administration in implementing the new system.

Supervisor C

In your opinion the problems in the redesigned school are attributable to one source: a failure to provide teachers with opportunities to fulfill their individual needs for autonomy and their natural desire to do competent work. You form this opinion on the basis of what you have learned about teachers in general as well as those at this troubled school. The teachers in this school, like those in your own school, are mature adults who, under the right motivating conditions, will want to do their best for the school; they want to enjoy their work and are capable of supervising themselves. Indeed, their performance record and their level of job satisfaction before the redesigning process prove that to be the case. The formula for success is simple and straightforward: Give people responsibility and authority to make decisions about how they are to work, and they respond with increased motivation. Provide them with opportunities to be successful in accomplishing their goals, and their performance improves. The best strategy is to provide the overall framework and let teachers figure out how to implement it. With the right climate, teachers respond to general expectations, need broad goals, and want to be held accountable if trusted and given the discretion to make the implementing decisions that make sense to them. In this school not enough attention was given to creating that climate.

In its plans to redesign the school, top administration has overlooked these facts and has chosen to treat employees like children. A new supervisor was brought in to monitor the work of teachers, and a new educational system was programmed to keep track of their comings and goings. The teachers were expected to meet new organizational goals for increased student performance while their needs for achievement, autonomy, self-direction, and a sense of fulfillment were ignored. Under the circumstances, a drop in performance was inevitable. You feel strongly that the present school attitude toward teachers is counterproductive, and you plan to make your feelings known during the upcoming meeting. The instructional system in the redesigned school cannot be salvaged in its present form. The overall goals and purposes may be okay and it may be appropriate to provide teachers with general frameworks and directions, but at the operational level a new system needs to be developed with teachers as full shareholders and decision makers in its design and implementation.

Supervisor D

You believe that the redesigned school was doomed from the start. The changes introduced were just not realistic. They did not reflect the way schools actually work or how teachers think and behave. The curriculum and instructional system and the teaching and evaluation design that were introduced featured discrete goals, structured tasks, easily measured outcomes, sure operating procedures, clear lines of authority, and single best ways to organize, teach, and evaluate. The problem, as you see it, is that these characteristics are suitable for teaching and learning environments that are stable and predictable and for instances in which student and teacher needs and styles are uniform. But schools have multiple and competing goals, unstructured tasks, competing solutions, difficult-to-measure outcomes, unsure operating procedures, and unclear and competing lines of authority. Further, teachers and students have diverse needs and styles. You hope to explain that these are characteristics of dynamic environments. What works in the first instance doesn't work in the second.

You remember reading somewhere that schools are "managerially loose and culturally tight," and you intend to build your arguments around this idea. What counts for teachers is not so much the management system that is provided but what they believe, the values they share, and the assumptions they hold. When values are held collectively, they become defining characteristics of the school's culture. Changing schools, as you see it, means changing school cultures.

You plan to recommend that the present system be abandoned. You also recommend that the faculty and administration spend the next year coming to grips with the values they share about teaching and learning, what schools are for, how best to evaluate, and how they might best work together. They should then conduct a needs assessment that identifies the norms and values that are now in place in the school as evidenced by what is now going on, and come to grips with what needs changing. This sort of reflection, you believe, will enable them to reinvent their school from top to bottom. You intend to point out that in this reinvented school less emphasis will need to be given to prescribing what needs to be done and to providing direct supervision. Shared values and purposes, a common perspective on what needs to be done to improve the school and a shared commitment to change, in your view, should function as substitutes for direct supervision and should help teachers to become self-managing.

Each of the recommendations of the four supervisors represents a different conception or "theory" of what supervision is, of how schools work, and of what is important to teachers. Make your selection by ranking the four in a way that reflects your view of supervision. Does a clear favorite emerge? Or do you feel more comfortable by combining some of the views? By deciding, you are revealing your own personal theory. The theories of each of the supervisors are described below.

SCIENTIFIC MANAGEMENT, HUMAN RELATIONS, AND NEOSCIENTIFIC MANAGEMENT SUPERVISION

Many of the supervisory practices found in schools today and many of the policies emerging from state governments and local school boards that influence these practices are based on one or a combination of two theories of supervision: traditional scientific management and human relations. These theories are reflected in the images of supervision portrayed by supervisors A and B. In our view, neither theory of supervision is adequate to provide a model for school supervision. Reasons for their inadequacy range from scientific limitations on the one hand to lack of fit with the realities of school supervision on the other. In later sections we propose human resources and normative supervision, the view of supervisors C and D, as theoretical approaches and models of practice that are more sound from a scientific point of view and more accurate in their fit to practice.

Scientific management supervision emerges from the thinking and work of Frederick Taylor and his followers during the early 1900s. Many of the ideas that shaped this theory stem from his experience and research in America's steel industries. For example, Taylor analyzed the loading of pig iron onto railroad cars at a Bethlehem, Pennsylvania, steel plant. Noting certain inefficiencies, he devised techniques for increasing the workers' productivity. His techniques were "scientific" in the sense that they were based on careful observation and task analysis. Taylor determined, for example, that the equipment the workers were using was inadequate to the task. He substituted standardized shovels and other work equipment designed specifically for the tasks to be done. Once the best way of doing something was established, he instructed workers to do exactly as they were told and only as they were told. By closely adhering to his methods and by using the equipment he provided, the workers were able to increase their average loading per day from 12 to 47 tons. Taylor felt that the secret to scientific management was a compliant worker who did not think too much but instead followed directions exactly.[2] The directions, of course, were to be based on "scientifically validated" methods of doing the job. The scientific management recipe is as follows: Identify the best way; develop a work system based on this "research"; communicate expectations to workers; train workers in the system; monitor and evaluate to ensure compliance.

Scientific management represents a classic autocratic philosophy of supervision within which workers are viewed as appendages of management and as such are hired to carry out prespecified duties in accordance with the wishes of management. These ideas carry over to school supervision when teachers are viewed as implementers of highly refined curriculum and teaching systems and where close supervision is practiced to ensure that they are teaching in the way in which they are supposed to and that they are carefully following approved guidelines and teaching protocols. Control, accountability, and efficiency are emphasized in scientific management within an atmosphere of clear-cut manager-subordinate relationships. Though vestiges of this brand of supervision can still be found in schools, by and large traditional scientific management is not currently in favor. Its basic premises and precepts, however, are still thought to be attractive by many policymakers, administrators, and supervisors. The ideas have not changed, as will be discussed later, but strategies for implementing these ideas have.

[2]See, for example, Frederick Taylor, *The Principles of Scientific Management.* New York: Harper & Row, 1911. Reprinted by Harper & Row in 1945. See also Raymond Callahan, *Education and the Cult of Efficiency.* Chicago: University of Chicago Press, 1962.

Human relations supervision emerged during the 1930s. The work of Elton Mayo, a social philosopher and professor at Harvard University, is considered to be important in the development of human relations supervision. Mayo believed that the productivity of workers could be increased by meeting their social needs at work, providing them with opportunities to interact with each other, treating them decently, and involving them in the decision-making process. His classic research study at the Western Electric Hawthorne plant during the 1920s gave testimony to these ideas.[3] Ultimately human relations supervision was a successful challenger to traditional scientific management. When it was applied to schooling, teachers were viewed as whole persons in their own right rather than as packages of needed energy, skills, and aptitudes to be used by administrators and supervisors. Supervisors needed to work to create a feeling of satisfaction among teachers by showing interest in them as people. It was assumed that a satisfied staff would work harder and would be easier to work with, to lead, and to control. Participation was considered to be an important supervisory method and its objective was to make teachers *feel* that they were useful and important to the school. "Personal feelings" and "comfortable relationships" were the watchwords of human relations.

Human relations supervision is still widely advocated and practiced today. Human relations promised much but delivered little. Its problems rested partly with misunderstandings as to how this approach should work and partly with faulty theoretical notions inherent in the approach itself. The movement actually resulted in widespread neglect of teachers. Participatory supervision became permissive supervision, which in practice was laissez-faire supervision. Furthermore, the focus of human relations supervision was and still is an emphasis on "winning friends" in an attempt to influence people. To many, "winning friends" was a slick tactic that made the movement seem manipulative and inauthentic, even dishonest. Though this approach developed a considerable following during the 1930s through 1950s, it became clear that increases in school productivity would not be achieved merely by assuring the happiness of teachers.

School reforms that began in the early 1980s and continue today suggest a new, renewed interest in scientific management thinking, though its shape and form in practice have changed considerably from the more traditional form. This *neoscientific* management is in large part a reaction against human relations supervision with its neglect of the teacher in the classroom and its lack of attention to accountability. Neoscientific management shares with traditional management an interest in control, accountability, and efficiency, but the means by which it achieves these ends is far more impersonal. For example, there is a renewed interest in closely monitoring what it is that teachers do, the subject matter they cover, and the teaching methods that they use. But checking daily lesson plans and visiting classes daily to *inspect* teaching often breeds resentment and results

---

[3]See, for example, Elton Mayo, *The Human Problems of an Industrial Civilization.* New York: Macmillan, 1933; F. J. Roethlisberger and W. J. Dickson, *Management and the Worker.* Cambridge: Harvard University Press, 1949.

in tension between teachers and supervisors. A more impersonal way to control what it is that teachers do is to introduce standardized criterion-referenced testing and to make public the scores by class and school. Since it is accepted that what gets measured gets taught, tests serve as an impersonal method of controlling the teacher's work. Within neoscientific management the task dimension, concern for job, and concern for highly specified performance objectives, all lacking in human relations supervision, are strongly emphasized. Critics feel that this emphasis is so strong that the human dimension suffers. Neoscientific management relies heavily on externally imposed authority and as a result often lacks acceptance from teachers.

Human relations supervision and the two versions of scientific management share a lack of faith and trust in the individual teacher's ability and willingness to display as much interest in the welfare of the school and its programs as that presumed by administrators, supervisors, and the public. Within traditional scientific management teachers are heavily supervised in a face-to-face setting in an effort to ensure that good teaching will take place. In human relations supervision teachers are provided with conditions that enhance their morale and are involved in efforts to increase their job satisfaction so that they might be more pliable in the hands of management, thus ensuring that good teaching will take place. In neoscientific management impersonal, technical, and rational control mechanisms substitute for face-to-face close supervision. Here it is assumed that if visible standards of performance, objectives, or competencies can be identified, the work of teachers can be controlled by holding them accountable to these standards, thus ensuring better teaching.

Sometimes neoscientific management and human relations are combined into one theory of action. For example, the work of teachers may be programmed by an impersonal system of regulation and control, but day-to-day supervision might emphasize pleasant and cordial relationships, building teachers up (telling them, for example, how important they are), encouraging positive attitudes, and rewarding teachers who conform.

HUMAN RESOURCES SUPERVISION

In 1967 the Association for Supervision and Curriculum Development's Commission on Supervision Theory concluded its 4-year study with a report entitled *Supervision: Perspectives and Propositions.*[4] In this report William Lucio discussed scientific management and human relations views of supervision and spoke of a third view—that of the revisionists—which sought to combine emphasis on both tasks and human concerns into a new theory. Standard-bearers of the revisionists were Douglas McGregor, Warren Bennis, Chris Argyris, and Rensis Likert.[5]

---

[4]William Lucio (ed.), *Supervision: Perspectives and Propositions.* Washington, D.C.: Association for Supervision and Curriculum Development, 1967.

[5]Douglas McGregor, *The Human Side of Enterprise.* New York: McGraw-Hill, 1960; Warren Bennis, "Revisionist Theory of Leadership," *Harvard Business Review,* vol. 39, no. 2 (1961), pp. 26–38;

Beginning with the second edition of this book, the concepts and practices associated with this new theory have been referred to as *human resources supervision*.[6] This is the theory of supervision that supervisor C relies upon. The distinction between human resources and human relations is critical, for human resources is more than just another variety of human relations. Human resources represents a higher regard for human need, potential, and satisfaction. Argyris captured the new emphasis succinctly as follows:

> We're interested in developing neither an overpowering manipulative organization nor organizations that will "keep people happy." Happiness, morale, and satisfaction are not going to be highly relevant guides in our discussion. Individual competence, commitment, self-responsibility, fully functioning individuals, and active, viable, vital organizations will be the kinds of criteria that we will keep foremost in our minds.[7]

Leadership within this new kind of supervision was to be neither directive nor patronizing but instead supportive:

> The leader and other processes of the organization must be such as to ensure a maximum probability that in all interactions and in all relationships within the organization, each member, in light of his background, values, desires, and expectations, will view the experience as supportive and one which builds and maintains his sense of personal worth and importance.[8]

Douglas McGregor, pointing out that every managerial act rests on a theory, provided a new theory more conducive to human resources management. Theory Y, as he called it, was based on optimistic assumptions about the nature of humankind and provided a more powerful basis for motivating workers than the older Theory X.

> Theory X leads naturally to an emphasis on the tactics of control—to procedures and techniques for telling people what to do, for determining whether they are doing it, and for administering rewards and punishments. Since an underlying assumption is that people must be made to do what is necessary for the success of the enterprise, attention is naturally directed to the techniques of direction and control. Theory Y, on the other hand, leads to a preoccupation with the *nature of relationships,* with the creation of an environment which will encourage commitment to organizational objectives and which will provide opportunities for the maximum exercise of initiative, ingenuity, and self-direction in achieving them.[9]

The assumptions about people associated with Theory X are as follows:

1 Average people are by nature indolent—they work as little as possible.
2 They lack ambition, dislike responsibility, prefer to be led.

Chris Argyris, *Personality and Organization.* New York: Harper & Row, 1957; and Rensis Likert, *New Patterns of Management.* New York: McGraw-Hill, 1961.

[6]This distinction was first made by Raymond Miles, "Human Relations or Human Resources?" *Harvard Business Review,* vol. 43, no. 4 (1965), pp. 148–163; and by Mason Haire, Edwin Ghiselli, and Lyman Porter, *Managerial Thinking: An International Study.* New York: Wiley, 1966.

[7]Chris Argyris, *Integrating the Individual and the Organization.* New York: Wiley, 1964, p. 4.

[8]Rensis Likert, op. cit., p. 103.

[9]McGregor, op. cit., p. 132.

3 They are inherently self-centered, indifferent to organizational needs.
4 They are by nature resistant to change.
5 They are gullible, not very bright, ready dupes of the charlatan and dem-
    agogue.[10]

One can find many instances in schools when the assumptions of Theory X
do indeed seem to be true. Teachers, for example, seem to work only minimally
and then only under close supervision. Few instances of teacher initiative can be
found. Instead teachers seem to be defensive and preoccupied with maintaining
the status quo. McGregor argued that when such conditions exist the problem
may be less with workers and more with the expectations that their administrators and supervisors have of them. Sensing negative assumptions and expectations, teachers are likely to respond in a negative way. This is an example of the
self-fulfilling prophecy. Fundamental to Theory X is a philosophy of direction
and control. This philosophy is administered in a variety of forms and rests
upon a theory of motivation that is inadequate for most adults, particularly professional adults.

The assumptions about people associated with Theory Y are as follows:

1 Management is responsible for organizing the elements of productive en-
    terprise—money, materials, equipment, people—in the interest of eco-
    nomic (educational) ends.
2 People are *not* by nature passive or resistant to organizational needs. They
    have become so as a result of experience in organizations.
3 The motivation, the potential for development, the capacity for assuming
    responsibility, the readiness to direct behaviors toward organizational
    goals are all present in people; management does not put them there. It is
    a responsibility of management to make it possible for people to recognize
    and develop these human characteristics for themselves.
4 The essential task of management is to arrange organizational conditions
    and methods of operation so that people can achieve their own goals *best*
    by directing *their* own efforts toward organizational objectives.[11]

Basic to Theory Y is building identification and commitment to worthwhile
objectives in the work context and building mutual trust and respect. Success in
work is assumed to be dependent on whether authentic relationships and the exchange of valid information are present.

Advocates maintain that school conditions created by human resources management result in a better life for teachers and more productive schooling. Satisfaction and achievement are linked in a new and more expansive way. Instead

---

[10]These assumptions are quoted from McGregor's essay, "The Human Side of Enterprise," which
appears in Warren G. Bennis and Edgar H. Schein (eds.), *Leadership and Motivation: Essays of Douglas
McGregor.* Cambridge, Mass.: MIT Press, 1966. The essay first appeared in *Adventure in Thought and
Action.* Proceedings of the Fifth Anniversary Convocation of the School of Industrial Management,
MIT, April 9, 1957.
[11]McGregor in Bennis and Schein, op. cit., p. 15.

of focusing on creating happy teachers as a means to gain productive cooperation, the new supervision emphasis is on creating the conditions of successful work as a means of increasing one's satisfaction and self-esteem. As Frederick Herzberg described the new emphasis:

> To feel that one has grown depends on achievement of tasks that have meaning to the individual, and since the hygiene factors do not relate to the task, they are powerless to give such meaning to the individual. Growth is dependent on some achievements but achievement requires a task. The motivators are task factors and thus are necessary for growth; they provide the psychological stimulation by which the individual can be activated toward his self-realization needs.[12]

HUMAN RELATIONS AND HUMAN RESOURCES SUPERVISION COMPARED

Neoscientific management and scientific management are really the same theory, though each has a slightly different look in practice. Human relations and human resources supervision, however, are two different theories. For example, though both are concerned with teacher satisfaction, human relations views satisfaction as a means to a smoother and more effective school. It is believed that satisfied workers are happier workers and thus easier to work with, more cooperative, and more likely to be compliant. Supervisors find it easier to get what they want from teachers when human relationships are tended to. Consider, for example, the practice of shared decision making. In human relations supervision this technique is used because it is believed it will lead to increased teacher satisfaction. This relationship is depicted as follows:

The human relations supervisor
$\downarrow$

adopts shared decision-making practices	$\rightarrow$	to	increase teacher satisfaction	$\rightarrow$	which in turn	increases school effectiveness

The rationale behind this strategy is that teachers want to *feel* important and involved. This feeling in turn promotes in teachers a better attitude toward the school and therefore they become easier to manage and more effective in their work.

Within human resources supervision, by contrast, satisfaction is viewed as a desirable *end* toward which teachers work. Satisfaction, according to this view, results from successful accomplishment of important and meaningful work, and this accomplishment is the key component to building school success. The human resources supervisor, therefore, adopts shared decision-making practices because of their potential to increase school success. The supervisor assumes that

---

[12]Frederick Herzberg, *Work and the Nature of Man.* New York: World Publishing, 1966, p. 78.

better decisions will be made, that teacher ownership and commitment to these decisions will be increased, and that the likelihood of success at work will increase. These relationships are depicted as follows:

The human relations supervisor
↓

adopts shared → to   increase   →   which in turn   increases
decision-making   school   teacher
practices   effectiveness   satisfaction

Human relations supervision is much more closely aligned with the assumptions of Theory X than with those of Theory Y, even though when experienced, they result in a softer form of control. This is evident when the two sets of assumptions are contrasted, as in Table 1–1.

Let us now revisit supervisors A, B, and C.

Scientific management and neoscientific management comprise the theory of practice that governs the thinking and practice of supervisor A. This supervisor supports a highly structured and finely tuned teaching and learning system characterized by close connections among objectives, curriculum, teaching methods, and testing. Supervisor A believes that if teachers do what they are supposed to, the system will produce the results that are intended.

Human relations comprises the theory of practice to which supervisor B gives allegiance. Supervisor B is concerned with the teaching system's insensitivity to teachers' needs. Further, teachers were not consulted about the system to be implemented and thus feel left out. The answer to this supervisor is to back off and try again, this time getting teachers involved and making compromises in the proposed changes that get in the way of teachers' social interaction and other needs. With the right human relations strategy, supervisor B believes, any school-improvement initiative will be successful. It is just a matter of how effectively you work with people.

Supervisor C comes closest to operating from within the human resources perspective. This supervisor believes that successful teaching and school improvement occurs when teacher motivation and commitment are high. Being in charge of one's work life and being held accountable to shared values and broad goals contribute to motivation and commitment. Authentic participation in decision making and providing responsibility are viewed as key supervisory strategies by supervisor C.

Supervisor D's analysis of the problems in Metro City represents a fairly new image of supervision. Supervisor D relies much less on direct supervision, whatever its form. No matter how enlightened such supervision might be, supervisor D reasons, it still depends largely upon some external force to make things happen. Even in the case of human resources supervision, at the base is an exchange of higher-level need fulfillment for some sort of work compliance. Instead, supervisor D seeks to build substitutes for supervision into the everyday

TABLE 1-1
SUPERVISORY ASSUMPTIONS

Theory X Soft Human Relations Model	Theory Y Human Resources Model
Attitudes Toward People	
1. People in our culture, teachers and students among them, share a common set of needs—to belong, to be liked, to be respected.	1. In addition to sharing common needs for belonging and respect, most people in our culture, teachers and students among them, desire to contribute effectively and creatively to the accomplishment of worthwhile objectives.
2. While teachers and students desire individual recognition, they more importantly want to *feel* useful to the school and to their own work group.	2. The majority of teachers and students are capable of exercising far more initiative, responsibility, and creativity than their present jobs or work circumstances require or allow.
3. They tend to cooperate willingly and comply with school goals if these important needs are fulfilled.	3. These capabilities represent untapped resources that are presently being wasted.
Kind and Amount of Participation	
1. The supervisor's basic task (or in reference to students, the teacher's basic task) is to make each worker believe that he or she is a useful and important part of the team.	1. The supervisor's basic task (or in reference to students, the teacher's basic task) is to create an environment in which subordinates can contribute their full range of talents to the accomplishment of school goals. He or she works to uncover the creative resources of subordinates.
2. The supervisor is willing to explain his or her decisions and to discuss subordinates' objections to the plans. On routine matters, he or she encourages subordinates in planning and in decision making. In reference to students, the teacher behaves similarly.	2. The supervisor allows and encourages teachers to participate in important as well as routine decisions. In fact, the more important a decision is to the school, the greater the supervisor's efforts to tap faculty resources. In reference to students, the teacher behaves similarly.
3. Within narrow limits, the faculty or individual teachers who make up the faculty should be allowed to exercise self-direction and self-control in carrying out plans. A similar relationship exists for teachers and students.	3. Supervisors work continually to expand the areas over which teachers exercise self-direction and self-control as they develop and demonstrate greater insight and ability. A similar relationship exists for teachers and students.

TABLE 1-1 (continued)

Theory X Soft Human Relations Model	Theory Y Human Resources Model

Expectations

Theory X Soft Human Relations Model	Theory Y Human Resources Model
1. Sharing information with teachers and involving them in school decision making will help satisfy their basic needs for belonging and for individual recognition.	1. The overall quality of decision making and performance will improve as supervisors and teachers make use of the full range of experience, insight, and creative ability that exists in their schools.
2. Satisfying these needs will improve faculty and student morale and will reduce resistance to formal authority.	2. Teachers will exercise responsible self-direction and self-control in the accomplishment of worthwhile objectives that they understand and have helped establish.
3. High faculty and student morale and reduced resistance to formal authority may lead to improved school performance. It will at least reduce friction and make the supervisor's job easier.	3. Faculty satisfaction and student satisfaction will increase as a by-product of improved performance and the opportunity to contribute creatively to this improvement.

Source: Adapted from Raymond E. Miles, "Human Relations or Human Resources?" Harvard Business Review, vol. 43, no. 4, (1965), pp. 148–163, esp. exhibits I and II.

life of the school. Substitutes enable teachers and supervisors to respond from within, to become self-managing.

It is hard to put a label on supervisor D's theory of supervision. Providing substitutes, for example, suggests that supervision as it is now being practiced should be replaced by something else. Supervisor D highlights shared values as one such substitute. Shared values can take many forms. Sometimes they are expressed as professional norms or community norms or the felt need for teachers to care about each other and to help each other. As schools are restructured as true learning communities, shared norms and ideas become the source of authority for what supervisors, teachers, and students do. These sources of authority replace bureaucratic and interpersonal authority by speaking to community members in a moral voice and calling them to do the right thing. These and other substitutes for supervision will be discussed in the next and subsequent chapters of this book.

This "normative" supervision that characterizes supervisor D's views is based on several premises that are at odds with more traditional approaches to supervision. One premise is that while self-interest may be an important source of motivation for teachers, most are capable of and willing to sacrifice self-interest for more altruistic reasons if conditions are right. Another premise is that preference, values, emotions, and beliefs are equally if not more powerful teacher motivators than are logic, reasoning, and scientific evidence. A third premise is that teachers and others do not make decisions simply as isolated individuals. Instead, what they think, believe, and ultimately do are shaped by their memberships in groups and their connections with other people. They are more responsive to norms than they are to either rules or needs—a condition that seems to apply to students as well.

Each of the supervisory models sketched above provides an oversimplification, and probably none is exclusively adequate. Successful supervision is shaped by the circumstances and situations that the supervisor faces, and at different times different models may be appropriate. Still, it matters greatly which of the general theories of supervision or which combination one accepts as her or his overarching framework. One important characteristic that defines each of the images of supervision is the source of authority for supervision. Supervision inevitably deals with control. Control is in turn a response to some form of authority. The source of this authority might be external, such as regulations, or internal, such as commitment to one's principles or values and one's sense of duty or obligation. Sources of authority for supervision are the theme of Chapter 3.

CHAPTER 2

SUPERVISION WITHIN THE RESTRUCTURING AGENDA

TRADITIONAL understandings of supervision assumed a school environment and structure that, with perhaps minor alterations, would define the context of the supervisor's work. Behind that environment and structure were assumptions about learning, the relationship between instruction and learning, the use of textbooks, the definition of curriculum, the testing of learning, technologies and logistical support systems (classroom size and groupings, daily and weekly class schedules, student placement in various curriculum tracks, utilization of media and computer technology, testing and grading and ranking technologies), pedagogical effectiveness, and teacher-evaluation criteria. While in many individual schools and school systems we can still find these assumptions guiding the practice of schooling, there has arisen a broad-based challenge to these beliefs and the school structures and environments they support. This challenge has called for the restructuring of schools to reflect new understandings about learning, about the relationship of instruction to learning, about what should constitute the curriculum, and about the assessment of learning. This restructuring agenda will redefine supervision, because the assumptions behind traditional forms of schooling that provided the context for supervision are being transformed.

WHAT IS THE RESTRUCTURING AGENDA?

It is difficult to understand the force and sustained energy behind the restructuring movement, unless one sees the movement as having multiple sources, some political, some economic, some philosophical, some based on various strands of research and theory. These sources contain ideologies that would conflict on many disparate issues, but that have coalesced around the conviction that schools must be restructured. Despite their different theoretical, ideological, and research bases, the forces behind the restructuring movement are in basic agreement about the restructuring agenda called for in schools.

In order to understand what the ingredients of the restructuring agenda are, it would help to map some of the sources that generated them. What follows is a brief overview of these sources, each one of which requires sustained study in order to grasp its full implication for the restructuring agenda. In subsequent chapters of this book, we will be touching upon many of them in greater detail.

Political Influences Federal, state, and local authorities call for school restructuring in light of international test data that they believe indicate American youth lag behind the youth of other countries on various measures of school achievement.

Economic Influences Business executives and government officials maintain that American youth are unprepared for the technological demands of the 21st-century workplace. Continued advances in economic productivity require investment in high-quality education, especially in developing workplace skills.

Cognitive Science Research This relatively new field has brought new understanding of how "experts" think and work in a variety of fields, which suggests how schools might prepare novice-experts. Cognitive science also has expanded our understanding of how the mind processes information, leading to suggestions on strengthening inquiry and reasoning skills and large frameworks (mental models, knowledge representations) for making and interpreting meaning. Research on multiple intelligences, especially in young children, has led to experimental learning settings that support the fuller development of these various intelligences, thus providing clues for an enriched curriculum that is more responsive to the diversity of talent children bring to their early classrooms.

Constructivist Learning Theory and Research This relatively new branch of psychology has shed light on how students actively produce knowledge and understanding, which suggests new approaches to designing learning tasks and activities. Constructivist research also has helped illuminate how background variables influence the way students process learning tasks and relate school learning to prior experiences.

Philosophy and Sociology There is widespread acceptance that knowledge is a social, cultural, and political construct. There has been a shift from "What we know is real" to "What is real is what we know." Instead of denying the existence of objective reality, this view accepts knowledge as partial and tentative, open to correction and modification, but in its present form simultaneously revealing and distorting reality. Knowledge is seen as both a product and a medium of socialization and power.

Research in Academic Disciplines   This study has more clearly identified methods of inquiry and strong inclusive frameworks that define the disciplines, thus suggesting new approaches to developing students as novice-experts in individual academic disciplines.

Curriculum Theory and Research   Such research has developed a new understanding of cultural, gender, and class bias in teaching materials and in curriculum tracking. This has led to various attempts to construct a curriculum that is more sensitive to gender, cultural, and language differences among students.

Legal Politics of Pluralism and Inclusion   Parents and other student advocates have forced new policies governing the treatment of special education, bilingual, and minority culture children, which in turn challenge traditional school structures and environments.

Research on Student Assessment   Research has introduced the notions of performance and authentic assessments, which in turn suggest a new understanding of learning. Following the dictum that what gets tested and how it gets tested directly influence (if not control) what gets taught and how, these new assessments substantially refocus the classroom on the active production and performance of student work.

Research on Professional Practice   Professional practice research has focused on how teachers respond intuitively to developments in the classroom, interpreting verbal and nonverbal signals from students, altering the lesson plan when it is not working, going off into unplanned tangents when the needs of the moment seem to dictate it, bringing their biases and stereotypes into play in what and how they teach, and so on. Studies contrasting expert with novice teachers reveal what teachers have to know and how they bring this knowledge to bear on their teaching strategies. These studies have also revealed how teachers can engage in action research to improve their understanding of and response to the students in their classes. It has also documented how teachers working together can recreate the curriculum and the learning environment of the school, when they are given the autonomy to do so. The implications of this research are that teachers have enormous reservoirs of knowledge and experience that enable them to solve many of the problems within the restructuring agenda, when they are given the proper autonomy and support.

Research on Second-Order Change   This research has provided new understanding about the dynamics of second-order change (deep, substantial, total institutional change—the kind of change demanded by the restructuring agenda), especially about the need to re-culture the institution as the restructuring is being attempted (changing assumptions, beliefs, and values as the community attempts to change structures and environments), as well as about the need for participation, ownership, and ongoing professional development.

Many different groups of scholars have been working in disparate areas of research over many years, not necessarily knowing about the work of other groups in related areas. As their findings have matured and been accepted, a broader pattern has begun to emerge, as the results of these various sources of ideas are combined. All of these studies have hinted at or elaborated on the educational implications of their conclusions. Simply by juxtaposing them we see a tapestry almost stitching itself together, as the findings, say, of the cognitive science researchers overlap with the findings of studies of expert thinking in the professions and in academic fields, or as the constructivist scholars' conclusions meld nicely with the sociology of knowledge conclusions. While no one of these developments constitutes a revolution in education, the combination and mutual influence of each of them on the others does begin to constitute a basis for such a revolution. No one has come up yet with a single best model for a restructured school, but there is widespread agreement that enough ingredients are known to enable educators and policymakers to launch a major overhaul of schooling in its traditional practice. Putting all these ingredients together, we have a clearer picture of what a restructured school agenda might look like, perhaps what it must look like if as a society we are to meet the challenges of the next century.

RESTRUCTURING PROPOSALS

David Conley has proposed a list of these ingredients, which he has subdivided into three sets: (1) central variables (learner outcomes, curriculum, instruction, assessment/evaluation), (2) enabling variables (learning environment, technology, school-community relations, time), and (3) supporting variables (governance, teacher leadership, variable personnel structures, working relationships).[1] Figure 2–1 expresses the relationship between these three sets of restructuring variables.

Conley asserts that in the restructured school the learner will be the center of the instructional process. Curriculum will be redesigned to respond to students' interests, abilities, and backgrounds, so that authentic learning will take place, learning that enables students to solve problems, create meaning, and express their appraisal of what they have learned. The world around the school—the family, the neighborhood, the community—will become one of the sources or contexts of the curriculum. Helping students to succeed at learning, rather than sorting students according to differentiated achievement, will be the focus of teaching; teachers will be expected to design learning experiences (sometimes with the students) that enable *all* students to succeed. Learning environments will be redesigned to encourage more learning and dialogue in pairs and in groups, as well as collaborative productions of learning. This will include cross-age and multiage grouping, parental involvement in learning tasks, learning activities in

---

[1]David T. Conley, *Roadmaps to Restructuring: Policies, Practices and the Emerging Visions of Schooling.* Eugene, Ore.: Eric Clearinghouse on Educational Management, 1993.

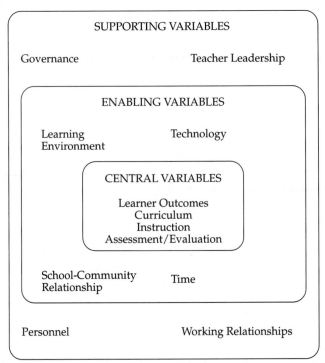

FIGURE 2–1 Dimensions of restructuring. *(Source: David T. Conley,* Roadmaps to Restructuring: Policies, Practices and the Emerging Visions of Schooling. *Eugene, Ore.: Eric Clearinghouse on Educational Management, 1993, p. 106.)*

the civic community, weekend enrichment learning, and extended day and year programs.

In the restructured school technology will be employed to stimulate and enhance learning in a variety of formats. The school will be engaged in multiple partnerships—with families, social agencies, civic authorities, local professionals, community service organizations, and business partnerships. There will be multiple leadership opportunities for teachers through enhanced valuing of their professional expertise and through numerous collaborative relationships. Finally, relationships between teachers and administrators, between schools and the central office, between unions and school authorities, and between school districts and state authorities will be redefined as teachers and individual schools seek greater autonomy to enhance the learning opportunities for all of their children.

Sounds idealistic? Conley cites examples of schools and school districts where many of these ingredients are already in place and where evidence of substantial gains in student learning is impressive.

David Perkins speaks of "smart schools," rather than restructured schools, although it is obvious that his smart schools can come into existence only by restructuring the vast majority of today's institutions as we know them.[2] He lists six dimensions of smart schools: (1) the consistent application of "Theory One" ("People learn much of what they have a reasonable opportunity and motivation to learn"); this means that students have clear information about the goals of the learning experience and the performance expected, an opportunity to engage actively and reflectively whatever is to be learned, clear feedback about their performance and how to proceed, and ample satisfaction from the learning experiences themselves; (2) a pedagogy for deep understanding (attending to the reasoning and explanations behind the answers students give); (3) attending to the metacurriculum (employing the language and strategies of thinking and inquiry as well as teaching for transfer and for the skills of learning how to learn); (4) attending to and employing distributed intelligence (the physical, social, symbolic, and collaborative distribution of intelligence that it takes for students to engage in complex learning tasks); (5) attending to the cognitive economy of learning (minimizing the costs to the student while maximizing the rewards of complex cognition); and (6) attending to the conditions and dynamics of change.[3]

Again, Perkins cites numerous examples of how these dimensions of smart schools are worked out in practice. He is not talking about what might be; rather, he is talking about changes that have already been shown to increase student achievement.

Fred Newmann and his associates at the Center on Organization and Restructuring of Schools at the University of Wisconsin speak of the ingredients for successful school restructuring as "circles of support."[4] The research on which these conclusions are based involved more than 1,500 schools throughout the United States, so we are looking at actual practices, not idealistic wishes. Figure 2–2 visualizes these circles of support, highlighting the four components of (1) high-quality intellectual work by the students (curriculum, instruction, assessment, scheduling, staff development, hiring, student advising, etc., must be oriented toward the core work of student learning); (2) authentic pedagogy that seeks to promote high-quality student learning (requiring students to think, to develop deep understanding, and to apply their learning to important, real-world problems); (3) a school organization that facilitates this kind of learning and teaching (organizational arrangements that promote a strong professional community among the teachers); and (4) external support from district, state, and federal authorities, as well as professional organizations, parents, and other citizens.

John Bruer's *Schools for Thought* represents a literature emerging from cognitive science that provides many insights into how students learn and offers

---

[2]David Perkins, *Smart Schools: Better Thinking and Learning for Every Child*. New York: Free Press, 1992.

[3]See Perkins, op. cit., pp. 231–235, for a synopsis of his six dimensions of smart schools.

[4]Fred M. Newmann and Gary G. Wehlage, *Successful School Restructuring*. Madison, Wis.: Center on Organization and Restructuring of Schools, 1995, p. 2.

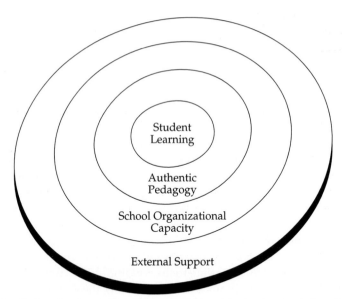

FIGURE 2–2   Circles of support—The context for successful school restructuring. *(Source: Fred M. Newmann and Gary G. Wehlage, Successful School Restructuring. Madison, Wis.: Center on Organization and Restructuring of Schools, 1995.)*

strategies to bring students to deep understanding and to the metacognitive tasks of learning how to learn.[5] His underlying message is that in all the mainline academic subjects of school (especially mathematics, the sciences, reading, writing, and literature), we know enough by now about how to develop students as intelligent novices in the academic subjects. That is, students can be taught to develop the ability to take charge of their own learning, at least as intelligent, scholarly beginners. They can become sufficiently knowledgeable of the various methodologies of inquiry and problem solving, of the criteria of acceptable evidence, and of the reasoning procedures for organizing the evidence, as well as of the major cognitive frameworks or maps of the disciplines, so that the teacher becomes less and less necessary as a constant guide and source of information. Although Bruer and other scholars provide impressive evidence of the peda-

[5]John T. Bruer, *Schools for Thought: A Science of Learning in the Classroom.* Cambridge, Mass.: MIT Press, 1993. The literature coming out of the cognitive sciences represents a variety of points of view on the teaching of thinking. See Raymond S. Nickerson, David N. Perkins, and Edward E. Smith, *The Teaching of Thinking.* Hillsdale, N.J.: Lawrence Erlbaum Associates, 1985; Lauren B. Resnick and Leopold E. Klopfer (eds.), *Toward the Thinking Curriculum: Current Cognitive Research.* Alexandria, Va.: Association for Supervision and Curriculum Development, 1989; Matthew Lipman, *Thinking in Education.* Cambridge: Cambridge University Press, 1991; Stuart Maclure and Peter Davies (eds.), *Learning to Think: Thinking to Learn.* Oxford: Pergamon Press, 1991; and James W. Keefe and Herbert J. Walberg (eds.), *Teaching for Thinking.* Reston, Va.: National Association of Secondary School Principals, 1992.

sters to develop the kind of novice-expert skills and understandings required in the workplace (and the universities), then the equally valid argument can be made that public life will become increasingly complex and that schools have to prepare citizens who will be called on to debate and vote on issues of enormous complexity and consequence. Will the schools graduate young people of voting age who know next to nothing about the public policy issues facing the nation and the community, who know nothing about how to participate in the political process, and who, by the school's inattention to practical involvement in the issues of public life, have inadvertently been taught not to care about the common good? Does not this void in the education of its future citizens also place the nation at risk? Since proponents for restructuring have already argued that mere knowledge of information is not enough, but applying that knowledge to real-life situations is what grounds that knowledge in deep understanding and makes it available for future applications, one could argue that knowledge of the lessons of political history is not enough. A curriculum that requires deep understanding through application in real-life situations would also be required for a curriculum in citizenship. This is not the place to propose such a curriculum. Those called upon to supervise the restructuring of schools, though, should be aware of the need.

This brings us to the second shortcoming of the restructuring proposals. One of the assumptions behind much of the thinking about restructuring is that the answer to the nation's and the world's problems, as well as to the major issues facing the individual, can be addressed by developing reasoning ability, inquiry skills, rational problem solving, and a deeper understanding of the academic disciplines and the applied sciences. This assumption brings us back to the Socratic belief that knowledge is virtue. Somehow, if we know enough and can think clearly enough, we will do the right thing. This was the promise of the Enlightenment, and upon that promise, mass education was constructed.

The belief that knowledge is virtue, however, is naive. It assumes that knowledge of reality is so compelling and unambiguous that it will inescapably lead to wise action. The history of the past century presents a rather uneven record of human wisdom, despite the spread of universal education. The Aristotelian notion that wise action or virtue is learned through practical participation in a community is only partially a corrective to the Socratic reliance on knowledge and clear thinking to produce wise action. Communities may produce actions that conform to their definition of wise action, but not conform to more universally recognized forms of human living (the recent inhumane actions of communities in the Balkans and in Rwanda are one example). Some explicit teaching of and concern for morality must be included in the restructuring agenda. While this is done with greater effect in the everyday experience of community, there needs to be some attention to universal moral principles that would apply to all communities. Again, this is not the place to develop such a curriculum. Supervisors, however, must be aware of its need.

What is taught in schools as knowledge, is a socially constructed knowledge, contained in the curriculum and the pedagogy of the school. The curriculum and pedagogy of the common school are supposed to communicate a knowledge of the world and its forms for understanding by which the individual is to locate himself or herself within the world. But this curriculum is not neutral. It is organized around and expressive of a form of economic nationalism and narrow cultural definitions of what life is supposed to be. These definitions express the relationships between the cultural and political elite and the rest of the world. The imposition of this knowledge through the curriculum and pedagogy is not effected through some evil conspiracy; it is simply the way all schools work in every modern nation.[8] This imposition of knowledge of the self and the world gives order and discipline, a predictable identity to social life. It is not imposed by force, but through the symbolic systems by which a society is educated and by which that society interprets, organizes, and acts in the world.[9] The key is to understand that these symbolic systems *interpret* reality rather than represent, in some universally objective fashion, what is real. This understanding about school knowledge needs to be included in the curriculum and pedagogy of restructured schools. Without it, we will have discouraged, if only by omission, the development of the critical faculties by which knowledge itself can be transformed into a more benign or inclusive interpretation that works better for the larger human community. This approach to knowledge implies a morality, a concern to continually transform knowledge for the larger benefit of the community.

The work of Howard Gardner can be cited to illustrate the point. Until Gardner challenged it, the notion of intelligence was associated with the conventional intelligence quotient. It was evaluated primarily by tests that measured mathematical and linguistic intelligence. Gardner's work with brain-damaged people led him to recognize that some individuals could function quite intelligently in particular areas but not in the area controlled by that part of the brain that had been damaged. He then developed a different interpretation of intelligence, one that was more inclusive of talents not previously interpreted as connected with intelligence.

Traditionally, schools accepted the monolithic notion of intelligence and tended to reward those youngsters whose talents lay in that direction and to ignore or accept in a secondary way youngsters whose talents were to be found in other intelligences such as musical intelligence, interpersonal intelligence, spatial intelligence, and bodily and kinesthetic intelligence. Because of Gardner's work, more school systems are beginning to explore ways of developing and strengthening the various intelligences youngsters bring to school so they can grow into the healthy and successful adults they are capable of being.[10] If Gard-

---

[8]See Herbert M. Kliebard, *The Struggle for the American Curriculum, 1893–1958.* Boston: Routledge & Kegan Paul, 1986.

[9]See Thomas S. Popkewitz, "Policy, Knowledge, and Power: Some Issues for the Study of Educational Reform," in Peter W. Cookson, Jr., and Barbara Schneider (eds.), *Transforming Schools.* New York: Garland Publishing, 1995, pp. 413–455.

[10]See Howard Gardner, *Frames of Mind.* New York: Basic Books, 1983; *The Unschooled Mind: How Children Think and How Schools Should Teach.* New York: Basic Books, 1991.

ner had not criticized the accepted understanding of intelligence, then we could not have developed more benign and inclusive interpretations of intelligence that work better for the community.

Youngsters need to be exposed to the self-correcting nature of knowledge, a truth that reveals it as always partial, as a limited interpretation of what is real. They also need to understand that knowledge represents power. Gardner's expansion of the notion of intelligence did not please those organizations that administer IQ tests nor those educators whose tidy assumptions about curriculum and student grading had to be changed. Yet his knowledge represented a new power that has begun to counter the power of an interpretation of intelligence that was found too distorting of a more inclusive understanding of intelligence. Even in this instance, however, we can discover competing interpretations about intelligence. For example, Gardner's list does not include political intelligence or the intelligence often referred to as "street smarts." Again, aboriginal people in Australia possess a spiritual intelligence and a survival intelligence that few white Australians can fathom.

The power to define what is considered legitimate knowledge, and therefore what will be rewarded in its representation, will always be contested. Schools that do not teach an openness to contesting the legitimacy of accepted knowledge are not being true to their own stated purposes. They are not teaching the inherent moral implications in claiming to know.

The point of suggesting this critical appraisal of the restructuring agenda is not to oppose it, but rather to enrich it. It can be argued that the restructuring agenda is difficult and challenging enough without adding concerns about citizenship, community, and morality. These can come later, after more important concerns have been dealt with. But that is like saying that redesigning a car should only take into account technical changes in the engine, rather than deal with pollution reduction measures, for instance, or ergonomic improvements. In both cases, it is a question of who defines what is "important."

We are suggesting that citizenship, community, and morality concerns are as important as the other ingredients of the restructuring agenda. It is this expanded vision that provides the framework for supervision throughout this book.

IMPLICATIONS FOR SUPERVISORS

As this brief overview of the restructuring agenda indicates, the traditional view of teaching and learning that stresses the activities of the teacher without considering the learning needs of all students, that approaches teaching as though one protocol can work for all or most of the students in the class, that approaches student learning as the relatively passive processing of information passed on by the teacher and the textbook for repetition on tests—this view of teaching and learning has been expanded considerably. The present view shows teaching and learning to be vastly more varied and complex. In this regard, the role of the supervisor as one whose job it was to pass out advice and handy tips for the teacher to follow has been transformed by the whole notion of the professional community of teachers.

Teachers today are expected to be actively engaged with their students, adapting classroom procedures to more effectively respond to the readiness of each student to the task at hand. Teaching is seen as being more dialogical, more tentative, more exploratory, and probably far less controlling than in the past. As a result, the supervisor may be viewed as less of an expert than the classroom teacher.

As this book unfolds, we will gain a better sense of what the restructuring agenda implies for today's supervisor. For now, we can say that the restructuring agenda has challenged and expanded many assumptions that helped define supervision in the past. Some of these assumptions had to do with the very definitions of knowledge, of learning, of intelligence, and of achievement. As we will see, restructured schools no longer hold to these earlier notions, but have developed much more complex and varied understandings in these areas. Furthermore, assumptions about the supervisor's authority, the accountability of teachers, the bureaucratic control of the school by an organization of hierarchies of responsibility, the legitimacy of the traditional measures of student achievement, and the social organization of the school have all been called into question. The restructuring agenda calls upon teachers to reshape their assumptions and work routines; it asks the same of supervisors. Hence, when we speak of the redefined perspectives of supervision, we are speaking of major transformations in the role and function of supervision, rather than a few cosmetic changes that will allow the traditional practice of supervision to remain, with perhaps minor modifications of management styles. We are suggesting that supervision be characterized by a *super vision*, that is, by an overview or expanded vision of the restructuring agenda. That vision will energize and direct the activities of the supervisor. The following chapters will attempt to define and develop that vision.

CHAPTER 3

SOURCES OF AUTHORITY
FOR SUPERVISION

THE four supervisors described in Chapter 1 share a common commitment to improving schools. Further, they realize that improving schools means changing existing ways of thinking about teaching and learning and changing existing teaching practices. Supervisors A and B choose slightly different paths but *follow a similar route* to achieve these goals. This is the case as well for supervisors C and D.

Each of the pairs of supervisors represents two very different conceptions of supervision, and each of the two different conceptions leads to different consequences in the school. Let us refer to these broad conceptions as *Supervision I* and *Supervision II.* Supervision I represents the traditional kind of supervision that has been in place in schools for most of this century. Supervision II, by contrast, represents an emerging pattern that can fundamentally change not only the way supervision is understood and practiced but also our understanding of how successfully to effect change, what really counts when it comes to motivating teachers, what leadership is, how to be helpful to teachers in the classroom, the meaning of staff development, and how to help teacher evaluation become more useful.

At the end of this chapter the assumptions and principles underlying Supervision I and Supervision II are compared. This comparison lays the foundation for developing a new kind of supervisory practice. To set the stage we first examine sources of authority for supervisory practice. The issue of authority is important not only in understanding different forms of supervision but also in handling the problems of change. Each of the four supervisors in Chapter 1, for example, sought to bring about change by relying on different sources of authority. "Authority" refers to the power to influence thought and behavior. The success or failure of any change strategy rests in a large measure on the match that exists between the source of authority relied upon and the situation at hand.

THE ISSUE OF CHANGE

Change does not come about easily and is very difficult to mandate from the top down or from the outside. Mandated change requires more checking and monitoring to sustain than is possible to provide. Further, for change to have meaning and effect it must change not only the way things look but also the way things work. And finally, too often efforts to change are directed only toward doing the same things better. Change that counts, by contrast, is typically that which alters basic issues of schooling such as goals, values, beliefs, working arrangements, and the distribution of power and authority. This kind of change requires more than just tinkering with the existing school culture.

Teacher evaluation provides a good example. In recent years those interested in improving teaching and learning have frequently relied upon state-mandated evaluation systems that feature checklists to track certain observed teaching behaviors. Yet the record to date suggests that such mandates have not made much of a difference in improving the quality of teaching and learning. For example, teachers may conform to the mandated system only when under scrutiny. Since constant checking and monitoring are not possible, such systems soon become time-consuming and expensive. Using such monitoring, the school can supply evaluation data that suggest teachers are acting in required ways and that point to an array of new policies and procedures that are in place in the school as further evidence. Nevertheless, the teaching and learning process continues as it did before.

In the case above, changes in teaching practice are superficial rather than real. One reason for this superficiality is that the source of authority chosen for implementing changes is too limited. Present supervisory practices emerge from a particular pattern of authority. Changing these practices means changing the authority base for supervision. If, for example, teaching is viewed as a profession within which practice is based on research, the wisdom of experience, careful analysis of the situation at hand, and commitment to professional virtue, then the sources of authority for what teachers do would be internal, knowledge oriented, and norm based. If, by contrast, teaching continues to be viewed as a technical field within which practice is based on set routines and practitioners are in need of constant direction and monitoring, then the sources of authority for what teachers do are external, process oriented, and management based.

THE SOURCES OF AUTHORITY

Supervisory policies and practices can be based on one or a combination of five broad sources of authority:

Bureaucratic, in the form of legal and organizational mandates, rules, regulations, job descriptions, and expectations. When supervisory policies and practices are based on bureaucratic authority, teachers are expected to respond appropriately or face the consequences.

Personal, in the form of interpersonal leadership, motivational technology, and human relations skills. When supervisory policies and practices are based on personal authority, teachers are expected to respond to the supervisor's personality, to the pleasant environment provided, and to incentives for positive behavior. Personal authority is enhanced by learning how to apply insights from psychology and human and organizational behavior.

Technical-rational, in the form of evidence derived from logic and scientific research in education. When supervisory policies and practices are based on the authority of technical rationality, teachers are expected to respond according to what is considered the truth. Research, for example, tells teachers what to do rather than informs the decision they make about what to do.

Professional, in the form of experience, knowledge of the craft, and personal expertise. When supervisory policies and practices are based on professional authority, teachers are expected to respond to common socialization, accepted tenets of practice, and internalized expertise. Research, in this case, does not tell teachers what to do but informs the decision that they make about what to do.

Moral, in the form of obligations and duties derived from widely shared values, ideas, and ideals. When supervisory policies and practices are based on moral authority, teachers are expected to respond to shared commitments and felt interdependence.[1]

Each of the five sources of authority is legitimate and should be used, but the impact on teachers and on the teaching and learning process depends on which source or combination of sources is prime. Authority underlying Supervision I is a combination of bureaucratic, psychological, and technical-rational. Supervision II is based primarily on professional and moral authority.

Each of the four supervisors described in Chapter 1 views authority for supervision differently. Supervisor A relies heavily on a combination of bureaucratic and technical-rational authority in implementing the instructional system in Metro City. The system itself, for example, is based on the school effectiveness and teaching effectiveness research in vogue during the 1970s and 1980s, and supervisor A appeals to the type of authority advocated in this research ("Research says that these are the indicators of effective teaching"; "Research says that tightly aligned curriculum and teaching to objectives and then testing for mastery produces better results"; and so on). Further, the teaching, supervisory, and

---

[1]The discussion of sources of authority for supervision in this chapter is based on Thomas J. Sergiovanni, "Moral Authority and the Regeneration of Supervision," in Carl Glickman (ed.), *Supervision in Transition.* Alexandria, Va.: Association for Supervision and Curriculum Development, 1992; and "The Sources of Authority for Leadership," in Thomas J. Sergiovanni, *The Moral Dimensions in Leadership.* San Francisco: Jossey-Bass, 1992, chap. 3.

testing processes to be followed are specified as rule-bound standard operating procedures. A system of monitoring is provided to check compliance, and penalties are levied for noncompliance. In the ideal, supervisor A reasons, the school should recruit teachers who are willing to go along with the desired instructional system at the outset. The reason is that bureaucratic and technical-rational sources of authority exist independent of people and of situations. It matters not what is unique about a particular classroom or what hunches the teacher has. Bureaucratic and technical-rational sources of authority are not defined by idiosyncrasy.

Supervisor B, on the other hand, recommends relying on certain kinds of knowledge about psychology and human behavior in developing personal authority, expressed as human relations leadership, to get the job done. The instructional system itself is not questioned, and the weight of bureaucratic and technical-rational authority is accepted but not emphasized. Bureaucratic and technical-rational sources of authority may motivate supervisors, but not teachers. Supervisor B might say: "Yes, research says so-and-so, but if you want teachers to follow the research, don't preach it, just treat them right"; "Procedures have to be followed, but in seeking compliance emphasize positive rewards rather than negative penalties"; or "Remember to involve teachers because they like to be involved and as a result are more likely to work within the system." Whether the research in question fits a particular teacher's personality or teaching situation is less important. Supervisor B sees rewards as better than reason and seeks to involve teachers in decision making because they will be more satisfied and thus less troublesome to supervise.

Supervisor C also relies on a form of personal authority but one that is different from that used by supervisor B. Bureaucratic and technical-rational sources of authority are not ignored, but they count less. Further, they are understood differently by supervisor C than by supervisor B. For example, supervisor C believes that it is okay to have a general sense of what is to be accomplished. Teachers are then involved in fleshing out this general sense into a more specific design. Bureaucratic rules in this case take the form of broad policies that guide the decision-making process. Research, too, plays a role, but is viewed less as a script to be followed and more as a series of revelations that can inform the shared decision-making process. Supervisor C relies heavily on developing the right interpersonal climate and on meeting teachers' needs for achievement, esteem, recognition, and autonomy within some general framework.

Supervisor D views sources of bureaucratic and technical-rational authority in a fashion similar to supervisor C. Personal authority also has its place, but what matters most are shared values and beliefs that become norms governing behavior. These norms are connected to the teacher's sense of professionalism, knowledge of the craft, and membership in the school as a learning community. Norms represent a form of moral authority. Professional and moral authority are the two sources relied upon most by supervisor D.

In the sections that follow we take a closer look at each of the five sources of authority, examining the assumptions underlying each one when it is used as the prime source, the supervision strategies suggested by each, and the impact each one has on the work of teachers and on the teaching and learning process.

BUREAUCRATIC AUTHORITY

As suggested above, bureaucratic authority relies heavily on hierarchy, rules and regulations, mandates, and clearly communicated role expectations as a way to provide teachers with a script to follow. Teachers, in turn, are expected to comply with this script or face consequences. There may be a place for this source of authority even in the most progressive of enterprises, but when this source of authority is *prime*, the following assumptions are made:

Teachers are subordinates in a hierarchically arranged system.

Supervisors are trustworthy, but you can't trust subordinates very much.

The goals and interests of teachers and those of supervisors are not the same; thus, supervisors must be watchful.

Hierarchy equals expertise; thus, supervisors know more about everything than do teachers.

External accountability works best.

With these assumptions in place it becomes important for supervisors to provide teachers with prescriptions for what, when, and how to teach, and for governing other aspects of their school lives. These are provided in the form of expectations. Supervisors then practice a policy of "expect and inspect" to ensure compliance with these prescriptions. Heavy reliance is placed on predetermined standards to which teachers must measure up. Since teachers often will not know how to do what needs to be done, it is important for supervisors to identify their needs and then to "in-service" them in some way. Directly supervising and closely monitoring the work of teachers is key in order to ensure continued compliance with prescriptions and expectations. To the extent possible, it is also a good idea to figure out how to motivate teachers and encourage them to change in ways that conform with the system.

The consequences of relying on bureaucratic authority in supervision have been carefully documented in the literature. Without proper monitoring, teachers wind up being loosely connected to bureaucratic systems, complying only when they have to.[2] When monitoring is effective in enforcing compliance, teachers respond as technicians who execute predetermined scripts and whose performance is narrowed. They become, to use the jargon, "deskilled."[3] When teach-

[2]See, for example, Karl Weick, "Educational Organizations as Loosely Coupled Systems," *Administrative Science Quarterly*, vol. 21, no. 2 (1976), pp. 1–19; and Thomas J. Sergiovanni, "Biting the Bullet: Rescinding the Texas Teacher Appraisal System," *Teachers Education and Practice*, vol. 6, no. 2 (Fall/Winter 1990–1991), 89–93.

[3]See, for example, Arthur E. Wise, *Legislated Learning: The Bureaucratization of the American Classroom*. Berkeley, Calif.: University of California Press, 1979; Susan Rosenholtz, *Teachers' Workplace: The Social Organization of Schools*. New York: Longman, 1989; and Linda McNeil, *Contradictions of Control: School Structure and School Knowledge*. New York: Routledge & Kegan Paul, 1986.

ers are not able to use their talents fully and are caught in the grind of routine, they become separated from their work, viewing teaching as a job rather than a vocation, and treating students as cases rather than persons.

Readers probably will have little difficulty accepting the assertion that supervision based primarily on bureaucratic authority is not a good idea. The validity of most of the assumptions underlying this source of authority are suspect. Few, for example, believe that teachers as a group are not trustworthy and do not share the same goals and interests about schooling as do their supervisors. Even fewer would accept the idea that hierarchy equals expertise. Less contested, perhaps, would be the assumptions that teachers are subordinates in a hierarchically arranged system and that external monitoring works best. Supervision today relies heavily on predetermined standards. Because of this, supervisors need to spend a good deal of time trying to figure out strategies for motivating teachers and encouraging them to change. Supervision becomes a direct, intense, and often exhausting activity.

PERSONAL AUTHORITY

Personal authority is based on the supervisor's leadership expertise in using motivational techniques and in practicing other interpersonal skills. It is assumed that as a result of this leadership, teachers will want to comply with the supervisor's wishes. When human relations skills become the prime source of authority, the following assumptions are made:

The goals and interests of teachers and supervisors are not the same. As a result, each must barter with the other so that both get what they want by giving something that the other party wants.

Teachers have needs; if these needs are met, the work gets done as required in exchange.

Congenial relationships and harmonious interpersonal climates make teachers content, easier to work with, and more apt to cooperate.

Supervisors must be experts at reading the needs of teachers and handling people in order to barter successfully for increased compliance and performance.

These assumptions lead to a supervisory practice that relies heavily on "expect and reward" and "what gets rewarded gets done." Emphasis is also given to developing a school climate characterized by a high degree of congeniality among teachers and between teachers and supervisors. Often personal authority is used in combination with bureaucratic and technical-rational authority. When this is the case very few of the things that the supervisor wants from teachers are negotiable. The idea is to obtain compliance by trading psychological payoffs of one sort or another.

Personal authority is also important to the practice of human resources leadership. In this case, however, as suggested in Chapter 1, it takes a slightly different twist. The emphasis is less on meeting teachers' social needs and more on providing the *conditions of work* that allow people to meet needs for achievement, challenge, responsibility, autonomy, and esteem—the presumed basis for finding deep psychological fulfillment in one's job.

The typical reaction of teachers to personal authority, particularly when connected to human relations supervision, is to respond as required when rewards are available but not otherwise. Teachers become involved in their work for calculated reasons, and their performance becomes increasingly narrowed. When the emphasis is on psychological fulfillment that comes from the work itself (emphasizing challenging work, for example) rather than the supervisor's skilled interpersonal behavior, teachers become more intrinsically motivated and thus less susceptible to calculated involvement and narrowing of performance. But in today's supervision this emphasis remains the exception rather than the rule.

Suggesting that using personal authority and the psychological theories that inform this authority as the basis for supervisory practice may be overdone and may have negative consequences for teachers and students is likely to raise a few eyebrows. Most supervisors, for example, tend to consider knowledge and skill about how to motivate teachers, how to apply the correct leadership style, how to boost morale, and how to engineer the right interpersonal climate as representing the heart of their work. It is for many supervisors the "core technology" of their profession.

We do not challenge the importance of psychologically based supervision and leadership. Indeed, we argued for its importance in earlier editions. We do question, however, whether it should continue to enjoy the prominence that it does. Our position is that personal, bureaucratic, and technical-rational sources of authority should do no more than provide support for a supervisory practice that relies on professional and moral authority. The reasons, we argue here and elsewhere in this book, are that psychologically based leadership and supervision cannot tap the full range and depth of human capacity and will. This source of authority cannot elicit the kind of motivated and spirited response from teachers that will allow schools to work well. We hope to build a case for this assertion in Chapters 6 and 7, where we examine what is important to teachers at work.

Another reason for our concern with the overuse of personal authority is that there are practically and morally better reasons for teachers and others to be involved in the work of the school than those related to matters of the leader's personality and interpersonal skills. Haller and Strike, for example, believe that building one's expertise around interpersonal themes raises important ethical questions. In their words

> We find this an inadequate view of the administrative role . . . its first deficiency is that it makes administrative success depend on characteristics that tend to be both intangible and unalterable. One person's dynamic leader is another's tyrant. What one person sees as a democratic style, another will see as the generation of time-wasting committee work. . . . Our basic concern with this view . . . is that it makes the administrative role one of form, not content. Being a successful administrator depends not on the adequacy of one's view, not on the educational policies that one adopts and how reasonable they are, and not on how successful one is in communicating those reasons to

others. Success depends on personality and style, or on carefully chosen ways of inducing others to contribute to the organization. It is not what one wants to do and why that is important; it is who one is and how one does things that counts. We find such a view offensive. It is incompatible with the values of autonomy, reason and democracy, which we see among the central commitments of our society and educational system. Of course educational administrators must be leaders, but let them lead by reason and persuasion, not by forces of personality.[4]

Carl Glickman raises still other doubts about the desirability of basing supervisory practice on psychological authority. He believes that such leadership creates dependency among followers.[5]

The perspectives of Haller and Strike and Glickman raise a nagging set of questions: Why should teachers follow the lead of their supervisors? Is it because supervisors know how to manipulate effectively? Is it because supervisors can meet the psychological needs of teachers? Is it because supervisors are charming and fun to be with? Or is it because supervisors have something to say that makes sense? Or because supervisors have thoughts that point teachers in a direction that captures their imagination? Or because supervisors speak from a set of ideas, values, and conceptions that they believe are good for teachers, for students, and for the school? These questions raise yet another question: Do supervisors want to base their practice on glitz or on substance? Choosing glitz not only raises moral questions but also encourages a vacuous form of leadership and supervisory practice. It can lead to what Abraham Zaleznik refers to as the "managerial mystique," the substitution of process for substance.[6]

TECHNICAL-RATIONAL AUTHORITY

Technical-rational authority relies heavily on evidence that is defined by logic and scientific research. Teachers are expected to comply with prescriptions based on this source of authority in light of what is considered to be truth.

When technical rationality becomes the primary source of authority for supervisory practice, the following assumptions are made:

Supervision and teaching are applied sciences.
Scientific knowledge is superordinate to practice.
Teachers are skilled technicians.
Values, preferences, and beliefs are subjective and ephemeral; facts and objective evidence are what matters.

When technical-rational authority is established, then the supervisory strategy is to use research to identify what is best teaching practice and what is best

[4]Emil J. Haller and Kenneth A. Strike, *An Introduction to Educational Administration: Social, Legal and Ethical Perspectives.* New York: Longman, 1986, p. 326.

[5]Carl D. Glickman, "Right Question, Wrong Extrapolation: A Response to Duffey's 'Supervising for Results,' " *Journal of Curriculum and Supervision*, vol. 6, no. 1 (Fall 1990), pp. 39–40.

[6]Abraham Zaleznik, *The Managerial Mystique Restoring Leadership in Business.* New York: Harper & Row, 1989.

supervisory practice. Once this is known, the work of teaching and supervision is standardized to reflect the best way. The next step is to in-service teachers in the best way. For the system to work smoothly, it is best if teachers willingly conform to what the research says ought to be done and how it ought to be done. Thus it is important to figure out how to motivate teachers and encourage them to change willingly.

When technical-rational authority is the primary source, the impact on teachers is similar to that of bureaucratic authority. Teachers are less likely to conform to what research says and more likely to act according to their beliefs. When forced to conform, they are likely to respond as technicians executing predetermined steps, and their performance becomes increasingly narrowed. When technical-rational authority is used in combination with personal authority, teachers tend to conform as long as they are being rewarded.

If criticism of a supervisory practice based on personal authority raises concerns, then suggesting that primary use of technical-rational authority is dysfunctional is also likely to raise concerns. We live, after all, in a technical-rational society where that which is considered scientific is prized. Because of this deference to science, the above beliefs and their related practices are likely to receive ready acceptance. "Supervision and teaching are applied sciences" has a nice ring to it, and using research to identify one best practice seems quite reasonable. But teaching and learning are too complex to be captured so simply. In the real world of teaching none of the assumptions hold up very well, and the related practices portray an unrealistic view of teaching and supervision.

For example, there is a growing sense among researchers, teachers, and policy analysts that the context for teaching practice is too idiosyncratic, nonlinear, and loosely connected for simplistic conceptions of teaching to apply.[7] Teaching cannot be standardized. Teachers, like other professionals, cannot be effective when following scripts. Instead they need to *create knowledge in use* as they practice, becoming skilled surfers who ride the wave of teaching as it uncurls.[8] This ability requires a higher level of reflection, understanding, and skill than that required by the practice of technical rationality—a theme to be further developed in Parts Three and Four.

The authority of technical rationality for supervisory practice does share some similarities with the authority of professionalism. Both, for example, rely on expertise. But the authority of technical rationality presumes that scientific knowl-

---

[7]See, for example, Linda Darling-Hammond, Arthur E. Wise, and S. R. Pease, "Teacher Evaluations in an Organizational Context: A Review of Literature," *Review of Educational Research*, vol. 53, no. 3 (1983), pp. 285–328; Thomas J. Sergiovanni, "The Metaphorical Use of Theories and Models in Supervision and Teaching: Building a Science," *Journal of Curriculum and Supervision*, vol. 2, no. 3 (Spring 1987), pp. 221–232; Lee S. Shulman, "A Union of Insufficiencies: Strategies for Teacher Assessment in a Period of Educational Reform," *Educational Leadership*, vol. 16, no. 3 (1988), pp. 36–41; and Michael Huberman, "The Social Context of Instruction in Schools." Paper presented at American Educational Research Association Annual Meeting, Boston, April 1990.

[8]Thomas J. Sergiovanni, "Will We Ever Have a TRUE Profession?" *Educational Leadership*, vol. 44, no. 8 (1987), pp. 44–51.

edge is the only source of expertise. Further, this knowledge exists separate from the context of teaching. The job of the teacher is simply to apply this knowledge in practice. In other words, the teacher is *subordinate* to the knowledge base of teaching.

PROFESSIONAL AUTHORITY

Professional authority presumes that the expertise of teachers counts most. Teachers, as is the case with other professionals, are always *superordinate* to the knowledge base that supports their practice. Professionals view knowledge as something that informs but does not prescribe practice.[9] What counts as well is the ability of teachers to make judgments based on the specifics of the situations they face. They must decide what is appropriate. They must decide what is right and good. They must, in sum, create professional knowledge in use as they practice.

Professional authority is based on the informed knowledge of the craft of teaching and on the personal expertise of teachers. Teachers respond in part to this expertise and in part to internalized professional values, to accepted tenets of practice that define what it means to be a teacher.

When professional authority becomes the primary source for supervisory practice, the following assumptions are made:

Situations are idiosyncratic; thus, no one best way to practice exists.

"Scientific knowledge" and "professional knowledge" are different; professional knowledge is created as teachers practice.

The purpose of "scientific knowledge" is to inform, not prescribe, the practice of teachers and supervisors.

Professional authority is not external but is exercised within the teaching context and from within the teacher.

Authority in context comes from the teacher's training and experience.

Authority from within comes from the teacher's professional socialization and internalized knowledge and values.

Supervisory practice that is based primarily on professional authority seeks to promote a dialogue among teachers that makes explicit professional values and accepted tenets of practice. These are then translated into professional practice standards. With standards acknowledged, teachers are then provided with as much discretion as they want and need. When professional authority is fully developed, teachers will hold each other accountable in meeting these practice standards with accountability internalized. The job of the supervisor is to pro-

---

[9]Thomas J. Sergiovanni, "The Metaphorical Use of Theories and Models in Supervision: Building a Science," *Journal of Curriculum and Supervision,* vol. 2, no. 3 (1987), pp. 221–232.

vide assistance, support, and professional development opportunities. Teachers respond to professional norms, and their performance becomes more expansive.

Though it is common to refer to teaching as a profession, not much attention has been given to the nature of professional authority. When the idea does receive attention, the emphasis is on the expertise of teachers. Building teacher expertise is a long-term proposition. In the meantime much can be done to advance another aspect of professionalism—*professional virtue.* Professional virtue speaks to the norms that define what it means to be a professional. Once established, professional norms take on moral attributes. When professional norms are combined with norms derived from shared community values, moral authority can become a prime basis for supervisory practice. These themes will be explored further in the next chapter, "Community as a Force for Change."

MORAL AUTHORITY

Moral authority is derived from the obligations and duties that teachers feel as a result of their connection to widely shared community values, ideas, and ideals. When moral authority is in place, teachers respond to shared commitments and felt interdependence by becoming self-managing.

When moral authority becomes the primary source for supervisory practice, schools can become transformed from organizations into communities. Communities are defined by their center of shared values, beliefs, and commitments. In communities, what is considered right and good is as important as what works and what is effective; teachers are motivated as much by emotion and belief as they are by self-interest; collegiality is understood as a form of professional virtue.

In communities, supervisors direct their efforts toward identifying and making explicit shared values and beliefs. These values and beliefs are then transformed into informal norms that govern behavior. With these in place it becomes possible to promote collegiality as something that is internally felt and that derives from morally driven interdependence. Supervisors can rely less on external controls and more on the ability of teachers as community members to respond to felt duties and obligations. The school community's informal norm system is used to enforce professional and community values. Norms and values, whether derived from professional authority or moral authority, become substitutes for direct supervision as teachers become increasingly self-managing. The five sources of authority for supervision with consequences for practice are summarized in Table 3–1.

Community and professional norms as expressions of moral authority play major roles in Supervision II, the recommended alternative to today's supervisory practice. They are described more fully in Chapter 4. Chapter 6, "Supervision as Moral Action," and Chapter 9, "Developing Teacher Leadership" extend the theme by examining how moral authority is expressed in day-to-day supervisory practice.

TABLE 3-1
THE SOURCES OF AUTHORITY FOR SUPERVISORY POLICY AND PRACTICE

Source	Assumptions When Use of This Source Is Prime	Leadership/Supervisory Strategy	Consequences
Bureaucratic authority Hierarchy Rules and regulations Mandates Role expectation Teachers are expected to comply or face consequences.	Teachers are subordinates in a hierarchically arranged system. Supervisors are trustworthy, but you cannot trust subordinates very much. Goals and interests of teachers and supervisors are not the same; thus, supervisors must be watchful. Hierarchy equals expertise; thus, supervisors know more than teachers. External accountability works best.	"Expect and inspect" is the overarching rule. Rely on predetermined standards to which teachers must measure up. Identify teachers' needs and "in-service" them. Directly supervise and closely monitor the work of teachers to ensure compliance. Figure out how to motivate teachers and get them to change.	With proper monitoring teachers respond as technicians in executing predetermined scripts. Their performance is narrowed.
Personal authority Motivation technology Interpersonal skills Human relations leadership Teachers will want to comply because of the congenial climate provided and to reap rewards offered in exchange.	The goals and interests of teachers and supervisors are not the same but can be bartered so that each gets what they want. Teachers have needs; if those needs are met, the work gets done as required in exchange. Congenial relationships and harmonious interpersonal climates make teachers content, easier to work with, and more apt to cooperate.	Develop a school climate characterized by congeniality among teachers and between teachers and supervisors. "Expect and reward." "What gets rewarded gets done."	Teachers respond as required when rewards are available but not otherwise. Their involvement is calculated, and performance is narrowed.

TABLE 3–1 *(continued)*

Source	Assumptions When Use of This Source Is Prime	Leadership/Supervisory Strategy	Consequences
	Supervisors must be expert at reading needs and handling people in order to successfully barter for increased compliance and performance.	Use personal authority in combination with bureaucratic and technical rational authority.	
The authority of technical rationality			
Evidence defined by logic and scientific research	Supervision and teaching are applied sciences.	Use research to identify one best practice.	With proper monitoring, teachers respond as technicians in executing predetermined scripts. Performance is narrowed.
Teachers are required to comply in light of what is considered to be truth.	Knowledge of research is privileged.	Standardize the work of teaching to reflect the best way.	
	Scientific knowledge is superordinate to practice.	"In-service" teachers in the best way.	
	Teachers are skilled technicians.	Monitor the process to ensure compliance.	
	Values, preferences, and beliefs don't count, but facts and objective evidence do.	Figure out ways to motivate teachers and get them to change.	
Professional authority			
Informed knowledge of craft and personal expertise.	Situations are idiosyncratic; thus, no one best way exists.	Promote a dialogue among teachers that makes explicit professional values and accepted tenets of practice.	Teachers respond to professional norms and thus require little monitoring. Their performance is expansive.
Teachers respond on basis of common socialization, professional values, accepted tenets of practice, and internalized expertness.	"Scientific" knowledge and "professional" knowledge are different; professional is created in use as teachers practice.	Translate above into professional practice standards.	

TABLE 3–1 (*continued*)

Source	Assumptions When Use of This Source Is Prime	Leadership/Supervisory Strategy	Consequences
	The purpose of "scientific" knowledge is to inform, not prescribe, practice.	Provide teachers with as much discretion as they want and need.	
	Authority cannot be external but comes from the context itself and from within the teacher.	Require teachers to hold each other accountable in meeting practice standards.	
	Authority from context comes from training and experience.	Make available assistance, support, and professional development opportunities.	
	Authority from within comes from socialization and internalized values.		
Moral authority	Schools are professional learning communities.	Identify and make explicit the values and beliefs that define the center of the school as community. Translate the above into informal norms that govern behavior.	Teachers respond to community values for moral reasons. Their performance is expansive and sustained.
Full obligations and duties derived from widely shared community values, ideas, and ideals	Communities are defined by their center of shared values, beliefs, and commitments.		
Teachers respond to shared commitments and felt interdependence.	In communities:		
	What is considered right and good is as important as what works and what is effective.	Promote collegiality as internally felt and morally driven interdependence.	
	People are motivated as much by emotion and beliefs as by self-interest.	Rely on ability of community members to respond to duties and obligations.	
	Collegiality is a professional virtue.	Rely on the community's informal norm system to enforce professional and community values.	

Source: Thomas J. Sergiovanni, "Moral Authority and the Regeneration of Supervision," in Carl Glickman (ed.), *Supervision in Transition,* 1992 ASCD Yearbook. Alexandria, Va.: Association for Supervision and Curriculum Development, 1992, pp. 203–214. © Thomas J. Sergiovanni. All rights reserved.

SUPERVISION II

In this section some of the basic assumptions and underlying operating principles that differentiate Supervision I from Supervision II are provided. Supervision II combines Theory Y from human resources supervision with the belief that people are morally responsive and able to sacrifice self-interests for the right reasons. Supervision I, by contrast, relies heavily on the assumptions of Theory X (scientific management) and Theory X soft (human relations), as described earlier.

In Supervision I a great deal of emphasis is given to understanding, researching, and improving supervisory behavior. As will be discussed in Part Two, Supervision II emphasizes action. Behavior is very different from action. Behavior is what we do on the surface. Action, by contrast, implies intentionality, free choice, value seeking, and altruism.

Because of this difference between behavior and action, Supervision II focuses more on interpretation. There is concern not only for the way things look but also for what things mean. The metaphors "phonetics" and "semantics" can help this distinction.[10] Tending to supervisory and teaching behaviors as they appear on the surface is an example of the phonetic view. It does not matter so much whether the supervisor is involved in leading, coaching, managing, evaluating, administering, or teaching. If the emphasis in these activities is on "the looks and sounds" of behavior, on the form or shape that this behavior takes as opposed to what the behavior means to teachers and students, the view is phonetic.

Identical behaviors can have different meanings as contexts change and as different people are involved. For example, a supervisor may walk through the classrooms of several teachers on a regular basis, making it a practice to comment to teachers about what is happening and to share her or his impressions. For supervisor A, teachers may consider this behavior inspectorial or controlling and view this supervisor as one who is closely monitoring what they do. For supervisor C this same behavior may be considered symbolic of the interest and support that the supervisor provides to teachers. In this case, supervisory behavior is interpreted as being caring and helpful. At one level, the phonetic, the behavior is the same for both supervisors. At another level, the semantic, the behavior carries different meanings. When concerned with different interpretations and meanings, one is tending to the semantic aspects of supervision.

Motivation in Supervision I focuses primarily on "what gets rewarded gets done." Supervision II is based on "what is rewarding gets done" and "what is believed to be right and good gets done." These latter emphases, as will be discussed in Chapter 5, not only reflect more completely what is important to teachers at work but also result in less emphasis on direct control-oriented supervision. When motivated by intrinsically satisfying and meaningful action, teachers become self-managing.

[10]Sergiovanni, *Educational Leadership*, op. cit.

In Supervision I it is assumed that supervisors and teachers make "rational" decisions on the basis of self-interest and as isolated individuals. Supervision II recognizes the importance of emotions and values in making decisions and the capacity for humans consistently to sacrifice self-interest as a result. Further, Supervision II recognizes that our connections to other people to a great extent determine what we think, what we believe, and the decisions that we make. These two themes will be explored further in Chapters 5 and 6.

Supervision I takes place in the context of hierarchically differentiated roles. "Supervision" and "designated supervisor" go together. Supervision is something that supervisors do to teachers. A teacher studies to become a supervisor, becomes licensed, and thus is allowed to practice supervision. Supervision, in other words, is a formal and institutionalized process linked to the school's organizational structure.

Supervision II views supervision as a process and function that is hierarchically independent and role-free. It may be linked to hierarchy and role, but it need not be. Supervision, in other words, is not necessarily shaped by organizational structure and is not necessarily legitimized by credentials. Instead, it is a set of ideals and skills that can be translated into processes that can help teachers and help schools function more effectively. Supervision is something that not only principals and hierarchically designated supervisors do but also teachers and others. Thus, such ideas as collegial supervision, mentoring supervision, cooperative supervision, and informal supervision are important in Supervision II. In a sense these processes are often in place in schools anyway. Teachers respect each other's craft knowledge and depend on each other for help. One of the purposes of Supervision II, therefore, is to deinstitutionalize institutional supervision and to formalize the informal supervision among teachers that now takes place in schools.

MODELS OF CONTROL

Supervision is a process designed to help teachers and supervisors learn more about their practice, to be better able to use their knowledge and skills to serve parents and schools, and to make the school a more effective learning community. For these goals to be realized, a degree of control over events is necessary, and in this sense supervision is about control. But it makes a difference how control is expressed in schools. The wrong kind of control can cause problems and lead to negative consequences despite the best of intentions.

Control is understood differently in Supervisions I and II. For example, the management theorist Henry Mintzberg proposed that the work of others can be controlled by providing direct and close supervision of what people are doing; by standardizing the work that needs to be done, then fitting people into the work system so that they are forced to follow the approved script; by standardizing outputs and then evaluating to be sure that output specifications have been met; by socializing people through the use of norms of one sort or another; and by arranging work circumstances and norms in a way that people feel a need to be interdependent.[11] When referring to socializing people, Mintzberg had in mind professional norms. The norms that come from common purposes and shared values provide still another control strategy that can be added to Mintzberg's list.[12]

In Chapter 1 supervisor A relied heavily on providing direct supervision, standardizing the work, and standardizing outputs as the preferred ways to control what teachers were doing and how. By contrast, supervisor D recommended relying on the process of socialization, building interdependencies, and developing purposes and shared values. Which of the two views makes the most sense? In part, the answer to this question depends upon the degree of complexity of the work to be supervised.

Fostering professional socialization, developing purposes and shared values, and building natural interdependencies among teachers are unique in that they are able to provide a kind of normative power that encourages people to meet their commitments. Once in place, the three become substitutes for traditional supervision, since teachers tend to respond from within, becoming self-managing. Since these strategies do not require direct supervision or the scripting of work, they are better matched to the complex behaviors that are required for teaching and learning to take place successfully. These are the strategies that provide the framework for control in Supervision II. The three are much more difficult to implement when schools are viewed as formal organizations. Such organizations tend to nurture control systems that rely on direct supervision, standardized work, and standardized outputs. In the next chapter we propose that one way to improve schools is to change the way they are understood, transforming them from organizations into communities.

THE IMPORTANCE OF CAPACITY BUILDING

From the discussion so far, it appears that Supervision II is the preferred method and no room exists for practices associated with Supervision I. Similarly, bureaucratic and personal authority should be abandoned for leadership and supervision based on professional and moral authority. But the reality is that ideas from both views of supervision have a place in a unified and contextually oriented practice. Most teachers have a natural inclination to respond to Supervision II. As this approach comes to dominate supervisory practice, schools will very likely be better places for teachers and students. But some teachers will not be ready to respond. Others may want to respond but lack the necessary knowledge and skill to function in this new environment. Furthermore, in many places the existing culture of teaching does not encourage the practices associated with Supervision II. What should supervisors do?

---

[11]Henry Mintzberg, *The Structure of Organizations*. New York: Wiley, 1979.
[12]Karl Weick, "The Concept of Loose Coupling: An Assessment," *Organizational Theory Dialogue*, (December 1986); and Thomas J. Peters and Robert H. Waterman, *In Search of Excellence*. New York: Harper & Row, 1982.

We believe the answer is to start with where teachers are now and to begin the struggle to change the existing norms in schools so that Supervision II becomes acceptable. Of particular importance in this struggle will be the emphasis supervisors give to capacity building. Take teacher leadership, for example. Before we can expect teachers to accept fuller responsibility for providing leadership, they must be encouraged to do so and they must know how to provide this leadership. Both of these goals are best achieved when teachers are members of a support network that strives to become a community of leaders. For teachers to be developers and supervisors of classroom learning communities, they must be part of a learning community themselves. Capacity building and changing school norms are what Michael Fullan describes as "reculturing."[13] Whatever is the focus of supervisory work, if Supervision II is to be the framework for embodying that focus, then reculturing will be at the heart of supervisory work.

[13]Michael Fullan, *Change Forces*. London: Falmer Press, 1993.

CHAPTER 4

COMMUNITY AS A FORCE
FOR CHANGE

WHAT should the basic purpose of supervision be in schools? Some supervisors would respond *control.* The basic purpose of supervision is to control both people and events to make sure that accepted ways of doing things are followed. Other supervisors might respond *development.* The basic purpose of supervision is to develop teachers so that they are better able to perform at higher levels. Building *professional community* might be a favorite of other supervisors. The basic purpose of supervision is to connect teachers to each other by building collegial relationships characterized by caring, inquiry, and shared practice. *Accountability* is another answer. The basic purpose of supervision is to make sure that everyone is fulfilling his or her responsibilities. *Leadership* would also be mentioned. The basic purpose of supervision is to inspire, motivate, and persuade people to do their best.

Advocates might differ on what the primary purpose of supervision is, but most would justify their choice for the same reasons. Accountability, leadership, development, control, and so on as the basis for supervision can help to improve schools so that students have better opportunities to develop and learn. Improving schools involves change. Supervision is widely viewed as a means to bring about this change. The change that matters in schools is that which results in a better developmental life for teachers and students and improved teaching and learning.

BRINGING ABOUT CHANGE

How can supervisors bring about successful change in schools? This is a question with many different answers, some of which follow. For example, supervisors can:

- Mandate that teachers do certain things thought to result in improvements and/or that schools meet certain standardized outcomes. They can then provide a management system complete with evaluation, rewards, and punishments to back up their mandate for change.
- Rely on corporate images of vision and leadership to motivate, inspire, or otherwise persuade teachers and schools to change.
- Apply market theories and principles to schools. These principles will allow the "invisible hand" of competition, backed by rewards for winners, to bring about change.
- Invest in capacity building to increase teacher professionalism. Professionalism, in turn, can increase the willingness of teachers to change.
- Change the culture of schools by helping them to become democratic communities that compel teachers to change.[1]

The answer a particular supervisor chooses depends on two things: how he or she understands the nature of schools and how he or she understands human nature. Different understandings lead to different change strategies. Not all strategies are equally effective in bringing about deep change. Deep change alters relationships among students, among teachers, and between teachers and students. It affects how teachers understand subject matter, pedagogy, and the way students learn and results in altered teachers' skills, teaching behaviors, and student performance. Deep change is contrasted with structural change, which influences the operation of schools without affecting what happens in classrooms. We will argue here that deep change results when the approach to change matches the unique cultural characteristics of schools. Changing schools, in other words, involves changing school cultures.

What are the views of schools that shape the way different supervisors think about change? Many supervisors view schools as formal organizations that share characteristics with other such organizations. This view allows for easy transfer to schools of assumptions and practices from the generic world of formal organizations. Thus, strategies for change (along with strategies for motivation, organization, accountability, and other aspects of supervisory leadership) that work well in the organizations found in the corporate world and in the formal organizations found in other sectors of society are generally assumed to apply

---

[1]This discussion of change is based on T. J. Sergiovanni, "Organization, Market and the Community as Strategies for Change: What Works Best for Deep Changes in Schools," in Andy Hargreaves (ed.), *International Handbook of Educational Change*. Washington, D.C.: American Educational Research Association, in press.

to schools.[2] This assumption explains why corporate restructuring, standards setting, accountability, and increased competition play such a large role in school reform efforts and why images from other sectors of society are often overlooked.

ORGANIZATIONAL TYPES

Many respected voices in organizational theory take a different view, believing that formal organizations represent only one of several conceptions of human association.[3] W. G. Ouchi,[4] for example, identifies three organizational types: bureaucracies, markets, and clans. He notes that bureaucracies get things done by developing rational systems of expectations; by placing value on members' contributions directed to achieving expectations; by providing supervision, rules, and other means to guide and enable the process; and by compensating fairly. Markets rely on the "natural" interdependence that emerges from interactions among people that take the form of trading compliance for desired incentives. Clans connect people to shared values and beliefs and rely on emergent norms that discourage opportunistic behavior and that promote commitment to the common good. To be consistent with our definitions in this edition, we will refer to Ouchi's distinctions as organizations, markets, and communities.

Differentiating among organizational types raises important questions for supervision. If different types exist, then a more effective approach in changing schools may be to first identify the type that best fits the school and then to adopt an approach to change that leads to the development of unique change strategies for the school—change strategies that match their special leadership and cultural requirements. Our present practice of treating all organized entities the same and thus indiscriminately transferring practices from one to the other can result in a category error that raises questions of validity. If schools should not be viewed as formal organizations but as something else (perhaps markets or communities), then a borrowed motivational, leadership, change, or other supervisory strategy that may have been valid in its original context may not be valid in schools. To put it another way, since educational practices are confirmed and validated by their underlying theories, what seems like reasonable and correct

---

[2]Sergiovanni, T. J. *Leadership for the School House* How is it Different? Why is it Important? San Francisco: Jossey-Bass, 1996.

[3]Blau and Scott make an important distinction between social organizations and formal organizations. They point out that "we would not call a family an organization, nor would we so designate a friendship clique, or a community, or an economic market, or the political institutions of our society" (p. 2). To them what differentiates formal organizations from more social enterprises is how human conduct becomes socially organized. By this Blau and Scott mean the regularities and behavior of people in the enterprise that are due to the social condition in which they find themselves rather than to their physiological or psychological characteristics as individuals. See P. M. Blau and W. R. Scott, *Formal Organization: A Comparative Approach.* San Francisco: Chandler, 1962.

[4]W. G. Ouchi, "Markets, Bureaucracies and Clans," *Administrative Science Quarterly*, vol. 25, no. 1 (1980), pp. 129–141.

practice may wind up being neither reasonable nor correct if the underlying theory is wrong.

CHANGE FORCES

Different ways of viewing schools can create different change realities. These realities become the basis for the policies and practices used to reform schools. We can think of these strategies as change forces.[5] Six change forces can be identified: bureaucratic, personal, market, professional, cultural, and democratic. Each of these forces relies on different strategies and practices to leverage change:

- Bureaucratic forces include rules, mandates, and other requirements intended to provide direct supervision, standardized work processes, and standardized outcomes.
- Personal forces include the personalities, leadership styles, and interpersonal skills of supervisors.
- Market forces include competition, incentives, and individual choice theories.
- Professional forces include standards of expertise, codes of conduct, collegiality, felt obligations, and other norms intended to build professional community.
- Cultural forces include shared values, goals, and ideas about pedagogy, relationships, and politics intended to build covenantal community.
- Democratic forces include social contracts and shared commitments to the common good intended to build democratic community.

Bureaucratic and personal change forces are favored by supervisors who view schools as "bureaucratic" or "organic" formal organizations.[6] Both types of change forces are organizationally oriented, with the first relying on patterns of rules and legal requirements aligned with management protocols and the second relying on the personalities, leadership styles, and interpersonal skills of

---

[5]Using force as the metaphor for change communicates both intent and inclusiveness. Force, for example, implies strength or energy brought to bear to move something or to resist movement. Force can also take many forms. It can be power understood in physical terms, organizational conventions understood in bureaucratic terms, mental strength or attraction understood in psychological terms, or felt obligations understood in moral terms. Leadership can be thought of as comprising a set of forces that include technical competence, human relations skills, educational know-how, symbolic messages, and cultural matters that school principals can use to influence people and events. See, for example, T. J. Sergiovanni, "Leadership and Excellence in Schools," *Educational Leadership*, vol. 41, no. 5 (1984), pp. 4–14. Michael Fullan coined the term "change forces" to communicate similar meaning aimed specifically at change issues. See his *Change Forces*. New York: Falmer Press, 1993.

[6]Organic organizations differ from bureaucratic in style but not substance. Instead of using rules, regulations, hierarchies, and so on to achieve bureaucratic ends, organic organizations rely on the leadership styles and skills and the motivational know-how of their leaders. They emphasize personal rather than bureaucratic authority.

leaders to either require or motivate change. Market forces, by contrast, are not organizationally oriented. Instead of using visible rules or direct leadership, they rely on the "invisible hand" of competition, incentives, and individual choice theories to motivate change.

Supervisors who view schools as communities are inclined to favor professional, cultural, and democratic forces to leverage change. These forces rely on standards of expertise, codes of conduct, collegiality, felt obligations, shared values, democratic social contracts, and shared commitments. Bureaucratic, personal, and market forces strive to motivate or otherwise induce change directly. Professional, cultural, and democratic forces seek to provide the conditions that result in the emergence of standards and norms that compel change.

KEY MEDIATING VARIABLES

The deciding factor in determining whether a chosen strategy is likely to be successful or not in bringing about deep change in schools is its ability to influence key mediating variables in the change equation. These variables include the extent to which teachers:

- Are connected to shared norms that support proposed changes.
- Understand differently the subjects they teach.
- Have an expanded understanding of how students learn.
- Have the necessary skills to teach differently.

If these key mediating variables are influenced positively by the change forces used, then enduring changes in relationships, teaching practice, and student learning are likely to occur. If not, then any change is likely to be structural rather than deep.

Bureaucratic, personal, and market forces generally result in changes in school structure. But because these three forces are only loosely connected to the mediating variables, they are less likely to result in any deep change. Professional, cultural, and democratic forces, on the other hand, may or may not result in changes in structure. But because these forces are tightly connected to the mediating variables, they are more likely to be powerful enough to result in deep change in relationships, teaching practices, and student learning.

Among the key mediating variables is the capacity of shared norms to influence change. Deep change requires that new pedagogical, relational, and political norms be cultivated.[7] Cultivating new beliefs points to the importance of

[7]See J. Oakes, "Normative, Technical, and Political Dimension of Creating New Educational Communities," in J. Oakes and K. H. Quartz (eds.), *Creating New Educational Communities*, Part I. Chicago: University of Chicago Press, 1995, pp. 1–15; K. H. Quartz, "Sustaining New Educational Communities Toward a New Culture of School Reform," in ibid., pp. 1–15, 240–252.

strategies for change that invest heavily in teacher development. New norms, for example, must not only be learned and believed in, but also be embodied in teaching practices. Embodiment in practice, in turn, presumes that teachers learn the new understandings and skills to practice differently. A situated model of teacher development, linked to the changes being proposed and anchored in teachers' constructing knowledge for themselves, is an important strategy for influencing the key mediating variables.

Change strategies based on bureaucratic, personal, and market forces overlook the importance of helping teachers to develop new understandings of the subjects they teach and new understandings of how students learn. Regardless of the presence of new norms that encourage change, unless teachers know how to change and are able to do so, such change is not likely to occur.

CONSEQUENCES FOR CHANGE

Which change forces are most appropriate for an individual school? The answer depends on how this question is framed. If the question is given as What works to bring about quick changes in a school? or What works to bring about changes in school structure and arrangements? then the best change forces are those based on views of the school as a formal bureaucratic organization, a formal organic organization, or a market. But when the question is framed as What works over the long term? or What works for leveraging deep change? then the best change forces are those based on the view of the school as a community. As suggested earlier, deep change involves changing the intrinsic school culture. And changing school culture requires a change in meanings that are individually and collectively held by teachers—requirements more likely to be met by the view of the school as a community. The six change forces and their consequences are summarized in Table 4–1.

Images of the school as a covenantal learning, professional, or democratic community are based on optimistic assumptions about human nature.[8] Those who advocate community change forces believe that given the opportunity and the right conditions (the right leadership, training, discretion, and support), principals and teachers will make the right decisions. They will be morally responsive. Control need not be externally provided, but will come from within. And given the opportunity, the needed training and support, and the needed connections to colleagues in a shared practice, principals and teachers will make the kinds of decisions about teaching and learning that will improve schools. Bring students, parents, and other administrators in as fellow citizens bound together by social contracts that define the school as a democratic community, say advocates,

---

[8]For an elaboration, see A. Etzioni, *The Moral Dimension: Toward a New Economics.* New York: The Free Press, 1988; T. Sowell, *A Conflict of Visions.* New York: Morrow, 1987; and T. J. Sergiovanni, *Moral Leadership.* San Francisco: Jossey-Bass, 1982.

TABLE 4–1
CHANGE FORCES AND THEIR CONSEQUENCES

Forces	Practices	Consequences	Observed Changes
Bureaucratic timetables,	Rely on rules, mandates, and requirements to provide direct supervision, standardized work processes, and/or standardized outcomes to prescribe change.	Teachers change just enough to avoid sanctions. Change stops when sanctions are removed.	Changes in structure, and arrangements.
Personal	Rely on personality, leadership style, and interpersonal skills of change agents to motivate change.	Teachers change just enough to receive gratification of needs. Change stops when rewards are not available.	Change in structures, timetables, and arrangements.
Market	Rely on competition, incentives, and individual choice to motivate change.	Teachers change just enough to win in the marketplace. Winning becomes less important after repeated losses.	Mixed but not enduring.
Professional	Rely on standards of of expertise, codes of conduct, collegiality, felt obligations, and other norms to build professional community.	Teachers internalize norms of competence and virtue that compel change.	Deep change that endures.
Cultural	Rely on shared values, goals, and ideas about pedagogy, relationships, and politics to build covenantal community.	Teachers internalize community norms that compel change.	Deep change that endures.
Democratic	Rely on social contracts and shared commitments to the common good to build democratic community.	Teachers internalize democratic norms that compel change.	Deep change that endures.

Adapted from Thomas J. Sergiovanni, "Organization, Market and Community as Strategies for Change: What Works Best for Deep Change in Schools?" in Andy Hargreaves, (ed.), *International Handbook of Educational Change,* Washington D.C.: American Educational Research Association, 1997.

and a revolution in change theory and practice will occur. Change in schools understood as organizations is rules driven. Change in schools understood as markets is incentives driven. But change in schools understood as communities is norms driven. In the next chapter we examine why community is such a powerful force for change in schools, discuss the characteristics of community, and identify what is involved in building a sense of community in schools.

CHAPTER 5

SUPERVISION AND THE STRUGGLE TO BUILD COMMUNITY

LET us begin this discussion of building community in schools by examining supervisor D's theory of supervision.

Supervisor D's analysis of the failed restructured school described in Chapter 1 relies heavily on the belief that though schools may be loosely connected in an organizational and management sense, they are tightly connected in a normative sense. Supervisor D commented, "The changes . . . did not reflect the way schools actually work or how teachers think and behave." And later, "What counts for teachers is not so much the management system but what they believe, the values they share, the assumptions they hold." Supervisor D's recommendation? View the school as a *community.* Develop a set of shared norms and values that define what this community is and how it works. Community norms, supervisor D believes, combined with the norms and values that define teachers as professionals, provide substitutes for management controls, instructional systems, and close supervision by helping teachers to become self-managed.

Supervisor D's ideas about schools and supervision do not make sense in schools understood as organizations. By the same token, the ideas of supervisors A and B do not make sense in schools understood as communities. For example, we often talk about the process of teaching and learning as if it were an instructional delivery system. This is an image generated by the metaphor organization. As you think about the idea of instructional delivery system, your thoughts tend to revolve around such themes as how to identify and carefully develop the targets, goals, steps, procedures, timetables, and schedules that will become the basis for establishing the best routes for delivering instruction; how to properly train deliverers and then provide them with clear instructions as to what to do and how to do it; how to develop a system of monitoring to ensure that instruction is delivered properly; how to provide additional training to correct mistakes and better align what deliverers do with what they are supposed to do; and how to put into place an evaluation scheme that measures the extent to which the system is working. But instructional delivery systems are larger than teachers. They are intended to reduce discretion and to force teachers to assume narrow roles. Since teachers don't like this narrowing, heavy reliance is placed on external motivation and monitoring. Instructional delivery systems, in other words, become supervisory-intensive.

Now imagine the issues that come to mind when schools are viewed as learning communities. In this case, it is likely you will be concerned with how this community will be defined; what the relationships will be among parents, students, teachers, and administrators; what the shared values, purposes, and commitments are that bond this community; how community members will work together to embody these values; what kinds of obligations to the community members should have; and how these obligations will be enforced.[1] These concerns require a kind of supervision different from that needed for instructional delivery systems.

UNDERSTANDING SCHOOLS AS LEARNING COMMUNITIES

We believe that schools should be understood as learning communities. At the heart of any community is its center of values, sentiments, and beliefs that provide the needed cement for bonding people in a common cause.[2]

A community center is an expression of what is valued by the individual school, and it provides a set of norms that guide behavior and give meaning to school community life. The norms become compass settings and sometimes road maps. They answer such questions as what is this school about? What is our image of learners? What makes us unique? How do we work together as colleagues? How does the school as community fit into the larger school community? How do parents fit into the picture? Why are all these questions worth asking and answering?"[3]

In a school, community norms are intermingled with the norms that define teaching as a profession. Together the two sets of norms provide the basis for what should be done and how. Teachers, for example, are not only responsive to shared values, conceptions, and ideals within the school but also bring to the school shared values, conceptions, and ideals that define them as professionals.

---

[1]Thomas J. Sergiovanni, *The Moral Dimension in Leadership*. San Francisco: Jossey-Bass, 1992.

[2]Edward A. Shils, "Centre and Periphery," in Edward A. Shils (ed.), *The Logic of Personal Knowledge: Essays Presented to Michael Polanyi*. London: Routledge & Kegan Paul, 1961, p. 119.

[3]Sergiovanni, op. cit., p. 46.

COMMUNITY AS A MODERN PROBLEM AND A POSTMODERN NECESSITY

Redefining the school as a community, however, is no easy matter. It will involve the supervisor and all the members of the school in a search for agreements on their core values. These core values may represent various interpretations, especially about the importance assigned to the individual, on the one hand, and to the community, on the other. The ambivalence surrounding both of these notions is a reflection of a shift taking place between a modern and a postmodern worldview.[4]

The modern world harbors a deep ambivalence toward the notion of community. What we define as the modern world began with a rebellion against the smothering of individuality and individual initiative by traditional communities of tribe or clan, or by the feudal communities that were governed by religiously legitimated rulers and hierarchically arranged systems of power and class. Within those traditional communities, people were assigned a place and required to keep that place. Individual social advancement and free inquiry were hindered by custom, tradition, and religious authority. In response, modernity embraced the individual as the primary social unit. Society or communities came to be seen as artificial creations of a social contract between individuals and the state whereby, in return for protection from others' invasion of their rights to property and the free pursuit of their own self-interests, they would surrender some of their freedom to state regulation. Communities were no longer understood as "natural," in the sense that they were intrinsic to the naturally social character of human beings. Human beings were declared individual by nature; social relations were pragmatic creations of self-interested individuals, who sought in these relations their own benefit.

Along with exalting the individual, the modern world, often referred to in its origins as the Enlightenment, championed the power of reason and its tool, science. Thus, by the use of his reason (the masculine is used here purposely, since the Enlightenment was more about the emancipation of men than of women), the individual was to be the primary source of truth, the primary player (through enlightened self-interest) in the game of economics, the primary arbiter of moral choice, and the primary figure (again, through enlightened self-interest) in democratic politics.

This belief in the powers of the individual developed into an ideology of "possessive individualism."[5] The individual came to think that he *possessed himself*, in much the same way as he possessed property and wealth. Talents such as intelligence, inventiveness, business acumen, and artistic facility were thought of as personal possessions to be used for the self-realization, satisfaction, and material betterment of their individual owner, independent of any social usefulness

---

[4]Robert J. Starratt, *Transforming Educational Administration: Meaning, Community, and Excellence.* New York: McGraw-Hill, 1996, pp. 87–103.

[5]See Charles B. McPherson, *The Political Theory of Possessive Individualism: Hobbes to Locke.* London: Oxford University Press, 1962.

they might have. This belief in possessive individualism was incorporated into a social and economic philosophy of laissez-faire. Thus, an individual, in seeking his own self-interest in economic, political, or cultural matters, would somehow, by a "hidden hand" of economic and political providence, improve society. By some providential dynamic, the collective efforts of self-seeking individuals within a free marketplace of economic and political striving would, according to this theory, produce the best results for the most people in society.

In such a view community is seen as an aggregate of self-serving individuals who *use* the community for their own individual purposes. Their obligations to the community are simply to avoid infringing on other individuals' rights to act in their own self-interest. Those who win out in the competition for wealth and power in the free marketplace have simply been wise stewards of their possessions. Whatever effects their competition have on the rest of society will somehow contribute to the improved social conditions of everyone. Without getting into the legitimation of this belief through the theological interpretation of predestination (those who succeed in material matters are those who are favored by the Divinity), it is easy to see how the Darwinian notion of the survival of the fittest came to be wedded to the idea of possessive individualism, giving rise, in turn, to the theory of social Darwinism. We hear versions of this theory proclaimed almost every day in the media by some prominent figure or other, sometimes in a subtly nuanced, understated argument about individual rights, sometimes in its more explicit "us versus them" rhetoric.

If we consider the present practice of education in most schools, we can hear clear echoes of possessive individualism. Success in school comes through competition among individuals using their talents for the top grades. Grading on a curve means that some will come out on top at the expense of those on the bottom; having winners, after all, implies having losers. Those who get good grades clearly used their talents to better themselves. Those who fail either did not have the talent or did not work hard enough. In either case, no one else is to blame for their ranking in school. In this system, collaborative learning arrangements are resisted, for teachers find it difficult to assign individual grades (and therefore rank students as superior or inferior) when the product is the result of a group effort. The whole system of competition for grades, competition to get into the better colleges, the focus through explicit schoolwide goals on the promotion of the fullest development of each individual's talents will ultimately place the individual on his own, against other individuals, and encourage him to use his talents as his own possession, for his own betterment, for his individual future, without any concern for those whose chances to get ahead diminish as his accelerate. This can be translated into a kind of collective individualism of winning (again, based on the assumption of a free marketplace) in interscholastic competitions. Chants of "we're number one" often take what should be friendly rivalries and turn them into a communal disparagement of opponents.

In many schools, youngsters are not socialized to see democracy as a way of bringing people together to create a community of neighbors and friends who want to share a mutually satisfying public life. Rather, democracy is presented as a system of protection of individual rights. Members are encouraged to use the democratic process to protect their property and to encourage legislation favorable to their own concerns. In this understanding of democracy, people exercise their basic freedoms by standing apart from the community and claiming their rights, or by competing against others for a larger share of the community's resources (e.g., calling for zoning regulations on property use and distribution, advocating tax breaks for certain business ventures, and supporting pork barrel projects) in a process in which the competition is negotiated not by mercenaries but by lawyers. Freedom is not seen as the opportunity to share life and possessions with others in community; rather, it is seen as freedom *from* other people, from their interference with the individual's life and economic welfare.

As generation after generation have been socialized independent of the community, independent of parents and extended family obligations, independent of tradition, the successes of individualism associated with modernity turn into tragedy. In freeing the individual from the group, the individual is left to learn the hard lessons of survival on his own. He is forced to enter into social contracts with other predators in uneasy and superficial communities where relationships, whether professional, economic, political, or simply neighborly, tend to be predominantly functional and defensive. Only in the nuclear family can the individual engage in intimate exchange (and even there, the focus on self-fulfillment can detract from the willingness to make sacrifices for spouse or children). Ironically, the banishment of community has brought an equally problematic reality, namely, the isolated individual. His freedom has become his prison.

Charles Taylor, however, reminds us that the modern quest for autonomy, personal responsibility, and individual expression has been fueled by a healthy intuition about human nature and that, despite its excesses, individualism contains an undeniable value as a human good.[6] Through the use of scientific research, the very tools of modernity, we know that the theory of isolated individualism is refuted by the evidence of the intrinsically social nature of human beings, whether this evidence is found in studies of language acquisition, cultural anthropology, social psychology, or, indeed, the sociology of knowledge. Those sciences reveal that the individual is, in one sense, constructed by the community. The genetic makeup of the individual is a gift—for better or worse—of his or her ancestors. The language and culture of the family shape the way the young individual perceives the world—for better or worse. The life experiences of the young individual, many of them scripted by cultural traditions and symbolic interpretations, shape and mold him or her—again, for better or worse. The individual, however, is not passive; each individual actively works with the genetic material and family culture and language and local life experiences in the shaping of his or her personality. Children from the same family reveal individual dif-

---

[6]Charles Taylor, *Sources of the Self: The Marketing of the Modern Identity.* Cambridge, Mass.: Harvard University Press, 1989.

ferences. In other words, while each individual is inextricably social, the community is likewise constituted by autonomous individuals. As John Dewey said, "If we eliminate the social factor from the child, we are left with an abstraction; if we eliminate the individual from society, we are left only with an inert and lifeless mass."[7]

Thus, we arrive at the present-day tension between community and individual. Whereas community was a modern problem and the individual a modern necessity, the individual is a postmodern problem and community a postmodern necessity. We find the ambivalence toward both notions in schools, because schools reflect the transitional tensions between the modern and the postmodern worlds.

CORE VALUES OF SCHOOLS AS COMMUNITIES

We suggested earlier that communities are defined by their centers. Centers are repositories of values, sentiments, and beliefs that provide the needed cement for bonding people in a common cause. As the sociologist Edward A. Shils explains,

> The center, or the central zone, is a phenomenon of the realm of values and beliefs. It is the center of the order of symbols, of values and beliefs, which govern the society [community]. It is the center because it is ultimate and irreducible.... The central zone partakes of the nature of the sacred. In this sense, every society [community] has an official "religion." . . . The center is also a phenomenon of the realm of action. It is a structure of activities, of roles and persons. . . . It is in these roles that the values and beliefs which are central are embodied and propounded.[8]

The core values of the school have always centered on three overriding foci, namely, the social, the personal, and the academic. The social focus was concerned with helping youngsters from different classes and ethnic backgrounds develop a sense of being American, of being citizens of a common polity who could learn to tolerate their differences while cooperating on making public life work reasonably well. The social focus also came to incorporate vocational concerns, namely, the preparation of youngsters to enter the workforce and be productive workers. The personal focus involved the development of the whole person as a social being who knew his or her rights and was respectful of the rights of others, into a cultured being (in the sense that one was functionally literate, had a sense of the nation's history and national values, and was literate enough to appreciate mass culture, if not high culture), into a person whose unique talents were initially developed to provide a satisfying life. The academic focus reflected core values about intelligent mastery of academic subjects so that the person would be able to express himself or herself, would appreciate the cultural

---

[7]John Dewey, "My Pedagogic Creed," in M. S. Dworkin (ed.), *Dewey on Education*. New York: Teachers College Press, 1959, p. 22.

[8]Op. cit., p. 119.

history of society, would understand the basic principles of science and mathematics, and, in many instances, would be prepared for higher learning.

These core values are what define the work of the members of the school community. The problem during this transition between modernity and postmodernity, as schools attempt to prepare youngsters for the 21st century, is that these core values are all subject to contested interpretations and each focus vies for primacy. One might argue that these core values have always been contested.[9] We seem to be in a period, however, of particularly intense shifts in the interpretations of all three foci. It is easy to understand, therefore, why building a community around agreed upon core values is so essential, if the schools are to move into deep and lasting change, if they are to be restructured around the principles elaborated in Chapter 2.

THE SCHOOL AS COMMUNITY

Since "community" means different things in different disciplines, we propose to define the term as follows: A community is a collection of individuals who are bonded together by natural will and who are together bound to a set of shared ideas and ideals. This bonding and binding is tight enough to transform the members from a collection of "*Is*" into a collective "we." As a "we," members are part of a tightly knit web of meaningful relationships. This "we" usually shares a common place and over time comes to share common sentiments and traditions that are sustaining.[10]

The concepts *gemeinschaft* and *gesellschaft* can help us understand this definition and the forms it takes as schools become communities. As used in sociology, the terms *gemeinschaft* translates as community and *gesellschaft* as society. Writing in 1887, Ferdinand Tonnies[11] used the terms to describe the changes in values and orientations that took place as humans moved first from a hunting and gathering society, to an agricultural society, and then to an industrial society. Each of these transformations resulted in a shift away from *gemeinschaft* and toward *gesellschaft*, away from a vision of life as sacred community and toward a more secular society. Though *gemeinschaft* and *gesellschaft* do not exist in pure form in the real world, they represent two ideal types—two different ways of thinking and living, two different types of cultures, two alternative visions of life.

Tonnies argued that as society moved toward the *gesellschaft* end of the continuum, community values were replaced by contractual ones. Among any collection of people, social relationships do not just happen; they are willed. Individuals decide to associate with each other. The reasons why they decide to

[9]See, for example, Thomas Popkewitz, *A Political Sociology of Educational Reform*. New York: Teachers College Press, 1991.

[10]This discussion of community follows T. J. Sergiovanni, *Leadership for the School House*. San Francisco: Jossey-Bass, 1996, pp. 48–51.

[11]F. Tonnies, *Gemeinschaft und Gesellschaft* [Community and Society], C. P. Loomis (ed. and trans.). New York: HarperCollins, 1957. (Originally published 1887.)

associate are important. In *gemeinschaft*, natural will is the motivating force. Individuals decide to relate to each other because doing so has its own intrinsic meaning and significance. There is no tangible goal or benefit in mind for any of the parties to the relationship. In *gesellschaft*, rational will is the motivating force. Individuals decide to relate to each other to reach some goal, to gain some benefit. Without this benefit there would be no relationship. Once the benefit is lost, the relationship ends. In the first instance, the ties among people are moral. In the second instance, the ties are calculated.

The modern corporation is an example of *gesellschaft*. Within the corporation, relationships are formal and distant, having been prescribed by roles and expectations. Circumstances are evaluated by universal criteria as embodied in policies, rules, and protocols. Acceptance is conditional. The more a person cooperates with and achieves for the corporation, the more likely he or she will be accepted. Relationships are competitive. Those who achieve more are valued more by the corporation. Not all concerns of members are legitimate. Legitimate concerns are bounded by corporate roles rather than personal needs. Subjectivity is frowned upon. Rationality is prized. Self-interest prevails.

Gesellschaft values make sense in the corporation and in other organizations such as the army, the research university, and the hospital. But applying the same values to a small church, a family, a social club, a neighborhood, a mutual aid society, a small town, a volunteer social action group, or a school, however, raises important questions of effectiveness and goodness.

Each social enterprise must solve the problem of connections among members if it is to function effectively. Members must be sufficiently connected to be able to communicate with each other, to understand each other, and to coordinate their activities. And members must be sufficiently connected to the enterprise's purposes and values so that, either willingly or unwillingly, they will function to reflect or achieve them.

Gesellschaft enterprises maintain connections by bartering rewards or punishments for loyalty and compliance. Members work for pay or for psychological rewards, and their involvement, as a result, is calculated. As long as they get what they want, they give what they must. But when they calculate otherwise, their involvement decreases.

Gemeinschaft enterprises, by contrast, strive to go beyond calculated to committed involvement. They do not ignore "what gets rewarded gets done," but they also strive to develop relationships among people that have moral overtones. They understand the importance of identifying with place and space over a period of time and providing members with security, sense, and meaning. And they recognize that in the end the ties that bind members together come from sharing with others a common commitment to a set of ideas and ideals.

Tonnies referred to these ties as community by relationships, community of place, and community of mind. *Community by relationships* characterizes the special kinds of connections among people that create a unity of being similar to that found in families and other closely knit collections of people. *Community of place* characterizes the sharing of a common habitat or locale. This sharing of place with others for sustained periods of time creates a special identity and a shared sense of belonging that connects people together in special ways. *Community of mind* emerges from the binding of people to common goals, shared values, and shared conceptions of being and doing. Together the three represent webs of meaning that connect people by creating a sense of belonging and a strong common identity.

As a school struggles to become a community, its members must address such questions as What can be done to increase the sense of family, neighborliness, and collegiality among the faculty of a school? How can the faculty become more of a professional community in which members care about each other and help each other to learn and to lead? What kinds of school-parent relationships need to be cultivated to include parents in this emerging community? How can the relationships that exist among and between teachers and students be defined so that they embody community? How can teaching and learning settings be arranged so that they are more like a family? How can the school itself, as a collection of families, be more like a neighborhood? What are the shared values and commitments that enable the school to become a community of mind? How will these values and commitments become practical standards that can guide the lives community members want to lead, what community members learn and how, and how community members treat each other? What are the patterns of mutual obligations and duties that emerge in the school as community is achieved?

Though not cast in stone, community understandings have enduring qualities. They are resilient enough to survive the passage of members through the community over time. They are taught to new members, celebrated in customs and rituals, and embodied as standards that govern life in the community. As suggested by R. N. Bellah and his colleagues,[12] enduring understandings create a fourth form of community: community of memory. In time, communities of relationships, of place, and of mind become communities of memory. Being a part of a community of memory sustains us when the going is tough, connects us when we are not physically present, and provides us with a history for creating sense and meaning.

It is important for supervisors to be clear about what they are doing to further the sense of community in the schools. The concern is not simply to facilitate the smooth running of a particular school, but to teach those life lessons needed to support a healthy polity or public life in the future. With this in mind, the promotion of school as community should do more than foster bonds of friendship and respect among students, emphasize the satisfaction of working together to achieve a successful completion of a team project or competition, teach the benefits of collaborative learning, or develop a proud sense of membership in a collective identity. Instead, the school as community must also fos-

---

[12]R. N. Bellah et al., *Habits of the Heart: Individualism and Commitment in American Life.* New York: HarperCollins, 1985.

ter those political skills needed to participate in the contested process of setting public policy, to partake in adjudicating and arbitrating community conflicts over policy implementation, and to join in those groups that concern themselves with managing the affairs of a self-governing polity. In other words, educating in and for community means not only developing satisfying relationships that embrace the wholeness of the persons involved, but teaching the responsibilities of membership in community, the responsibilities of citizenship.

WHY COMMUNITY THEORIES INSTEAD OF MARKET THEORIES?

From what has been said earlier about market theories of education, it is clear that their core values reside in the modern ideology of possessive individualism and laissez-faire understanding of the market. The proponents of this view continue to find a sympathetic audience.[13]

Many advocates of market change forces seem comfortable with community ideas. They argue that while promoting community-oriented schools cannot be guaranteed as the outcome of using market forces, it is a possible and perhaps even a likely outcome. Teachers, students, and their parents, they argue, would have free choice in an open market to build community-oriented schools. All they need is to be successful enough to win as they compete with other conceptions of schooling. Such reasoning has appeal, but, as will be discussed below, the prospects for the success of market forces over the long run are dim.

Market forces, for example, may be more efficient than democratic forces, but they may not be appropriate given schools' special role in promoting societal interests. Choice is an important feature in both market and democratic images of schools. In markets, individuals, motivated by self-interest, act alone in making preferred choices. Democratic choice, by contrast, is collective, complex, cumbersome, time consuming, and sometimes combative. Furthermore, unlike markets, where the will of the majority is not supposed to be imposed on everyone, once a democratic decision is made, it applies to everyone.

Despite inefficiencies, democratic decision making should be preferred for the things that society values—like defense, legal codes, transportation, and health care. "When, however, the things we are talking about are trivial—designer jeans, compact discs, deodorant soaps, different types of breakfast cereals—then democratic decision making is a waste of effort. . . . Democratic politics should be the system we use for the distribution of everything important, and economic markets should be the system we use for the distribution of everything trivial."[14] Given this reasoning, schools belong in the first category. There is a danger that, over time, market values will drive out virtue. This tendency is particularly wor-

[13]J. E. Chubb and T. M. Moe, *Politics, Markets, and America's Schools*. Washington, D.C.: Brookings Institute, 1990.

[14]B. Schwartz, *The Costs of Living: How Market Freedom Erodes the Basic Things in Life*. New York: Norton, 1994, p. 21.

risome among the professions and for societal institutions that hold a special place in our culture. The commercialization of sports is an example.[15] Professional sports have long been considered American pastimes that enshrined loyalty, self-sacrifice, devotion to the game, and duty. Today's professional sports, however, are characterized by strikes and lockouts, team hopping as a result of free agent bidding, and the switching of franchises from city to city at the drop of a dollar.

Imagine a group of educational marketeers switching school franchises from an economically deprived neighborhood to an affluent neighborhood as a way to attract more desirable customers. Imagine our best teachers operating as free agents, switching from school to school to get "better" students to teach. Imagine schools recruiting new students from one part of town rather than another in search of pupils who are thought more likely to be successful. While business may be business, this sort of thinking is unacceptable for schools and other social organizations. But the danger is there none the less. The very same market values that work so well for some sectors of society can erode other sectors.

Similarly, the same strategies for change that might make sense for some sectors of society seem not to work well for other sectors. Schools are a case in point. Deep change in schools is difficult to achieve when using change forces that emerge from views of schools as formal bureaucratic organizations, formal organic organizations, or markets. This difficulty is exacerbated by the negative effects that constrained theories and practices can have on teachers. Instead of nurturing professional community, constrained views breed cynicism, erode civic virtue, and encourage the development of human nature's passionate side at the expense of its rational side. In Chapter 4 and in this chapter we have argued that deep change may well require two things. First, the basic metaphor for schools must be changed from formal organizations or markets to communities. Once this is done, then leadership strategies and change forces must be matched to the unique cultural requirements of schools understood as communities.

FOCUSING ON COMMUNITY

While by no means in the majority, a growing number of scholars have begun to consider the need to move beyond possessive individualism in schools to a focus on community as the overarching context for developing both the academic and the personal. The work of Lynn Beck and Nell Noddings has dealt with the theme of caring as a necessary centerpiece of schooling.[16] Others have dealt with community as connected to the democratic purposes of schooling, such as Ernest Becker, David Bricker, and Orit Ichilov.[17] Others, such as Thomas Sergiovanni,

---

[15]Ibid.

[16]Lynn G. Beck, *Reclaiming Educational Administration as a Caring Profession*. New York: Teachers College Press, 1994; Nell Noddings, *The Challenge to Care in Schools*. New York: Teachers College Press, 1992.

[17]Ernest Becker, *Beyond Alienation: A Philosophy of Education for the Crisis of Democracy*. New York: George Braziller, 1967; David Bricker, *Classroom Life as Civic Education*. New York: Teachers College

David Purpel and H. Svi Shapiro, and Robert Starratt, link the building of community to the moral purposes of schooling.[18] Still others, such as Anthony Bryk and Michael Driscoll, Gregory Smith, and Ralph Peterson, link concern for community in schools specifically to the making of a learning community.[19]

Clearly, these authors present convincing evidence that some attempt at redefining the core values of schools is under way. Our argument is that, at the very least, supervisors need to recognize the legitimate claims of community as one of the most important perspectives for shaping the restructuring agenda. Schools should be considered as communities, not simply as people who do a lot of things together. The theme of community should become integrated into the formal and informal curricula of schools. In this way, schools truly become learning communities whose members are given a fulfilling sense of being part of something larger than themselves.

IMPLICATIONS FOR SUPERVISORS

In regards to community what are the implications for supervisors on how they understand schools and how they arrange for teaching and learning? With community as the theory, restructuring would take place in such a way that schools are not defined by brick and mortar but by ideas and tight connections. Creating communities of relationships and of place, for example, might well mean splitting large high schools into several smaller schools that do not exceed 400 or so students. The importance of creating sustained relationships would require that students and teachers stay together for longer periods of time. Traditional teaching in 50-minute periods would have to be reevaluated. Elementary schools would have to give serious consideration to organizing themselves into smaller and possibly multiaged units. Discipline problems would no longer be resolved on psychological principles but on moral ones. The use of moral principles would require schools to abandon such taken-for-granted ideas as having explicit rules linked to clearly stated consequences that are uniformly applied. Instead, school administrators would have to develop social contracts, constitutions, and normative codes. In-service education and staff development would move from the administrative side of the ledger to the teacher side as part of teachers' ongoing commitment to practice at the edge of their craft. Extrinsic reward systems would

Press, 1989; Orit Ichilov (ed.), *Political Socialization, Citizenship Education, and Democracy.* New York: Teachers College Press, 1990.

[18]Thomas J. Sergiovanni, *Building Community in Schools.* San Francisco: Jossey-Bass, 1994; David E. Purpel and H. Svi Shapiro (eds.), *Schools and Meaning: Essays on the Moral Nature of Schooling.* New York: University Press of America, 1985; Robert J. Starratt, *Building an Ethical School: A Practical Response to the Moral Crisis in Schools.* London: Falmer Press, 1994.

[19]Anthony Bryk and Michael Driscoll, *The High School as Community: Contextual Influences and Consequences on Students and Teachers.* Madison, Wis.: National Center on Effective Secondary Schools, 1988; Gregory Smith (ed.), *Public Schools That Work: Creating Community.* New York: Routle, 1991; Ralph Peterson, *Life in Crowded Places.* Portsmouth, N.H.: Heinemann, 1992.

have to disappear. The number of specialists would probably be reduced a
pullouts would be less common as "families" composed of teachers and students
began to take fuller responsibility for solving their own problems. And all of these
changes would necessitate the invention of new standards of quality, new strategies for accountability, and new ways of working with people—the invention of
a new kind of supervision.

SUPERVISION AS MORAL ACTION

A generation ago scholars and professionals in the field of supervision would have been embarrassed by talk of supervision as moral action. The literature on supervision had been dominated by language and imagery borrowed from the mainstream social sciences of psychology and sociology. Those fields had attempted to model themselves on the natural sciences in an effort to reproduce "value-free" facts and theories generated by methods that were supposed to screen out ideological points of view, imaginative speculation, philosophical perspectives, and all such impressions deemed subjective and nonempirical.

More recently this positivistic, reductionistic approach to explaining social systems has been challenged. Sociologists and social psychologists have begun to include considerations of human beings in all their complexity as a central factor in their study of how social systems do or do not work.[1] In these emerging perspectives, the person is seen in a much richer light, as someone seeking meaning and purpose in daily life. Moreover, life in organizations is coming to be seen as far more complex, as involving not only rational thinking but also emotional responses, moral ambiguity, political influence peddling and defensive ego investment. Organizational culture can suppress creativity and extra effort, distort

---

[1]See, for example, the August 1996 issue of *Educational Administration Quarterly* (vol. 32, no. 3, edited by Colin W. Evers and Gabriele Lakomski), which contains articles themed to "Post-Positivist Conceptions of Science in Educational Administration."

the interpretation of events impinging on the organization from the outside world, and support sexist and racist attitudes and a host of other undesirable ingredients in the life of the organization. Needless to say, supervision takes place in schools where these morally implicating situations occur. There are even deeper reasons for considering supervision as moral action, however, and these have to do with the intrinsic morality involved in the core work of the school: teaching and learning.

THE MORAL IDEAL OF TEACHING

We will not argue for the need of supervisors to encourage the moral commitment of teachers, as though that is lacking on the part of teachers. On the contrary, the action of supervision takes place within an existing moral environment created by the professionalism of teachers. We will better understand the moral dimensions of supervision by a close look at the moral dimensions involved in the ideal of teaching, an ideal to which the large majority of teachers subscribe and which makes up the core of their general concept of professionalism.[2]

When first thinking about professionalism, attention is drawn to issues of competence. Professionals are experts, and this expertise entitles them to be autonomous. But expertise is not enough to earn one the mantle of professionalism. Though society often refers to expert safecrackers, hairdressers, gamblers, and baseball players as being professionals, the reference is colloquial. Being a professional has to do with something else besides being competent. Society, for example, demands not only that physicians, physicists, teachers, and other professionals be skilled but also that their skills be used for good intentions. Professionals enjoy privileges because they are trusted. It takes more than competence to earn trust. One might refer to this "something else" as professional virtue.[3]

What are the dimensions of professional virtue? At least four are related to this discussion.[4]

A commitment to practice in an exemplary way
A commitment to practice toward valued social ends
A commitment not only to one's own practice but to the practice itself
A commitment to the ethic of caring

[2]Magdalene Lampert and Christopher M. Clark, "Expert Knowledge and Expert Thinking in Teaching: A Response to Floden and Klinzing," *Educational Researcher*, vol. 19, no. 5, (June–July 1991), pp. 21–23.

[3]This discussion of professional virtue follows Thomas J. Sergiovanni, *The Moral Dimensions of Leadership*. San Francisco: Jossey-Bass, 1992, pp. 52–56.

[4]The first two dimensions are from Alastair McIntyre, *After Virtue*. Notre Dame, Ind.: Notre Dame University, 1981. The third is from Albert Flores, "What Kind of Person Should a Professional Be?" in Albert Flores (ed.), *Professional Ideals*. Belmont, Calif.: Wadsworth Publishing, 1988. The fourth is from Nel Noddings, *Caring: A Feminine Approach to Ethics and Moral Education*. Berkeley, Calif.: University of California Press, 1984.

The four dimensions of professional virtue provide the roots for developing a powerful norm system that, when combined with the norm system that defines the school as community, can greatly diminish if not replace supervision as it is now practiced. For this reason establishing the virtuous side of professionalism should be a high priority for supervision.

A commitment to exemplary practice, for example, means practicing on the cutting edge of teaching, staying abreast of the latest research in practice, researching one's own practice, experimenting with new approaches, and sharing one's craft insights with others. Once established, this dimension results in teachers accepting responsibility for their own professional growth, thus greatly reducing the need for someone else to in-service them or to plan and implement staff development programs for them. The focus of professional development shifts from "training" to providing opportunities for self-renewal, for interacting with others, for learning and sharing. Much of what happens in this kind of professional development is informal and built into the everyday life of the school. Teachers accept a greater share of the responsibility for planning and carrying out both formal and informal activities and programs.

The second dimension of professional virtue, a commitment to practice toward valued social ends, represents a commitment to place oneself in service to students and parents and to agreed-upon school values and purposes. Such a commitment raises the issue of purpose to a prime position in ongoing conversations about the school and its work and in planning, doing, and evaluating teaching and learning.

When relying on purposes, an idea and value structure emerges in the school that can greatly reduce the need for hierarchically based controls or for supervisors working hard to provide deft interpersonal leadership. Teachers, for example, would do things not because they are forced to by controls or cajoled by personality but because they are persuaded by merit defined by purposes. When compliance for teachers must be required and the weight of this compliance comes from school purposes rather than rules of personality, professional and moral sources of authority are activated. These sources of authority have the capacity to transform the work of the school from something technical and secular to something sacred.

The third dimension of professional virtue, a commitment not only to one's own practice but also to the practice of teaching itself, forces teachers to broaden their outlook. On the one hand, teachers become concerned with the broad issues of teaching policy and practice. On the other, teachers become concerned with the practical problems and issues of teaching and learning faced every day in their own school as seen in relationship to these issues and policies. Such a commitment requires that teaching be transformed from individual to collective practice. In collective practice, for example, it would not be acceptable for one teacher to teach competently in the company of others having difficulty, without being concerned, without offering help. It would not be acceptable to have special insights into teaching and not to share them with others. It would not be acceptable to define success in terms of what happens in one's own classroom when the school itself may be failing.

When teaching is conceived as collective practice, then collegiality emerges as an expression of professional virtue. Teachers feel compelled to work together not so much because interpersonally they enjoy relief from isolation and not because administrative arrangements (teaming or cooperative teaching and learning) force them together but because of internally felt obligations. With professional virtue intact, collegiality becomes a reciprocal form of meeting obligations in a collective practice. Its source of authority becomes professional and moral.

A commitment to the ethic of caring, the fourth dimension of professional virtue, shifts the emphasis from viewing teaching as a technical activity involving the execution of validated teaching moves to viewing teaching as a professional activity involving concern for the whole person. The word "person" is key. Too often technical conceptions of teaching, complete with their language systems of labels and categories, regard students as cases to be treated rather than persons to be served. The caring ethic speaks not only to how students should be regarded and to the quality of relationships but also to teaching itself. Teachers, as Nell Noddings observes, act as models of caring when they model "meticulous preparation, lively presentation, critical thinking, appreciative listening, constructive evaluation, general curiosity."[5] The ethic of caring, in sum, provides still another substitute for direct, close, formal supervision. As the ethic is internalized, teachers are motivated more from within, thus requiring less external supervision.

A DEEPER LOOK AT MORAL AGENCY

Moral agents act with a sense of how the integrity of their own lives is tied up in relationships with people and circumstances at home, at work, and in the neighborhood, as well as in relationships to public organizations. Those relationships provide for the individual's sense of personal fulfillment and moral identity through family bonds, friendships, colleagueship, client relationships, and even the loose fellowship of shared public concerns, shared material resources, shared public spaces, and shared cultural communities. The relationships impose obligations of trust, honesty, respect, acceptance, and loyalty. The humanity of shared personal and public existence is preserved and supported when people behave in ways that we traditionally label as moral, namely, in ways that respect the integrity of persons with whom we interact in specific circumstances and contexts (which themselves dictate and shape the appropriate, moral response).

These ways of behaving become codified into systems of ethical principles, standards, and values. The study of ethics explores the intelligibility and reasonableness of these standards, values and principles—not simply for the general establishment and acceptance of such principles in public life, but also for guidance in those circumstances when it is not clear which moral path to follow.

---

[5]Nel Noddings, "Fidelity in Teaching, Teacher Education, and Research for Teaching," *Teacher Education and Research for Teaching,* vol. 56, p. 503, Nov. 4, 1986.

Whether these ethical systems are understood as grounded in natural law (somewhat the way engineering principles are based on the laws of physics or medical practices are based on biochemical laws) or understood as socially constructed guides derived from the pragmatic and humanitarian concerns and interests of the civil community is a question long argued by philosophers and social theorists.

While we do not pretend to settle that argument, we do assert that concerns over the moral dimensions of public life are essential to the integrity of any educational process, and that therefore the work of supervisors should reflect the moral dimensions of their roles within the educational process. As we have suggested, a supervisor's moral agency derives in large part from his or her involvement with teachers' work, which we have suggested is intrinsically moral or virtuous. In order to understand the moral implications of teachers' work, we need to see it as grounded in the morality of the very production of knowledge.

THE MORAL DIMENSIONS OF KNOWLEDGE PRODUCTION AND TRANSMISSION

Knowledge is produced by scholars whose work involves them in studying a piece or element of reality and deciphering its intelligibility, either in its elemental structure or in relationship to other frameworks of meaning. The scientific ideal is to be very meticulous in gathering and weighing the data involved before proposing an interpretation or explanation of that piece or element of reality. The ideal is to let the reality speak for itself, without the scholar's imposing an opinion or a fanciful explanation that does not respect the evidence available. There is an unspoken moral obligation upon the scholar to represent that reality as truthfully and as accurately as possible. To fabricate an interpretation or explanation that would intentionally deceive the audience as to the true nature of the object of the scholar's study would be considered an immoral act. Such misrepresentation of knowledge is seen as a serious violation of the public's trust in the role of the scholar, who has traditionally been viewed as committed above all else to the pursuit of truth. Scholars are supposed to report the findings of their studies forthrightly, cleansed of their own biases and interests—to report their knowledge as they found it, not as they might want it to appear. Where their findings represent one possible interpretation among many, they should report them that way, citing the evidence that points to their own conclusion and noting other evidence that might support another interpretation.

An artist is allowed some license to distort reality in order to highlight one or more features or aspects of reality, or to reveal a subjective feeling or state of mind related to that reality, or even to express free-floating feelings or imagery. Even there, the artist is attempting to express an aspect of a reality, however subjective. The artist cannot be untrue to the reality that seeks expression through his or her work. There is a moral bond to express that reality as fully and richly as possible. Clearly, the achievement of that expression is relative; the work may or may not be considered successful. The role of the art critic is to judge the relative perfection of the artist's expression.

One might say, therefore, that scholars and artists are responsible *to* what they know. That is, they have to respect the integrity of what they know as they attempt to report it. In addition, scholars are responsible *for* what they know. Often their knowledge has important implications in the public life of the community (the discovery of a new disease or cure for a known disease, the revelation of evidence that could reverse an earlier judgment about a person or group of persons, the knowledge of a chemical process that will benefit food production; the uncovering of misconduct by a person in public office, etc.). The image of "pure science" is debated: Are scholars excused from the public debate about what to do with the new knowledge they have produced? Are those who discovered the potential use of atomic power, for instance, absolved of any say in how that power is to be used? Are those who discover the harmful effects of hydrofluorocarbons to be excused from the policy debates on environmental legislation? Are historians of the colonizing of the United States who know how the lands of Native Americans were expropriated excused from the public debates over redressing those injustices? And, of course, what are the responsibilities of the general public appraising the new knowledge? We would argue that knowledge of reality entails responsibility for that knowledge when its use can prevent the continuation of injustice or harm to the community or can lead to clear benefits to the community.

THE MORAL AGENCY OF THE TEACHER

Since the work of the teacher is very much related to the production and representation of knowledge he or she suffers similar moral obligations. These obligations entail the duty to know the work of scholarship that supports the knowledge the teacher is attempting to impart, to be aware of the kind of evidence and information that supports that knowledge and the legitimacy of the methodology employed to produce that knowledge, and to understand the large interpretative scaffolding of the scholarly disciplines within which such work takes on meaning. That is what university preparation is supposed to equip the teacher with, and what continuing education should continue to develop. A teacher is supposed to be responsible to what he or she knows. The educator cannot exercise that responsibility except by his or her own continuous learning.

Similarly, a teacher needs to be responsible for what he or she knows. This implies that the educator must raise with students the implications that their common learning has for their participation in the larger community. Knowledge of the injustices suffered by various groups in this country, for example, ought to lead to discussions about antidiscrimination legislation, about already successful community building practices, about a deeper understanding of the residue of bitterness or anger one finds in the collective memory of these groups. Knowledge of political abuses should lead to class discussions about the role of citizen watchdog committees or legislative oversight committees in fighting corruption. Knowledge of genetics, of atomic radiation, of deteriorating water tables, of harmful effects of certain methods of food processing, of the devastating effects of addictive drugs, of questionable activities of banks and large corporations, to mention but a few additional examples, should lead to class discussions of potential legal and political remedies available to citizen groups. The point of all this is to underscore that knowledge of how the world works brings responsibilities of stewardship into play; we are responsible for what we know.

Consider the content knowledge that is required to carry on the activity of teaching in a normal class. This knowledge is not a linear collection of concepts and facts, although textbooks tend to present knowledge that way. It is, rather, knowledge of and within a dynamic, existential field. A piece of knowledge can be abstracted from the field for purposes of analysis and discussion (for example, a discussion in a social studies class of a piece of legislation such as prohibition against alcohol), but in isolation from the dynamic field of social history, that piece of knowledge is decontextualized. A teacher has a responsibility to both the field of knowledge from which the material is selected and to the students who are to learn something from studying the material. The teacher is always involved with a specific context at a particular moment of time, trying to sort out a plan of action that respects and responds to the content being studied and to the multiple contextual strands of the tapestry that make up any classroom moment.[6] That construction of a unit of the curriculum by the teacher implies a moral responsibility both to present the material in nondistorted fashion and to present it in such a way that it is useful to the students as they encounter this piece of social history.

Responsiveness to the context of students implies a sensitivity to their life connections. When a situation involves the need, for example, to clean up toxicity in a lake, the expert has to consider the sources of toxicity, the impact of various treatments on the whole ecology of the lake, the current chemical composition of the lake, the support of a food chain for various living systems, and the seasonal variations in relation to rainfall and drainage. When the situation involves a teacher and an individual student, it involves understanding the student's family background, his or her talent and interests, fears and aspirations, as well as the student's developmental capabilities for cognitive and affective responses. The teacher must take into account this constellation of student variables when assessing the potential of a variety of learning activities to stimulate learning readiness within each student. That knowledge of all these variables does not exist "out there" in some uniform, objective package, as though it could be fed into 20 computers, all of which would prescribe the same learning activities. Teachers are not separated from their knowledge of the content and of the context. It is something that they generate from their own prior education and their embedded personal understanding of the subject matter, as well as their diagnostic understanding and sensitivity, which in turn are colored by their cultural

[6]For a treatment of the moral implications of teaching see John I. Goodlad, Roger Soder, and Kenneth A. Sirotnik, *The Moral Dimensions of Teaching*, San Francisco: Jossey-Bass, 1990; M. Buchmann, "Role Over Person: Morality and Authenticity in Teaching," *Teachers College Record*, vol. 87, (1986), pp. 529–544; David E. Purpel and H. Svi Shapiro (eds.), *Schools and Meaning: Essays on the Moral Nature of Schooling.* New York: University Press of America, 1985.

and class background, their own values and beliefs, and their degree of understanding of or attending to other potential variables that might enter into their decision-making processes. The knowledge upon which professional teaching decisions are based is partly derived from the knowledge base of the profession (which is itself imperfect and inconsistent), but it is also a knowledge that is personal, intuitive, and interpersonal. By saying that a teacher's knowledge is interpersonal, we add a further complication to the teacher's ability to arrive at professional decisions. The teacher knows only what each student chooses to disclose about himself or herself. A student may reveal a problem in understanding what the teacher is trying to teach but may not be able to say why he or she does not understand. The cause of the problem may be one of several possibilities.

When we compound the difficulties involved in decision-making knowledge when teaching one student, by considering that most teachers deal with from 20 to 120 students a day in classes of approximately 20 to 30, then we begin to understand some of the complexity of teaching and the complexity of the professional expertise required of teachers. Being responsive simultaneously to the enormous variety of interests, talents, learning blocks, emotional states, and cultural backgrounds within any given classroom requires an artistry of high complexity.

The large majority of experienced teachers manage to meet this challenge. They engage in this professional activity driven not simply by knowledge but by a sense of responsibility. That sense of responsibility derives from an intuitive ideal of what teachers are supposed to be doing for youngsters, namely, finding the appropriate interaction that will trigger insight, understanding, skill acquisition, curiosity, motivation, and interest in learning. Just as doctors are concerned with bringing their patients to a condition of health, so teachers must bring their students to a condition of learning. That ideal places certain obligations on teachers:

1   To know their students well enough to create learning opportunities for them that do in fact bring them to a condition of learning
2   To understand their subject matter well enough so that they can bring out its internal relationships and its connections to other bodies of knowledge
3   To discover the various illustrations, analogies, metaphors, stories, experiences, sensory representations, and learning activities that will enable the students to connect with the subject matter
4   To develop a large repertory of teaching strategies that can be employed in a variety of circumstances to develop conditions of learning for their students
5   To influence, by their example and counsel, a broad array of learning that extends beyond academic learning to a variety of personal and social learning including, but not limited to, social manners, acceptance of differences, self-esteem, and a sense of social responsibility for the quality of life of the community

In other words, teachers experience their work as driven by a moral ideal. That ideal activates their integrity as human beings. That ideal is imbedded in the understanding of teaching as a profession. It is what teachers are called to do; it is their vocation.

Because teaching is a moral activity, supervision partakes of its moral qualities. Supervision is supposed to support, nurture, and strengthen the moral ideals embedded in teaching. Supervision as a professional activity, therefore, is intimately tied to both the knowledge expertise of the teacher and the moral responsibility of the profession of teaching. The supervisor must understand the complexities of teaching, its multilayered and multidimensional artistic knowledge base. Beyond appreciating that complex knowledge base and being able to converse with teachers about it, the supervisor is obliged to participate with teachers in the task of bringing youngsters to the condition of learning. The supervisor does this by supporting the teachers' search for improved responsiveness to their students.

That support will clearly bring the supervisor's professional knowledge base into play. In subsequent chapters we will deal with various aspects of that knowledge base. Supervision as moral activity, however, involves more than the supervisor's knowledge; it involves the supervisor's ability to engage teachers at a level of moral discourse that mirrors the moral responsibility teachers model for their students. Ultimately, what teachers try to accomplish with their students is not simply the acquisition of knowledge, although that is central to their task; teachers also want the experience of knowing they have opened up students to an appreciation of life, an experience of themselves as connected to a world that is challenging and complex, filled with beauty and pain and joy.[7]

Underneath all the specifics of what they are teaching, teachers basically want to share a deep part of their life with youngsters, the joy and fascination that they experience in understanding and engaging the world through a variety of perspectives. Teachers are happy enough when their students score well on exams; however, they are most fulfilled when their students delight in what they are learning. It is at this level that a supervisor engages teachers in the moral dimension of teaching. At this level supervisors engage in one of the fundamental aspects of empowerment.

EMPOWERING AS A MORAL ACTIVITY OF SUPERVISION

Teacher empowerment is a term with many uses and various meanings, depending on whether it is employed by teacher unions, school administrators, or school reformers.[8] We use it here to indicate a moral basis for teacher autonomy and pro-

---

[7]Among other testimonies of this moral commitment to the human growth of students, see Tracy Kidder, *Among Schoolchildren.* New York: Avon, 1989; Philip Lopate, *Being with Children.* New York: Poseiden, 1975; Jay Mathews, *Escalante,* New York: Holt, 1988; Jo Anne Pagano, *Exiles and Communities: Teaching in the Patriarchal Wilderness.* Albany, N.Y.: State University of New York Press, 1990.

[8]See Gene I. Maeroff, "A Blueprint for Empowering Teachers," *Phi Delta Kappa,* vol. 69, no. 7 (March 1988), pp. 472–477; Vicki J. Karant, "Supervision in the Age of Teacher Empowerment," *Educational Leadership,* vol. 46, no. 8 (May 1989), pp. 27–29.

fessionalism. In order to understand this usage, we need to consider what "power" means.

For many people, power has negative overtones. It is associated with coercion, force, threat, and sometimes violence. Power is often viewed as something only a few possess; "the powerful" are thought to be able to control or influence the affairs of the community. From that vantage point, empowering people implies that those who hold power over others give them some of their power. Yet the reality is that no one person has power over another unless that person is allowed to have that power. If everyone refuses to comply with those "in power," then they have no power, as governments all over the world eventually discover. Even the power of persuasion implies that the listeners assent to the reasonableness of the persuader's argument. The power of the judge to impose a prison sentence is based on an assumed agreement of the people to live according to the law.

Instead of thinking of power as "power over," we may think of power as something every person possesses: a power to be and a power to do. The most unique power each person possesses is the power to be herself or himself. No one else has the power to be you. Only you can exercise that power. You may fail to use that power and instead try to live up to an idea that others have of you, or to some fantasy image provided by popular culture. The power is the power to accept and reject such images. The power may be heavily circumscribed by circumstances in your present context, but it is a power you never lose. You may turn it over to other people, but it always belongs to you. It is the power to be yourself, to sing your own song, dance your own dance, speak your own poetry. It is the power to be true to your best self, rather than to the self that is fearful, jealous, or spiteful.

The paradox about this power is that although it is yours, it is given you for the benefit of the community. You can exercise the power to be you only in relationship to your community. Some mistakenly think that the power to be an individual is a power against the community, a power that necessarily defies the community.[9] Although isolation from all social contacts, real or imaginary, is impossible except, perhaps, for autistic people, some people attempt to live as though other people are not necessary for their own fulfillment or even for their own existence. That attitude leads to varieties of narcissistic isolation, which are actually self-destructive.

You can be yourself only in relation to others, to other selves whom you value as they value you. You can express yourself only in relation to the world, to another person, to a particular circumstance that at that moment is part of your de-

[9]For interesting perspectives on this point, see Robert N. Bellah, Richard Madsen, William M. Sullivan, Ann Swidler, and Steven M. Tipton, *Habits of the Heart*. New York: Harper & Row, 1985; Kenneth A. Strike, "The Moral Role of Schooling in a Liberal Democratic Society," in Gerald Grant (ed.), *Review of Research in Education*, vol. 17. Washington, D.C.: American Education Association, 1991, pp. 413–483; Gregory Bateson and Mary Catherine Bateson, *Angels Fear: Towards an Epistemology of the Sacred*. New York: Macmillan, 1987; Edward Shils, *Tradition*. Chicago: University of Chicago Press, 1981.

finition (such as your family, your workplace, your neighborhood, your garden).[10] You express yourself by responding to persons and events in your immediate surroundings, and that expression is an expression of giving or of taking, an expression of gratitude or of greed, an expression of celebration or of complaint, an affirmation of life or a denial of life. Insofar as your expression of yourself is giving, thankful, celebratory, and affirming, you yourself receive life, grow, and are nurtured. Insofar as your expression of yourself is taking, hoarding, complaining, and denying, you hurt yourself and those around you. The person you express in negativity is an expression of self-destruction. Hence, the power to be yourself is a moral power. It is either an enormously creative power, a power to create yourself while adding to the life around you, or an enormously destructive power, a power to destroy yourself (even though that takes place by minuscule choices) and smother and depress life around you. That is why some people choose not to exercise that power; they sense the moral risk involved. Better to leave the choices in the hands of others.

There are few people for whom the power to be themselves, freely and spontaneously, is unlimited. People are victims as well as beneficiaries of their socialization, habituated to guiding their actions by the cues they pick up from those around them, especially from authority figures such as parents, older relatives, teachers, and public figures. When people have been taught not to trust their own feelings, they rarely rely on their own intuitions or wants. Maxine Greene writes about the socialization of teachers as follows:

> Classroom teachers, assigned a relatively low place in the hierarchy, share a way of seeing and of talking about it. They are used to watching schedules, curricula, and testing programs emanate from "the office." They take for granted the existence of a high place, a seat of power. . . . The reality they have constructed and take for granted allows for neither autonomy nor disagreement.[11]

For a wide variety of reasons, some psychological, some cultural, some political, people are limited in their power to be themselves. Yet the most basic moral task in life is precisely to be uniquely oneself. It is a task never fully achieved.

TEACHING AS AUTOBIOGRAPHY

Recent studies of teachers seem to be pointing in the same direction: Each teacher brings his or her unique constellation of personality traits, interests, talents, prior educational and psychological influences, and prior professional experiences to bear on classroom practice.[12] Even when teachers experience uniform staff de-

---

[10]See John MacMurray, *Persons in Relation.* London: Faber and Faber, 1961; David E. Hunt, *Beginning with Ourselves.* Cambridge, Mass.: Brookline Books, 1987.

[11]Maxine Greene, *Landscapes of Learning.* New York: Teachers College Press, 1979, pp. 44–45.

[12]See Michael G. Fullan, "Staff Development, Innovation, and Institutional Development," in Nancy B. Wyner (ed.), *Current Perspectives on the Culture of Schools.* Cambridge, Mass.: Brookline Books, 1991, pp. 181–201; Michael Huberman, "The Social Context of Instruction in Schools." Paper presented at the American Educational Research Association Annual Meeting, Boston, April 1990; David E. Hunt, "From Single Variable to Persons-in-Relation," in L. Fyans (ed.), *Achievement Motivation: Recent Trends in History and Research.* New York: Plenum, 1980, pp. 447–456.

velopment programs and agree to implement schoolwide changes, their class-room activity reflects elements of their personality and their unique ways of re-sponding to perceived needs of students. Whereas previously that may have been perceived as an unavoidable deficit by those attempting to implement teacher-proof innovations, it is now being seen as an asset to be encouraged.[13] Clearly, the power to be themselves, when combined with experience and a professional teaching culture, enables teachers to enrich the learning experiences of their stu-dents through, for example, self-constructed or self-discovered learning activi-ties, through references to life lessons from their own experience, and through the teachers' obvious excitement and commitment associated with various units of the curriculum.[14] This is not to glorify an extreme form of individualism and isolationism on the part of teachers; clearly, teacher professionalism requires col-laboration on instructional and curricular improvements. What these studies are emphasizing is the need to balance collaboration with individual autonomy in the practice of everyday life in school.[15] The mix of teachers' personalities, back-grounds, personal histories, talents, and interests creates a rich experience of adult community for students, an experience that profoundly educates in its own tacit manner throughout the students' years in that community.

SUPERVISORS AND EMPOWERMENT

While no one can give a person the power to be herself or himself, it is possible to limit or enlarge that power, especially when one is perceived to have "power over" that person. Supervisors, by creating a trusting and supportive relation-ship with teachers, can enlarge the relational space that teachers need to be more fully themselves. That relational space allows for a mutual process of discover-ing what the power to be and the power to do means in a particular school, what positive qualities are attached to the exercise of that power, and what limitations are imposed by the circumstances of the communal effort at schooling. Such a process of empowerment involves mutual respect, dialogue, and invitation; it im-plies recognition that each person enjoys talents, competencies, and potentials that are being exercised in responsible and creative ways for the benefit of the students. It implies that teachers legitimately and necessarily model what it means to be genuine in the way they conduct their relationships with their students and in the way they engage them in the learning material itself. In this empowering relationship, both teachers and supervisors invite one another to

---

[13]D. Jean Clandinin and F. Michael Connelly, "Rhythms in Teaching: The Narrative Study of Teachers' Personal Practical Knowledge of Classrooms," *Teaching and Teacher Education,* vol. 2 (1986), pp. 377–387; Freema Elbaz, *Teacher Thinking: A Study of Practical Knowledge.* New York: Nichols, 1983; Virginia M. Jagia, *Teachers' Everyday Use of Imagination and Intuition.* Albany: State University of New York Press, 1994, esp. chap. 5.

[14]Virginia Richardson, "Significant and Worthwhile Change in Teaching Practice," *Educational Researcher,* vol. 19, no. 7 (October 1990), pp. 10–18.

[15]Andy Hargreaves, "Individualism and Individuality: Reinterpreting the Teacher Culture." Paper presented at the American Educational Research Association Annual Meeting, Boston, April 1990.

exercise their power to be themselves in the specific relationship of teacher and supervisor. This process requires some exploration of what the relationship is supposed to entail. This leads to considerations about the moral "underside" of supervision.

THE UNDERSIDE OF SUPERVISION

Many stories told by teachers of their experiences of "being supervised" are anything but uplifting.[16] Again and again teachers tell of being placed in win-lose situations, of experiencing powerlessness, manipulation, sexual harassment, and racial and ethnic stereotyping. At best, their encounters with supervisors lead directly to evaluative judgments based on the skimpiest of evidence. At worst, they are destructive of autonomy, self-confidence, and personal integrity. Unfortunately, supervision as practiced by some supervisors is not only nonprofessional, it is dehumanizing and unethical.

The most traditional exercise of supervision is the formal observation of a teacher in his or her classroom. Despite some semblance of clinical supervision, most encounters result in the supervisor's making evaluative judgments about the appropriateness and effectiveness of various teaching behaviors. These judgments are usually recorded and placed in the teacher's file. Classroom observations that start out with preconceived formulas for what constitutes good practice tend not to be very helpful.[17] Moreover, the supervisor's underlying but unspoken assumptions about teaching and learning frequently defeat the supervisory experience right from the start, because they tend to be simplistic and reductionistic. Teachers' decision making, whether flawed or appropriate, is based on an awareness of an extremely complex, multilayered field of human beings in dynamic interaction over extended periods of time. Supervisors who observe that group of human beings interacting in one slice of time cannot be aware of all that is going on.[18] Hence, evaluation of teachers' performance is a very complex and imperfect art that, in practice, few have mastered.

Beyond professional issues, there are other attitudes and behaviors that undermine supervisors' activities. These have to do with the desire to dominate and control others; with insecurities that must be covered over by aggressive and controlling actions and words; and with racial, sexual, and ethnic stereotypes that prevent genuine communication and mutual respect. Some older teachers are disdainful of younger supervisors; some older supervisors are disdainful of younger teachers. A black supervisor raises problems for a white teacher; white supervisors raise problems for black teachers. Women supervising men and men su-

---

[16]See *Impact*, New York State Association for Supervision and Curriculum Development, vol. 19, no. 1 (Fall 1983). The whole issue is devoted to dealing with these less than altruistic motives. Arthur Blumberg raises penetrating questions in his treatment of the "cold war" between teachers and supervisors in *Supervisors and Teachers: A Private Cold War*. Berkeley, Calif.: McCutcheon Publishing, 1974.

[17]Susan Stoldowsky, "Teacher Evaluation: The Limits of Looking," *Educational Researcher*, vol. 13, no. 9 (November 1984), pp. 11–18.

[18]Jane Juska, "Observations," *Phi Delta Kappa*, vol. 72, no. 6 (February 1991), pp. 468–470.

pervising women have to deal with agendas beyond the explicit professic agenda. When racial and cultural differences are mixed with gender differences, the possibilities for misunderstanding and harm are multiplied.

The expanding literature by women about the challenges of being a woman teacher deserves much greater attention within the field of supervision. As more and more women teachers find their voice and explore ways of being more fully themselves in their work, rather than acting according to the roles they have been socialized to assume, supervisors need to be much more sensitive to this growth process.[19] For some women, this exploration of new personal terrain is a moral challenge. Male supervisors may be unprepared for this emerging phenomenon among women teachers. Our advice would be to begin the dialogue with women about what is afoot. This valued, growing female voice points to a need for more women supervisors.

When these negative issues dominate the supervisory experience, they subvert any possibility of open, trusting, professional communication and can lead to manipulative words and actions on the part of the supervisor, the teacher, or both. Sometimes the supervisor and the teacher are not aware that they are being offensive to each other. Sometimes one consciously seeks to control, dominate, or intimidate the other. Often teachers go through the motions, play a superficial role, act as though everything is perfectly understandable, and keep feelings and honest communication at a safe distance. More often than not, supervisory encounters take place without either teachers or supervisors revealing their true feelings toward each other or toward the game they are playing. It is simply an organizational ritual that must be completed to satisfy some political or legal necessity. In the above instances, supervision is the opposite of moral action, implying hypocritical, dishonest, disloyal, vicious, or dehumanizing intentions. Sometimes supervision is immoral simply because it wastes so much time of so many people.

THE MORAL HEURISTICS OF SUPERVISORY PRACTICE

If supervision is to be moral action, it must respect the moral integrity of the supervisor and the supervised. That is to say, the exchange between the supervisor and the teacher must be trusting, open, and flexible in order to allow both persons to speak from their own sense of integrity and to encourage each person to respect the other's integrity. The exchange must begin with an honest discussion of what will be helpful for the teacher and the students. For this to happen, supervisors need to explore those conditions necessary to establish and maintain trust and honesty and open communication. This means that supervisors need to discuss the ground rules ahead of time. Hence, supervisors need to explore with teachers what procedures will be followed, what rights and re-

---

[19]Nell Noddings, "Feminist Critiques in the Professions," in Courtney Cazden (ed.), *Review of Research in Education,* vol. 16 (1990), esp. pp. 406–416; Madeleine R. Grumet, "Women and Teaching: Homeless at Home," *Teacher Education Quarterly,* vol. 14, no. 2 (1987), pp. 39–46.

l be defined, who controls what, whose needs are being served,
he exchange, etc. This discussion in itself is a kind of moral ac-
n of guidelines to be followed so that fairness and honesty can
These exploratory discussions on how to initiate and maintain a
ge comprise the heuristics of moral action.

Beyond the heuristics of setting the parameters and guidelines, there is the exchange itself, an engagement of another person in all his or her complexity, fragility, and ambiguity. Embedded in the process of making contact with that other person are the moral imperatives of acceptance, honesty, respect, and care. These comprise the moral activity of empowerment, the willingness to let people be who they are, and beyond that willingness, an appreciation of what they have to contribute. These moral imperatives are not experienced as some abstract, Kantian principles, reference to which deductively leads to specific conclusions. Rather, they are intuitive, instantaneous responses to the other person in the ebb and flow of the interaction. After the fact, through reflection, both supervisor and teacher can understand the moral aspects of those responses.

PROMOTING A MORAL COMMUNITY

Besides concern for the empowerment of individual teachers, supervisors have a responsibility to nurture the moral environment of the individual school. In fact, both moral concerns support each other. Everyday life in the school contains within it many moral challenges, but often supervisors do not know how to name them. Often institutional practices in the school convey a sense of impersonality. Communications contained in faculty memos, announcements to the students over the intercom, administrative changes in student disciplinary policies, average class sizes, or the length of the school day can convey paternalistic, authoritarian, or adversarial attitudes. School practices—in grading and testing, in assigning students to tracked curriculum groups, in choosing textbooks and assembly speakers—can be questioned in terms of fairness, equity, respect for cultural pluralism, and other moral criteria. The imposition of uniform class schedules, the labeling of some children as gifted and others as disabled, the practice of suspending students from class and from school attendance, the absence of important topics and points of view in textbooks, the process of calculating class rank, the absence of alternatives in student assessments, the criteria for student and faculty awards—these and other institutional procedures carry moral implications, because the ends or purposes they were intended to serve are at least implicitly moral.

As with most institutions, in schools, standard operating procedures tend to rigidify and to take on a life of their own. Instead of regarding these procedures as human constructs put in place to serve a larger purpose, school personnel tend to allow means to become ends, to allow procedures to define the way things have always been and the way they are supposed to be. When institutional procedures become more important than the human beings the institution is supposed to serve, then the danger for moral mischief spreads. The institutional environment becomes inimical to human life. Values such as uniformity, predictability, efficiency, obedience, and conformity can tend to override other values, such as freedom of conscience, creativity, diversity, inventiveness, risk taking, and individuality. Individuals should not be forced to serve institutional procedures when those procedures violate human values. Institutional procedures should serve human beings. When they do not, they should be changed.

To speak of supervisory action as necessarily moral, but at the same time restrict that activity exclusively to activity with individual teachers, is to ignore the institutional context of teaching and supervising and its potential for demoralizing, in the literal sense, the teaching-learning situation. It is also to ignore the supervisor's position within the institution. The supervisor's position often is an institutional position in a way that differs from the teacher's institutional position. The teacher's primary responsibility is to the students: to see that they learn what he or she and the school community has determined they should learn. The supervisor's responsibilities are more to the total community: to see that schoolwide goals are being achieved. Institutional arrangements impinge very directly on the teaching-learning situation, and individual teachers are not in a position to change them.

Supervisors, however, enjoy a multiplicity of institutional opportunities to initiate and sustain conversations among various groups within the school community. They can challenge the appropriateness of institutional practices that unfairly affect various segments of the community.[20] Supervisors function at a variety of institutional levels, and their activities intersect with a variety of offices. Because they are relatively free to structure their day, they can attend a variety of administrative and faculty meetings to bring these institutional moral concerns before the community. To ignore these issues is to allow institutional practices and policies to disempower teachers and students, to thwart the very work supervisors carry on with individual teachers.

COMMITMENT TO LARGE EDUCATIONAL VALUES

Supervisors are among those in the school and the school system who have to be committed to a vision of what the school can become. Most schools have mission statements, which hold up high moral purposes to the learning community. Those mission statements tend to be forgotten unless people within the community refer to them and use them to plan and to debate school policies. Teachers and students, as well as all administrative staff, need to hear references to the higher purposes at which their collective activity is aimed. That sense of purpose is needed to encourage the school community when the aggravations of everyday school life wear down the patience and enthusiasm for the tasks at hand.

---

[20]For a more extensive discussion of this responsibility of supervisors, see Robert J. Starratt, "Building an Ethical School: A Theory for Practice in Educational Leadership," *Educational Administration Quarterly*, vol. 27, no. 2 (May 1991), pp. 195–202.

In schools it is customary for people to compete for scarce resources, whether they be library materials, larger classrooms, brighter students, or better class schedules. Moreover, affiliations among teachers based on narrow self-interest build up and lead to group rivalry and conflict, especially when some teachers appear to have greater status and power within the school. Add to those tensions petty grievances that arise daily—a missed meeting, a favorite parking place usurped by a rival, a misconstrued remark overheard in the teachers' room—and it is easy to see how these minor problems can lead to conflicts or loss of morale.

When teachers have a deep ownership of the larger goals of the school, though, attention to those goals can lead them to lay aside irritations and to work as a team. Grievances need to be cleared up, to be sure. However, there will always be someone assigned the last-period class, lunchroom duty, or a less desirable classroom. Appeals to the larger goals of the educational community and frequent reminders of the larger moral purposes being served by the community's collective action will draw teachers' focus away from these small grievances and invite pride in being part of such a community. That is clearly one of the continuing moral activities of supervisors.

THE POLITICS OF THE POSSIBLE

This treatment of supervision as moral action can be viewed as hopelessly idealistic, as out of touch with the realities of schooling. In discussing supervision as moral action, however, it was not our intention to present it as something beyond the reach of every person who serves in a supervisory capacity. Supervision can be moral action, although it can perhaps never be untainted by traces of self-interest or manipulation. The context of schooling is a context of limited rationality, of limited altruism, of limited power, of limited efficiency—as is the context of every organization. Moral action in this context is therefore itself limited. This limitation is no reason to deny its importance and its possibility.

In any given example used in the above treatment of supervision as moral action, the exercise of moral action will be limited by the circumstances of that particular experience. Some teachers may never enter into a supervisory exchange with genuine trust. In that case, supervisors simply do what is possible. In other instances, supervisors will find that their advice to policymakers is neither wanted nor attended to. Again, supervisors can do only what is possible. Perhaps next year will be a more favorable time to seek a change in policy. In any given school, supervisors will find different chemistries among groups of faculty. Those chemistries will make things either possible or impossible. Because circumstances change every year, new chemistries and hence new possibilities emerge. Because the exercise of moral action will not always be possible at any given time does not mean that it should be ruled out altogether. There will always be opportunities for some form of moral action at one level or another. The challenge and the need never go away. What is possible at any given time will always be in flux.

SUMMARY

This chapter addressed the work of supervisors as moral activity. It focused primarily on the moral implications embedded in the empowerment of teachers. The teachers' sense of the professional ideal of teaching leads to the awareness of a kind of moral imperative embedded in that ideal, an imperative to do their best to see that students learn what they are capable of. Besides working with teachers to improve their knowledge base, supervisors are called upon to nurture the empowerment of teachers so that the teachers' sense of self, their self-confidence, and their excitement about their own learning can be more easily transmitted to their students, thereby enriching the learning experiences of their students. The creation of such enabling relationships poses intrinsically moral challenges, challenges to protect the relationship from distortions and challenges to carry on the relationship with integrity and care.

Beyond their work with individual teachers, supervisors must be sensitive to the moral implications of institutional practices that destroy or limit the empowerment of teachers and students in the learning situation. In other words, supervisors have the responsibility to promote a moral environment in which the school can better function as a community of learners and a community of moral agents.

PART TWO

FOUNDATIONS FOR SUPERVISORY LEADERSHIP

CHAPTER 7

TEACHING AND LEARNING

$\mathbf{A}$S earlier reviews of the restructuring agenda indicate, the individual learner and the activities of learning have become more of a focus of education. Previously, the curriculum appeared to be fixed, as something uniform and completely codified, simply there for the students to master. Now learning itself is being emphasized. Let us expand on this important change.

The curriculum can be thought of as a body of knowledge codified by the academic disciplines and translated into course syllabi, textbooks, and demonstration materials. This is the *curriculum-as-planned*. Teachers take the curriculum-as-planned and adapt it to their own perspectives, supplement it with commercial or personal materials, emphasize some elements, and give less attention to others. They may have developed clever ways to teach certain parts of the curriculum; other parts they teach with less creativity and verve. This is the *curriculum-as-taught.*

Students encounter the curriculum-as-taught, misunderstand or misinterpret certain parts of it, relate other parts of it to their prior knowledge (which itself is limited and fallible), memorize certain parts to be repeated verbatim on exams, are absent from class on some days when crucial concepts are treated, and are oblivious to the significance or meaning of certain other parts. Some students find the material interesting, while others find it boring but tolerable in the short run. Still others have not learned the previous material well enough to build bridges to the new material. This is the *curriculum-as-learned.* It will be different for every student in the class, even though the majority of students may have acquired a sufficient common vocabulary of the material to talk about it with the teacher.

Students are then tested on what they have learned. The tests cover only selected parts of the curriculum thought to be representative of the material that should have been learned. Often tests are constructed to measure simple recall of information and definitions. Other tests are constructed with some easy questions, some moderately complicated questions, and some difficult questions that can only be understood by students functioning at the metacognitive level. Some tests attempt to find out what the students do not know, others to find out what they know well. Many tests are constructed on the conviction that achievement is reflective of the so-called normal curve of intelligence and that the job of the test is to sort out the brighter from the less bright, so that the teacher's grade sheets can reflect this normal curve. Many teachers have learned that too many high grades are interpreted by parents and administrators as a sign of insufficient rigor and that too many low grades are interpreted as a sign of unrealistically demanding (and unfair) expectations. This is the *curriculum-as-tested.*

To be sure, in this system creative and stimulating pedagogical techniques may be encouraged, and some personal interpretations by students may be allowed, especially in literature, social studies, and the fine arts. (Creative algebra, on the other hand, is almost as unthinkable as a creative fire drill.) Despite concessions for creativity and interpretation, by and large the curriculum content and the methodologies associated with distinct subject matters are established by curriculum experts, to be taught and learned as they are presented in textbooks and outlined in the school's or district's syllabus.

DEEP UNDERSTANDING FOR ALL STUDENTS

This traditional understanding of the curriculum and the teaching of it have been altered by the importance given to the curriculum-as-learned. Now the emphasis is on the success of *all* students in acquiring a deep understanding of the material. Under the traditional system a school could maintain the easy assumption of the normal curve of achievement: 10 to 20 percent of the students receive an A; around 30 percent receive a B; around 30 percent receive a C; the rest receive either a D or an F. Now, however, that is unacceptable. Virtually all students are expected to achieve at an A or a B level. It is further assumed that, if they do not, there is something wrong with the way the material is being presented and taught. The explanations that students don't care, that they are lazy and unfocused, no longer settle the issue. It must be asked *why* they don't care, *why* they are unfocused, *why* they are apathetic. The answers to these questions imply that the school (not simply one particular teacher) has failed to entice them to care, has failed to explain or present the material in ways that facilitate cognitive clarity and attention, has failed to stimulate and excite in students the curiosity and involvement needed to connect with the material and tasks at hand. The curriculum is no longer considered exclusively as what has been institutionally constructed for the relatively passive, uncontaminating reception by the students;

now the curriculum is seen primarily as what works for these students on this day in this context, as this part of a broader understanding-in-process of a larger framework of knowledge. Today's curriculum is what the students can learn today, with an eye on its connection to yesterday's and tomorrow's learning.

The emphasis is on the activity of the students as they attempt to construct the knowledge and understanding implied in the curriculum unit. Whereas in the traditional system the emphasis in classroom learning seemed to be on the students' absorbing what the teacher was saying or demonstrating, now the emphasis is on the students' actively interacting with the material at hand to *draw out* the knowledge and understanding called for by the curriculum task. In this way, students from an early age learn attack skills and inquiry strategies to make sense out of new material. They build up a repertoire of problem-solving alternatives, habits of looking at material from several points of view, processes of building on earlier understandings to piece together a new puzzle. This does not mean that the teacher never provides a demonstration or an overview or a theoretical explanation. Instead, the emphasis is on teaching the students to become more independent learners. Even in cases where the teacher does provide the initial demonstration, researchers have shown that students must work over that instruction in their own minds, using previously understood categories and skills to reconstruct for themselves what the teacher is trying to show.[1] Students cannot be said to understand what the teacher was demonstrating without such active internal processing. Moreover, it is only by developing their mental images of the material by making applications, by providing explanations, by giving multiple examples of the concept or principle involved, and by connecting that to larger networks of meanings that lasting or deep understanding is achieved. This is a different understanding of learning; rather than attempting to remember what someone else told them, students must work over the material, and work at it in a variety of formats, and produce a variety of performances.[2]

Research is showing that students have a wealth of prior learnings and experiences that they call on to grasp new material.[3] Teachers, however, seldom encourage students to call on that prior learning, nor do they teach students specific strategies for making those connections. As a result, youngsters attempt a hit-or-miss process of making connections, often distorting or misinterpreting the

[1]See Bonnie Shapiro's research in *What Children Bring to Light: A Constructivist Perspective on Children's Learning in Science.* New York: Teachers College Press, 1994. See also the illuminating essays of teachers doing research on their teaching in Marilyn Corchran-Smith and Susan L. Lytle (eds.), *Inside/Outside: Teacher Research and Knowledge.* New York: Teachers College Press, 1993.

[2]See the work of David Perkins and his associates at Harvard Project Zero, as elaborated in his *Smart School: Better Thinking and Learning for Every Child.* New York: The Free Press, 1992. John Bruer underscores the importance of challenging students to develop their own understandings as they grapple with knotty problems. See his *Schools for Thought: A Science of Learning in the Classroom.* Cambridge, Mass.: MIT Press, 1993.

[3]For an illustrative example of such research with kindergarten children, see Irmie Fallon and JoBeth Allen, "Where the Deer and the Cantaloupe Play," *The Reading Teacher,* vol. 47, no. 7 (1994), pp. 546–551. See also the research reported in Corchran-Smith and Lytle, op. cit.

material at hand. By carefully listening to students as they explain how they arrived at certain conclusions, teachers can come to understand the common errors children make on their way to figuring something out.[4] Their "wrong" answers are frequently "correct" when one understands the premises under which they have been working. Teachers need to consider youngsters' descriptions of their academic performances to understand how the patterns of their thoughts are formed and shaped.[5]

Children are constantly constructing their world out of the conversations of their parents and friends, and out of the meanings and associations picked up in their everyday experience in school and at home. This internalized world picture, in turn, shapes their subsequent perspectives and interpretations. Schoolwork often asks them to realign those perspectives with new understandings. Unless a teacher is somehow aware of how a child is making sense of the world, he or she may not know how the prior understandings of that particular child are distorting or preventing the appropriation of the new material.

AUTHENTIC TEACHING AND LEARNING

There appears to be a shift of major proportions occurring in our understanding of teaching and learning, namely, that authentic learning goes well beyond the passive intake of information to active engagement of the learner in producing or reproducing knowledge and understanding. Recent research is showing that authentic learning does not take place until the learner has come to an understanding of the material by organizing information into meaningful categories and into networks of categories, by having to explain what the material looks like from different perspectives, by providing various examples, by applying the understanding to new problems or contexts, and by evaluating the significance of new information in the light of this understanding. Even then a student's understanding is incomplete. It must be complemented by a placing of that understanding within the perspectives of an academic discipline, then showing how that understanding is related to other understandings considered essential in that field. The understanding is more mature when it can be connected to the world beyond the school, when it can be used to explain or explore issues in the civic community, and when the student can discuss his or her understanding with an adult audience in that larger community.[6]

The focus on the student as the active producer of knowledge has been pushed even further. Some well-documented research indicates that children can move

---

[4]Shapiro, op. cit.

[5]Again, the accounts of teacher research documented in Corchran-Smith and Lytle, op. cit., are instructive.

[6]See the work of the Center on Organization and Restructuring of Schools, as reported in Fred M. Newmann and Gary G. Wehlage, *Successful School Restructuring*. Madison, Wis.: Center on Organization and Restructuring of Schools, 1995.

to the metacognitive level in their learning. That is to say, they can discover the very processes by which they come to learn something. They can reflect back on what they have been learning to grasp how they came to learn the material, by seeing the methods they have used to construct bridges from earlier knowledge to new material and by coming to understand the process of knowing (metacognition). Groups of youngsters engaged in the jigsaw method of peer teaching can be guided to discuss how they came to the understandings they were trying to communicate to one another.[7]

David Perkins calls this attention to metacognition "the metacurriculum," thereby situating this form of learning as the crowning achievement of the students' active learning process.[8] He cites the following examples of attention to the metacurriculum:

- Encouraging students to think about the kinds of questions they would pose for themselves when faced with new material (e.g., What is this? How does it work? What is this like?).
- Encouraging students to describe their general problem-solving strategies (e.g., divide a problem into subproblems).
- Getting students to use terms such as hypothesis and sources of evidence as they try to make sense out of new material.
- Understanding that what is accepted as evidence varies across subject matters (formal proof in mathematics, experimental results in science, argument from the text and historical context in literary criticism, etc.).

This practice of reflective learning, usually carried on verbally with other students and the teacher, provides the foundation for the appropriate transfer of learning in new situations and for developing the general skills of learning how to learn. When carried out within a collaborative context, students also learn the important lesson of relying on the cumulative intelligence of the group, where everyone has some important insight or perspective to contribute, oftentimes correcting an oversimplification or distortion of understanding presented by other individuals in the group or filling in some unattended spaces in the group's thinking. The presence of the teacher allows for challenges to the misconceptions or distortions still remaining in the group's deliberations. The point is that the activity does not begin with the teacher's explaining the metacognitive content and skills; instead, the students are asked to come up with their own understandings, thus developing the habit of processing their work for the metacognitive scaffolding around it.

---

[7]L. Baker and A. L. Brown, "Metacognitive Skills and Reading," in P. D. Pearson (ed.), *Handbook of Reading Research*, vol. 2. New York: Longman, 1984, pp. 353–394; A. L. Brown and A. S. Palinscar, "Reciprocal Teaching of Comprehension Strategies: A Natural History of One Program for Enhancing Learning," in J. D. Day and J. G. Borkowski (eds.), *Intelligence and Exceptionality: New Directions for Theory, Assessment, and Instructional Practices.* Ablex Publishing, 1987.

[8]Perkins, op. cit., p. 101.

Fred Newman and Gary Wehlage add another dimension to the metacurriculum by insisting that this knowledge have some value beyond the school, beyond the simple achievement of competence.[9] Student learning should issue in more public products or performances that have aesthetic, pragmatic, or personal value. Students should be able to apply their understanding in public performances in their communities and to discuss these performances with adults in the community, using the understanding of the frameworks and methods of the disciplines. Unfortunately, society seldom expects schoolchildren to have anything important to contribute to the life of the community. One of the reasons youngsters become disaffected with schoolwork is that they believe that no one outside the school seems to need what they are working on. Youngsters are told that their efforts are supposed to prepare them for some distant future use, "when they grow up." By insisting that schoolwork issue in some kind of public performance outside the school, Newmann and Wehlage provide the missing link for motivating youngsters to take their school projects seriously. Furthermore, the concentration and effort required to produce something worthy of public scrutiny will necessarily deepen the students' appropriation of the metacurriculum. Barbara Presseisen refers to this aspect of higher-order thinking as conation, the motivating influence of doing a task when learning applies to the real world of the student.[10]

In order for students to develop the habits required for their full attention to the activity of learning, many researchers who deal with the metacurriculum stress a division of the learning activity into three stages: (1) the anticipatory activities, (2) the learning exercise itself, and (3) the follow-up activities.[11] In the anticipatory stage students are asked to recall earlier learnings about both content and learning procedures, which are connected to the learning at hand. These will serve as a bridge to the new material. The new material will be introduced with initial probing questions to begin focusing on the nature of the problems to be encountered. Again, students will be asked to recall a variety of attack skills that can be employed as they seek to make sense of the task. This is sometimes called a rehearsal of the learning activity. If grouping and collaboration are called for, specific responsibilities and subtasks are clarified, as well as the expected results of the exercise.

In the learning activity itself, students will engage the material by setting up the task, identifying the key components of the new materials, asking questions of the material, and applying various previously acquired categories such as cause-effect analyses, comparison-contrast analysis, explanatory hypotheses, species/genus categories, narrative structural elements, the influence of contextual variables, cultural values and ideologies, taxonomies, sources of evi-

---

[9]Newman and Wehlage, op. cit., pp. 9–11.

[10]Barbara Z. Presseisen, "Thinking Skills in the Curriculum," in James W. Keefe, and Herbert J. Walberg (eds.), *Teaching for Thinking*. Reston, Va.: National Association of Secondary Principals, 1992, p. 4.

[11]This is a summary of several suggestions contained in essays in Keefe and Walberg, ibid.

dence and weighing of evidence, and appropriate boilerplate formulas and equations. As the learners come to a deeper understanding of the new material and make sense of it, they move toward the completion of the task, whether it is to write an expository paragraph in plain language about the material, to report on the conclusion of an experiment to peers working on other experiments, to evaluate a political debate, to compare two poets or painters, to write an interpretation of a historical event that had been reported from three different perspectives, or to argue the public policy merits of a proposal for a new sewage treatment plant in the community. Before completing the task, they might review an explicit or tacit checklist, asking themselves such questions as Do my results relate to the definition and purpose of the exercise? What procedures did I follow? Did I skip any steps in the analysis or argumentation? Is my report well organized so that the main points are clear? Is my presentation grammatically correct and stylistically graceful? Self-checks such as these allow for revision of the jagged edges of a report and further cement the cognitive grasp of the learning.

In the follow-up activities, students should be called upon to explain their conclusions or findings, defend the methods they used to derive their conclusions, or explain how their findings relate to the larger field or academic discipline (e.g., as illustrating a general principle, or as filling in some information or perspective missing from, but consistent with, earlier learnings about the discipline). Other students should be asked to evaluate the group's report, and the group should be expected to comment on the appositeness of those evaluations. Finally, they should be asked to explain what they learned in the exercise, both in terms of subject matter and of the learning processes employed, and explain what use their learning might have for the real world and for them personally. When appropriate, they should be asked to speculate about future applications of their learning to other new learning tasks.

In elaborating on the above, it may seem that these three stages of the metacurriculum are more appropriate for doctoral students in their final year of completing their dissertation, but not for students in elementary and middle schools. Yet research is showing that students of these ages are capable of thinking their way through these activities—not with the complex vocabulary of adults, but nonetheless still reflecting the underlying metacognitive processes.[12]

THE CONTEXT OF THE LEARNER

While the recommendations coming from the research on successful or smart schools provides invaluable insights into the process of learning, we have to situate these recommendations within an understanding of the various contexts of the learner. These contexts involve those kinds of long-standing and deeply personal influences on the self-perception, the expressive style, the language, the so-

---

[12]See the remarkable achievements of formerly low-achieving minority students in the learning projects designed by Ann Brown and her colleagues, as reported in Ann L. Brown and Joseph C. Campione, "Students as Researchers and Teachers," in Keefe and Walberg, op. cit., pp. 49–57.

cial perspectives, and the sense of family and group belonging of the learner. The students' race, ethnic identification, social class, gender, and family background, therefore, are major influences on basic attitudes toward school, toward authority, toward the so-called mainstream culture, and toward the traditional academic tasks of classroom learning. If it is important to link new learning tasks to prior experience and to the real-life circumstances of the learner, then a school setting that conveys little regard for, or in fact shows disregard for, race, culture, ethnicity, language community, or social class differences will not succeed in bringing students to other than superficial compliance with academic demands.

Signithia Fordham and John Ogbu, for example, have documented how school success for an African-American student is judged by his or her African-American peers as "acting white."[13] For many African-American youngsters, then, especially in early and mid adolescence, complying with the academic demands of teachers and school authorities to get high grades and placement in honors programs is equated with adopting white, middle-class language and culture, with acting superior to their peers. Hence, many African-American youngsters engage in cultural resistance in schools, insisting on speaking "Black English" and in staying together in exclusively African-American groups. Hispanic or Latino students likewise perceive a disparagement of their cultural and linguistic heritage, as do Asian students, often to a lesser extent. When, to the cultural differences one adds class differences, then culturally different students from impoverished families face a school environment that is dominated by white middle-class culture and attitudes that, subtly or directly, labels them as "other," and thus inferior.[14] Add to this the even more consistent and less acknowledged absence of the feminine voice and perspective in the curriculum, and it becomes clearer that the learning context of a female, minority, poor child is perhaps the least attended to in the schools.

The solution is to train teachers to be more attuned to the life world of these children and to relate the learning tasks to that life world in such a way that that life world is honored and respected in all its human dimensions. The problem is that teachers bring the same cultural and class baggage to their work as does the general population. Teachers by and large represent the mainstream of American culture and see their job as bringing these children into the mainstream. What they usually do not realize is that they convey to their students that the mainstream is better, superior, more legitimate than the student's life world. Moreover, the textbooks, the testing and grading system, the behavioral norms of the school—just about all institutional aspects of the school—convey a similar message. That is why we have stressed early in this book the importance of community as a necessary and essential environment for learning. Teachers will need to partner with parents and leaders of the minority communities in order

---

[13]Signithia Fordham and John U. Ogbu, "Black Students' School Success: Coping with the Burden of 'Acting White,' " *Urban Review*, vol. 18 (1986), pp. 161–176.

[14]See the penetrating analysis of the Teach for America project by Thomas Popkewitz, "Policy, Knowledge, and Power: Some Issues for the Study of Educational Reform," in Peter W. Cookson and Barbara Schneider (eds.), *Transforming Schools*. New York: Garland, 1995, pp. 415–455.

to understand the realities of the students' life world, both the different values and assumptions embedded in that context and the struggles involved in dealing with joining the mainstream while attempting to maintain and protect all that is good in their own cultural communities.

Based on that understanding, teachers can build bridges between their students and the learning agenda of the schools. This will involve incorporating more multicultural components in the curriculum as well as creating reference points between the students' life world and the material under study. It will also mean supporting learning performances that use the life worlds of the students as an arena for legitimate research (e.g., the economics of the housing projects, the history of immigration in their communities [including the oral history of grandparents, grand uncles and aunts, etc.], the classical poetry of their language community, the art and dance of their cultural community, the political struggles of their communities, the geography of the country of origin of their forebears, and the contribution of women in their cultures). If the school is a community of learners, then teachers will allow themselves to be taught by their students and by their students' parents and will be able to reinforce the comparisons among the struggles and heroics of several cultures. "Being different," then, becomes a way of contributing to an enlarged sense of community among people who are seeking ways to live in harmony, where differences as well as deeper unities are honored.

IMPLICATIONS FOR TEACHING

The focus on active student learning and on the curriculum-as-learned obviously will present new challenges to teachers. To be sure, excellent teachers have already been engaged in the kind of facilitating pedagogy that enhances active student learning and deep understanding of the curriculum. They have done so, by and large, in school systems that have encouraged a model of teaching that promotes student passivity in learning, with the resulting alienation from and apathy toward the work of learning. The evidence of the failure of the schools to bring about in the majority of students the kind of deep understanding and metacognition called for by the public and by scholars is quite conclusive. The blame should be shared by school boards, by parents, and by textbook publishers, as well as by school administrators, teachers, and professors preparing teachers for their work. The effort to right the situation will require a broad-based effort by the school board, the textbook publishers and technology specialists, the school administrators, the universities, and, of course, the teaching profession itself.

For the moment, let us assume that all other stakeholders in the school are willing to support teachers' efforts to restructure the learning environment. In such an ideal situation, what kind of teachers are we looking for?

Ideally, schools need teachers who

- Are committed to the principle that all children can succeed at learning and who will do all in their power to bring that about.

- Are convinced that significant learning is only achieved by the active engagement of the learner in the production or performance of multiple expressions of authentic understanding.
- Are committed to collaborating with other teachers in the school to build a flexible, responsive, and dynamic learning environment that engages every student.
- Know the content of the academic disciplines they are teaching as well as the methodologies of inquiry of these disciplines.
- Know the components of the metacurriculum—the aspects of higher-order thinking; the major conceptual frameworks, models, and methodologies of the disciplines—and can recognize productions and performances that authenticate learners' relative proficiency in the metacurriculum.
- Have executive control of a wide variety of instructional protocols and strategies for opening up the curriculum to youngsters.
- Can design a variety of learning activities, for individuals as well as groups, that will maximize autonomous, active involvement with the material.
- Continually monitor students' work through dialogue and action research so as to assess whether an individual student is experiencing difficulties, to discover what the source of those difficulties are, and to respond in ways that will facilitate the mastery of the learning tasks.
- Are committed to working with parents as partners in supporting the learning tasks in which their children are engaged.
- Can evaluate in both formative and summative procedures a variety of assessment performances and portfolios.
- Can reconstruct, in collaboration with parents, administrators, and the school board, the school's learning environments whenever necessary.

Obviously, this profile of the kind of teacher needed for the work of restructuring requires a transformation of the professionals currently working in the classrooms of most schools in the country. The job of supervisors is to encourage teachers to work together as colleagues in their own transformation. Supervisors will not be able to legislate this transformation; it must be achieved by the teachers themselves. Again, we come back to the important foundation of community as the environment for change. If, in the formation of a professional community, the teachers come to some agreements about working together to develop approaches to stimulate more authentic student learning, then the climate for their own transformation will be set. Supervisors need to facilitate the formation of this kind of professional community.

STANDARDS FOR AUTHENTIC PEDAGOGY

Newmann and Wehlage offer a concise definition of what they term authentic pedagogy.[15] By this they mean the kind of teaching that leads to authentic learning or performance. Authentic student learning is the result of active engagement

---

[15]Newmann and Wehlage, op. cit., p. 17.

TABLE 7–1
STANDARDS FOR AUTHENTIC PEDAGOGY: INSTRUCTION

Construction of Knowledge
Standard 1. Higher-Order Thinking: Instruction involves students in manipulating information and ideas by synthesizing, generalizing, explaining, hypothesizing, or arriving at conclusions that produce new meaning and understanding for them.

Disciplined Inquiry
Standard 2. Deep Knowledge: Instruction addresses central ideas of a topic or discipline with enough thoroughness to explore connections and relationships and to produce relatively complex understanding.
Standard 3. Substantive Conversation: Students engage in extended conversational exchanges with the teacher and/or their peers about subject matter in a way that builds an improved and shared understanding of ideas or topics.

Value Beyond School
Standard 4. Connections to the World Beyond the Classroom: Students make connections between substantive knowledge and either public problems or personal experiences.

Source: Fred M. Newmann and Gary G. Wehlage, *Successful School Restructuring.* Madison, Wis.: Center on Organization and Restructuring of Schools, 1995, p. 17. Used with permission.

of the student with the material of the curriculum. Authenticity calls for student accomplishment to reflect (1) the construction of knowledge (2) through disciplined inquiry (3) to produce discourse, products, and performances that have meaning beyond success in school.[16] The criteria of authenticity require students to show successful analysis of the material, an understanding of the disciplinary concepts that ground the essential meanings of the discipline, and elaborated performances that are concerned with the world beyond the school. Newmann and Wehlage's standards for authentic pedagogy are summarized in Table 7-1.

Newmann, Secada, and Wehlage propose a three-pronged strategy for assessing authentic pedagogy: assessing tasks that teachers give students to complete, assessing the dynamics of teaching and learning, and assessing the work students actually do.[17] They then provide research-based standards and scoring criteria for assessing tasks, teaching and learning, and student work. The protocols for assessing tasks are provided in Appendix 7-1. Teaching/learning and student work protocols are available from the Wisconsin Center for Educational Research.

Newmann and Wehlage's categories—construction of knowledge, disciplined inquiry, and value beyond school—appear deceptively simple, but they provide for a wide expression of teaching strategies and interventions. Their focus on the

---

[16]Ibid., p. 11.
[17]Fred M. Newmann, Walter G. Secada, and Gary G. Wehlage, *A Guide to Instruction and Assessment: Vision, Standards and Scoring.* Madison: Wisconsin Center for Educational Research, 1995.

student's role in the production of knowledge and understanding stands in sharp contrast with the previously assumed, more passive role of the student in receiving curriculum "delivered" by the teacher. This approach emphasizes the teacher's understanding of how students process the academic tasks before them and of the students' prior knowledge that can be built on to introduce new material. Also, in this approach the student is the main actor. In contrast, the teacher is much more of the director, who connects various forms of structured activity into cohesive wholes that are consistent with the frameworks and methodologies of the academic disciplines, who continually raises questions about matters not being addressed by the learners in their inquiry activities, and who gets students to reflect on what and how they are learning.

The effectiveness of teachers in this system is enhanced by the kind of networking that they engage in with their colleagues. Working collaboratively, they can explore new approaches, discuss problem areas, look into research findings, engage in their own research to find out what students are thinking and feeling about their work, and make use of new resources such as the Internet and CD-ROM databases.

CONCERN WITH OUTCOMES

Carl Vigeland tells about a discussion several golf afficionados were having about the perfect golf swing. In comparing different golfers, someone mentioned Lee Trevino's swing. The others objected that Trevino's swing was hardly classic. Trevino's defender retorted, "Look where the ball ends up; the ball tells you who has the best swing." Indeed, in his prime, Trevino could put the ball where he wanted it more consistently than other golfers who appeared to have the more perfect swing.[18] The moral of this story for teachers is that no matter how imaginative or "perfect" their teaching plan seems, the key is whether all students are learning successfully. Teachers have to be able to read the readiness and interest and prior learning of their students so well that they get them successfully involved all the time. Obviously, Trevino did not win every tournament he played in; neither will teachers always succeed. That is why they have to keep studying their game, getting better at it, practicing a variety of approaches until they develop the kind of mastery that enables them to consistently hit the mark with their students.

The moral applies equally well to students. A student may not appear particularly flashy or creative. He or she may not follow the model problem perfectly, and the style and methods used may be unorthodox. But look at the results. Do the results indicate a profound and personalized grasp of the deep structures and frameworks of the material under study? Trevino's coach had enough sense to see where Trevino put the ball, even though his swing was not picture perfect. The good teacher will have enough sense to understand the learning strategies and processes that enable a student to produce an answer so true to the mark, even though his or her learning style may be different or unorthodox, or even slightly outrageous.

---

[18]Carl Vigeland, *Stalking the Shark*. New York: Norton, 1996, p. 23.

IMPLICATIONS FOR SUPERVISORS

An important theme in understanding supervision and evaluation is that it is difficult to separate what one considers to be effective teaching from questions of ideology. What a supervisor or a teacher, for example, considers to be evidence of good teaching is a function of both questions of meaning and truth. Further, truth is always a function of the meaning attributed to the evidence in the first place. What people believe, in other words, is what they see. Many of the practices of Supervision I are based on a particular set of beliefs about teaching and learning. The practices of Supervision II are based on different beliefs. It is not likely that teachers and supervisors will change their practices without first changing what they believe to be true about teaching and learning.

Consider, for example, the seven pairs of beliefs about teaching and learning listed below.[19] For each pair distribute 10 points to indicate the extent to which

---

1. (a) Learning is a process of accumulating of information and skills   (a) _____
   (b) Learning involves active construction of meaning and
   understanding.   (b) _____ = 10
2. (a) Students are like empty vessels who receive and store information
   that is taught.   (a) _____
   (b) Students' prior understandings influence what they learn during
   instruction.   (b) _____ = 10
3. (a) Learning is defined as a change in student behavior.   (a) _____
   (b) Learning is defined as a change in a student's cognitive structure
   and worldview.   (b) _____ = 10
4. (a) Successful learning is reflected in high test scores of the students.   (a) _____
   (b) Successful learning is reflected in the construction of meaning by
   students.   (b) _____ = 10
5. (a) Competition between individual learners provides the major
   motivation for learning.   (a) _____
   (b) Learning in cooperation with others is more important in
   motivating students and in enhancing outcomes.   (b) _____ = 10
6. (a) Teachers must work hard at delivering instruction to students to
   be successful.   (a) _____
   (b) Teachers must arrange for students to do the work of learning.   (b) _____ = 10
7. (a) Thinking and learning skills are generic across content areas and
   context.   (a) _____
   (b) Teaching and learning skills are content- and context-specific.   (b) _____ = 10
                                                                70

---

you believe each statement is true. For the first pair, if you believe that the *a* statement ("Learning is a process of accumulating information and skills") and the *b* statement ("Learning involves active construction of meaning and understand-

---

[19]The assumptions are adapted from James Nolan and Pam Francis, "Changing Perspectives in Curriculum and Instruction," in Carl Glickman (ed.), *Supervision in Transition*, 1992 Yearbook of the Association for Supervision and Curriculum Development. Alexandria, Va.: Association for Supervision and Curriculum Development, 1992, pp. 11–59.

ing") are both equally true, give each 5 points. If you believe that the *a* statement is much more true than the *b*, give the first 9 or 8 points and the second 1 or 2 points and so on.

Supervision I is based on the beliefs about teaching and learning implied by the *a* statement of each pair. Given these beliefs, Supervision I takes the form of tightly linking teachers to detailed objectives, content scripts, schedules, and evaluation schemes and then checking to be sure that teachers are following through according to the required specifications. The act of teaching itself is thought to be expressed in the form of research-validated generic behaviors. The behaviors comprise lists that supervisors use in observing teachers to be sure that they are teaching the way in which they are supposed to.

Supervision II is based on the beliefs implied by the *b* statements. The *b* statements comprise a reality that leads to a different kind of supervisory and teaching practice. In making the case for the *b* statements, Harriet Tyson explains:

> School structures and routines should be shaped more by students' needs than by the characteristics of the disciplines, and less by teachers' and administrators' need for control and convenience. Young children learn best when they become active workers rather than passive learners. They make more progress, and are much more interested in schoolwork, when they are permitted to work together in groups to solve complex tasks, allowed to engage in class discussions and taught to argue convincingly for their approach in the midst of conflicting ideas and strategies. Even young children can do these things well with a little encouragement . . . many children, particularly those with little home support, learn best in a more familial school atmosphere.[20]

Believing that teaching is not the same as telling, Tyson concludes:

> Generic pedagogy, which has spawned generic in-service training programs and generic teacher evaluation systems, overlooks the intimate and necessary connection between a discipline and teaching methods. Powerful, subject-specific and topic-specific pedagogy, most of it in mathematics and science, is becoming available. These new techniques make the battles over relative importance of content knowledge and pedagogical knowledge seem futile. Effective teaching requires both kinds of knowledge, developed to a high degree, and applied flexibly and artistically to particular topics and students.[21]

Much of the new research on teaching leads to the conclusion that teaching is much more than following a script and supervision is much more than making sure that those scripts are being followed.[22] As teaching becomes more and more context-specific and subject-matter-dependent, supervision becomes more con-

---

[20]Harriet Tyson, "Reforming Science Education/Restructuring the Public Schools: Roles for the Scientific Community." Prepared as a background paper for the New York Academy of Sciences and the Institute for Educational Leadership Forum on Restructuring K-12 Education, New York Academy of Sciences, New York, March 1990, p. 22.

[21]Ibid., p. 24.

[22]See, for example, Lee S. Shulman, "Knowledge and Teaching: Foundations of the New Reform," *Harvard Educational Review*, vol. 57, pp. 1–22; and S. M. Wilson and A. E. Richart, "150 Different Ways of Knowing: Representations of Knowledge in Teaching," in J. Calderhead (ed.), *Exploring Teachers' Thinking*. London: Cassell, 1987.

textually constructed and teacher-dependent. There is no template held by supervisors to which teachers must try to fit themselves. What makes sense is not something that can be determined beforehand and presented as a script. Instead, what makes sense in teaching must be constructed from within the act of teaching itself. For example, much depends on the teacher's understanding of the subject matter he or she is teaching; as this subject-matter understanding changes, so does what makes sense. Subject-matter knowledge consists of the facts, concepts, principles, and theories underlying the structure of the discipline. "Pedagogical content knowledge" counts too.[23] This kind of knowledge refers to the teacher's ability to transform subject-matter understandings into learning activities that make sense to students.

By totaling a and b scores, you can get a rough idea of the degree to which you agree with each of the two views of teaching and learning. The newer research on teaching and the b beliefs about teaching and learning that underlie Supervision II have important implications for how supervision should be thought about and practiced. Nolan and Frances list some of these implications as follows:

1 Teachers will be viewed as active constructors of their own knowledge about teaching and learning.
2 Supervisors will be viewed as collaborators in creating knowledge about teaching and learning.
3 The emphasis in data collection during supervision will change from almost total reliance on paper and pencil observation instruments [designed] to capture the events of a single period of instruction to the use of a wide variety of data sources to capture a lesson as it unfolds over several periods of instruction.
4 There will be greater emphasis on content specific knowledge and skills in the supervisory process.
5 Supervision will become more group oriented rather than individually oriented.[24]

To this list we add that supervision will increasingly be viewed as a role-free process. For teachers to be active participants in knowledge and collaborators in creating new knowledge about teaching and learning, they must assume roles not only as co-supervisors with principals and other administrators but also as co-supervisors with other teachers. Indeed, the future will show that supervision involving principals and other administrators as lead people will be less important than collegial supervision involving peers.

THE BOTTOM LINE

As was mentioned earlier, supervisors must consider the bottom line at all times, that is, whether all students are successfully engaged in learning. As we will see

---

[23]Shulman, op. cit.
[24]Nolan and Francis, op. cit., p. 58.

in later chapters, successfully engaging all students in learning involves both supervisors and teachers in an ongoing quest to improve specific instructional strategies as well as

- Working relationships both vertically and horizontally among teachers.
- Partnerships with parents.
- The utilization of space, time, and technology within the school.
- The way the learning community supports experimentation.
- The moral commitment to learning.
- The professional development opportunities of teachers.

For now, it may be clear that supervisors have to pursue their own professional development as they shift from Supervision I to Supervision II. The research literature on student learning and teacher action research is growing rapidly, and there is much to absorb as supervisors attempt to gain a deeper appreciation of the change in focus from teacher work to student work. As this professional development for supervisors continues, we believe that a much deeper appreciation of the complexity of teaching will emerge, and with it a greater appreciation of how teachers intuitively are moving in the right direction.

Appendix 7–1:
Standards and Scoring Criteria for
Assessment Tasks

Overview and General Rules

The main point here is to estimate, for a given task, the extent to which the teacher communicates to students expectations consistent with the standards. To what extent does successful completion of the task require the kind of cognitive work indicated by each standard?

The seven standards reflect three more general standards for authentic achievement as follows:

Construction of knowledge:	Organization of information
	Consideration of alternatives
Disciplined inquiry:	Disciplinary content
	Disciplinary process
	Elaborated written communication
Value beyond school:	Problem connected to the world beyond the classroom
	Audience beyond the school

A. If a task has different parts that imply different expectations (e.g., worksheet/short answer questions and a question asking for explanation of some conclusions), the score should reflect the teacher's apparent dominant or overall expectations. Overall expectations are indicated by the proportion of time or effort spent on different parts of the task and by criteria for evaluation stated by the teacher.

B. Scores should take into account what students can reasonably be expected to do at the grade level.

Source: Fred M. Newmann, Walter G. Secada, and Gary G. Wehlage, *A Guide to Authentic Instruction and Assessment: Vision, Standards and Scoring.* Madison: Wisconsin Center for Educational Research, 1995, pp. 80–85. Reprinted with permission.

Standard 1: Organization of Information

The task asks students to organize, synthesize, interpret, explain, or evaluate complex information in addressing a concept, problem, or issue.

Consider the extent to which the task asks the student to organize, interpret, evaluate, or synthesize complex information, rather than to retrieve or to reproduce isolated fragments of knowledge or to repeatedly apply previously learned algorithms and procedures. To score high, the task should call for interpretation of nuances of a topic that go deeper than surface exposure or familiarity.

> 3 = high
> 2 = moderate
> 1 = low

When students are asked to gather information for reports that indicates some selectivity and organizing beyond mechanical copying, but are not asked for interpretation, evaluation, or synthesis, give a score of 2.

Standard 2: Consideration of Alternatives

The task asks students to consider alternative solutions, strategies, perspectives, or points of view as they address a concept, problem, or issue.

To what extent does success in the task require consideration of alternative solutions, strategies, perspectives and points of view? To score high, the task should clearly involve students in considering alternatives, either through explicit presentation of the alternatives or through an activity that cannot be successfully completed without examination of alternatives implicit in the work. It is not necessary that students' final conclusions include listing or weighing of alternatives, but this could be an impressive indicator that it was an expectation of the task.

> 3 = high
> 2 = moderate
> 1 = low

Standard 3: Disciplinary Content

The task asks students to show understanding and/or use of ideas, theories, or perspectives considered central to an academic or professional discipline.

To what extent does the task promote students' understanding of and thinking about ideas, theories or perspectives considered seminal or critical within an academic or professional discipline, or in interdisciplinary fields recognized in authoritative scholarship? Examples in mathematics could include proportion, equality, central tendency, and geometric space. Examples in social studies could include democracy, social class, market economy, or theories of revolution. Reference to isolated factual claims, definitions, algorithms—though necessary to inquiry within a discipline—will not be considered indicators of significant disciplinary content unless the task requires students to apply powerful disciplinary ideas that organize and interpret the information.

  3 = Success in the task clearly requires understanding of concepts, ideas, or theories central in a discipline.
  2 = Success in the task seems to require understanding of concepts, ideas or theories central in a discipline, but the task does not make these very explicit.
  1 = Success in the task can be achieved with a very superficial (or even without any) understanding of concepts, ideas, or theories central to any specific discipline.

Standard 4: Disciplinary Process

The task asks students to use methods of inquiry, research, or communication characteristic of an academic or professional discipline.

To what extent does the task lead students to use methods of inquiry, research, communication, and discourse characteristic of an academic or professional discipline? Some powerful processes of inquiry may not be linked uniquely to any specific discipline (e.g., interpreting graphs), but they will be valued here if the task calls for their use in ways similar to important uses within the discipline.

  3 = Success in the task requires the use of methods of inquiry or discourse important to the conduct of a discipline. Examples of methods of disciplinary inquiry would include looking for mathematical patterns or interpreting primary sources.
  2 = Success in the task requires use of methods of inquiry or discourse not central to the conduct of a discipline.
  1 = Success in the task can be achieved without use of any specific methods of inquiry or discourse.

Standard 5: Elaborated Written Communication

The task asks students to elaborate on their understanding, explanations, or conclusions through extended writing.

This standard is intended to measure the extent to which a task requires students to elaborate on their ideas and conclusions through extended writing in a discipline. Expectations for elaborated communication can vary between disciplines. We indicate criteria for mathematics and social studies.

  4 = Analysis/Persuasion/Theory.
    Mathematics: The task requires the student to show his/her solution path and to justify that solution path, that is, to give a logical argument, explain his/her thinking, or to justify results.
    Social studies: The task requires explanations of generalizations, classifications, and relationships relevant to a situation, problem, or theme. Examples include attempts to argue, convince, or persuade and to develop or test hypotheses.
  3 = Report/Summary.
    Mathematics: The task requires some organization of material. The student is asked to give clear evidence of his/her solution path but is not required to give any mathematical argument, to justify his/her solution path, or to explain his/her thinking.
    Social studies: The task calls for an account of particular events or series of events ("This is what happened"), a generalized narrative, or a description of a recurrent

pattern of events or steps in a procedure ("This is what happens"; "This is the way it is done").

2 = Short-answer exercises.

Mathematics: The task requires little more than giving a result. Students may be asked to show some work, but this is not emphasized and does not request much detail.

Social studies: Only one or two brief sentences per question are expected.

1 = Multiple choice exercises; fill-in-the-blank exercises (answered with less than a sentence).

Standard 6: Problem Connected to the World Beyond the Classroom

The task asks students to address a concept, problem, or issue that is similar to one that they have encountered, or are likely to encounter, in life beyond the classroom.

To what extent does the task present students with a question, issue, or problem that they have actually encountered, or are likely to encounter, in their lives beyond school? In mathematics, estimating personal budgets would qualify as a real-world problem, but completing a geometric proof generally would not. In social studies, defending one's position on compulsory community service for students could qualify as a real-world problem, but describing the origins of World War II generally would not.

Certain kinds of school knowledge may be considered valuable as cultural capital or cultural literacy needed in social, civic, or vocational situations beyond the classroom (e.g., knowing how a bill becomes a law, or how to compute interest on an investment). However, task demands for culturally valued, "basic" knowledge will not be counted here unless the task requires applying such knowledge to a specific problem likely to be encountered beyond the classroom.

When students are allowed to choose topics of interest to them, this might also indicate likely application of knowledge beyond the instructional setting. But tasks that allow student choice do not necessarily connect to issues beyond the classroom. To score high on this standard, it must be clear that the question, issue, or problem which students confront resembles one that students have encountered, or are likely to encounter, in life beyond school.

3 = The question, issue, or problem clearly resembles one that students have encountered, or are likely to encounter, in life beyond school. The resemblance is so clear that teacher explanation is not necessary for most students to grasp it.

2 = The question, issue, or problem bears some resemblance to real world experiences of the students, but the connections are not immediately apparent. The connections would be reasonably clear if explained by the teacher, but the task need not include such explanations to be rated 2.

1 = The problem has virtually no resemblance to questions, issues, or problems that students have encountered, or are likely to encounter, beyond school. Even if the teacher tried to show the connections, it would be difficult to make a persuasive argument.

Standard 7: Audience Beyond the School

The task asks students to communicate their knowledge, present a product or performance, or take some action for an audience beyond the teacher, classroom, and school building.

Authenticity increases when students complete the task with the intention of communicating their knowledge to an audience beyond the teacher and when they actually communicate with that audience. Such communication can include informing others, trying to persuade others, performing, and taking other actions beyond the classroom. This refers not to the process of working on the task, but to the nature of the student's final product.

4 = Final product is presented to an audience beyond the school.
3 = Final product is presented to an audience beyond the classroom, but within the school.
2 = Final product is presented to peers within the classroom.
1 = Final product is presented only to the teacher.

CHAPTER 8

CURRICULUM AND ASSESSMENT

IN the last chapter we distinguished between curriculum-as-planned, curriculum-as-taught, curriculum-as-learned, and curriculum-as-tested. This chapter focuses on the sense of curriculum-as-learned and examines the assumptions and intentions behind the curriculum-as-taught and the curriculum-as-tested. As we will see, the curriculum-as-taught can vary considerably from the curriculum-as-planned and in this way directly influences the curriculum-as-learned. Likewise, the assessment of student learning can emphasize the wrong things and indirectly misdirect subsequent student learning away from a more authentic understanding of the curriculum and the metacurriculum. The intention of this chapter is to align supervisors' thinking about the curriculum-as-planned, the curriculum-as-taught, the curriculum-as-learned, and the curriculum-as-tested with their understanding of authentic learning, so that supervisors can have some sense of perspective as they work with teachers to improve learning for all students. We will explore how teaching can induce authentic learning, which in turn is reflected in authentic assessments.

OBSERVING THE CURRICULUM-AS-TAUGHT

Suppose you are having a busy day supervising. You visit the classes of five physics teachers. You discover that each teacher is using quite different methodologies. One teacher has divided the class into small groups that spend most of

115

the time discussing what kind of experiments they would have to construct to study light as a particle and light as a wave. In another, the teacher is showing an animated cartoon that illustrates the different properties of light, and concludes by leaving the students in a quandary over which theory of light is correct. This teacher assigns groups of students to teams that will argue one point of view over another. In another class, the teacher is relating Newtonian particle physics to individualistic theories of society, then contrasting that with field theory physics and more communal views of society; toward the end of the class the students get into a lively discussion of the low level of student morale and the prevailing tendencies of people at the school to "do their own thing." In the fourth class you find the students in the physics laboratory performing an experiment with a ripple tank, carefully following the instructions in their lab books and recording their measurements carefully in their notebooks. There is no class discussion; the teacher merely walks around the lab, occasionally pointing out a faulty measurement notation or telling one student team to stop "goofing off." In the fifth class the students have been reading a biography of Isaac Newton and the teacher has assigned teams to prepare a model replication of Newton's laboratory. The class begins with the teacher questioning the students about the antecedent scientific knowledge to which Newton had access that might have shaped much of Newton's approach to his experiments.

You come back to your office at the end of the day with a half hour before you must leave to referee a basketball game in the league quarter finals. Tomorrow you are scheduled for individual conferences with all the teachers you have observed today. Besides the routine aspects of class management and pupil attentiveness, what will you say about the approach each teacher is using, especially as that relates to the school's curriculum? Granting the observable strengths and weaknesses of each teacher in putting on the instructional performance (self-confidence, good tone of voice, good use of questions, etc.), can you say that one approach was better than another? If you say none of the approaches is necessarily better, do you mean that they are all interchangeable, that it does not really matter which approach one uses? Or does each approach originate from a different idea of what the curriculum actually is or is supposed to be? Are these approaches mutually exclusive? Is the content learned in one approach totally different from the content learned in another? Or are there some common learnings one finds embedded in each approach? Is it fair to give one departmental exam covering material taught in such divergent ways? How would these students score on a national physics test? Does it make much difference to you if the teacher does not care much about national test scores? Before you begin to sort out these vexing questions, the bell rings and you must dash over to the gym to catch the bus for the basketball tournament.

At this point we can leave our imaginary supervisor to the vagaries of the basketball tournament and look more closely at the curriculum-as-taught by the five physics teachers. We want to remain focused on the bottom line consideration—authentic learning—in each of these classes. We want to ask some questions of the curriculum-as-taught, so as to draw out some of the deeper assumptions behind what we observed. The analysis of learning activities by Jere Brophy and Janet Alleman provides a basis for these questions.[1] Their principles can be summarized as follows.

I. **Primary principles**
   A. The activity must be clearly and developmentally related to an important program goal, such that the completion of the activity leads to the achievement of the program goal clearly and unambiguously.
   B. The activity must be sufficiently difficult to stretch the student in the intended area of learning, but not so difficult as to frustrate the student. This may require some initial structuring and scaffolding of the activity differentially provided for different students.
   C. The activity must be feasible within the constraints of space, time, equipment, type of students.
   D. The benefits derived from the activity must justify its anticipated costs in time and effort. These benefits can relate to specific program goals, cross-disciplinary goals, or schoolwide goals.
II. **Secondary principles** (desirable, but not absolutely necessary)
   A. Activities that simultaneously accomplish many goals are preferred.
   B. Learnings that connect subject fields make certain activities desirable.
   C. Activities that develop the understanding of central ideas and their applications are preferred over isolated skill or concept-focused activities.
   D. Activities that require whole-task completion are preferred over activities that deal with partial or limited learnings.
   E. Activities that involve students in higher-order thinking (interpretation, debate, generation of alternatives, sustained argument, etc.) are preferred.
   F. Activities that enable students of various degrees of ability to participate are preferred over those that cannot.
III. **Implementation principles** (how teachers structure activities)
   A. Each activity should have a clear introduction, then some scaffolding so that students understand what they are expected to do and can begin the activity intelligently.
   B. Each activity should involve students working independently from the teacher, although the teacher monitors and intervenes when necessary.
   C. Each activity should conclude with assessment, feedback, reflection, and debriefing, so that both student and teacher have a sense of whether the learning goals were reached.

It should be noted at the outset that Brophy and Alleman stress the close connection between instruction and student activities, indicating that learning oc-

---

[1]Jere Brophy and Janet Alleman, "Activities as Instructional Tools: A Framework for Analysis and Evaluation," *Educational Researcher,* vol. 20, no. 4, pp. 9–23; see also Vito Perrone (ed.), *Expanding Student Assessment.* Arlington, Va.: Association for Supervision and Curriculum Development, 1991.

curs in the doing, in the engagement with the learning task, rather than in the passive listening to prepackaged units of information. We would argue along with Fred Newmann[2] that active engagement by students in the learning process is the essential ingredient, without which the most detailed, most enthusiastic, most creative teacher classroom preparation will flounder. Hence the curriculum that the teacher plans and presents must be centered on curriculum-as-learning activities, the immediate precursor of the curriculum-as-learned. The principles outlined by Brophy and Alleman can be turned into questions that the supervisor in our case study could discuss with each teacher. Better still, the supervisor could suggest the reading of the Brophy and Alleman essay for all five teachers, with a follow-up discussion of how helpful they might have found it in raising questions about assumptions behind their lesson plans. These teachers could use the principles as a self-evaluation check as they prepare various curriculum units.

As noted in Chapter 7, Fred Newmann and Gary Wehlage have concluded that "authentic pedagogy" involves students constructing knowledge for themselves, being involved in disciplined inquiry, and seeing the value of what they are learning beyond the classroom.[3]

As was stated in Chapter 6, learning carries moral implications. There is the question of intellectual honesty, whereby the learner attempts to present the knowledge he or she has acquired as honestly and without personal bias as possible. There is an implied caring for what one knows and how one uses it. There is the general morality of respecting the truth, however unpleasant or surprising it might appear. Beyond that there is the moral responsibility to use one's knowledge for the betterment of the community, even at some expense to one's own advantage. When group learning tasks are at hand, each member of the group is obliged to make a contribution; everyone will feel responsible in making the final product as good as possible. As regards the relationship between teacher and learner, there is the moral requirement of respect and caring. Again, these normative statements about the intrinsic morality of the curriculum can be turned into questions and topics for discussion.

POSTOBSERVATION REFLECTION WITH THE TEACHER

Let us assume that you are going to conduct the postobservation conversation with the physics teachers whose classes you have observed. What follows are possible responses to some of the questions generated by the principles mentioned above.

---

[2]Fred M. Newmann (Ed.), *Student Engagement and Achievement in American Secondary Schools.* New York: Teachers College Press, 1992.

[3]Several standards have been proposed by Newmann and Wehlage. The supervisor and five teachers in our case study could use these standards to assess the extent to which authentic pedagogy has taken place in their classrooms.

Postobservation Conference #1

Supervisor: Maureen, I was intrigued by your approach to teaching that class on the wave and particle interpretations of light. Do you usually encourage the students to figure out experiments that way?

Maureen: Yes. Whenever we are starting a new unit, before we read the textbook, I explain some of the properties of the elements to be studied and try to generate at least three experiments by which we might verify the presence of these properties. So this class was following a familiar pattern for the students. You see, I want them to think like scientists, to use their imaginations as well as their logical reasoning in designing experiments. Actually, I believe some of the most creative scientific work is done in the area of designing experiments, rather than in the methodologies of measurement, which often get associated with the "real work" of science.

Supervisor: How do you respond to a student who suggests an experimental design that simply won't work?

Maureen: I encourage full discussion among the class on every design suggestion the students offer. Everyone is expected to contribute reasons why a design would work or would not work. Students are evaluated much more on their reasoning and creativity than on whether the design would work. I want them to understand that doing science involves tons of exploratory searches, the majority of which don't work.

Supervisor: That's fascinating. Your students are getting an experience closer to the real-life experiences of scientists than they would by simply memorizing the information provided in the textbook. What do you expect them to do with the design ideas they generate?

Maureen: For extra credit, students actually design their experiment and then demonstrate how it works to the class. This gives students a real pride in their accomplishment. We have been able to send six or more students to the regional science fair for the past four years, mainly, I believe, because this approach generates the imagination required to come up with the kind of science projects the fair supports. Another thing: I try to emphasize to my students that this work on designing experiments will help them in all kinds of careers, not simply in careers as scientists, because it has all kinds of problem-solving applications to other contexts.

Supervisor: Are your labs, then, made up of student demonstrations?

Maureen: Not entirely. We usually do the experiments referred to in the textbooks. On this one, we'll get to the ripple tank that Joe Schwartz is currently working on with his kids by the middle of next week.

As you can see, this conversation with Maureen has yielded significant information about the teacher's platform, continuity with earlier and later classes in the course, student readiness for the learning, expected outcomes of the class, etc.

We will break away from this conference to look at the conference with the third teacher, the one comparing the wave and particle theory of light to theories of society.

Postobservation Conference #3

Supervisor: Frank, I was fascinated by the far-ranging discussion in your class. Is this a regular feature of your classes?

Frank: Not exactly a regular feature. Usually at the end of a unit in the course I will spend a class like the one you saw today. I usually stick fairly close to the textbook sequence and supplement the textbook with occasional readings of the cultural history behind some of the advances in physics. What you were seeing today is something I feel strongly about as a science teacher, namely, that all the knowledge we have of the physical universe has a larger message for us as human beings. It's like a metaphor of something human. When we deal with energy, fusion, fission, relativity—concepts like that—I spend time exploring the possible human significance those realities might have for us. It's not something manufactured, simply to relieve boredom, or to conjure up an image for them to hang their scientific understanding on. Human beings are part of nature. Nature is in us. When we understand how the natural universe works, we understand ourselves better, not simply as natural beings, but as human beings, because I think that physical realities are qualitatively transformed in human experience. I know that this may sound kind of far out, but I find that after the first few discussions, kids see the point. It somehow changes the whole way they study science. I've tried sharing my approaches with other teachers in the department, but they don't seem to want to get involved.

Supervisor: Go on, Frank. Tell me how this gets worked into the classroom discussion I witnessed.

Frank: Well, it's like this. If you think that physical reality is made up of discrete things—atoms, molecules, rocks, chairs, human beings—then the problem is to understand how they can affect one another. Newton's understanding of the atom, as the smallest piece of matter, was as a discrete thing, so to speak, whose motion and speed was affected by other atoms. It would be possible to isolate each atom as discrete. I believe his view of the physical universe was consistent with the social theories of subsequent social philosophers, namely, that society is made of discrete, independent individuals, whose relationship to each other is entirely instrumental. So society, from that perspective, is nothing more than a collection of self-sufficient individuals who interact out of self-interest. But notice what happens when a different view of the physical universe becomes the metaphor for a view of society. In quantum physics, all particles make up a field of energy in which every particle is somehow connected to every other particle, and no one particle can act independently of the field. When that view of physical reality becomes a metaphor for human society, then the individual human being is connected to everyone else in that society, not by rational choice, but by nature.

Supervisor: This is pretty heavy stuff. You think the kids can grasp it?

Frank: Some of them struggle with it, but I encourage those who grasp the idea first to explain it in their own words, and then the other kids start to catch on. Some understand what I'm driving at but think that it is too poetic or fanciful.

Their earlier education in science has led them to totally disassociate scientific knowledge from knowledge about human affairs.

Supervisor: What do you expect them to do with this kind of learning, Frank? In other words, if you succeed in this effort, how would this new understanding change them?

Frank: I would hope that they would see how much they depend on other people, and on the natural environment for their very existence, and that they would understand their responsibilities to honor their connections with other people. For example, I am extending this discussion to examine how the student government here in the school works. I think that kids here are struggling with the ambivalence of wanting to belong, to be accepted, and on the other hand of believing in extreme individualism, letting everyone do their own thing. I think that the way the student government works around here reflects the view of society as a collection of independent individuals. If they saw themselves differently, as a community of people who naturally belonged to one another, would they want a different student government?

Supervisor: I can see that these are pretty powerful ideas. From field theory to a new student government! Tell me, do you think that spending time on these discussions distracts from their covering the required syllabus in physics? Other teachers complain that they never have enough time to finish their course.

Frank: As a matter of fact, I think that the discussions help them to understand the physical concepts better. Unfortunately, none of the standard tests of knowledge of physics seem to be interested in these applications of concepts from physics. I find that the interest these discussions generate, even though they take up precious time, add to the motivation of the students to tackle the next chapters in the text.

This is quite a different platform from Maureen's. Nevertheless, Frank's discussion of his approach seems to flow from a profound understanding of the connections between scientific knowledge and human understanding. Note how both Frank's and Maureen's sense of the curriculum flows out of their personal convictions and values.[4]

Yet another set of reflections emerges when the supervisor engages the fifth teacher in a postobservation conference.

Postobservation Conference #5

Supervisor: I learned a lot about the relatively primitive laboratory methods of the 17th century yesterday. It is interesting, Marvin, how you can get across to the kids many of the early principles of scientific laboratory experimentation.

---

[4]For a clear example of this in the literature, see George H. Wood, "Teachers as Curriculum Workers," in James T. Searles and J. Dan Marshall (eds.), *Teaching and Thinking About Curriculum*, New York: Teachers College Press, 1990, pp. 97–109.

Marvin: Yeah. I think the textbook explanation of physics hides the difficulties people like Newton had to face in their work. Seeing it in its historical context helps them understand the genius of someone like Newton, as well as how much the effort of science requires the slow, painstaking work of many, many scientists who build on one another's work. Taking the time to look closely at the historical development also helps kids understand that prevailing worldviews and even language limits the ability of scientists to even frame the right questions. One of the amazing things the study of Newton's writings shows us is that he was aware of some of the wavelike properties of light. It was his followers who concentrated on his corpuscular explanations, creating the impression that Newton saw only that explanation. By studying the history, we can correct the inaccurate statement of our own textbook.

Supervisor: So you use this historical approach throughout your course?

Marvin: I would like to, but it is too time-consuming. Tomorrow, for example, we're going to do Newton's experiment with the convex lens and how it creates circles of various colors. The problem is that the textbook skips that experiment and the work of Huygens and goes right to Young's experiment. So after we do Newton's experiment, and Huygen's experiment of refraction of light in water, and then set up Young's experiment, I will have spent a week and a half on what the textbook expects to be covered in two classes. On the other hand, when we get to the ripple tank experiment, my kids will have a much deeper grasp of the physical properties of light than they would have had by racing through the text. So I speed up in some other places of the textbook in order to finish up with the other teachers.

Supervisor: Do your kids end up knowing as much as the kids in the other physics courses?

Marvin: Yes and no. The way I look at it, there are an almost infinite number of things to learn in physics. No matter who teaches the first course in physics, he or she has to choose. I try to achieve two things. One is that students have a sense of how science really got done, through years of trial and error, painstakingly building on the work of others, always with partial results. Second, that they know a good sample of physical concepts and theories reasonably well. We add to these two basic learnings a more superficial exposure to other concepts and theories, which is usually enough for them to score well on standard, multiple-choice tests of physics. You can only do so much in one course.

In each of the three postobservation conferences, you can see how the classes that were observed were part of a larger continuum of classes as designed in the plans of the three teachers. Although different, each class fit into a larger rationale of each teacher. As educators, they were each convinced that they were providing valuable learnings for their students. The question facing the supervisor is, How do I respond to these teachers?

One difficulty with this exercise is that as the supervisor, you do not have a complete transcript of each class. You do not know how teachers performed in specific teaching strategies, such as the review of prior information, the creation of a readiness set, the presentation of leading questions, the wait time after each question, the use of media to illustrate the main points, and the inclusion of positive and negative reinforcement of student responses. With more detail, you might be able to explore other possibilities with each teacher. For the moment, however, put aside considerations on technique and stay with the curriculum questions. What are the curriculum questions raised by these supervisory episodes?

The first question that arises concerns the quality of student learnings. Are the students in all these different physics classes learning the essentials of physics? How would they score on a standard test of physics? Would the scores of students in one class be higher than the scores in the other four classes? Would that mean that one teacher's arrangement of the curriculum is superior? Would a pretest and a posttest be required of each class in order to determine which class learned the most?

Yet each teacher was covering more than concepts and theories of physics contained in the textbook. What about the learnings in each course that were legitimately related to learning physics but were not tested by the standard test? Is not the physics test itself a reflection of what a curriculum in physics should be? But who makes up the test, and does that person have the agreement of the teachers in question that it is a legitimate test for their students? Does the school not have general goals such as the promotion of democratic values, community concern, and the application of knowledge to problems of living? Are not all teachers expected to teach for growth in these areas as well as in academic subjects? Of the five teachers, whose students would probably have attended to those goals more successfully? Should a department seek to have all students learn the same thing? Does a preset list of learnings assume that all teachers will create the same curriculum to produce those learnings? Shouldn't teachers in that department get together more often to discuss their differences and arrive at some common learning outcomes? Even if they were to agree on common learning outcomes, given their different approaches, would the learnings, in fact, be common? What does a "common learning" mean—a memorized definition of a theory, or choosing the same item on a multiple-choice test? Or does it mean that the students in all five classes could discuss their learnings in physics intelligently, so that their differences in understanding would not defeat their ability to agree on the meaning of basic concepts in physics?

A DEEPER ANALYSIS

Other curriculum questions emerge out of a deeper analysis of what is going on in these physics courses. What is being communicated about the way scientific knowledge is achieved? Is the scientist pictured as a person who stands apart from the object of scientific study, dispassionate, objective, in control of the material under study? Is the curriculum communicating an accurate picture of how scientific knowledge is achieved, a picture of what scientific knowledge consists of, or rather a philosophical or ideological interpretation of scientific knowledge? Furthermore, is scientific knowledge presented as the purest form of knowledge, the most exact form of knowledge, such that all other forms of knowledge (e.g., the knowledge of the painter or musician or theologian or parent or friend) are seen as less exact, flawed, subjective, mixed with emotions? Does the curriculum ever include discussions of the public policy implications of scientific knowledge and application (e.g., discussion of the pros and cons of nuclear energy plants)? Are questions posed concerning public policy decisions when the scientific evidence is contradictory or inconclusive (e.g., What are the effects of radiation due to atmospheric changes caused by fluorocarbons)? Is the authority of the scientist presented as absolute, or at least more validly grounded than that of the average person? Is there an implied assumption that the ordinary citizen ought to leave more complicated technological, economic, and political decisions in the hands of experts who have access to and really understand scientific knowledge?

Is the natural universe of physical objects and forces presented as simply "out there," waiting, as it were, for human minds and scientific technologies to bump into them and discover their essential material properties, and to use this knowledge to control them and put them to productive use? Or is scientific knowledge presented as a human construct, influenced as much by the instrumentation and metaphors that human beings use to study the object as by what is out there? In the science curriculum, how often are the students encouraged to maintain a sense of reverence and stewardship for the natural universe they are studying?

Underneath the surface of the curriculum being taught, there is a substratum of ideas, assumptions, and beliefs that also makes up the curriculum. Often this substratum is not at all attended to by either the teacher or the supervisor. It might be named the "tacit curriculum"; it is very much present in the teaching and learning of the classroom, but neither student nor teacher is explicitly attending to it. It is like subliminal advertising.

The answers to these questions are not easy to come by. Upon reflection, it becomes apparent that the superficial appearance of a uniform curriculum intentionally planned and agreed to by teachers and administrators does not hold up to scrutiny. Using the example of a physics curriculum presents the matter rather simply. An analysis of social studies, or literature, or art classes would likely reveal much greater diversity and variability in the way a curriculum actually is taught and learned.[5] Research that stresses the importance of teaching cognitive and metacognitive processes across the curriculum reveals a wide variety of instructional approaches, cued by both contextual factors of students' age and

[5]See C. Evertson, "Differences in Instructional Activities in Higher- and Lower-Achieving Junior High English and Math Classes," *Elementary School Journal*, vol. 82, no. 4 (1982), pp. 329–350; William H. Clune, "Three Views of Curriculum Policy in the School Context: The School as Policy Mediator, Policy Critic, and Policy Constructor," in Milbrey W. McLaughlin, Joan E. Talbert, and Nina Bascia (eds.), *The Context of Teaching in Secondary Schools: Teachers' Realities.* New York: Teachers College Press, 1990, pp. 256–270; A. Gamoran, "The Stratification of High School Learning Opportunities," *Sociology of Education*, vol. 60 (July 1987), pp. 135–155.

previous educational opportunities as well as by personal frames of reference and metaphors used to model the curriculum content.[6]

ADDITIONAL CURRICULUM CONCERNS

New voices have been raised in the curriculum field to challenge traditional views on curriculum. African-American, Hispanic, Native American, and other scholars have recently challenged the exclusion of relevant material about their culture and communities from the school curriculum. The school curriculum, they argue, is unbalanced in favor of a Eurocentric, or white, male, middle-class perspective. These scholars would encourage a greater diversity of historical and cultural material that would provide students of various cultures with a sense of the contribution of their communities in human affairs and would promote a greater understanding of and respect for the cultures and histories of various groups in society. More and more states are requiring courses in multicultural education for teacher certification, as well as revising textbooks to be more sensitive to multicultural concerns. These are steps in the right direction, but it is obvious that the multicultural curriculum agenda will continue to evolve, and more than likely involve local and national controversy. Feminists also have raised their voices about a curriculum that excludes a representative number of women role models and ignores women's perspectives on a number of issues.[7] While some textbook revision is under way to make learning materials more inclusive of women, developments of this agenda appear to be going slowly. Nonetheless, supervisors and teachers need to be more sensitive to sexist patterns in the curriculum that omit relevant historical information or present predominantly male perspectives. As many feminists have pointed out, sexism involves not only exclusionary language in the curriculum but also the absence of awareness of women's ways of knowing.[8] As the research

[6]See Beau Fly Jones, Annemarie Sullivan Palinscar, Donna Sederburg Ogle, and Eileen Glunn Carr (eds.), *Strategic Teaching and Learning: Cognitive Instruction in the Content Areas.* Alexandria, Va.: Association for Supervision and Curriculum Development, 1987; Robert J. Marzano, Ronald S. Brandt, Carolyn Sue Hughes, Beau Fly Jones, Barbara Z. Presseisen, Stuart C. Rankin, and Charles Suhor (eds.), *Dimensions of Thinking: A Framework for Curriculum and Instruction.* Alexandria, Va.: Association for Supervision and Curriculum Development, 1988; Lauren B. Resnick and Leopold E. Klopfer (eds.), *Toward the Thinking Curriculum: Current Cognitive Research.* Alexandria, Va.: Association for Supervision and Curriculum Development, 1989.

[7]For a sample of such authors, see Jane Roland Martin, "Sophie and Emile: A Case Study of Sex Bias in the History of Educational Thought," *Harvard Educational Review,* vol. 51, no. 3 (August 1981), pp. 357–372; Jane Roland Martin, *Reclaiming a Conversation: The Ideal of the Educated Woman.* New Haven, Conn.: Yale University Press, 1985; Madeleine R. Grumet "Women and Teaching: Homeless at Home," in William F. Pinar (ed.), *Contemporary Curriculum Discourses.* Scottsdale, Ariz.: Gorsuch Scarisbrisk, pp. 531–539; Madeleine Grumet, "Conception, Contradiction, and the Curriculum," *Journal of Curriculum Theorizing,* vol. 3, no. 1 (Winter 1981), pp. 21–44; Lillian Robinson, "Treason Our Text: Feminist Challenges to the Literary Canon," in Elaine Showalter (ed.), *Feminist Criticism: Essays on Women, Literature & Theory.* New York: Pantheon, 1985; Jo Anne Pagano, *Exiles and Communities: Teaching in the Patriarchal Wilderness.* Albany: State University of New York Press, 1990.

[8]Jo Anne Pagano, op. cit.; Carol Gilligan, "In a Different Voice: Women's Conception of Self and Morality," *Harvard Educational Review,* vol. 47 (1977), pp. 481–517.

and analysis by women continues to develop and reach wider audiences, some lively conversations will ensue among teachers, supervisors, and curriculum developers.

Still other voices are raised in criticism of a curriculum that is excessively technocratic,[9] as reproducing the ideologies and structures of oppression found in society at large, as excessively vocational or instrumental in orientation.[10] These critics argue that the curriculum tacitly reflects ideological definitions of the way the world works. Hence the curriculum communicates values and attitudes toward authority, property, material acquisition, social conformity, work and leisure, and the like, which support the economic and political status quo.[11] Citing recent national school-reform reports, these critics indicate the domination of school-reform efforts by economic interests in an effort to maintain national economic hegemony/competitiveness. School learning is seen as instrumental in securing employment and achieving technical literacy for the workplace. Critics cite the lack of concern for developing citizen participation skills and understandings, or environmental literacy.[12]

When their voices are added to those of the environmentalists, one can begin to get a sense of how much is missing from current school curricula.[13] Noel Gough suggests that a postmodern epistemology of knowing points to an older tradition going back to Aristotle of "phronesis"—knowing as practical judgment, a kind of knowing linked to the exercise of politics, which, in Aristotle's view, is the community seeking to come up with practical judgments about how to live its life as a community. Gough points to a new paradigm of education in which the curriculum would present the study of the natural environment as an interconnected whole.[14] This new paradigm of education would invite the community of men and women of all races and cultures to consider and seek practical judgments about how to survive and live their lives in some kind of harmony with each other and with their environment.[15]

[9]See Robert V. Bullough, Jr., Stanley L. Goldstein, and Ladd Holt, *Human Interests in the Curriculum*. New York: Teachers College Press, 1984.

[10]See William Bigelow, "Inside the Classroom: Social Vision and Critical Pedagogy," in Steven Tozer, Thomas H. Anderson, and Bonnie B. Armbruster (eds.), *Foundational Studies in Teacher Education: A Reexamination*. New York: Teachers College Press, 1990, pp. 139–150; Michael W. Apple, "The Culture and Commerce of the Textbook," *Journal of Curriculum Studies*, (July–September 1979), pp. 191–202; and Henry A. Giroux, "Critical Pedagogy, Cultural Politics, and the Discourse of Experience," *Journal of Education*, vol. 167 (1985), no. 2, pp. 22–41.

[11]See Robert Dreeben's book, *On What Is Learned in School*. Reading, Mass.: Addison-Wesley, 1968, as evidence by a "mainstream" scholar that supports the critics' contention.

[12]See the work of the Institute for Democracy in Education, associated with the School of Education at Ohio University, for examples of curriculum efforts to counteract this void in contemporary school-reform efforts.

[13]See C. A. Bowers and David J. Flinders, *Responsive Teaching*. New York: Teachers College Press, 1990.

[14]Noel Gough, "From Epistemology to Ecopolitics: Renewing a Paradigm for Curriculum," *Journal of Curriculum Studies*, vol. 21, no. 3 (1989), pp. 225–241.

[15]For an approach to curriculum as embedded in a social environment, see the interesting essays contained in Joe L. Kincheloe and William F. Pinar (eds.), *Curriculum as Social Psychoanalysis: The Significance of Place*. Albany: State University of New York Press, 1991.

This places knowledge–school knowledge—at the service of human and environmental needs first, and only in the light of these needs at the service of commercial needs. Hence supervisors who would carry those concerns into classrooms would ask very different questions at the outset of their conversations with teachers.

Seen from this perspective, curriculum takes on a sense of drama. The script of this drama is concerned with human survival and the survival of the ecosphere. Schooling is seen as a drama in which the future of a society gets played out in anticipation. The curriculum can be seen as the script for this drama, but it is a script that is only imperfectly written. Teachers and students will have to improvise, experiment, and complete the script.[16] The teacher adopts a variety of postures toward instruction within this drama: at one time serving as director in rehearsing several versions of the script; at another time serving as critic of the students' performance of a script; at yet another time coaching students as they work through a problem presented by the script. From within this metaphor of schooling as a drama, teachers have to enter in as players in their own right, for they also have a stake in the outcome of this curriculum.

The above perspectives on curriculum, while calling for modifications or transformations of what most would consider the traditional understanding of curriculum, nevertheless continue to reveal that the teacher is the one who shapes the curriculum, according to very basic beliefs about the purposes of schooling, the nature of knowledge, and the varieties of learnings that make that knowledge useful or functional for the student. This theme is underscored in recent studies of teachers as shapers of curriculum based on their own personal history.[17] These studies indicate that teachers' personal histories shape how they think and feel about what they are teaching. Their own education, the teachers who influenced them, their way of seeing the world through the frames and experiences of their intellectual journey, their fears, disappointments, and hopes—all feed into what and how they teach. The studies point out that it is important for teachers to reflect on how their biographies influence their teaching in order to better understand themselves as teachers. This approach to understanding teachers' choices and actions relative to the curriculum they organize and teach allows supervisors to connect with a reservoir of material in the teachers' experience that can enable them to converse and make meaning out of classroom events.

What the above considerations point to is an agenda for supervision that goes beyond a narrow concern with specific teaching techniques or technologies to a

---

[16]See Robert J. Starratt, *The Drama of Schooling/The Schooling of Drama.* London: Falmer Press, 1990.
[17]See David E. Hunt, *Beginning with Ourselves,* Cambridge, Mass.: Brookline Books, 1987; Peter Woods, "Teacher, Self and Curriculum" in Ivor F. Goodson and Stephen J. Ball (eds.), *Defining the Curriculum: History and Ethnographies,* London: Falmer Press, 1984, pp. 239–261; William Pinar, "Whole, Bright, Deep with Understanding: Issues in Qualitative Research and Autobiographical Method," *Journal of Curriculum Studies,* vol. 13, pp. 173–188, July–September, 1981; F. Michael Connelly and D. Jean Clandinin, *Teachers as Curriculum Planners: Narratives of Experience,* New York: Teachers College Press, 1988.

larger educational conversation with teachers. Such conversations, we contend, provide a much greater opportunity for teachers to consider what they are doing and to explore new possibilities for both teaching and learning.

REFLECTIVE PRACTICE OF THE TEACHER

Donald Schön's work on the reflective practice of expert professionals has caused widespread interest among teacher educators and researchers into teacher practice.[18] The widespread interest in reflective practice has also spawned some misapprehensions of what Schön meant by the term.[19] Schön emphasizes that the traditional understanding of how professionals work, namely, that they take theoretical knowledge learned in their own professional studies and apply that knowledge to individual cases they encounter in their practice, is erroneous. His studies show that expert practitioners generate knowledge as they engage in the particulars of a case, spontaneously forming intuitions about what is called for in a given situation. Those intuitions are formed through experience of successes and failures in their past practice. Their theoretical knowledge, such as it affects their practice, is tacit; only after the fact, when questioned by others, can they come up with explanations of their actions that are framed in intelligible theory. Even then, they may not be able to express all they know in a given situation, because so much is assumed in the activity of their practice. Their reflective practice is reflection in action; that is, it takes place *in* the action, simultaneously *with* the action. Schön did not mean reflection *on* action, which usually takes place after the fact, either alone or in discussion with a colleague. When the professional is dealing with another person or a group of people, the activity takes place in active dialogue with the client(s) being served or treated. Thus, as the professional's treatment of the client unfolds, it involves instantaneous feedback and exchange of information, so that the treatment is continually being shaped by the response of the client to the action of the professional. Reflection is a kind of intense presence to the person being served and to all the cues that are being sent in response to the initiatives of the professional. The practitioner knows what is going on in the action he or she is performing and knows the effect those actions are having on the client.

Applying this understanding of reflective practice to the supervisor-teacher relationship, you can see how the supervisor engages the teacher in the postobservation conference in reflection on the observed classroom episode, so that the supervisor can understand the *teacher's* reflective practice—the knowledge/intuitions-in-action—of that classroom episode. The supervisor is also helping

---

[18]Donald Schön, *The Reflective Practitioner: How Professionals Think in Action.* New York: Basic Books, 1983; *Educating the Reflective Practitioner: Toward a New Design for Teaching and Learning in the Professions.* San Francisco: Jossey-Bass, 1987.

[19]See Hugh Munby and Tom Russell, "Educating the Reflective Teacher: An Essay Review of Two Books by Donald Schön," *Curriculum Studies*, vol. 21, no. 1 (1989), pp. 71–80.

the teacher to consider the teacher's own reflective practice. A double reflection is going on here, in which the teacher is reflecting on and explicitating his or her own tacit knowledge that was operative in the teaching activity of the observed class. This exercise helps both the supervisor and the teacher to understand the tacit knowledge influencing the teacher's action in the classroom and to see whether that tacit knowledge is reasonably accurate, adequately responsive to the students in that classroom episode, and appropriate to the curriculum outcomes being sought.

REFLECTIVE PRACTICE OF THE STUDENT

What the supervisor models for the teacher by encouraging the teacher's reflective practice is something that the teacher should be doing with each student. As a student progresses through the learning tasks, the teacher should be asking such questions as How did you come to that conclusion? What are your reasons for holding that interpretation? Can you apply your reasoning to this other topic? What were you thinking when you were working on that problem? What was the first question you asked when you finished the experiment? Can you compare this result with the results of last week's work? How do you answer this objection to your hypothesis? What would happen if the relationship between the variables was reversed? Of what use is this piece of knowledge? What did you learn in this exercise? What did this class mean to you? How would you apply this to your own life? What kind of problem in the community does this remind you of? Contrast this measurement with another; what is similar and what is different? How would you teach this to a younger student?

Getting students to reflect on their learning often involves them in the metacurriculum, in higher-order thinking that relates the learning to the larger frames of reference in the discipline, to real-life applications, and to methodological considerations associated with problem solving and inquiry. Matthew Lipman refers to this as complex thinking, that is, thinking about procedures or methodology as well as the subject matter.[20] He suggests that this kind of reflective thinking should take place in collaboration with peers. Citing a phrase from the philosopher Charles Sanders Pierce, Lipman urges teachers to convert the classroom into "a community of inquiry in which students listen to one another with respect, build on one another's ideas, challenge one another to supply reasons for otherwise unsupported opinions, assist each other in drawing inferences from what has been said, and seek to identify one another's assumptions."[21] Referring back to the case study of the five physics teachers, then, which ones seem to exemplify such a community of inquiry?

---

[20]Matthew Lipman, *Thinking in Education.* Cambridge: Cambridge University Press, 1991, pp. 23–24.

[21]Ibid., p. 15.

ASSESSING THE CURRICULUM-AS-LEARNED

As we have stressed earlier, the curriculum-as-planned, the curriculum-as-taught, and the curriculum-as-learned should be woven together tightly. The same is true for the curriculum-as-tested (or assessed). We prefer the word "assessed" rather than "tested" because of the many negative connotations associated with tests and testing. Assessment suggests multiple approaches to the inquiry of what was learned. The term "authentic assessment" signifies that the assessment is close to the planned and taught curriculum as well as to the learned curriculum. Authentic assessment usually involves the completion of a whole task, one that reflects the complex and multileveled learning that has been necessary to produce the product for assessment.

Just as the supervisor needs to review the kind of learning activities the teacher designs to engage the students with the curriculum, so too should the supervisor review the kind and quality of assessments of student learning the teacher requires. In fact, the assessments alone will reveal much about the curriculum-as-planned and the curriculum-as-taught, as well as about the curriculum-as-learned.

To sharpen the supervisor's attention to issues of assessment, we will first look at some postulates offered by Grant Wiggins, review Lauren Resnick's criteria for assessment, then move on to examples of student self-assessment. This will lead to considerations of the teacher's assessment of the curriculum-as-taught and the curriculum-as-planned. The chapter ends with an appendix of some exemplary authentic assessments cited in the literature.

Grant Wiggins, one of the leaders in promoting authentic assessments, offers nine postulates for a more thoughtful assessment system.[22] His postulates assume an approach to teaching that stresses the active engagement of the student with the curriculum material. They apply not only to end-of-semester exams but also to shorter assessment tasks. As you read the postulates, try to come up with some authentic assessments for the physics students in the case study.

Postulate 1: Assessment of thoughtful mastery should ask students to justify their understanding and craft, not merely to recite orthodox views or mindlessly employ techniques in a vacuum.

Here Wiggins would have students be required to explain or defend their product, whether a term paper or lab report.

Postulate 2: The student is an apprentice liberal artist and should be treated accordingly, through access to models and feedback in learning and assessments.

Students need models of excellence and an opportunity to imitate those models. This implies cycles of exposure to a model of excellence, practice of the model, feedback, and refinement of the work. Whatever assessment products the student creates should exhibit an appropriate level of excellence that has already been modeled in their earlier learning activities.

---

[22]Grant Wiggins, *Assessing Student Performance.* San Francisco: Jossey-Bass, 1993, pp. 47–67.

Postulate 3: An authentic assessment system has to be based on known, clear, public, nonarbitrary standards and criteria.

This postulate implies that students know in advance the scoring criteria and have seen models, whether papers or videotaped performances. Advanced placement exams provide such scoring rubrics so that students will know ahead of time the criteria for the scores to be given.

Postulate 4: An authentic education makes self-assessment central.

This implies that self-assessment is a frequent, normal occurrence. For major pieces of work, students could be asked to hand in a self-assessment with their work.

Postulate 5: We should treat each student as a would-be intellectual performer, not as a would-be learned spectator.

This postulate does not deny that we want students to be capable critics of artistic, political, or scientific performances. It asserts that the emphasis in our assessments, however, should be on the students creating a product or a performance of their own.

Postulate 6: An education should develop a student's intellectual style and voice.

This implies that work will be returned not only for grammatical or methodological mistakes, but also work that is boring, disorganized, bland, without some fingerprint of the student. Peer readings and critiques of reports can help here.

Postulate 7: Understanding is best assessed by pursuing students' questions, not merely by noting their answers.

This postulate suggests that students should be judged by the questions they raise, their criticisms of accepted opinions, their probing for the unattended to, and their asking for an alternative view.

Postulate 8: A vital aim of education is to have students understand the limits and boundaries of ideas, theories, and systems.

In assessments, we should have students be able to point to the partiality or tentative nature of knowledge or systems of knowledge so as to avoid the absolutizing of any particular discipline. This can be done by exposing them to the history of the disciplines or by indicating the disputed areas in those disciplines.

Postulate 9: We should assess students' intellectual honesty and other habits of mind.

This implies self-assessment, as well as an expected candor about what students really know and what they are faking. Assessments that attend to this postulate would have students document their project from its inception, describing the difficulties and successes along the way. In group projects, this would require students to say what they have learned with the help of others in the group.

ASSESSMENT AS PART OF CURRICULUM

As we ponder Wiggins's nine postulates, we come to realize that assessment is not primarily something done after the learning has taken place in order to assign a grade. It does serve that purpose, but that purpose should be secondary. Assessment is part of the teaching and learning process itself. It provides students with a clear task to be achieved as they engage the material at hand. When completed, it provides the opportunity for the all-important feedback and reflection on the learning expressed in the assessment.

Educators tend to think that learning has taken place *only* when the students get the task right. Most learning, however, takes place when they do not get it right. When they do not get it right, students have to figure out what they need to do to learn. That review of learning often leads to crucial insights into the correct procedure, the clearer expression, the deeper relationship to patterns that have not been recognized. The history of science is instructive here. Most successful scientific breakthroughs occur after many false starts and misguided hunches in the laboratory. The same holds true for many artistic works. The masterpiece or successful composition takes place only after many revisions of unsatisfactory attempts.

Learning involves moving forward by inches, and often only after many false starts. Progress is a matter of making mistaken connections that are corrected only after trying them out and finding that they do not work or that they make only superficial sense. Understanding is initially partial, muddy, disjointed. It becomes sharper as the learner clears away the unrelated associations, the unworkable applications, the confusion of one thing for another. Learning progresses only by stumbling, groping in the darkness, muddling through until it is time to quit for the day, and coming back the next day for more of the same.

While all of this is going on, the learner is extremely vulnerable. After all, no one wants to appear stupid in front of others and certainly not to oneself. As a result, the learner often fakes it, trying to maintain the impression that he or she knows the material at hand.

This vulnerability is exposed by the teacher in such often asked questions as, "Who is having trouble understanding this?" or "Is this clear now so we can move on?" The problem here is that most youngsters are reluctant to admit that they are confused. Teachers must convince them that it is normal to find learning difficult and that the asking of questions should be the expected protocol rather than the exception. Unfortunately, teachers can become impatient when youngsters ask a lot of questions; they sometimes send the unspoken message that questions are not really welcomed. Many teachers have forgotten how they felt as young students—afraid of being considered stupid by their peers, let alone by their teacher. It is true that teachers feel pressured to cover the material and therefore become impatient when the class gets slowed down by two or three youngsters who are struggling to keep up. Finding flexible ways to assist these students while keeping the others moving forward is not easy, especially when teachers are working with supervisors who expect relatively uniform teaching procedures to be sufficient for the whole class or who expect that a certain percentage of students will fail as a matter of course.

Research by Ames,[23] following up on work by C. I. Diener and Carol Dweck, has indicated that children adopt early on in their school experience either a *performance motivation* or a *learning motivation.*[24] Those with a performance motivation concentrate on finishing the task, getting a high grade, and winning teacher and parental praise. Those with a learning motivation derive satisfaction from the learning experience itself, finding it intrinsically rewarding to solve new problems or work on new material. When faced with problems they cannot solve, the two groups tend to interpret the cause of their failure differently. The performance-motivated students tend to say that they are not smart enough and that there is nothing they can do about it. Consequently, they tend to give up easily. The learning-motivated students tend to keep working at the problem, trying other approaches. For them, it is not a matter of a lack of intelligence. The performance-oriented group tends to present a static view of intelligence (you either are smart enough or you are not); the learning-oriented group tends to think of intelligence developmentally or incrementally. Ames's research shows that the static view of intelligence and the performance motivation are taught inadvertently starting in the early grades. Her research shows that altered classroom protocols can develop in the students a deeper learning motivation and a belief that intelligence can be built incrementally, as they work through successively more satisfying solutions to the learning task.

These findings point out the need to use frequent informal assessments to determine which students are succeeding and which are having problems in carrying out a particular learning task. Teachers must listen sensitively to students' explanations of their difficulties and their way of approaching the task. They must also devise alternative approaches to clarifying a topic or task. These on-the-spot assessments can significantly reduce the remediation required after more formal assessments reveal the unattended misunderstanding. Moreover, a student who clears up a misunderstanding while the learning is in progress should not subsequently receive a negative grade on the formal assessment. This is part of the formula of working for the success of all children in the learning task.

Nevertheless, more formal assessments are still necessary. With the current emphasis in schools on the active production of student understanding, all assessments should be aimed at high-quality learning. Testing for the simple recall of information will no longer serve this focus on learning. Instead, assessments, both formal and informal, should focus on the performance of some intellectual task. Wiggins suggests that assessments that are intended to measure

[23]Carol A. Ames, "Motivation: What Teachers Need to Know," *Teachers College Record,* vol. 91 (1990), pp. 409–421.

[24]C. I. Diener and Carol S. Dweck, "An Analysis of Learned Helplessness: Continuous Changes in Performance, Strategy, and Achievement Cognitions Following Failure," Journal of Personality and Social Psychology, vol. 36 (1978), pp. 451–462.

competent understanding might be designed using Lauren Resnick's criteria for higher-order thinking.[25]

Resnick's criteria assert that higher-order thinking

- Is nonalgorithmic (the path of action is not fully specified in advance).
- Is complex (the total path is not visible from any single vantage point).
- Often yields multiple solutions, each with costs and benefits.
- Involves nuanced judgment and interpretation.
- Involves the application of multiple criteria, which sometimes conflict with one another.
- Often involves uncertainty (not everything that bears on the learning task is known).
- Involves self-regulation of the thinking process.
- Involves imposing meaning, finding structure in apparent disorder.
- Is effortful (there is considerable mental work involved).[26]

In preparing formal assessments, teachers should review these criteria, brainstorming ahead of time two or three student responses that would satisfy some or all of these criteria for each question in the assessment. After students have engaged in the performance assessment, teachers might again review Resnick's criteria to see whether the assessment in fact drew out these various characteristics of higher-order thinking and understanding.

SELF-ASSESSMENT

Let us turn to Wiggins's postulate dealing with student self-assessment. The following example may help supervisors realize how rich a source of teaching and learning such exercises involving the curriculum-as-learned can be.

Consider an ordinary class setting, say, a self-contained high school honors poetry class with one teacher and 24 students. The class has just concluded a comparison of two poems. Previous classes have dealt with aspects of poetry, such as mood, figures of speech, rhythm, unity, image, and symbol. The students have read a variety of poems and have done some analysis using these critical concepts. The objective of today's class is to have students use these critical concepts to compare two poems and to argue why one poem is "better" than the other. This objective fits into the larger goal of the course, which is for students to learn to discriminate between superior and inferior literary expression.

Toward the end of the class the teacher feels satisfied that most if not all of the students have demonstrated a good grasp of the analytical concepts and have applied them well in arguing for the superiority of one poem over the other. In an attempt to further reinforce the learning and to test out her impressions that the class has achieved the instructional objectives, she says, "Now let's all pause

---

[25]Wiggins, op. cit., p. 215.

[26]Lauren B. Resnick, *Education and Learning to Think.* Washington, D.C.: National Academy Press, 1987, p. 3.

a minute and reflect on what it is we learned today. What new thing struck us? What have we understood with greater clarity? How does what we've done today fit with what went on before? Of what practical use was this whole experience, anyway?"

The following answers come back:

- "I learned that it makes a difference when you read a poem out loud. I could *hear* how superior that first poem was to the other one."
- "I learned that you can still like an inferior poem—I mean, yeah, the first poem is a better poem, by all the measures we apply to it, but I like the second poem because it expresses a feeling about being alone that I've had many times. Just because a poem is a mediocre poem doesn't mean it's no good at all."
- "I learned that I had to read both poems at least four times before they made any sense to me. It seems that with poetry, kinda like music, you gotta acquire a kind of familiarity with it before it really says anything to you."
- "I learned that all this art stuff isn't entirely a matter of feeling, you know, all from inside someone's fantasy. There's something to it, some kind of intelligence. And you can talk about poetry intelligently, instead of simply leaving it to subjective feelings of like or dislike."
- "I learned that I have no poetic imagination. I never thought those kinds of thoughts. And I'm wondering how one gets to be a poet—are you born that way, or can you develop poetic imagination?"
- "I'm really having a hard time understanding what makes a poem "unified." It's a word that seems to me to mean perfect, or perfection. Like a perfect circle or something. So if a poem has unity, then it must mean that every word, every line is in a perfect place. But who could ever decide that? Maybe I need to see examples of *really* unified poems and some that are a little off-center and maybe I'll catch on."
- "I learned that it feels good to discover that a lot of people agree with my conclusions. Before the class started, I wasn't sure whether my picking the first poem as better was the right answer, you know. But when other people gave the same reasons as I had, I really felt good, because I figured— yeah, for the first time—that I'm understanding all the stuff we've been doing on poetry."

The teacher then continues the class by picking up on one student's question about what makes a poem unified. Other students are asked to come up with responses to the question, and a disjointed class discussion ensues about poetic unity. The teacher cites another student's comment that poetry is like music, and asks how one would know that a song is unified. That leads to further examples, and the class moves into a distinction between narrative unity and a unity of impression, which then leads to the deeper question of whether the poem itself is unified, or whether it creates a sense of unity in the reader. The teacher then asks the class whether they have experienced their life as a unity each day. This leads to several humorous responses, and the teacher challenges them to write a poem about an experience that conveys to them a sense of completeness.

This example illustrates a range of student learnings that reflect not only the achievement of the teacher's objectives but also the many idiosyncratic, ancillary learnings that always occur. The example points to the importance of taking time to let students reflect on what they have learned. Obviously, the students in this honors poetry class have relatively high levels of motivation and of verbal and abstractive abilities. Students in third or fourth grade will come up with simpler responses, to be sure. But getting them into the habit early of evaluating what they are learning will pay enormous dividends as it develops into ongoing reflective habits of mind and a genuine satisfaction over knowing that they are making progress.

Students' evaluation of their appropriation of the curriculum can lead to both cognitive and affective results. By reflecting on their grasp of the learning task, they can clarify what they know. Frequently, simple recall of the class material or unit will reinforce a student's grasp of the material. When this reflection is done in a nonthreatening environment, students can also clarify and admit what they have not yet grasped or understood. They can trace back the instructional sequence until they get to the point where the teacher or the textbook lost them. This clarification of what one does not know will often lead to a desire to learn that material.

On the affective level, students can be encouraged to review what they have learned, not so much for intellectual understanding but simply for enjoyment. The youngster who felt the need to read the poems many times was discovering how poems are meant to be enjoyed. This kind of enjoyment is not limited to those subjects within the humanities. A sensitive biology teacher or a physical education teacher can lead students into a kind of repetitive appreciation of what they have learned. Sometimes that leads to genuine wonderment.

On either a reflective or an affective level, student evaluation of this learning can lead to ownership. Recognizing what they have learned, what it means, how it is related to what they have learned before, how they can use it, what a sense of excitement or enjoyment comes with that mastery of a skill or discovery of a surprising piece of information—all of this leads students to appropriate that learning as theirs. Once appropriated, the learning tends to be effective, which is to say that the student owns it and can use it in many ways in the immediate future. Unfortunately, many teachers fail to take the time to encourage this sense of ownership. What they miss by not encouraging student self-evaluation is the genuine satisfaction of knowing how much their students have actually absorbed and the fascination of observing the individual subtleties in learning that manifest themselves through such feedback. Moreover, much of the formal evaluation the teacher engages in does not pick up the obvious clues that students put forth in their self-evaluation. A supervisor who helps a teacher to initiate student self-evaluation may have provided a stimulus for instructional and program improvement more effective than several semesters of in-service lectures on the topic.

In the example of the honors poetry class, the teacher used a spontaneous assessment of the students' learning to carry the lesson forward, to get them to probe for deeper understandings of the material. She was also able to employ their self-assessments to relate the material to their own personal experience, then to use that for writing their own poetry. In this example, one can see how easily spontaneous assessment can flow into curriculum elaboration. Assessment becomes part of the curriculum-as-learned.

AUTHENTICITY IN ASSESSMENT

Besides the informal or formal assessment, teachers must design a more independent form of assessment to which the student must be held accountable. Tests, often contain one or more faulty design features that end up sending the wrong message about the nature and purpose of school learning.[27] What we are looking for are *authentic* tests. Another of Wiggins's postulates on authenticity can help us here. Wiggins states in Postulate 3 that an authentic assessment system has to be based on known, clear, public, nonarbitrary standards and criteria. Among his criteria for authenticity are the following:

- The assessment task is like the problems faced by adult citizens, consumers, or professionals in the field.
- The assessment includes contextual factors found in real life, such as access to resources, variable time windows and restraints, and clear contextual parameters (e.g., audience, budget, and purpose). This criteria attempts to eliminate the false certainties of decontextualized learning.
- The assessment task presents real problems, not formulaic, boilerplate responses. Real problems require the application of various kinds of knowledge and skills and the prioritizing and organizing of stages of the work.
- The assessment is a *learning* task. There has been thorough preparation for performing the task; there is built-in self-assessment and self-adjustment by the student; the task may be discussed, clarified, and even modified by discussion with the assessor. There is concurrent feedback and the possibility of self-adjustment during the test. The results of the assessment (the judgments of the assessor) are open to discussion and possible revision. After completion of the assessment, teachers and students will discuss whether and why the assessment was a good assessment.
- The assessment requires students to justify and explain answers or choices. Each student is expected to understand what he or she knows and to elaborate on that knowledge.
- The assessment is one of many assessments that look for consistent patterns of work, for habits of mind across various performances.

---

[27]See Richard J. Stiggins, "Revitalizing Classroom Assessment: The Highest Instructional Priority," *Phi Delta Kappan*, vol. 69, no. 5 (January 1988), pp. 363–368, for a commentary of teachers' faulty construction of classroom assessments.

THE FORCE OF PRIOR ASSUMPTIONS

Behind any evaluation activity are values and assumptions about the nature of teaching and learning and the curriculum. Contrast the above criteria for authenticity with another set of assumptions and beliefs, listed below, which seem to stand behind the test protocols of many teachers.

- Knowing or understanding something means giving this particular response to that question.
- This curriculum design or this text contains the most legitimate, or the only legitimate, approach to this area of knowledge (e.g., modern Latin American history seen from a North American perspective), and therefore a test of the student's knowledge of this approach indicates that he or she knows something true or objective or valid about that area of knowledge.
- Using the language of public discourse in evaluation is the best means of measuring what the student has learned (rather than using poetry or music or graphics to measure it).
- Teachers and other school officials have the authority and competency to decide the criteria for evaluating and ranking students.
- Learning primarily involves learning what others have discovered (and seldom the way they discovered it), and so evaluation monitors learning on that level.
- There is always a causal connection between learning and instruction (rather than learning and the *students'* search, inquiry, practice, trial and error, or logical deduction); hence evaluation of learning implies an evaluation of instruction.
- The proper place for most learning is a classroom, and so evaluation never compares classroom learning (with all its constraints) with learnings in other settings.

One could go on and on, describing the assumptions behind assumptions. The point of listing these is to encourage supervisors to create distance from the evaluation activity so that both they and the teacher can perceive the value assumptions that are embedded in their evaluation procedures.

Because these assumptions rarely surface for discussion, they remain a strong, constant shaper of teacher tests and assessments. Bringing teachers together to explore alternative approaches to authentic assessment will enable them to work together to reshape their assessment practices. If a healthy sense of community among teachers has begun to be developed, then the foundation of professional trust will support the difficult efforts in changing these deep-seated assumptions.

SUMMARY

We hope by now it will be clearer what kind of fundamental changes are in the wind, both nationally and internationally, as educators and policymakers chart the course for schools for the 21st century. As we have seen in the last two chapters, major changes in traditional views of education have shifted. They can be listed as follows:

- All children can and must learn at a much higher standard of performance than has been previously accepted. What was expected for top students is now expected for all.
- The whole school community must be mobilized to support this first principle of success for all, including the school board, the central office staff, the school administration, the teachers, the parents, and the students themselves. No longer can accountability for success or failure be placed exclusively on the shoulders of individual teachers, when the schoolwide conditions and supports and incentives for high-quality learning are not present.
- The work of students, their active engagement with the curriculum, and their performance of the curriculum are seen as the core business of the school. The teachers' role is to assist, guide, facilitate, coach, direct, stimulate, encourage, motivate, assess, and remediate this work. The essential focus of school restructuring is on improving the quality of student learning performances.
- A corollary of the above is that the teachers' focus is on the curriculum-as-learned, namely, the students' production and performance of knowledge and understanding, contextualized (1) by the students' gender, culture, stage of development, class, family background, learning style, interests, and prior experience; (2) by the "real-life" variables associated with the learning tasks; and (3) by the methodologies and conceptual frames of the academic disciplines. This focus displaces the more passive memorizing of the curriculum-as-taught. What counts is the knowledge of the student, not the knowledge on the page of the textbook.
- Testing and assessment procedures will reflect this different understanding of and approach to student learning, in order to promote authentic performance and production of the curriculum-as-learned.
- Schools will be reorganized around this core work of learning and the facilitation of learning in such a way that resources of professional staff, daily, weekly, and yearly schedules, space, student groupings for learning, home-school partnerships, community resources, administrative arrangements, budgets, and assessments will be refashioned to support and maximize student learning.
- The work of supervision, then, becomes more complex and more subtle. Authority, responsibility, and accountability will be shared with teachers. While retaining a concern for improving individual classroom performance, a greater emphasis will be placed on the collaborative work of recreating a more user-friendly, learning-friendly school environment that will support more flexible and more responsive teaching and more consistently high-quality learning for all students.

Wiggins, in citing the work of Gagne,[28] provides a helpful bank of various roles and situational challenges that could be used in the construction of more authentic assessments.[29] This chapter concludes with Appendix 8–1, which suggests the professional roles and situations through which students can "perform with knowledge."

Appendix 8–1: Authenticity, Context, and Validity

PROFESSIONAL ROLES AND SITUATIONS THROUGH WHICH STUDENTS CAN "PERFORM WITH KNOWLEDGE"

Roles

Museum curator: design museum exhibits on a given topic; compete for "grant" money with other designers.

Engineering designer.
1. Bid and meet "specs": largest-volume oil container, MIT egg drop, and so on.
2. Apply theory: design and build a working roller coaster, a catapult, a herbarium, or anything else that requires application of theory studied.
3. Map/survey: focus on a region around school or school buildings, perhaps.

U.N. representative: design model U.N. tasks and activities, particularly those that require a careful analysis of the interplay of "knowledge" and culture.

Characters in historical reenactments.
1. Trials: Socrates, Scopes, *Brown v. Board of Education,* the Pied Piper.
2. "Meeting of the Minds": on a shared event or theme.
3. Diaries: made up as if by a historical person present from another era.
4. "What if . . . ?": writing/acting out a historical scenario.

Ad agency director: design advertising campaigns, book jackets, blurbs, and so on for the book(s) read in class.

Tour organizer/cultural exchange facilitator: design travel, logistics, and cultural guides for a world tour—within a specific budget and time frame and for a particular purpose.

Psychologist/sociologist: conduct surveys and statistical analysis, graph results, write newspaper article on the meaning of the results.

Bank manager: structure budgeting exercises needed in running a bank.

Document archaeologist: "From what text/culture/time frame is this fragment?"

Person archaeologist: "Who Am I?" (given clues).

Essayist/philosopher, student of essential questions. "History: evolution or revolution?" "When is a generalization a stereotype and when not?" "Is a mathematical system an invention or a discovery?" "Does the 'heart know things the mind cannot'?" "Does history repeat itself?" "Are there Great Books, and if so by what criteria?" Consider these (and similar) questions through research and debate products; present conclusions in writing.

Newspaper editor and writer.

---

[28]Robert Gagne, "Learning Outcomes and Their Effects: Useful Categories of Human Performance," *American Psychologist,* vol. 39 (1984), pp. 377–385.
[29]Wiggins, op. cit., pp. 223–225.

1. Research and write articles as if set in the studied historical time.
2. Make complex ideas and/or facts accessible to readers (magnitude of the Kuwait oil spill, Middle East background history, and so on).
3. Attempt to address a single issue from multiple perspectives: for example, write an editorial, a straightforward article, and letters to the editor from a wide variety of readers.

Historian.
1. "Biased, or just different?" Analyze and assess *controversial* accounts of historical events.
2. Conduct an oral history.
3. Review accounts of an event in three different textbooks for accuracy.
4. Outline the design of a "meaningful" textbook on U.S. history for kids.
5. Predict a future event (simulate CIA or State Department analysis) in an existing country.

Product designer: Conduct research, design an ad campaign, run focus groups, and present a proposal to a panel.

Job applicant: Prepare a portfolio with which to attempt to get hired for a specific job related to skills of the current course (with an interview by other students or the teacher).

Teacher: "If you understand it, you should be able to teach it." Teach younger children something you "know."

Expert witness: Give expert testimony to "Congress" on such issues as, Are all aspirin alike? Are advertising claims accurate? Should children's television viewing be regulated?

Speaker-listener: successfully communicate directions.

Debug expert: address problems with a car engine, an experimental design, an incomplete or garbled "text" (fragment of a book, radio transmission, incomplete translation, and so on).

Reviewer: "The medium is the message." Compare and contrast two presentations of one work— a book and its movie, a poem and song, play and musical, and so on.

Commercial designer: propose artwork for public buildings.

Situational Challenges

Discern a pattern.	Infer a relationship.
Adapt to and reach an audience.	Facilitate a process and result.
Empathize with the odd.	Create an insightful model.
Pursue alternative answers.	Disprove a common notion.
Achieve an intended aesthetic effect.	Reveal the limits of an important theory.
Exhibit findings effectively.	Successfully mediate a dispute.
Polish a performance.	Thoroughly rethink an issue.
Lead a group to closure.	Shift perspective.
Develop and effectively implement a plan.	Imaginatively and persuasively simulate a condition or event.
Design, execute, and debug an experiment.	Thoughtfully evaluate and accurately analyze a performance.
Make a novice understand what you deeply know.	Judge the adequacy of a superficially appealing idea.
Induce a theorem or principle.	Accurately self-assess and self-correct.
Explore and report fairly on a controversy.	Communicate in an appropriate variety of media or languages.
Assess the quality of a product.	Complete a cost-benefit analysis.
Graphically display and effectively illuminate complex ideas.	Question the obvious or familiar.

Rate proposals or candidates.
Make the strange familiar.
Make the familiar strange.

Analyze common elements of diverse products.
Test for accuracy.
Negotiate a dilemma.
Establish principles.

Source: Adapted from Grant P. Wiggins, *Assessing Student Performance.* San Francisco: Jossey-Bass, 1993, pp. 223–225.

CHAPTER 9

DEVELOPING TEACHER
LEADERSHIP

THE preceding chapters have progressively moved the supervisory process into the heart of the educational enterprise: teaching, curriculum, and student learning. The supervisory process is seen not so much as the performance of bureaucratic functions, such as rating teacher and student performance according to prescripted behaviors, but as facilitating both teacher and student progress in the learning tasks at hand. We have moved into the essential meaning of Supervision II. However, the more we explored what Supervision II might mean, the more it became apparent that the process of supervision could not be tied to any one role or position. It could be exercised by a principal, a district supervisor, a lead teacher, a teaching colleague, and indeed, by a student. What is essential to the process is reflection on the significance of what is happening.

As a process, supervision involves a "standing over," a "standing above," in order to achieve a larger or deeper view of the educational moment, to gain a vision of the whole as it is reflected and embodied in its parts. In short, supervision is not so much a view of a teacher by a super-ior viewer; it is a super-vision, a view of what education might mean at this moment, within this context, for these particular people. Perhaps more accurately, the process of supervision is the attempt by a segment of the community of learners to *gain* this super-vision of the educational moment within their reflective practice, so that their insight into the possibilities of that moment can lead to the transformation of that moment into something immensely more satisfying and productive for them.

What becomes more apparent in the exploration of the significance of Super-vision II is that the process requires an open, flexible, inquiring attitude. The process is not directed at judging behaviors according to a fixed, seemingly ob-jective set of standards. Rather, the process leads to the construction of under-standing and practical judgment, which leads to tentative, experimental choices that the participants see as responsive to the particulars of the context in which they find themselves. The participants, in their reflective practice, decide whether those choices are appropriate and productive for them. This is not to say that those pragmatic choices, guided by reflective practice, will be perfect. On the con-trary, teaching and learning are carried forward in the reflective give-and-take concerning, in this particular situation, what works and what does not work, what makes sense and what does not make sense, what facilitates student per-formance and what does not. Neither the teacher, the students, nor the supervi-sor knows ahead of time what will result until they engage the material in a spe-cific way.[1] They are constantly constructing the teaching-learning moment. Supervision is the attempt to see that teaching-learning moment in all its multi-dimensionality and all its possibility.

THE SUPERVISOR AS A PROFESSIONAL

Although it is possible and desirable for students to participate in this process of supervision, the responsibility for the more formal exercise of supervision is a professional responsibility of members of the educational staff—teachers, ad-ministrators, and professional support staff. In order to exercise this professional responsibility, those engaged in the supervisory process need to have some sense (by no means ever complete) of the substance of the super-vision. In other words, they have to have some vision of an ideal educational moment or an ideal edu-cational tapestry woven of many threads. As will be discussed in the next chap-ter, one's educational platform is usually the unspoken foundation of such a vi-sion, namely, a sense of how children learn, a sense of what is most valuable to learn, a sense of the social significance of what is learned, a sense of the ways to orchestrate learning, a sense of the importance of community and self-governance and social character in learning and for learning. Many teachers possess this vision tacitly, but the vision becomes narrowed by the daily routine of fragmented learning tasks. Through collaborative, reflective conversations in a supervisory process, teachers can regain that super-vision for themselves and for their students.

As professional educators, those who engage in supervision need to have a larger sense of the purposes of schooling. They have to bring to the supervisory process a sense of how *this* educational moment of *these* students and this teacher might embody the larger purposes of this school, given its neighborhood con-

---

[1]Michael Huberman, "The Social Context of Instruction in Schools." Paper presented at the An-nual Meeting of the American Educational Research Association, Boston, April 1990.

text, the socioeconomic realities of the community, the cultural makeup of its families, and the human potential and social capital such a community represents. Such an educational awareness does not come with state certification. It requires a sustained effort to be present to the cultural and social realities of the students, an attempt to understand emphatically what their world feels like and means to them. It also requires an understanding of the learning task from the inside, as it were, not simply as a proposition on a page in a textbook or course outline. Supervisors must imagine a variety of ways of entering into and working at the learning task. They must be willing to learn by trial and error what teaching strategies work in a particular instance. When one approach does not work, then both supervisor and teacher should say openly, "This isn't working. Let's try another way of looking at this."

Gaining super-vision through the reflective practice of teaching is not a deductive, logical, linear type of reasoning, moving from a clearly spelled out vision to a three- or four-step process that ends up choosing a specific learning activity. Rather, it is a highly specific involvement with the task at hand that is illuminated by an intuition of how it is working, and by further intuitions flowing from the exchanges with the students that enable the teacher to see that this is an instance of the larger purpose or value that the school is promoting. The super-vision flows out of the task, rather than from a temporary pause in the level of reasoning. The experienced teacher knows the super-vision tacitly in the particularity of the task, as Michael Polanyi would say.[2]

Such intuitions, however, come only with time, experience, and reflection. Having a sense of these complex realities is not easily gained. It requires intelligent inquiry, reflective assessment, and deep familiarity with the material being taught. It also requires a critical assessment of the institutional barriers to teaching and learning, given all the contextual variables just mentioned. In other words, the work of supervision is intellectual work. Not exclusively intellectual work, but certainly work that must be enlightened by an effort to understand, to develop intelligible frameworks for interpreting what happens between teachers and students and for proposing how it might happen more felicitously. It should not be characterized as work that relies on checklists of supposedly correct teacher behaviors, or on assumptions of superior knowledge granted by administrative position, or on a romanticized personal experience as a teacher. The practice of Supervision II places challenging demands on those who exercise it.

The practice of Supervision I tends to promote incremental changes within the status quo. Hence relatively uniform formulas define "good teaching." A relatively superficial notion of what constitutes academic knowledge suffices as a measure of effectiveness. A complacency with institutional arrangements of classroom schedules, physical arrangements of the learning space, procedures for grading and promotion, and so forth, assumes that teaching and learning must take place within these boundaries. A view of knowledge as something that

---

[2]Michael Polanyi, *The Tacit Dimension*. Garden City, N.Y.: Doubleday/Anchor, 1967.

exists independently somewhere—in the textbook, in the library, in the teacher's head—and is to be communicated to the students, all of whom will receive it as some uniform package suitable for testing, informs the way Supervision I judges and rates the work teachers do.

The practice of Supervision II challenges all these assumptions. But these assumptions cannot be challenged unless one is prepared to argue intelligently for their displacement. When we say, then, that Supervision II requires a larger professional commitment, we mean that it requires a profound grasp of child and adolescent development, a commitment to a studied understanding of teaching and learning, a new view of the variety of settings and stimuli that can nurture learning, a new awareness of the complexity of student assessment, a revised concept of professional authority as a necessary complement to hierarchical, legal authority, an understanding of adult learning, and an imaginative sense of the possibilities for flexible redesign of the process of schooling itself.

Supervision II requires of those who implement it to shift from the traditional roles defined by Supervision I to those of facilitator, policy innovator, resource finder, inventor, collegial experimenter, intellectual, critic, coach, institutional builder, community healer, visionary. Supervision II views the work with individual teachers and groups of teachers as but one aspect of a large, communal effort of transforming the school into a learning community.

In earlier editions of this book, we tended to treat supervisory leadership as the domain of the administrator-supervisor or central office supervisor. We recognize now that teachers are supervisors in their own right—supervisors of students' production and performance of knowledge. In Chapter 6 we saw how much of the morality of supervisory work derives from its involvement with the intrinsically moral enterprises of learning and of teaching. In this chapter, we similarly propose that much of the leadership of supervisor-administrators and central office supervisors derives from their involvement with teacher leaders of student learning and the nurturing of that kind of teacher leadership.

EMERGING PERSPECTIVES ON TEACHER LEADERSHIP

The literature on teacher leadership has only begun to emerge recently. American education has long labored under the mistaken notion that leadership was something for administrators to exercise, not teachers. Indeed, since most teachers worked in isolation, it was assumed there was no one to lead. Lee Bolman and Terrence Deal cite Michael Scriven's pronouncement that leadership skills "are entirely unnecessary for good teaching."[3] That statement appears to derive from the association of leadership with the work of administrators. As the following review of some recent literature on the topic of teacher leadership reveals, there is no agreement on what teacher leadership means.

---

[3]Lee G. Bolman and Terrence E. Deal, *Becoming a Teacher Leader: From Isolation to Collaboration.* Thousand Oaks, Calif.: Corwin Press, 1994, p. 1.

Bruce Cooper seems to imply that teachers exercise leadership in jobs and activities outside the classroom.[4] He speaks of a kind of "upward mobility" of teachers who assume leadership in their union, who join a school-site management team or a districtwide governance committee, or who move up to administrative responsibilities. In all of these instances, teachers exercise leadership by moving out of the classroom or by becoming involved in leadership activities at a distance from the classroom. They exercise leadership in nonteaching work. It is not surprising that Cooper and the other authors in this collection focus on these types of nonteaching leadership, since the book was written by professors of educational administration for an audience of professors of educational administrators. This is not to deny that teachers exercise leadership in these other nonteaching positions. However, we want to consider whether it is possible, indeed desirable, to think of teacher leadership primarily as involving classroom teaching.

Bolman and Deal offer four categories of organizational leadership (human resource development, political, structural, and symbolic) for classifying the types of leadership teachers may employ in their work.[5] While the examples of teacher leadership in their book often originate in classroom episodes, the leadership work itself tends to take place with other teachers outside the classroom. Again, we do not find the authors using the categories of leadership to analyze how teachers exercise leadership *with the students* in their individual classrooms. We believe that those categories could indeed be used to analyze how teachers lead their students in their common endeavor to reach their learning goals within the classroom. For instance, teachers are concerned with the development of youngsters in their classroom. They engage in a subtle form of classroom politics as power alignments and control of classroom work shift from groups of students back to the teacher, then back again to other students. Teachers structure the work arrangements in the classroom; indeed, moving from teacher-dominated structures and procedures to learning-focused activities is the most significant structural shift in the whole schooling enterprise. Finally, the symbolic, or cultural, category of leadership touches on the very heart of learning. Teachers are not only creating a classroom culture, they are teaching youngsters the very meaning of culture and the mastery of symbolic communication. Again, we do not want to deny the validity of the leadership exercised by the teachers described by Bolman and Deal. Indeed, that type of leadership promotes and supports the outstanding commitment of other teachers in the school and helps in the search for ways to make teaching more effective.

Whereas Bolman and Deal see leadership as involving teachers in the organizational life of the school, Leonard Pellicer and Lorin Anderson focus on leadership as involving teachers working with other professionals in workshops and

---

[4]Bruce S. Cooper, "When Teachers Lead," in Terry A. Astuto (ed.), *When Teachers Lead*. University Park, Pa.: University Council for Educational Administration, 1993, pp. 7–13.

[5]Bolman and Deal, op. cit.

collaborative projects that deal with curriculum and instructional issues.[6] The authors focus on concerns for improving classroom teaching, but, again, the teachers exercise their leadership outside the classroom, with other teachers. Even though in their introductory chapter they clearly refer to the leadership activities of teachers with their students, Pellicer and Anderson spend the rest of the book speaking of teacher leadership with and among other teachers. Furthermore, their suggestions for this kind of leadership work tend to focus more on the technical aspects of teaching and curriculum development. To cite but one instance:

> Simply stated, an effective teacher is one who is able to bring about intended learning in his or her students. This definition implies that the teacher is able to identify what he or she intends students to learn, structure learning experiences to facilitate student learning, and determine whether or to what extent the intended learning has occurred.[7]

The authors go on to suggest a series of helpful teaching strategies.

Although the many suggested ways of improving teaching to be found in Pellicer and Anderson's book are useful and are backed up by studies that indicate their applicability, we are not convinced that this focus on workshops and collaborative projects can be equated with teacher leadership. In this model, outside experts or consultants are simply supplanted by an inside teacher expert who marches the rest of the teachers through instructional improvement strategies. The bulk of Pellicer and Anderson's book focuses on workshops aimed at developing more effective instructional strategies, all good in themselves. However, the authors do not propose these teaching strategies as the strategies of teacher leadership; rather, leadership is exercised in running the workshops for other teachers. Again, it appears that leadership is conceived exclusively in terms of leading other teachers.

Patricia Wasley brings us closer to our own understanding of leadership in her analysis of three teachers.[8] In two of the three instances the teachers attempt to use their own classrooms as a basis for engaging other teachers in improving student learning. Wasley highlights this classroom leadership. In each case, the leadership is based on the teacher's own instructional practice and focuses on the investigation of challenging instructional strategies both by themselves and by the colleagues they were working with. Wasley stresses the importance of having these teacher leaders continue to work in the classroom while they are working with other teachers. This allows for ongoing experimentation and testing of ideas in the work setting.

Even Wasley, though, seems to fall back on the notion that teacher leadership means leadership with other teachers rather than leadership of students. She de-

[6]Leonard O. Pellicer and Lorin W. Anderson, *A Handbook for Teacher Leaders*. Thousand Oaks, Calif.: Corwin Press, 1995.

[7]Ibid., p. 92.

[8]Patricia A. Wasley, *Teachers Who Lead: The Rhetoric of Reform and the Realities of Practice*. New York: Teachers College Press, 1991.

fines teacher leadership as "the ability of the teacher leader to engage colleagues in experimentation and examination of more engaged student learning."[9] Adapting her words, we would prefer the definition to read as follows:

Teacher leadership involves the experimentation and examination of more powerful learning activities with and for students, in the service of enhanced student productions and performances of knowledge and understanding. Based on this leadership with and of students, teacher leaders invite other teachers to similar engagements with students in the learning process.

TEACHER LEADERSHIP IN THE CLASSROOM

For the moment, we want to focus on teacher leadership in the classroom setting. Consider the typical situation on the opening day of school. The teacher, in most cases, does not know the students and the students do not know the teacher. Many of the students do not want to be there; they would rather be outside playing with their friends or pursuing a hobby. The students know that they are in a relative position of powerlessness. The teacher can make their lives miserable—piling on the homework, telling their parents when they get in trouble, meting out detentions and other forms of punishment. After the first or second grade, however, most students know that they can, to some extent, make the teacher's life difficult, or at least frustrate the teacher's attempt to totally control what goes on in the classroom. They can pass notes, throw spitballs, drop their books on the floor, ask silly questions, copy homework, misrepresent their teacher to their parents, and engage in other obstructionist forms of resistance. Good teachers know that. They also know that the youngsters are vulnerable to criticism and failure, are unsure of themselves, are easily embarrassed, and need the approval of their classmates.

The leadership challenges for the teacher on the opening day of school are numerous. The teacher has to invite the students to believe that their time together can be satisfying, enjoyable, exciting, and rewarding. The teacher has to communicate to the children that they are cared for and respected in their own right. The teacher has to be able to mix the distribution of "warm fuzzies" with gentle demands for responsibility and accountability. The teacher has to convince the youngsters that they can derive deep personal satisfaction, both individually and as a class, in the production of quality work. The teacher has to convince them that this is significant, valuable work they will be attempting together. The teacher has to get to know the strengths and shortcomings of each student so that those strengths can be developed and those shortcomings minimized, bringing out the leadership qualities of the students themselves, so that they can develop the self-confidence and pride that comes with achievement. The teacher has to communicate a belief in these youngsters, an expectation that they can do high-quality work, that together they can become an outstanding class, a class that others in the school will take notice of and admire. The teacher, in other words,

[9]Wasley, op. cit., p. 170.

has to turn around potential hostility, apathy, and resistance into enthusiasm, collective self-confidence, interest, and pride in accomplishment.

Scan the book titles on corporate leadership in any bookstore and you will see references to these very same challenges: serving the customer well; managing by values; leadership through human development; managing with courage and conviction in an age of uncertainty; leading with a vision of the possible; cooperating to compete; working it out; disciplining without punishment; arousing the heart; discovering the soul; the power to be extraordinary; values to humanize the way we work; managing chaos; management by meaning; knock-your-socks-off service; imagination engineering.

Many teachers are reasonably good technicians. They can come up with a good lesson plan, develop three or four ways to get across a concept, and devise a sophisticated grading scheme. Teacher leaders are good technicians too, but they are also a lot more. They bring to their work with youngsters an excitement about learning, a belief in the sacredness of each child and in his or her untapped potentialities, an obvious caring for each child, and a commitment to create satisfying possibilities for the achievement of each child. Youngsters in their classes perceive this caring and respond readily to it. To be sure, there will be some students whose home experiences may have been so damaging as to require lots of time and effort to create the requisite trust. Teacher leaders take the long view with these children and eventually find ways to tease them into involvement.

Teacher leaders tend to focus on the profound significance of what students are doing and, by implication, on the profound significance of their own work as teachers. In the next chapter we will discuss the notion of the teacher's educational platform. Here we can say, by anticipation, that the teacher leader's platform will be based on at least a tacit understanding that their work with youngsters is involved with the ongoing self-creation of each student. Likewise, the teacher leader somehow knows that in the learning experiences of the students in that classroom, the culture is being recreated, the human experiment is again becoming self-conscious, and a little piece of human history is moving from drift and accident to a clearer conscious direction. The teacher leader understands that work in the classroom is involved with what John Dewey termed the transformation of experience—where raw experience moves toward intelligent understanding and this understanding is put at the service of intelligent action on both an individual and a group basis.

Without necessarily using the above terminology, we know that the teacher leader works out of these understandings and commitments when we observe the deep satisfaction of the teacher when the student looks up from his or her work and says, "That's it, isn't it? I got it! I never thought I could do it," or "I get it now, I know how it works," or "We did it! Wait till we show our parents!" Those are the moments the teacher leader works for and the moments he or she continually reminds the students of.

The teacher manager tends to be someone who arranges the students' work around the mastering of the syllabus. The achievement of good grades on standardized or teacher-made tests provides the necessary evidence for the teacher manager that the work has been accomplished. The teacher leader, on the other hand, goes beyond the mastery of the common syllabus and good grades on tests to push for a more personal and profound appropriation of the material under study. He or she will ask the student, "What does this mean to you, in terms of how you define yourself, in terms of your relationship to the community or to nature?" Furthermore, the teacher leader tries to bring the whole class to a reflective appreciation of the significance of learning in its own right—as a sacred activity, as an emancipatory activity, as an activity that bonds them to each other and to their world. For the teacher leader, the student performance of knowledge is not simply the production of right answers. It involves a sense of personal appropriation, of personal reconstruction, as something that bears the stamp of the student's lived experience, as something needed by the community, as something worthy of celebration.

To be sure, this description of the teacher leader is idealized. Yet we all know teachers who have approached this ideal. A little reflection reveals that these teachers did indeed lead the class to an unusually high level of performance, not simply in achieving the standard requirements of learning the school syllabus, but in achieving a sense of both individual and group pride in the work done together and in the improved sense of self-esteem and self-confidence of the class. These teachers possessed those same qualities of leadership we recognize in other leaders in other fields of endeavor.

David Berliner offers the insight that teachers perform many executive-type functions in the classroom.[10] For instance, teachers engage in planning, in communicating goals, in regulating the activities of the workplace, in creating a pleasant atmosphere for work, in educating newcomers to the work group, in relating the work of the site to other units in the system, in supervising workers and other staff, and in motivating those being supervised and evaluating the work performance. Berliner comments that teaching requires ongoing management of the workplace by a talented executive. His analysis is consistent with the shift in understanding already alluded to in earlier chapters in this book, namely, that the students are workers involved in the production and performance of knowledge. Teachers facilitate (manage, if you will) this work. This executive work of teachers becomes leadership when it is suffused with a view of the learner as a bearer of unlimited and heroic possibilities as well as a view of learning as a transformative and sacred activity, not only for the individual student but for the community of learners. That vision transforms the technical work of teaching into something special, which is what any kind of leader does: elevate the conception of the work to a deeper significance than it previously had; connect the work to something intrinsically important for the carrying on of human life. That new sense of the significance and meaning energizes the workers more enthusiastically and wholeheartedly to transform the work itself.

Our insistence that we begin by grounding teacher leadership in the teacher's leadership of his or her students rests on the conviction that teaching demands an autonomy and discretion that is unique to the profession. Lee Shulman brings

[10]David Berliner, "The Executive Functions of Teaching," *Instruction*, vol. 43, no. 2 (1983), pp. 38–40.

out the need for teacher autonomy and discretion as he describes the multiple demands teachers face in their classroom.[11] Teachers are expected to diagnose every student's learning readiness as well as learning handicaps or weaknesses for every new unit of the curriculum, in order to provide the appropriate stimulus and motivator for the learning involved. Shulman points out that when one student is having difficulty completing the reading project, for example, there could be any number of reasons for the difficulty: ignorance of a basic phonic rule; failure to apply the phonic rule even though already known; a misunderstanding of the point of the story; a confusion of the vocabulary with a similar-sounding word in the student's first language; an emotional upset at home the night before; a distraction caused by a classmate who was fooling around; a misunderstanding of the directions for the project given the day before, and so forth. The teacher has to spend sufficient time with that student to figure out what is causing the difficulty in order to respond with the appropriate guidance.

Teachers have the added challenge to balance mastery of skills and understandings by every student with the demand to cover the syllabus in a limited amount of time. Moreover, they are to attend to the needs of mainstreamed students and bilingual students, with the often cumbersome record keeping required for administrative oversight. They are responsible for detecting the signs of child abuse, protecting all the children from the possibility of infection by an undisclosed student in the classroom with AIDS, teaching impulse control and providing appropriate sanctions for violations of classroom rules, teaching basic ethical principles such as fairness, respect and honesty, and balancing a firm application of the rules and of academic accountability with the common fact that youngsters have their bad days when they are feeling out of sorts with everything and everybody. In other words, teachers not only have to know their stuff, but they have to be responsive to the messy and unpredictable swirl of emotions, surprises, disasters, and the multifaceted levels of realities being experienced by their students.

Teacher leaders somehow manage, most of the time, to provide the individual attention and motivation while leading the class to high-quality learning. They do not lead by providing uniform teacher protocols for every group of students every day in class. Rather, their work is characterized by versatility, inventiveness, improvisation, caring, laughter, multiple methodologies simultaneously employed for various subgroups in the class, willingness to throw away a lesson plan on the spot when it is not working, instantaneous restructuring of class activities when the moment presents itself. The teacher leader keeps his or her finger on the pulse of the class, to determine the way students are responding to the day's learning activities. This is not to say that the teacher forgets about the mandated curriculum outcomes; on the contrary, the effort to have every student achieve those outcomes is precisely why the teacher leader adapts the

---

[11]Lee S. Shulman, "Autonomy and Obligation: The Remote Control of Teaching," in L. S. Shulman and G. Sykes (eds.), *Handbook of Teaching and Policy*. New York: Longman, 1983, pp. 484–504.

flow of classroom activities. The teacher leader knows that each child will come to those learning outcomes in individual and personal ways and is continually seeking for the door that will open their minds to the lessons being attempted.

Because of that essential need for autonomy and discretion in the structuring and restructuring of the classroom work, teacher leaders who subsequently may attempt to exercise leadership with their colleagues know ahead of time how crucial that autonomy and discretion are for their colleagues as well. Hence, in their work with other teachers, they will present any specific protocols as requiring a multitude of adaptations and applications, for they know that there is no magic teaching formula that works for all children, nor for any children on the same two days. Teacher leaders explore a variety of approaches to the subject matter, some of which may, at one time or another, prove useful. The larger lesson teacher leaders teach their colleagues is to trust in the ability of their students to do high-quality work once they are motivated and trust in the mutual exploration with the teacher of how to do the work. Unlocking that potential of their students will always be different for different youngsters. Teacher leaders can help their colleagues to develop the ability to improvise on the spot, rather than to follow a model of teaching that does not work for several of the students in their class. Obviously, such improvisation will develop over time, with practice, through trial and error, with greater understanding of the subject matter and of the many ways youngsters come to knowledge. As Wasley also brings out, teacher leaders find that they grow in the exchange with their colleagues as they explore together alternative ways of approaching a learning unit.[12]

THE NEXT STEP

The next type of teacher leadership remains very close to this concern for transformative student learning, when the teacher leader begins to work with one or more teachers whose work is similar or overlaps with their own, or who, in the case of younger teachers, ask for help. Teacher leaders who begin to collaborate with a few other teachers (who might or might not be leaders in their own classrooms) in discussing common problems, sharing approaches to various learning situations, exploring ways to overcome the structural constraints of limited time, space, resources, and restrictive policies, or investigating motivational strategies to bring the students to a deeper engagement with their learning then begin to expand their leadership power exponentially.

When teacher leaders work closely with other teachers who are struggling with both the technical and the motivational side of teaching, they begin to bring the force of their classroom leadership to bear on the work in other classrooms. We need to be clear, however, that their focus, at this point, is on the enhancement of student learning in the immediate contexts of those classrooms, rather

[12]Wasley, op. cit.

than on other matters such as the reorganization of the bylaws of the local chapter of the teacher union or on the workings of a site-based management team. That type of leadership may or may not come later. For now we want to concentrate on teacher leadership as it is involved with instructional concerns. Teacher leadership at this level—both within the teachers' own classrooms and among teachers—does not receive enough attention, appreciation, or support. Very often the collaboration among teachers at this level is spontaneous and not structured by any administrative demands. At first administrators may not be aware of it. When they do become aware of it, there is little guarantee that they will actively encourage it. In some schools the culture is indifferent or disdainful of efforts to improve teaching.[13] Nonetheless, this spontaneous reaching out to support and collaborate with other teachers, while by no means the norm, is sufficiently widespread. Many teachers will refer to other professionals in the early years of their career, veterans who help them to develop ever more responsive approaches to their students.[14]

SUPERVISORY RESPONSE

We propose that the development of this kind of teacher leadership ought to be the first priority of supervisors. When a supervisor encounters a teacher leader in an initial classroom visit, the supervisor's response should be one of enthusiastic praise and support. Even though a supervisor might feel an obligation to make at least one recommendation for improved instruction (for does not that define the role of supervisor?), that impulse must be stifled. Teacher leaders already know that few of their classes are perfect. More often than not, the instructional gem that the supervisor wants to suggest is already familiar to and often practiced by the teacher. The proper response is to be supportive and to build an ongoing working relationship with that teacher, exploring ways in which the teacher would be comfortable sharing that talent with other teachers. There is no guarantee that these teacher leaders will be competent directors of workshops in instructional strategies for other teachers. But they can usually model their leadership with their students for other teacher observers. The one-to-one conversations with another teacher are sometimes the most helpful ways to bring that teacher leader's influence into play. Where there are one or two natural teacher leaders in a school, supervisors ought to arrange for beginning teachers to visit their classes often, assuming that this is an agreeable arrangement.

---

[13]P. Wasley, *Teachers Who Lead: The Rhetoric of Reform and the Realities of Practice.* New York: Teachers College Press, 1991; Judith Warren Little, "Conditions of Professional Development in Secondary Schools," in M. W. McLaughlin, J. E. Talbert, and Nina Bascia (eds.), *The Contexts of Teaching in Secondary Schools.* New York: Teachers College Press, 1990, p. 201.

[14]Bolman and Deal, op. cit.; Milbrey W. McLaughlin and S. M. Yee, "School as a Place to Have a Career," in A. Lieberman (ed.), *Building a Professional Culture in Schools.* New York: Teachers College Press, 1988, pp. 23–44.

ADDITIONAL ROLES FOR TEACHER LEADERS

It is important to recognize that most teacher leaders value their classroom teaching and only reluctantly surrender that primary commitment.[15] At least initially, therefore, some significant time should be reserved for that important work, even as teacher leaders are invited to take up broader responsibilities. As they acquire experience in their leadership roles, they will become more comfortable with the opportunities to use their accumulated expertise in arenas outside the classroom, and in fact will find their expertise stretched by the demands of these new leadership roles.[16]

The second caution to observe is the enormous workload teachers are already carrying. The teacher workweek averages well over 50 hours, according to a study by the National Education Association, with little or no time for formal, ongoing professional development.[17] Often teachers are asked to perform leadership roles that add to an already exhausting workload. With little time for planning, with little time to network with other teacher leaders, teachers are often given a herculean task to perform when they are asked to share their expertise with other teachers in after-school workshops and seminars, especially when these are spread out over several months. Supervisors who ask teacher leaders to conduct such workshops must find ways to relieve the workload in other areas. They must also see to it that the teachers have access to budgets and materials to adequately support such seminars. Furthermore, some attention must be given to legitimating the teacher leadership position. The teacher leader will often possess the requisite credibility among his or her colleagues; a title, an office (however tiny), and a budget, however, always help to provide legitimacy.

Often this kind of teacher leadership carries the title of master teacher, or sometimes instructional leader. In some schools, master teachers occupy a position of prestige and honor. They are considered to be the ones who are outstanding in the classroom and who possess a broad knowledge of their professional area (early childhood education, middle-school education, special education, or one or more subject-area specializations). They are looked to as a source of ideas and for sage advice. A supervisor should build strong partnerships with them, for in many ways, the teacher leaders will carry out the professional development work that the supervisor is often unable to do because of other responsibilities, or because of the large number of people the supervisor is responsible for.

TEACHER LEADERSHIP AND THE RESTRUCTURING AGENDA

By and large, teachers have been kept out of the broad discussions on school restructuring. In some districts, it is true that teachers have been exposed to work-

---

[15]Mclaughlin and Yee, op. cit.; Little, op. cit.
[16]McLaughlin and Yee, op. cit.; S. J. Ball and Ivor F. Goodson (eds.), *Teachers Lives and Careers*. London: Falmer Press, 1985.
[17]National Education Association, *Status of the American Public School Teacher 1985–86*. Washington, D.C.: Author, 1986.

shops on constructivist learning theory and appropriate pedagogies, but the focus tends to be confined to their individual classroom practice. Teachers have not been encouraged to work collaboratively with building and district administrators on the local restructuring of the core work (teaching and learning) of *the whole school*, and the developing of institutional structures and policies needed to support such second-order changes. For that matter, neither have supervisors been particularly vocal in the restructuring conversation.

We want to suggest that the supervisor take an important initial step as an active player in the restructuring effort by intensively working with teacher leaders at the local level. Beyond the effort to encourage mentoring and to develop appropriate teacher experiments that increase students' active engagement in learning, the supervisor can introduce the broader focus on schoolwide efforts to multiply the kind of engaged learning that may be found in two or three classrooms in the school. At present, most classroom teacher leadership takes as a given the current allocation of space and time in the school day and school week; takes as a given the grading, assessment, and promotion processes; takes as a given the grouping of students by grade levels; takes as a given the isolated classroom as the locus of instruction and curriculum development. The supervisor, once a feeling of trust and partnership has been established with teacher leaders, can engage them in discussions of other possibilities for organizing learning time and space and student groups and instructional resources that might better support the more active engagement of students in the learning tasks. The teacher leaders do not have to suggest any radical changes to the school administration and the rest of the teachers. Rather, they can look at their immediate situation and begin there.

By starting with a small team of teachers who want to work together to create an enhanced learning environment for their students, the supervisor can begin to build a culture of collaboration and inquiry. Over time the confidence and talent of the group will grow, and the teacher leaders will build a strong base from which to expand their influence throughout the school, or at least throughout one or more subunits within the school. This does not mean that their efforts will automatically be met with their colleagues' universal and enthusiastic approval. There is enough evidence in the literature on school change to suggest precisely the opposite. By marshalling support, sometimes teacher by teacher, by encouraging administrative endorsement, and by providing time for teachers to discuss the benefits of increased student engagement in their learning, the supervisor can help to encourage the growth of a critical mass of teachers who will become involved. As that group of teachers grows, then the institutional obstacles to restructured learning and teaching will become more apparent. With that critical mass of teachers, the school is prepared to begin experimenting with different daily and weekly schedules, different groupings of students, different arrangements for student teams to work on class projects in the community during the school day, different arrangements in the use of computer technology outside the classroom—all in the interest of enhancing the productivity of students in their learning tasks.

As more and more teachers expand their thinking about teaching and learning beyond their own classroom, they will come to realize the need for major restructuring of the way the school conducts its primary business—the production and performance of knowledge. To become engaged in the restructuring agenda, the supervisor has to create these kinds of partnerships with the emerging teacher leadership of the school. As those partnerships mature, the readiness for schoolwide restructuring grows.

Cooper's helpful categories for teacher leadership now come into play.[18] Teachers can exercise leadership, for example, when serving on school committees on computer technology and curriculum development, the principal's advisory council, or the local site-based management committee. Membership in these committees does not of itself constitute leadership, however. A broader vision of what schools are for, a feel for strategic planning, an ability to create coalitions among disparate subgroups in the school, a passion for home-school partnerships—these and other characteristics are what will make the leadership difference. Similarly, these characteristics and others will contribute to teachers' leadership in districtwide committees, another arena for teachers' involvement in school-improvement efforts. Likewise, teacher leadership within the local union or professional association will carry concerns for teachers' roles in the restructuring agenda.

While supervisors have no direct influence over these other forms of teacher leadership, they can exert indirect influence through their ongoing collaborative efforts to improve the core work of the classroom and the school. By focusing on the quality of student learning, supervisors can reinforce the basic commitments of teacher leaders no matter where they exercise their leadership.

SUMMARY

In this chapter we have attempted to shift the more traditional focus on the supervisor's leadership role to the teacher's role. We believe that the emerging understanding of the core work of the school, namely, teaching for the enhanced student production and performance of knowledge, requires a greater attention to partnerships with and among teacher leaders. The leadership of a supervisor is increasingly tied to his or her work with teacher leaders in supporting and encouraging their leadership with their students and with their colleagues. Supervisors who want to lead will see their work linked to the restructuring agenda of the whole school, and therefore will see the importance of their bringing that perspective to their work with teacher leaders. That work of leadership involves building, in partnership with teacher leaders, a critical mass of teachers who feel collectively empowered to engage in the slow but exciting work of transforming the school into an environment that promotes high-quality learning for all students.

[18]Cooper, op. cit.

CHAPTER 10

THE SUPERVISOR'S
EDUCATIONAL PLATFORM

THROUGHOUT the book we are emphasizing the link between supervision and the involvement of teachers in the restructuring of the core work of the school. By distinguishing between what we term Supervision I and Supervision II, we want to draw attention to a different way of being a supervisor and to a different process that encourages and supports the reflective practice of teachers. Supervision II appears to be the more effective way to elicit teachers' involvement in the restructuring agenda. Supervision II encourages teachers to draw on the collective wisdom of their craft and to collaborate on the redesign of student learning activities that progressively engages students in the active production and performance of knowledge. The collaborative reflection on the complexities of the teaching-learning work enables teachers to explore the conceptual maps they use to define and shape the curriculum they teach.[1] In this chapter, we suggest that this reflective practice needs, at some point, to engage each teacher's educational platform. Unless teachers and supervisors uncover their platforms, they will not establish a base of mutual understanding that is necessary to ground their collaborative efforts.

Besides the technical understandings that emerge from a blend of intuition and conceptual schemata, there is a floor of beliefs, opinions, values, and attitudes that provides a foundation for practice. These beliefs, opinions, values, and atti-

---

[1]Donald A. Schön, *The Reflective Practitioner.* New York: Basic Books, 1983.

tudes make up what has been called a "platform."[2] Just as a political party is supposed to base its decisions and actions on a party platform, so too educators carry on their work, make decisions, and plan instruction based on their educational platform. When a teacher is asked why a child was disciplined in a certain way, he or she frequently will respond with a generalization about how all children should be disciplined. When asked about the social usefulness of learning a certain lesson, a teacher frequently will frame his or her explanation according to a set of more general beliefs about the socialization of children.

A teacher's platform is rarely explicit. Neither is it static or one-dimensional. It is derived from life experiences, from formal education, and especially from trial-and-error experience in classrooms. Teachers are not accustomed to pausing before walking into their first class of the day and recalling the elements of their platform. Rather, their platform is seen, if at all, in their patterns and habitual ways of interacting with students.

Whether or not a platform position is right or wrong is not the issue here. Knowing *what* the platform position is, understanding the relationship between teaching practices and platform elements, perceiving inconsistencies between platform and practice, appreciating differences between one's own platform and that of another—these are the points of emphasis in this chapter. Both teacher and supervisor need to know what their respective platforms are. They need to examine where they agree and where they differ and whether the differences are so substantial as to inhibit the collaborative work of redesigning the teaching-learning process. In the effort to encourage reflection in practice, teachers and supervisors need to take the time to articulate their platform. Most teachers tend to resist the exercise simply because they are not used to making their platform explicit. They simply act according to the feel of the situation. Yet when they do write out their platform, they experience the satisfaction of naming what they do and why they do it. Greater sense of task identity and task significance strengthens motivation, satisfaction, and commitment to one's work.[3]

What follows are several examples of at least partially developed platforms. In practice, a teacher's platform might take more of a narrative, or more of a disjointed style, than the examples below. What is presented here is more a skeletal form, which tends to focus on the primary emphasis of the platform.

THE BASIC COMPETENCY PLATFORM

1 The purpose of schooling is to ensure a minimal competency in prescribed skills and understandings for all children. Enrichment of students' learning beyond these minimum competencies is an important but secondary aim of schooling.

---

[2]Decker Walker, "A Naturalistic Model for Curriculum Development," *School Review,* vol. 80, no. 1 (1971), pp. 51–65.

[3]J. Richard Hackman and Greg R. Oldham, "Motivation Through the Design of Work: Test of a Theory." *Organizational Behavior and Human Performance,* vol. 16 (1976), p. 256.

2 Schools can make a great difference in the achievement of these minimum competencies; people who do not achieve them end up as unproductive citizens living on the margins of society.

3 Present and future civic and employment demands point to the absolute necessity of acquiring basic competencies. Mastery of these competencies will assist the person in other areas of personal and social growth.

4 The educator's job is to construct a highly organized environment to promote the gradual mastery of basic competencies in reading, writing, computation, and scientific processes. This implies a careful definition of learning objectives for each major unit of an intentionally sequenced series of learnings, careful assessment of entry-level skills and understandings with built-in correction of start-up deficiencies, careful monitoring of student progress with built-in remediation phases, a requirement of mastery before moving on to the next unit, and a sequential progression to broader and deeper levels of mastery of the competencies as defined by graduation requirements.

5 Almost all students, except a small percentage of children with severe disabilities, are capable of mastery levels of learning in these minimum competencies, given sufficient time and appropriate instruction.

6 The most significant factor in learning is "time on task." This means that much of class time will be spent on drills and exercises that strengthen the target competency, that additional time will be afforded to those students needing it, and that daily homework will be assigned on the target competency.

7 While one approach to learning a competency may be initially stressed, alternative methodologies will be employed for students experiencing difficulty.

8 Higher-level learnings and cultural enrichment activities will tend to receive less attention, especially in the earlier grades, except for those students who have achieved mastery of the minimum competencies.

9 Classroom discipline will be controlled more by the intense concentration on the learning task than by teacher's imposition of punishments and repetition of rules.

10 All the reward systems of the school should serve to promote academic achievement as the highest priority. Rewards for other desirable behaviors or achievement should be secondary to this priority.

THE SOCIAL DRAMA PLATFORM

1 Schools prepare young people for the social drama of public life. Adult life involves people in a number of social roles, such as worker, neighbor, citizen and voter, consumer, tourist, group member, and cultural participant. Schools prepare youngsters for the social drama by exposing them to the scripts, language, costuming, cues, spoken and unspoken rules, ways of framing situations, perspective-taking, etc. The challenge, of course, is

somehow to be a real person while playing one's part in the social drama, to retain one's autonomy and spontaneity while keeping the social drama moving forward.

2 Youngsters need to learn large blocks of the plot of the drama, such as the economics, the history, the ecology, and the geography of the social drama, in order to make intelligent decisions while playing their part. They are made aware that the social drama is a human construct, and as such can be changed to ensure a better outcome for the characters in the play. They are urged to take responsibility for the social drama.

3 Youngsters need to master the language and symbols used in expressing their roles.

4 Youngsters also need to develop into authentic characters in the play; hence they need to be able to improvise on the cultural scripts they are given. Improvisation and personal appropriation of one's script will be a learning that runs throughout the curriculum.

5 Teaching involves aspects of coaching, in which the teacher helps individual groups of youngsters to play out scenes in the drama. Teaching also involves directing a whole class in a variety of rehearsals of the drama. The teacher is also a critic who comments on the actors' performance. And finally, the teacher is also a player in the drama, who teaches by example.

THE HUMAN GROWTH PLATFORM

1 Students are unlike input factors in system designs of industrial or military organizations; for example, they are not pieces of steel that arrive at the "input station" all neatly measured and stable. Steel, wood, and stone do not grow and change during the very time when the production worker is trying to manipulate them. Students do.

2 The school makes a difference in a child's growth, but not *that* much difference. If the school were nonexistent, other influences and experiences would "educate" the child. Besides, human beings are dynamic and constantly growing. The school simply speeds up the growth process and channels it in supposedly beneficial directions, rather than leaving the student to random, trial-and-error growth.

3 Curricular-instructional programs should be designed in conformity with the growth patterns of students. The human growth needs of students should never be subordinated to objectives dictated by the needs of society and the demands of the discipline. Theoretically, these three concerns—human growth, achievement of disciplined skills and knowledge, and fulfillment of social responsibilities—should not be in conflict. In practice, however, they frequently are in conflict, and the concern for human growth usually is the one to be sacrificed.

4 The educator's primary function is to become obsolete. The job of the educator is to so influence students that the students will gradually but eventually reach the point where they do not need the teacher, where they can

pursue their own learning on the basis of their acquired knowledge and skills.

5 *Active* pursuit of knowledge and understanding, an actual dialogue with reality, will produce the most significant and long-lasting types of learning. Whenever possible, therefore, the student must actively search, actively inquire, actively discover, and actively organize and integrate. The teacher's job is to guide and direct this activity toward specified goals.

THE DEMOCRATIC SOCIALIZATION PLATFORM

1 The primary aim of education is to enable the individual to function in society. Assuming a democratic society, the school should promote not only those qualities necessary for survival (employment, getting along with people, managing one's financial affairs, being a responsible family person, etc.) but also those qualities necessary for a healthy democratic society (political involvement that seeks the common good, willingness to displace self-interest for a higher purpose, skills at community building and conflict resolution, an understanding of how the political process works and how to influence public policy, etc.).

2 The school should intentionally arrange itself so that learning takes place primarily in a community context. Students should be taught to collaborate on learning tasks rather than compete with one another. Team projects, peer tutoring, group rewards, and discussion of community problems should have priority even while encouraging the development of individual talents. Individual talents, however, should be prized more for what they contribute to the community than for the exclusive enrichment of the individual.

3 Learning is best nurtured in a community context. Language skills are developed by regular and varied group communication. A sense of history and culture is nurtured by a focus on the group's history and culture. Psychological needs such as self-esteem and assertiveness are best met through active involvement in the community. Acceptance of differences and the development of individuality are negotiated best when there is a sense of community. Values, laws, and social customs are best taught within the context of the community.

4 The educator stands within the learning community and yet holds a special place of authority. The educator facilitates and directs the learning tasks of the younger members of the community but allows the agenda of community dynamics to intrude on the more academic tasks when the need arises.

5 Teachers and students function best when they work in relatively small, relatively self-contained, relatively autonomous learning communities. Hence those schools with large enrollments should be broken down into manageable learning communities that allow for closer and more continuous contact between a team of teachers and their students.

6 The curriculum should be controlled by a set of schoolwide learning outcomes for each year, but the learning community should have considerable autonomy in the ways it achieves these outcomes. The teams of teachers should be accountable for promoting required learnings but should be allowed to devise the particular learning activities that best address the students in their communities.

7 Wherever possible, the learning communities should be involved with the larger civic community through parental involvement, by using the civic community as a learning laboratory, by discussing problems in the civic community, and by promoting the value of community service.

THE CRITICAL AWARENESS PLATFORM

1 Traditionally, schools reproduce the unequal relationships found in society; schools also promote the perspectives of vested interests in the larger society. In both the language of the curriculum as well as its content one finds stereotypes, cultural/racial/ethnic and gender bias, blind spots, and distortions. To counteract this, students should be taught a "hermeneutics of suspicion," that is, a way of questioning the official curriculum by asking: Whose interests are being served by this point of view? Who is in charge of defining the world as working in this particular way? What perspectives are left out? What are the relationships of this knowledge with social and political power?

2 Schools traditionally teach as though knowledge is "out there" waiting to be grasped by the inquiring mind. Rather, knowledge is produced by elites as a way of describing a reality which places them in a position of privilege, power, and control. True knowledge is acquired by taking action on the problems in one's life and then reflecting on the consequences.

3 Schools traditionally require students to be passive reproducers of the knowledge made available to them. Rather, they should actively create knowledge that is useful for living. Learning, moreover, should flow from dialogue, from imaginative inquiries into social possibilities, and from debate about current realities.

4 Schools traditionally stress individual achievement in competition with peers. Rather, they should stress cooperation and collective action, which encourages each student to make a contribution to the life of the community. Out of that group activity will emerge the knowledge of what is necessary for further emancipatory activity.

5 School learning should involve a struggle to define meanings in the face of cultural definitions of truth which are simply contemporary methods of containment and control; schooling should involve the questioning of the power structure within the school, which disenfranchises some students from the start.

6 Pedagogy belongs to the realm of politics. One teaches either on the side of the oppressors or on the side of the oppressed. Hence teaching will al-

ways involve going beyond the surface of the curriculum to the underlying social and political structural dynamics that support competing interpretations of the curriculum materials being presented. Specific strategies include debate, role-playing various power relationships, investigative reporting, problematizing everyday experience, and inquiring into alternative possibilities.

THE ECOLOGICAL PLATFORM

1 The primary reality is neither the individual nor human society, but the entire ecosphere. Hence, the survival demands of the ecosphere and the concomitant implications for human society should comprise the primary focus of schooling.

2 Human culture can be understood analogously in ecological imagery. Human beings live within a culture as organisms in a natural environment of food chains, cycles of life, and rhythms of seasons. Human beings understand themselves as human through the rituals, traditions, artifacts, and relationships that are elements of a living culture. Hence schools, besides teaching the primary systems and structures of the ecosphere, should teach the cultural ecology by which human survival and development is possible.

3 The individual does not stand outside of the natural or cultural environment; rather, the individual is embedded in the natural and cultural environment. Human fulfillment does not mean escaping from this environment but discovering harmonious ways to live with those two environments. Learning itself is a discovery of one's relationship to and embeddedness in the cultural and natural environment.

4 The social purposes of schooling are not so much to achieve technical control over nature or to master the culture in the service of some instrumental purpose, but to overcome those social practices and social arrangements that destroy the natural and cultural environment. This is achieved by exploring those public policies and practices that sustain and respect the natural rhythms and patterns of nature and culture. Ethnocentric, nationalistic, sexist, racist, and all exploitative relationships deny the unity and integrity of the natural and human environment. When society harms the environment, it literally harms itself; similarly, when society damages the natural bonds between human beings, it damages itself. People are inextricably embedded in their cultural bonds; those bonds support humanity and feed the human spirit. People's understanding of who they are collectively is embedded in their culture.

5 Knowledge, then, is not something one individual achieves or possesses; it is the achievement and heritage and energy of all human beings. When one knows something, one knows it as one's culture names it. One knows something because the relationships that are grasped in knowledge contain oneself as much as one contains those relationships. Human beings

always know much more than they can articulate because most knowledge is tacit and is experienced at subliminal levels of intuition. The human body knows at least as much as the human mind does; the mind has different ways of articulating that knowledge than the body does.

6 Relationships to the environment and culture are known through experience. Using a language to describe those relationships frames those relationships in ways that distort as well as clarify. Language is not a neutral tool for expression; language carries interpretations constructed and imposed by the culture. Hence part of the task of schools is to make explicit the point of view embedded in taken-for-granted cultural understandings. Everyday language contains many class, sexist, rationalistic, economic, and ethnocentric distortions, which in turn reveal distortions and disharmonies between human beings and the natural environment, within the culture and within human beings themselves.

7 The classroom itself represents an artificial cultural ecology that distorts how youngsters view the natural environment, how they view themselves, how they view science and rationality. Current school curricula promote values that are antithetical to both the survival of the ecosphere and the cultural unity and integrity of the human race. Hence the pedagogy employed and the curriculum and the assessment of learning must be transformed to reflect the survival demands of both the natural and the human environment.

ELEMENTS OF A PLATFORM

In stressing the importance of explicating the platform, we realize that many teachers will find the exercise difficult. Their platform statements may or may not come out as clearly as the ones given here. On the other hand, the effort to elucidate the platform can help teachers become more reflective about their practice. Such reflection can help teachers puzzle their way through instructional problems which their intuitions cannot solve. It also enables teachers to acknowledge some inconsistencies in their practice that, although not previously acknowledged consciously, may have created an occasional sense of dissatisfaction. Recognizing such inconsistencies opens up the space for changes in practice.

Furthermore, platform clarification brings greater, more explicit intelligibility to what teachers do in class everyday. It gives teachers names and words for telling their story. It enables them to talk with greater clarity among themselves, with parents, and with supervisors about what they do. The examples above provide some idea of what a platform entails. In general terms we can say that a platform contains about eight elements. All platforms need not contain all these elements; some may be expressed more in narrative form, some in a sequence of terse sentences; some may be better expressed in pictures or cartoons. Furthermore, platforms need not be cast in stone. From year to year, new elements will be added, or some stressed more than others. The important thing is to have a sense of what one's platform is, rather than to construct a prize-winning statement for the school board.

General Elements of a Platform

1 *The aims of education.* Set down, in order of priority, the three most important aims of education—not simply education in the abstract, but education for the youngsters in your school system.

2 *Major achievements of students this year.* Bring these aims down to more specific application; identify the major achievements of students by the end of the year (e.g., mastery of some academic skills up to a certain level; the acquisition of certain basic principles that would govern behavior; more personal achievements, such as increased self-awareness or self-confidence, or trust and openness).

3 *The social significance of the student's learning.* Some teachers emphasize vocational learning, or the utilization of learning for good citizenship, or the acquisition of a particular cultural heritage.

4 *The image of the learner.* This element tries to uncover attitudes or assumptions about how one learns. Is the learner an empty vessel into which one pours information? Some may view the learner in a uniform way—as though all learners are basically the same and will respond equally to a uniform pedagogy. Some may use "faculty" psychology to explain how students learn. Some will focus on operant conditioning; others on targeting instruction to the cognitive developmental stages of concrete operations. Still others will differentiate among various styles and dispositions for learning that point to a greater emphasis on individualization of learning. Obviously, we are emphasizing here the active engagement of the learner in the production and performance of knowledge.

5 *The image of the curriculum.* This element touches upon attitudes about *what* the student learns. Some say that the most important learnings are those most immediately useful in "real" life. Others say that any kind of learning is intrinsically valuable. Others qualify the latter position and consider some learnings, such as the humanities, to be intrinsically more valuable because they touch upon more central areas of our culture. Others would claim that the learning of subjects has value only insofar as it categorizes people of different abilities and interests and channels them in socially productive directions. Here we emphasize the curriculum-as-learned and performed.

6 *The image of the teacher.* What is a teacher? Is a teacher an employee of the state, following the educational policies and practices dictated by the local, state, and federal government? Or is a teacher a professional specialist whom a community employs to exercise his or her expertise on behalf of youngsters? Or is a teacher a spokesperson for tradition, passing on the riches of the culture? Or is a teacher a political engineer, leading young-

sters to develop those skills necessary to reform their society? Here we emphasize the teacher's role as facilitator and guide of student learning.

7 *The preferred pedagogy.* Will the teacher dominate the learning experience? Some assume that inquiry learning is the best way to teach. Others assume that each discipline lends itself better to some forms of pedagogy than others. Some would opt for much more student-initiated learning, while others favor group projects. Although there may be some reluctance to focus on *one* pedagogical approach to the exclusion of all others, teachers tend to settle on two or three as the more effective approaches.

8 *The preferred school climate.* This element brings various environmental considerations into play, such as the affective tone to schoolwide and classroom discipline, feelings of student pride in the school, faculty morale, the openness of the school community to divergent lifestyles, expressive learnings, and individualistic ways of thinking and behaving. Some would describe an environment reflective of a learning community: open, caring, inquisitive, flexible, collaborative. Some would opt for order and predictability. Others would prefer a more relaxed climate, perhaps more boisterous but also more creative and spontaneous. This element is very much related to what is valued in the curriculum and to the social consequences of learning.

It becomes obvious to teachers when they test out their assumptions under each of the categories listed above that there tends to be an intrinsic logic to them. That is, there tends to be a consistency between assumptions about the nature of the learner and the preferred kind of teacher-student relationship, which in turn relates logically to teachers' beliefs about the aims of education. As educators clarify their assumptions, beliefs, and opinions under each of these eight categories, the platform they use in practice should become apparent to them. That is to say, educators usually make practical decisions about professional practice based upon convictions, assumptions, and attitudes that are not clearly or frequently articulated. Nevertheless, they do influence, some would even say dominate, actions. By bringing these convictions, assumptions, and attitudes out into the open for their own reflection, educators can evaluate internal consistency and cogency. They can also check whether they are satisfied with their platform, or whether they have not taken important factors into consideration. By clarifying the underlying intelligibility of their actions, educators might see a need to grow in specific areas in order to increase their effectiveness as well as to broaden their capacities.

THE SUPERVISOR'S PLATFORM

The above analysis of key elements in a platform deals with an educational platform. This educational platform focuses on what one believes ought to happen in a process of formal education. It could belong to a teacher, a student, an administrator, or a supervisor. The supervisor can elaborate his or her own educational platform, but it becomes complete when the supervisor adds his or her beliefs about the activity of supervising. Two categories that concern supervision are the following: the purpose of supervision and the preferred process of supervision.

1 *The purpose or goal of supervision.* Some would answer from a neoscientific orientation. Others would speak from a human relations perspective. Some would tend to stress the moral activity of teacher empowerment and enriched student learning.
2 *The preferred process of supervision.* Some would express a preference for the clinical supervision approach. Others would prefer a more eclectic process that responds to the contingencies of the situation. Others would stress the development of teacher leadership in service of the restructuring agenda.

Again, the point of clarifying one's convictions and unspoken assumptions about the nature of supervision is to open the door for growth, for the sharing of ideas, and for supervisory performance grounded in basic beliefs. Ideally, these last two elements of the supervisor's platform should be written down before one reads this book, and again after one has read the book. If the analysis of supervision presented between these covers has an effect, it would show up in the differences between the two platform statements.

APPROACHES TO PLATFORM CLARIFICATION

Many teachers may find the initial efforts at platform clarification very frustrating. It is not something they do often, and there can be a feeling of awkwardness. Yet everyone has an unexpressed platform. Were a sensitive observer to follow a teacher around for a day or two on the job, it would be relatively easy to guess that teacher's beliefs about how youngsters learn best, about what is important to learn, about good teaching and inferior teaching, and so on. People's actions usually reveal their assumptions and attitudes quite clearly.

Two different approaches offer supervisors and teachers a way to construct their platforms. One approach would be to work with all the teachers or a group of them in a staff-development format. The other approach would entail a supervisor and a teacher working in a one-on-one situation.

Group Approaches to Educational Platform Development

In a staff-development framework, supervisors can work with a group of teachers. Some explanation of what platforms are and how platform clarification might assist their practice should be given. Examples of platforms should then be provided. Teachers would then write out their own platform. They should be encouraged to try out a unifying image or metaphor around which all their platform elements might cluster. David Hunt, in his work with teachers, has found that metaphors help teachers bring out the theory embedded in their practice.[4] Metaphors of teaching such as guiding a journey, conducting an orchestra, pulling rabbits out of a hat, mining gold, tending a garden, captaining a ship, and directing a play contain beliefs and assumptions about learning, curriculum, social purposes of schooling, and pedagogy. Many others find the orderly process of filling out where they stand on the eight elements of the platform the most convenient beginning for the exercise. After the first draft, they may want to re-arrange and amplify. Putting words onto paper may then enable them to see their guiding metaphor. Teachers can also check the internal consistency between el-ements of the platform and note points to pursue with themselves or with oth-ers during subsequent exercises. Others will prefer a less structured approach, letting their assumptions come out as they are felt and recognized, rather than having to force them into categories with which they are uncomfortable.

Some find it helpful to find a quiet place to write down their reflections. Nor-mally, these thoughts will come out in no particular order of priority. Once teach-ers have written down the elements of their platform, they can with further re-flection begin to group them in clusters and place them in some order of importance. Almost everyone with any experience in education, however, will feel several times during this exercise the need to qualify and add nuance to those general statements: "Which teaching strategy I'd use in a given situation depends a lot on a youngster's background. But by and large, I'd choose this approach." "While I'd place my major emphasis on mastery of basic intellectual skills, I still think it's important to spend some time teaching kids good manners." "I almost always prefer to start a lesson with a colorful advance organizer. That usually stirs up the pupils' curiosity. But there are times when I run plain, old-fashioned memory drills."

Others will find the writing exercise too tedious and will seek out a colleague with whom to discuss this whole question. The free flow of shared ideas fre-quently stimulates the process of clarification. In those instances, a tape recorder may help for subsequent transcription of the conversation. Others may find a combination of dialogue and writing the better way. Still others may refer to a formal statement of goals that the school or system has in print to begin the process. By studying the goals and *probing the assumptions behind them,* the teacher may discover areas of disagreement or agreement.

However teachers go about clarifying their platform initially, two other steps will prove helpful. After the first tentative statement of the platform, the teach-ers should compare their platform with two or three colleagues, to test out areas of agreement or disagreement. Sometimes this may lead to modification of their own platforms. It may also lead to a greater acceptance of diversity of perspec-tives. It certainly will help teachers to build teamwork. Knowing the biases be-hind one another's approach will enable teachers to work together in areas where they agree or might complement one another.

---

[4]David E. Hunt, *Beginning with Ourselves.* Cambridge, Mass.: Brookline Books, 1987.

When the teachers have discussed their platforms together, they should then compare them with the school's or the system's platform. That may not exist in a written document, but, as in their own cases, it exists implicitly in the operational policies of the school or school system. They may find some genuine discrepancies between what the school's goal statements profess and what the school practices. Bringing those discrepancies to light, in itself, would be a service to the school. The purpose of examining the expressed and unexpressed (but operative) platforms of the school, however, is aimed more at a comparison between the school's platform and the teachers' platforms. If they find striking divergences between them, then the teachers and supervisors will have to seek some means of reconciling the discrepancies, modifying one or the other to make them more compatible.

The point of this exercise is not to introduce frustration and cynicism but, on the contrary, to reduce it. If supervisors and teachers are to work toward restructuring the educational process in their schools and school systems, then this exercise may be a good place to begin. As Michael Fullan suggests, school improvement and classroom improvement necessarily overlap, and teachers must be involved with both levels of improvement.[5]

The group activity with platforms can continue on to a variety of discussions. Teachers may use the discussions as a basis for considering curriculum restructuring as well as new configurations for instructional space and time arrangements. They may also use the sharing of their platforms as a launching pad for discussions about including other student learning outcomes that their present teaching is ignoring or slighting, or other ways of evaluating student learning. These follow-up discussions will depend on the particular context and frame of mind the teachers are in, or on perceived student or professional needs within the school. Discussions about platforms among groups of teachers, while worthwhile in themselves, also can lead to a variety of additional staff-development initiatives.

Individual Use of Platform Development

Supervisors can also use the group platform exercise to work with individual teachers. Discussions about the teacher's platform enable both supervisor and teacher to clarify what teaching episodes mean to the teacher. Such discussions can enable teachers and supervisors to interpret and explore possibilities within such teaching episodes and series of episodes. Making one's platform explicit also enables both supervisor and teacher to explore discrepancies between the teacher's platform in theory and the platform in use. That is to say, in particular instances, teachers may act in class in contradiction to their stated platform. Supervisors and teachers then have to discuss the apparent discrepancy and see

---

[5]Michael G. Fullan, "Staff Development, Innovation, and Institutional Development," in Bruce Joyce (ed.), *Changing School Culture Through Staff Development*. Alexandria, Va.: Association for Supervision and Curriculum Development, 1990, pp. 3–25.

whether such practices need to be changed to conform to their stated platform. The emphasis here is not so much on correcting faults, however, as it is on clarifying the intelligibility and intentionality of the teacher's work with youngsters. As teachers become more reflective about their work, under the influence of exercises like platform clarification, they will grow in their sense of consistency and in their responsiveness to students as well. Moreover, through discussions about the teacher's platform, supervisors will be working out of a framework of collegial conversation with the teacher based on the teacher's language and perspectives, rather than a framework of some generalized format for teaching. Such a basis of understanding between supervisor and teacher facilitates ongoing positive conversations, which teachers can feel comfortable with because they are dealing with their own agenda rather than a bureaucratic agenda of filling out forms containing categories constructed by someone else.

SUMMARY

In this chapter we have taken up the concept of the educational platform. When examples of educational platforms were given, it became apparent that a platform is made up of those basic assumptions, beliefs, attitudes, and values that are the underpinnings of an educator's behavior. It also became apparent that the platform tends to shape the educator's everyday practice. By encouraging teachers to clarify their platform, supervisors can stimulate a variety of teacher reflections on their practice. Some of these reflections can take place in a group setting, generating possibilities for restructuring the work of the school. Other reflections on practice in the light of the platform can take place on an individual basis. Such reflection can provide some common language and understanding between supervisor and teacher out of which can grow new insight into teaching and new possibilities for student learning.

PART THREE

THE CONTEXT FOR PRACTICE AND RENEWAL

SCHOOL CLIMATE, CULTURE, AND CHANGE

IN Chapter 4 we discussed forces for change that could be used to leverage restructuring in schools. The changes we had in mind were more institutional than individual. We tried to provide answers on how can schools across the country be improved. Six different change forces were identified: bureaucratic, personal, market, professional, cultural, and democratic. Professional, cultural, and democratic change forces that seek to transform schools into learning communities were proposed as being more appropriate and more effective than bureaucratic, personal, or market change forces, which are used in the corporate world and in other nonschool sectors of society. In this chapter we focus more specifically on individual changes. Individual changes affect the way teachers think about themselves and about each other as colleagues in a given school. Individual changes affect the way students think about themselves and each other, as well as the way they are connected to the school and its work. School climate and culture are the avenues used to explore change at this level.

LEVELS OF CHANGE

Improving schools requires changing them. But as pointed out in Chapter 4, change takes place at two levels—the way things look and the way things actually work. Changes at the first level are *structural,* resulting in altered arrangements. Changes the second level are *normative*, resulting in altered beliefs.[1] When only first-level changes are introduced in schools it may appear that things are being done differently, but results seem not to be effected, at least not for very long.

A supervisor, for example, wants to encourage teachers to be more deliberate in their teaching and to make a better effort to teach to agreed-upon curriculum outlines. Working with a committee of teachers, she introduces a series of inservice workshops on the content of the curriculum, how to select objectives, and how to write effective lesson plans. She then establishes a policy requiring teachers to submit their lesson plans weekly for her perusal. Although she finds that the lesson plans seem to match the curriculum outlines, teachers seem to be making little progress toward improving the fit between what they teach and what they are supposed to teach. In this example, the supervisor was successful in implementing change in how teachers constructed their plans, but she was not successful in changing what they were actually teaching. Normative change alters how teachers look at things, what they believe, what they want, what they know, and how they do things. Normative changes are much more likely to affect outcomes.

Although structural changes can be important, in themselves they seem not to matter much. Too often, they become "nonevents." When a junior high school changes its name to a middle school and abandons academic departments for teams that "turn teach" by subject-matter specialization, this is an example of a nonevent. The introduction of supervisory and evaluation systems that elicit changes in how teachers teach when under surveillance but not otherwise is another example of a nonevent. Nonevents become events when changes are not only structural but normative as well.

Many of the practices of Supervision I involve structural, but not normative, changes. Normative changes take into account the aspects of human nature. It is helpful to think about human nature having two sides: the psychological and the symbolic. Psychologically speaking, people have needs and seek opportunities to meet these needs. (Chapter 12 examines in more detail the important topic of needs and how they play out for individual teachers and can improve teachers' capacity and commitment to provide effective teaching and learning.) Symbolically speaking, people seek to make sense of their lives by searching for meaning. The psychological side of human nature is more readily affected by *school climate* and the symbolic side is more readily affected by *school culture.* In this chapter we examine school climate first and then school culture. In each case we assess their importance in bringing about school improvement.

THE IMPORTANCE OF SCHOOL CLIMATE

School climate can help or hinder teachers as they attempt to satisfy their needs at work. One way to understand school climate is by examining your own ex-

---

[1]See, for example, Michael Fullan with Suzanne Stiegelbauer, *The New Meaning of Educational Change,* 2d ed. New York: Teachers College Press, 1991.

perience with groups in schools. Recall, for example, a group that you belonged to or know about that seemed best to encourage members to learn, solve problems, and take reasonable chances. Now recall a second group that most hindered learning, problem solving, and risk taking. Briefly describe the two groups. Who were the members? What was the group trying to accomplish? How did group members work together? How did they treat one another? What were the leaders like? Using the questionnaire in Exhibit 11–1, evaluate each of the groups you recalled. Start first with the most effective learning group. Circle the number for each category that best describes this group. Now evaluate the less effective group, using check marks to indicate responses. Compare your circled and checked responses.

By describing groups that help and hinder learning and then evaluating them, you are describing and measuring dimensions of school climate. The seven categories shown in Exhibit 11–1 are composed of several dimensions that social psychologists have found to be important in determining whether a climate is open (is supportive of learning) or closed (hinders learning). To obtain an overall climate score for the two groups you evaluated, total the score values given for each of the seven items. Reverse the scores given to item 1, conformity, for in this case a low score suggests a supportive climate. The higher the score, the more open or supportive the group is likely to be. Now, using the categories and scores, write a few sentences that describe the helpful and hindering groups you recalled. You are now describing climate in the language of social psychologists.

Since the climate of the school is a matter of impression, it is often difficult to define with precision. Climate can be viewed as the enduring characteristics that describe the psychological makeup of a particular school, distinguish it from other schools, and influence the behavior of teachers and students, as well as the "feel" that teachers and students have for that school. George Litwin and Robert Stringer, for example, define climate as "the perceived subjective effects of the formal system, the informal 'style' of managers, and other important environmental factors on the attitudes, beliefs, values, and motivation of people who work in a particular organization."[2]

Climate provides a reading of how things are going in the school and a basis for predicting school consequences and outcomes. Such a barometer represents an important tool for evaluating present conditions, planning new directions, and monitoring progress toward new directions. Indeed, school climate is a key dimension of human resources supervision as described in earlier chapters.

THE HEALTHY SCHOOL

Climate can also be understood by applying the metaphor of health to the school. Matthew Miles describes the "healthy" school as one that exhibits reasonably clear and reasonably accepted goals (goal focus); communication that is relatively

---

[2]George H. Litwin and Robert A. Stringer, Jr., *Motivation and Organization Climate.* Boston: Harvard University, Division of Research, Graduate School of Business Administration, 1968, p. 5.

EXHIBIT 11–1
ORGANIZATIONAL CLIMATE QUESTIONNAIRE

Introduction
For each of the seven organization climate dimensions described below place an (A) above the number that indicates your assessment of the organization's current position on that dimension and an (I) above the number that indicates your choice of where the organization should ideally be on this dimension.

1 Conformity The feeling that there are many externally imposed constraints in the organization; the degree to which members feel that there are many rules, procedures, policies, and practices to which they have to conform rather than being able to do their work as they see fit.

| Conformity is not characteristic of this organization. | 1 2 3 4 5 6 7 8 9 10 | Conformity is very characteristic of this organization. |

2 Responsibility Members of the organization are given personal responsibility to achieve their part of the organization's goals; the degree to which members feel that they can make decisions and solve problems without checking with superiors each step of the way.

| No responsibility is given in the organization. | 1 2 3 4 5 6 7 8 9 10 | There is great emphasis on personal responsibility in the organization. |

3 Standards The emphasis the organization places on quality performance and outstanding production including the degree to which the member feels the organization is setting challenging goals for itself and communicating these goal commitments to members.

| Standards are very low or nonexistent in the organization. | 1 2 3 4 5 6 7 8 9 10 | Challenging standards are set in the organization. |

4 Rewards The degree to which members feel that they are being recognized and rewarded for good work rather than being ignored, criticized, or punished when something goes wrong.

| Members are ignored, punished, or criticized. | 1 2 3 4 5 6 7 8 9 10 | Members are recognized and rewarded positively. |

5 Organization clarity The feeling among members that things are well organized and goals are clearly defined rather than being disorderly, confused, or chaotic.

| The organization is disorderly, confused, and chaotic. | 1 2 3 4 5 6 7 8 9 10 | The organization is well organized with clearly defined goals. |

6 Warmth and support The feeling that friendliness is a valued norm in the organization; that members trust one another and offer support to one another. The feeling that good relationships prevail in the work environment.

| There is no warmth and support in the organization. | 1 2 3 4 5 6 7 8 9 10 | Warmth and support are very characteristic of the organization. |

7 Leadership The willingness of organization members to accept leadership and direction from qualified others. As needs for leadership arise, members feel free to take leadership roles and are rewarded for successful leadership. Leadership is based on expertise. The organization is not dominated by, or dependent on, one or two individuals.

| Leadership is not rewarded; members are dominated or dependent and resist leadership attempts. | 1 2 3 4 5 6 7 8 9 10 | Members accept and reward leadership based on expertise. |

Source: David A. Kolb, Erwin M. Rubin, and James M. McIntyre. *Organizational Psychology: An Experiential Approach,* 3d ed., Englewood Cliffs, N.J.: Prentice-Hall, 1979, pp. 193–194. Reprinted by permission of Prentice-Hall, Englewood Cliffs, N.J.

distortion-free vertically, horizontally, and across boundary lines (communication adequacy); equitable distribution of influence to all levels of the organization (optimal power equalization); and effective and efficient use of inputs, both human and material (resource utilization). The healthy school reflects a sense of togetherness that bonds people together (cohesiveness), a feeling of well-being among the staff (morale), self-renewing properties (innovativeness), and an active response to its environment (autonomy and adaptation). Finally, the healthy school maintains and strengthens its problem-solving capabilities (problem-solving adequacies).[3]

The 10 dimensions of health as described by Miles are listed below.[4] As you review the list, think about how you would describe the two groups you evaluated earlier according to each of the 10 dimensions.

1 *Goal focus.* In a healthy organization, the goal (or more usually goals) of the system would be reasonably clear to the system members, and reasonably well accepted by them. This clarity and acceptance, however, should be seen as a necessary but insufficient condition for organizational health. The goals must also be *achievable* with existing or available resources, and be *appropriate*—more or less congruent with the demands of the environment.

2 *Communication adequancy.* Since organizations are not simultaneous face-to-face systems like small groups, the movement of information within them becomes crucial. This dimension of organizational health implies that there is relatively distortion-free communication vertically, horizontally, and across the boundary of the system to and from the surrounding environment. That is, information travels reasonably well—just as the healthy person "knows himself" with a minimum level of repression, distortion, etc. In the healthy organization, there is good and prompt sensing of internal strains; there are enough data about problems of the system to ensure that a good diagnosis of system difficulties can be made. People have the information they need and have gotten it without exerting undue efforts.

3 *Optimal power equalization.* In a healthy organization the distribution of influence is relatively equitable. Subordinates (if there is a formal authority chart) can influence upward, and even more important—as Rensis Likert has demonstrated[5] —they perceive that their boss can do likewise with *his* boss. In such an organization, intergroup struggles for power would not be bitter, though intergroup conflict (as in every human system known) would undoubtedly be present. The basic stance of persons in such an or-

[3]Matthew Miles, "Planned Change and Organizational Health: Figure and Ground," *Change Processes in the Public Schools.* Eugene, Ore.: University of Oregon, Center for the Advanced Study of Educational Administration, 1965.

[4]The 10 dimensions of health are abridged from ibid., pp. 18–21.

[5]Rensis Likert, *New Patterns of Management.* New York: McGraw-Hill, 1961, cited in Miles, op. cit.

ganization, as they look up, sideways, and down, is that of collaboration rather than explicit or implicit coercion.

4 *Resource utilization.* We say of a healthy person, such as a second-grader, that he is "working up to his potential." To put this another way, the classroom system is evoking a contribution from him at an appropriate and goal-directed level of tension. At the organization level, "health" would imply that the system's inputs, particularly the personnel, are used effectively. The overall coordination is such that people are neither overloaded nor idling. There is a minimal sense of strain, generally speaking (in the sense that trying to do something with a weak or inappropriate structure puts strain on that structure). In the healthy organization, people may be working very hard indeed, but they feel that they are not working against themselves, or against the organization. The fit between people's own dispositions and the role demands of the system is good. Beyond this, people feel reasonably "self-actualized"; they not only "feel good" in their jobs, but they have a genuine sense of learning, growing, and developing as persons in the process of making their organizational contribution.

5 *Cohesiveness.* We think of a healthy person as one who has a clear sense of identity; he knows who he is, underneath all the specific goals he sets for himself. Beyond this, he *likes himself;* his stance toward life does not require self-derogation, even when there are aspects of his behavior which are unlovely or ineffective. By analogy at the organization level, system health would imply that the organization knows "who it is." Its members feel attracted to membership in the organization. They want to stay with it, be influenced by it, and exert their own influence in the collaborative style suggested above.

6 *Morale.* The implied notion is one of well-being or satisfaction. Satisfaction is not enough for health, of course; a person may report feelings of well-being and satisfaction in his life, while successfully denying deep-lying hostilities, anxieties, and conflicts. Yet it still seems useful to evoke, at the organization level, the idea of morale: a summated set of individual sentiments, centering around feelings of well-being, satisfaction, and pleasure, as opposed to feelings of discomfort, unwished-for strain, and dissatisfaction.

7 *Innovativeness.* A healthy system would tend to invent new procedures, move toward new goals, produce new kinds of products, diversify itself, and become more rather than less differentiated over time. In a sense, such a system could be said to grow, develop, and change, rather than remaining routinized and standard.

8 *Autonomy.* The healthy person acts "from his own center outward." Seen in a training or therapy group, for example, such a person appears nearly free of the need to submit dependently to authority figures, *and* from the need to rebel and destroy symbolic fathers of any kind. A healthy organization, similarly, would not respond passively to demands from the outside, feeling itself the tool of the environment, and it would not respond

destructively or rebelliously to perceived demands either. It would tend to have a kind of independence from the environment, in the same sense that the healthy person, while he has transactions with others, does not treat their responses as *determinative* of his own behavior.

9 *Adaptation.* The notions of autonomy and innovativeness are both connected with the idea that a healthy person, group, or organization is in realistic, effective contact with the surroundings. When environmental demands and organization resources do not match, a problem-solving, restructuring approach evolves in which *both* the environment and the organization become different in some respect. More adequate, continued coping of the organization, as a result of changes in the local system, the relevant portions of the environment, or more usually both, occurs. And such a system has sufficient stability and stress tolerance to manage the difficulties which occur during the adaptation process.

10 *Problem-solving adequacy.* Finally, any healthy organism—even one as theoretically impervious to fallibility as a computer—*always* has problems, strains, difficulties, and instances of ineffective coping. The issue is not the presence or absence of problems, therefore, but the *manner* in which the person, group, or organization copes with problems. Chris Argyris has suggested that in an effective system, problems are solved with minimal energy; they stay solved; and the problem-solving mechanisms used are not weakened, but maintained or strengthened.[6] An adequate organization, then, has well-developed structures and procedures for sensing the existence of problems, for inventing possible solutions, for deciding on the solutions, for implementing them, and for evaluating their effectiveness.

Though Miles uses the language of organizational theory in his analysis of health, the basic ideas seem to fit schools as well. The dimensions of health for any school operate in a system of dynamic interaction characterized by a high degree of interdependence. Clear goal focus, for example, depends upon the extent to which the school communicates its goals and permits inhabitants to modify and rearrange them. At another level, a high degree of health encourages school adaptiveness, while school adaptiveness contributes to, and is essential to, the health of the school.

CLIMATE AND LEARNING

An important question is, does school climate make a difference in improving learning opportunities? Susan Rosenholtz provides convincing evidence that it does. She found that the quality of work relationships that existed in a school had a great deal to do with that school's ability to improve. She defines quality

---

[6]Chris Argyris, *Integrating the Individual and the Organization.* New York: Wiley, 1964, cited in Miles, op. cit.

as the degree of openness, trust, communications, and support that is shared by teachers. These factors encourage not only learning but job satisfaction and improved performance as well. Rosenholtz refers to schools that possess these qualities as being "learning enriched" to differentiate them from "learning impoverished" schools.[7]

Climate focuses attention on the school's interpersonal work life as it affects teachers, administrators, and supervisors. But climate affects students as well. For example, one important line of inquiry links assumptions that teachers and administrators hold for *students* to climate dimensions. This research uses the Pupil Control Ideology (PCI) scale developed by Donald Willower and his associates.[8] This scale measures the assumptions and attitudes of teachers and supervisors toward students on a continuum from custodial to humanistic. "Custodial schools" tend to be rigidly controlled and concerned with maintenance and order. Within custodial schools students do not participate in decision making and are expected to accept decisions without question. Further, they are viewed as being irresponsible, undisciplined, untrustworthy, and trouble-prone. As a result, strong emphasis is given to controlling students through the development and use of punitive methods. "Humanistic schools," on the other hand, resemble communities that include students as fuller members and seek their cooperation and interaction. Self-discipline is emphasized and learning is considered to be promoted and enhanced by obtaining student identity and commitment. In schools with humanistic climates teachers are more likely to cooperate with one another as they work together, to have higher morale, and to enjoy a sense of task achievement. Social interaction among teachers is also high. In custodial schools these characteristics are not found and students are likely to be more alienated. Teachers are more likely to view the school as a battlefield. Wayne Hoy and James Appleberry found that in schools with more custodial climates, teachers were significantly less engaged in their work, showed less esprit, and were more aloof.[9] These are important findings that point to the link between climate and factors that directly effect the quality of teaching and knowing.

A study by researchers at Claremont Graduate School's Institute for Education and Transformation points to the quality of relationships between teachers and students and to other relationship themes as the most important leverage points for school improvement. Studying students, teachers, parents, and others in two elementary schools, one middle school, and one high school, the researchers determined that the data strongly suggest "that the heretofore identified *problems* of schooling (lower achievement, higher dropout rates and problems in the teaching profession) are rather *consequences* of much deeper and

[7]Susan Rosenholtz, *Teachers' Workplace: The Social Organization of Schools.* New York: Longman, 1989.

[8]Donald J. Willower, Terry I. Eidell, and Wayne K. Hoy, *The School and Pupil Control Ideology,* Pennsylvania State University Studies no. 24. State College: Pennsylvania State University, 1967.

[9]Wayne K. Hoy and James B. Appleberry, "Teacher-Principal Relationships in 'Humanistic' and 'Custodial' Elementary Schools," *Journal of Experimental Education,* vol. 39, no. 2 (1970), pp. 27–31.

more fundamental [relationships] problems."[10] They concluded that efforts to change schools, no matter how sensible, were not likely to be successful unless relationships too were changed for the better. Improving school climate and building community in schools can help. The findings of this important study are summarized in Exhibit 11–2.

Many studies of highly successful schools confirm the importance of climate. For example, in their now famous study of 12 inner-London secondary schools, Michael Rutter, Barbara Maughan, Peter Mortimer, and Janet Ouston found that important differences in climate existed between those schools that were more or less effective.[11] Effectiveness in this case was defined as higher scores on national examinations, better behavior, and better attendance. In the more effective schools teachers worked harder and had better attitudes toward learning, spent more time in actual teaching, relied more heavily on praising students, and were better able to involve students as active learners. Studies of highly successful schools that emphasize ethnographic techniques and the importance of culture reach similar conclusions.[12]

Finally, the work of Patricia Ashton and Rodman Webb that links teachers' sense of efficacy, motivation, and commitment to teacher behavior, student behavior, and student achievement provides further evidence.[13] Their findings are summarized in Chapter 12. In the accompanying discussion it is noted that students of more efficacious teachers are more enthusiastic, are more likely to initiate interactions with teachers, and score higher on mathematics and language tests. A supportive school climate is one important contribution to a teacher's sense of efficacy.

SCHOOL CLIMATE AND GROUP BEHAVIOR

The concept of school climate is collective, born of the sum of teacher perceptions of the interpersonal life of the school as the faculty lives and works together. Membership in groups is important to teachers, and the norms that develop as a result influence what they believe and do. From a psychological point of view group membership provides the means for meeting many of the needs of teachers. And, from a symbolic point of view groups provide the means to enable teachers to construct their realities and to find meaning and significance. Both are important conditions that enable teachers to find satisfaction in work and to work to full potential. Amitai Etzioni suggests that teachers tend to make deci-

---

[10]Institute for Education and Transformation, *Voices from the Inside: A Report on Schooling from Inside the Classroom—Part I: Naming the Problem.* Claremont, Calif.: Claremont Graduate School, 1992, p. 11.

[11]Michael Rutter, Barbara Maughan, Peter Mortimer, and Janet Ouston, *Fifteen Thousand Hours: Secondary Schools and Their Effects on Children.* Cambridge, Mass.: Harvard University Press, 1979.

[12]See, for example, Joan Lipsitz, *Successful Schools for Young Adolescents.* New Brunswick, N.J.: Transaction Books, 1984; Sara Lightfoot, *The Good High School.* New York: Basic Books, 1983.

[13]Patricia T. Ashton and Rodman B. Webb, *Making a Difference: Teachers' Sense of Efficacy and Student Achievement.* New York: Longman, 1986.

EXHIBIT 11–2

THE IMPORTANCE OF RELATIONSHIPS:
A SUMMARY OF FINDINGS

The Claremont researchers concluded that low student performance, high dropout rates, problems in the teaching profession, and other school difficulties were *consequences* of deeper, more fundamental problems that pointed to seven major issues, as summarized below. Relationship themes are imbedded in each of the issues, with relationships being the most important.

1. *Relationships.* Participants feel the crisis inside schools is directly linked to human relationships. Most often mentioned were relationships between teachers and students. Where positive things about the schools were noted, they usually involve reports of individuals who care, listen, understand, respect others, and are honest, open, and sensitive. Teachers report their best experiences in school are those where they connect with students and are able to help them in some way. They also report, however, there is precious little time during the day to seek out individual students. . . . Students of color, especially older students, often report that their teachers, school staff, and other students neither like nor understand them. Many teachers also report they do not always understand students ethnically different than themselves. When relationships in schools are poor, fear, name calling, threats of or incidents of violence, as well as a sense of depression and hopelessness exist. This theme was prominently stated by participants and so deeply connected to all other themes in the data that it is believed this may be one of the two most central issues in solving the crisis in schools.
2. *Race, culture, and class.* A theme which ran through every other issue, like that of relationships, was that of race, culture, and class. This is a theme with much debate and very little consensus. Many students of color and some Euro-American students perceive schools to be racist and prejudiced, from the staff to the curriculum. Some students doubt the very substance of what is being taught. . . . Teachers are tremendously divided on such issues. Some are convinced that students are right about racism, others are not. . . . Students have an intense interest in knowing about one another's culture but receive very little of that knowledge from home or school.
3. *Values.* There are frequently related conversations in the United States that suggest people of color and/or people living in economically depressed areas hold different basic values than others, and that it is these differences which create conflicts in schools and society. While cultural differences clearly do exist in the expression or prioritization of values, our data hold no evidence that people inside schools have significantly different fundamental values. Our data suggest that parents, teachers, students, staff, and administrators of all ethnicities and classes, value and desire education, honesty, integrity, beauty, care, justice, truth, courage, and meaningful hard work. Participants' writings and transcripts of discussions are filled with references to basic values. However, very little time is spent in classrooms discussing these issues, and a number of restrictions exist against doing so. In the beginning of our research many participants initially assumed other participants held different values. The more we talked, the more this assumption was challenged. Students desire a network of adults (parents and teachers) with whom they can "really talk about important things," and want to have these conversations about values with one another.

EXHIBIT 11–2 *(continued)*

4. *Teaching and learning.* Students, especially those past fifth grade, frequently report that they are bored in school and see little relevance of what is taught to their lives and their futures. Teachers feel pressure to teach what is mandated and sometimes doubt its appropriateness for their students. Teachers also are often bored by the curriculum they feel they must teach. . . . Students from all groups, remedial and advanced, high school to elementary, desire both rigor and fun in their schoolwork. They express enthusiasm about learning experiences that are complex but understandable, full of rich meanings and discussions of values, require their own action, and those about which they feel they have some choice.

5. *Safety.* Related to disconnected relationships and not knowing about one another's differences is the issue of safety. Very few participants on campus or parents feel schools are safe places. This is particularly true in our middle school and high school. Teachers, students, and staff fear physical violence. The influence of drugs, gangs, and random violence is felt by students. Students feel physically safest inside classrooms and least safe in large gatherings between classes or traveling to or from school.

6. *Physical environment.* Students want schools that reflect order, beauty, and space and contain rich materials and media. The desire for clean, aesthetically pleasing, and physically comfortable spaces is expressed by all. The food served to students is a persistent complaint. Many would like foods more typical of their homes and home cultures. The lack of any significant personal space such as lockers is problematic to students and also leads to feelings of being devalued. The depressed physical environment of many schools, especially those in lower socioeconomic areas, is believed by participants to reflect society's lack of priority for these children and their education.

7. *Despair, hope, and the process of change.* Many participants feel a hopelessness about schools that is reflected in the larger society and in the music and art of our youth. Paradoxically, hope seemed to emerge following honest dialogues about our collective despair. Participants are anxious for change and willing to participate in change they perceive as relevant. We have strong indications that change inside schools might best be stimulated through participatory processes. In these self-driven research processes, participants came to openly discuss their hopes and dreams. Through this process, we understood there were shared common values around which we could begin to imagine a more ideal school.

Source: Institute for Education and Transformation, *Voices from the Inside: A Report of Schools from Inside the Classroom—Part I: Naming the Problem.* Claremont, Calif.: Claremont Graduate School, 1992, pp. 12–16.

---

sions not as isolated individuals but as members of collectivities.[14] Their teaching preferences, how they are likely to respond to school improvement initiatives, and even how cooperative they are likely to be with supervisors are all shaped by such memberships. To a great extent, changing individuals means changing groups. For this reason understanding the faculty as a work group is important.

[14]Amitai Etzioni, *The Moral Dimension Toward a New Economics.* New York: Free Press, 1988.

Further, helping faculties become effective work groups is an important purpose of supervision and a critical part of the school improvement process.

How can supervisors judge the extent to which faculty groups are working effectively? One indicator is the kind and nature of group outcomes. What is the group supposed to be accomplishing and to what extent is it accomplishing these aims? If outcomes are being accomplished, the group is judged to be *efficient*. But the problem with viewing effectiveness in this way is that efficiency is only one necessary component. The other component is *growth*. An effective group is concerned not only with accomplishing its tasks but also with improving its ability to accomplish even more difficult tasks in the future. Many studies have shown that giving primary attention to efficiency and neglecting growth may result in short-term increases in productivity, but over time the work group loses its productive edge.[15] The relationship between effective supervision and group effectiveness is becoming increasingly important as the work of supervision takes place more and more within the context of groups. Examples include peer-collegial supervision; clinical supervision; team-oriented staff-development programs; curriculum-development projects; and team, family, or group teaching.

THE SYMBOLIC SIDE OF HUMAN NATURE

Supervision II seeks to give a fuller account of what matters to teachers and of what is involved in helping them to think more carefully about their practice. A fuller account means giving attention to the symbolic side of school life as well as the psychological side.

One way to appreciate the complexity of human nature is by examining the research traditions of scholars engaged in its study. Different traditions are based on different assumptions, and different assumptions lead to different supervisory practices. Behaviorists, for example, view teachers as responders to external forces—forces in the environment and forces created for them and applied to them by their supervisors. Teachers are presumed to respond to these forces in highly predictable and determinate ways. To be helpful, supervisors provide structures and incentives that elicit the proper response. Phenomenologists, by contrast, view teachers as intentional beings who create their own reality and then direct their energies toward living this reality in some meaningful way. Teachers are presumed to derive sense and direction from interactions with others and from norm systems that they help to create. To be helpful, supervisors encourage teachers to reflect on the realities they create and to provide mirrors of their behaviors that test these realities.

Gareth Morgan and Linda Smircich identify the assumptions about human nature that emerge from six different scholarly traditions.[16] These assumptions

---

[15]See, for example, Rensis Likert, *The Human Organization*. New York: McGraw-Hill, 1967; and Likert, *New Patterns of Management*, op. cit.

[16]Gareth Morgan and Linda Smircich, "The Case for Qualitative Research," Academy of Management Review, vol. 5 (October 1980), pp. 491–500.

are illustrated in Exhibit 11–3. Assumptions that view human beings as information processors, adaptive agents, and responding mechanisms tend to focus on the psychological side of human nature and suggest a practice in which school climate is considered to be of particular importance. Assumptions that view human beings as transcendental beings, creators of their own reality, and social actors tend to focus on the symbolic side of human nature and highlight the importance of school culture. Though legitimate arguments exist over which of the six views best captures the essence of human nature, few would deny that each captures some aspect of human nature. Human beings are all these things, and the practices of supervision therefore should not be limited to those from the psychological perspective. Giving attention to all six views means giving attention to school culture as well as school climate.

SCHOOL CULTURE

Climate is to the psychological side of school life what culture is to the symbolic side. Teachers respond to work not only as a result of psychological needs but also as makers of meaning. Thus, studying school culture means studying how events and interactions come to be meaningful.[17] *Culture* can be defined as a set of understandings or meanings shared by a group of people. Typically these meanings are tacitly held and serve to define the group as being distinct from other groups.[18]

Communities are one kind of culture. Organizations are another kind of culture. As suggested in Chapter 4, the values and shared meanings of community cultures are more deeply held and elicit stronger feelings of loyalty and affection than is the case for organizations. Though admittedly some organizations (for example, L.L. Bean) engender in many employees and customers alike passion that stems from deeply held community values, most organizations are decidedly more instrumental and secular. Cultures of schools that are understood as communities are decidedly more sacred, having been defined by their centers of shared values. By contrast, the cultures of schools understood as organizations are more secular. Often they are contrived, having been invented and engineered by school administrators, and as a result they speak less to deeply held values of teachers, parents, and students than they do to the instrumental values of management. In chapter 4 we discussed Edward A. Shils' use of the concept of "central zone" to illustrate the importance of shared values in understanding cultures. His description of central zone is repeated here:

---

[17]Linda Smircich, "Is the Concept of Culture a Paradigm for Understanding Ourselves?" in Peter J. Frost et al. (eds.), *Organizational Culture.* Beverly Hills, Calif.: Sage Publications, 1985, pp. 55–72.

[18]M. R. Louis, "Organizations as Culture Bearing Milieux," in Louis Pondy et al. (eds.), *Organizational Symbolism.* Greenwich, Conn.: JAI, 1980, pp. 76–92.

EXHIBIT 11–3
ASSUMPTIONS ABOUT HUMAN NATURE

	Humans as Transcendental Beings	Humans Create Their Realities	Humans as Social Actors
Assumptions about human nature	Human beings are viewed as intentional beings, directing their psychic energy and experience in ways that constitute the world in a meaningful, intentional form. There are realms of being, and realms of reality, constituted through different kinds of founding acts, stemming from a form of transcendental consciousness. Human beings shape the world within the realm of their own immediate experience.	Human beings create their realities in the most fundamental ways, in an attempt to make their world intelligible to themselves and to others. They are not simply actors interpreting their situations in meaningful ways, for there are no situations other than those which individuals bring into being through their own creative activity. Individuals may work together to create a shared reality, but that reality is still a subjective construction capable of disappearing the moment its members cease to sustain it as such. Reality appears as real to individuals because of human acts of conscious or unwitting collusion.	Human beings are social actors interpreting their milieu and orienting their actions in ways that are meaningful to them. In this process they utilize language, labels, routines for impression management, and other modes of culturally specific action. In so doing they contribute to the enactment of a reality; human beings live in a world of symbolic significance, interpreting and enacting a meaningful relationship with that world. Human beings are actors with the capacity to interpret, modify, and sometimes create the scripts that they play upon life's stage.
Scholarly tradition	Phenomenology	Ethnomethodology	Social action theory
Overall perspective	Symbolic	Symbolic	Symbolic

EXHIBIT 11-3 (continued)

	Humans as Information Processors	Humans as Adaptive Agents	Humans as Responding Mechanisms
Assumptions about human nature	Human beings are engaged in a continual process of interaction and exchange with their context—receiving, interpreting, and acting on the information received, and in so doing creating a new pattern of information that affects changes in the field as a whole. Relationships between individual and context are constantly modified as a result of this exchange; the individual is but an element of a changing whole. The crucial relationship between individual and context is reflected in the pattern of learning and mutual adjustment that has evolved. Where this is well developed, the field of relationships is harmonious; where adjustment is low, the field is unstable and subject to unpredictable and discontinuous patterns of change.	Human beings exist in an interactive relationship with their world. They influence and are influenced by their context or environment. The process of exchange that operates here is essentially a competitive one, the individual seeking to interpret and exploit the environment to satisfy important needs, and hence survive. Relationships between individuals and environment express a pattern of activity necessary for survival and well-being of the individual.	Human beings are a product of the external forces in the environment to which they are exposed. Stimuli in their environment condition them to behave and respond to events in predictable and determinate ways. A network of causal relationships links all important aspects of behavior to context. Though human perception may influence this process to some degree, people always respond to situations in a lawful (i.e., rule-governed) manner.
Scholarly tradition	Cybernetics	Open systems theory	Behaviorism Social learning theory
Overall perspective	Psychological	Psychological	Psychological

Source: Adapted from G. Morgan and L. Smircich, "The Case for Qualitative Research," *Academy of Management Review 5* (October 1980), pp. 494–495. Copyright © 1980 by the Academy of Management. Reprinted by permission.

The central, or the central zone, is a phenomenon of the realm of values and beliefs. It is the center of the order of symbols and values and beliefs, which govern the society. . . . The central zone partakes of the nature of the sacred. In this sense every society has an official "religion." . . . The center is also a phenomenon of the realm of action. It is a structure of activities, of roles and persons, within the network of institutions. It is in these roles that the values and beliefs which are central are embodied and propounded.[19]

As repositories of values these centers are sources of identity for individuals and groups and the means by which their work lives become meaningful. Centers provide a sense of purpose to seemingly ordinary events and bring worth and dignity to human activities within the organization.

LEVELS OF CULTURE

It is useful to think about dimensions of school culture as existing at at least four levels.[20] The most tangible and observable level is represented by the *artifacts* of culture as manifested in what people say, how people behave, and how things look. Verbal artifacts include the language systems that are used, stories that are told, and examples that are used to illustrate certain important points. Behavioral artifacts are manifested in the ceremonies and rituals and other symbolic practices of the school.

The next level of school culture to be understood is the *perspectives* of people. Perspectives refer to the shared rules and norms, the commonness that exists among solutions to similar problems, how people define the situations they face, and the boundaries of acceptable and unacceptable behavior.

The third level is that of *values.* Values provide the basis for people to evaluate the situations they face, the worth of actions, activities, their priorities, and the behaviors of people with whom they work. The values are arranged in a fashion which represents the covenant that teachers share. This covenant might be in the form of an educational or management platform and statements of school philosophy. Platforms and philosophy were discussed in more detail in Chapter 10.

The fourth level is that of *assumptions.* Assumptions are more abstract than each of the other levels because they are typically implicit. Craig C. Lundberg describes assumptions as "the tacit beliefs that members hold about themselves and others, their relationships to other persons, and the nature of the organization in which they live. Assumptions are the nonconscious underpinnings of the

---

[19]Edward A. Shils, "Centre and Periphery," in *The Logic of Personal Knowledge: Essays Presented to Michael Polanyi.* London: Routledge & Kegan Paul, 1961, p. 119.

[20]The levels are from Craig C. Lundberg, "On the Feasibility of Cultural Interventions in Organizations," in Peter J. Frost et al., *Organizational Culture.* Beverly Hills, Calif.: Sage Publications, 1985. The four levels are based on the work of Schein and Dyer as follows: W. G. Dyer, Jr., *Patterns and Assumptions: The Keys to Understanding Organizational Culture,* Office of Naval Research Technical Report TR-0 NR-7; and Edgar H. Schein, *Organizational Culture and Leadership.* San Francisco: Jossey-Bass, 1985.

first three levels—that is, the implicit, abstract axioms that determine the more explicit systems of meanings."[21]

IDENTIFYING THE CULTURE OF YOUR SCHOOL

The four levels of culture provide a framework for analyzing a school's history and tradition, patterns of beliefs, norms, and behaviors. For example, the questions below can help supervisors identify and describe important aspects of the culture of their schools.

The School's history. How does the school's past live in the present? What traditions are carried on? What stories are told and retold? What events in the school's history are overlooked or forgotten? Do heroes and heroines among students and teachers exist whose idiosyncrasies and exploits are remembered? In what ways are the school's traditions and historical incidents modified through reinterpretation over the years? Can you recall, for example, a historical event that has evolved from fact to myth?

Beliefs. What are the assumptions and understandings that are shared by teachers and others, though they may not be stated explicitly? These may relate to how the school is structured, how teaching takes place, the roles of teachers and students, discipline, the relationship of parents to the school. Perhaps these assumptions and understandings are written somewhere in the form of a philosophy or other statement.

Values. What are the things that your school prizes? That is, when teachers and principals talk about the school, what are the major and recurring value themes underlying what they say?

Norms and standards. What are the oughts, shoulds, do's, and don'ts that govern the behavior of teachers, supervisors, and principals? Norms and standards can be identified by examining what behaviors get rewarded and what behaviors get punished in the school.

Patterns of behavior. What are the accepted and recurring ways of doing things, the patterns of behavior, the habits and rituals that prevail in the school?

Corwith Hansen suggests that teachers be asked the following questions in seeking to identify the culture of their school.[22] Describe your work day both in and outside of the school. On what do you spend your time and energy? Given that most students forget what they learn, what do you hope your students will retain over time from your classes? Think of students you are typically attracted to—those that you admire, respect, or enjoy. What common characteristics do these students have? What does it take for a teacher to be successful in your school or in your department? What advice would you give new teachers? What do you remember about past faculty members and students in your school or depart-

[21]Lundberg, *ibid.*, p. 172.
[22]Corwith Hansen, "Department Culture in a High-Performing Secondary School." Unpublished dissertation. New York: Columbia University, 1986.

ment? If you were to draw a picture or take a photo or make a collage that represented some aspect of your school, what would it look like? How are students rewarded? How are teachers rewarded? What might a new teacher do that would immediately signal to others that he or she was not going to be successful?

"The School Culture Inventory: Identifying Guiding Beliefs" appears as Exhibit 11–4. This inventory is designed to help faculties tackle the task of identifying their culture by examining their school's belief structure. Depending on responses, a school can be classified generally on a continuum from having a strong to very weak culture.

From this discussion of school culture one might reasonably conclude that the concepts of culture and climate are similar. But still they are unique in many ways. Earlier we discussed the PCI scale and its use in identifying custodial and humanistic schools. These schools differed with respect to the assumptions and beliefs that teachers made about students, discipline, and control. In many respects the PCI conception of climate is concerned with aspects of school culture suggesting that the two concepts share commonalities. Still, the climate metaphor leads one to think more about the interpersonal life in schools. Culture leads one deeper into the life of the school, into the tacit world of beliefs and norms, into the realm of meaning and significance.

PLANNING FOR CHANGE TEACHER BY TEACHER

Acknowledging both the psychological and symbolic sides of human nature redefines the problem of how to introduce change; the problem of how to overcome the resistance of individual teachers becomes the broader problem of how to alter the culture of the school. An effective change strategy gives attention to both.

W. J. Reddin views individual teacher concerns as falling into three broad categories:

1 How will the proposed change affect the individual?
2 How will the proposed change affect relationships with others?
3 How will the proposed change affect the individual's work.[23]

He maintains that though these concerns are real, they are often not considered to be "legitimate" reasons for favoring or opposing a change. For this reason, teacher concerns often remain unstated. Instead the talk of resistance has to do with such issues as whether what is being proposed makes "educational sense or not."

Consider, for example, a teacher who is faced with the prospect of having to give up the safety and autonomy of teaching in a self-contained classroom for teaming with others. She may be worrying about what others will think about her teaching and about the additional time and interpersonal pressures involved

---

[23]W. J. Reddin, *Managerial Effectiveness*. New York: McGraw-Hill, 1970, p. 163.

EXHIBIT 11–4
THE SCHOOL CULTURE INVENTORY: IDENTIFYING GUIDING BELIEFS

Before a school's culture can be understood, evaluated, or changed, it needs first to be described. The list of questions which comprise this inventory can help faculties describe the culture of their school. The questions are patterned generally after those which appear in Jerry Patterson, Stuart C. Purkey, and Jackson Parker's, *Productive School Systems for a Nonrational World*. Though presented in the form of an inventory, the questions will have the most meaning when discussed by faculty. When individual and group ratings are obtained from teachers they should be supplemented by examples. To help acquaint you with the inventory items, try evaluating a school with which you are familiar using the following scale:

(*Always, Most* of the time, *Part* of the time, *Never*)

School Purposes
To what extent does the school:
  1 Communicate a set of purposes that provide a
    sense of direction and a basis for evaluating?   A M P N
  2 Value the importance of teachers and students
    understanding the purposes?   A M P N
  3 Want decisions to be made that reflect purposes?   A M P N
Give examples:

Empowerment
To what extent does the school:
  4 Value empowering teachers to make decisions
    that are sensible given circumstances they face?   A M P N
  5 Link empowerment to purpose by requiring that
    decisions reflect the school shared values?   A M P N
  6 Believe that teachers, supervisors, and
    administrators should have equal access to
    information and resources?   A M P N
  7 Believe power to be an expanding entity that
    increases when shared?   A M P N
Give examples:

Decision Making
To what extent does the school:
  8 Believe that decisions should be made as close to
    the point of implementation as possible?   A M P N
  9 Believe that value decisions should be made by
    those directly affected by them?   A M P N
  10 Believe that decisions should be made by those
    who are most expert, given the circumstances or
    problem being considered, regardless of
    hierarchical level?   A M P N
Give examples:

Sense of Community
To what extend does the school:

EXHIBIT 11–4
THE SCHOOL CULTURE INVENTORY: IDENTIFYING GUIDING BELIEFS *(continued)*

11 Value a "we" spirit and feeling of ownership in the school?   A M P N

12 Consider teachers and other employees as shareholders and stakeholders in the school?   A M P N

13 Demonstrate commitment to helping and developing school members?   A M P N

Give examples:

Trust

To what extent does the school:

14 Believe that given the opportunity teachers will want to do what is best for the school?   A M P N

15 Have confidence in the ability of teachers to make wise decisions?   A M P N

Give examples:

Quality

To what extent does the school:

16 Value high standards and expectations for teachers and students?   A M P N

17 Believe in a "can do" attitude in teachers and students?   A M P N

18 Value an atmosphere of sharing and encouraging within which school members "stretch and grow"?   A M P N

Give examples:

Recognition

To what extent does the school:

19 Value recognizing teachers and students for taking chances in seeking new and better ideas?   A M P N

20 Value recognizing the achievements and accomplishments of teachers and students?   A M P N

Give examples:

Caring

To what extent does the school:

21 Value the well-being and personal concerns of all school members?   A M P N

22 Take a personal interest in the work concerns and career development of teachers?   A M P N

Give examples:

EXHIBIT 11–4
THE SCHOOL CULTURE INVENTORY: IDENTIFYING GUIDING BELIEFS *(continued)*

Integrity
To what extent does the school:

23 Value honesty in words and actions?   A M P N

24 Adopt a single standard of norms and
expectations for teachers, students, and other
school members?   A M P N

25 Value consistency?   A M P N

26 Demonstrate commitment to highest personal and
ethical convictions?   A M P N

Give examples:

Diversity
To what extent does the school:

27 Value differences in individual philosophy and
personality?   A M P N

28 Value differences in teaching style?   A M P N

29 Value flexibility in teaching and learning
approaches in response to student differences?   A M P N

30 Link diversity in style and method to common
school purposes and values?   A M P N

Give examples:

Sum of column tallies   _ _ _ _

Scoring directions: To score the school climate inventory, multiply the sum of tallies in column A by 4, column M by 3, column P by 2, and column N by 1. Now sum the scores for each column to get a grand score. The scale below provides a *rough* indicator of the strength of your school's professional culture:

110 to 120	Strong
90 to 110	Moderately strong
60 to 90	Weak
Below 60	Very weak

Source: Adapted from Jerry Patterson, Stuart Purkey, and Jackson Parker, "Guiding Beliefs of Our School District," in *Productive School Systems for a Nonrational World.* Arlington, Va.: Association for Supervision and Curriculum Development, 1986, pp. 50–51. Reprinted with permission of the Association for Supervision and Curriculum Development and Jerry Patterson, Stuart Purkey, and Jackson Parker. Copyright © 1986 by the Association for Supervision and Curriculum Development. All rights reserved.

in having to negotiate with others what will be taught, how it will be taught, and when. Furthermore, she may be worrying about whether her chances of becoming an assistant principal in the school will be enhanced or diminished as a result of this new teaching arrangement. But given the formal roles played in schools, it is typically not socially acceptable to state publicly such personal concerns. Thus instead of speaking to these *real* issues, the teacher complains that students are likely to find team teaching to be impersonal, that clear lines of authority will become clouded, that discipline problems will increase, and that students will find it burdensome to adjust to several different teaching styles.

Not surprisingly, these more organizationally legitimate concerns are not real in and of themselves but are proxies for the more personal concerns of teachers. This is unfortunate, because as teachers make peace with personal concerns, the proxies have a way of disappearing. One advantage of a healthy school climate is that levels of trust and openness among colleagues are such that it becomes acceptable to raise these less legitimate reasons for being concerned about proposed changes.

You can test Reddin's ideas by applying his categories to your own personal experience. Recall, for example, an occasion when a significant change was being proposed. What was your initial reaction to this change? Think less about what you said to others about the change and more about what you actually thought about and felt. Use Reddin's list below to identify the items that were of most concern to you:

Concern for self

How will my advancement possibilities change?
How will my salary change?
How will my future with this company change?
How will my view of myself change?
How will my formal authority change?
How will my informal influence change?
How will my view of my prior values change?
How will my ability to predict the future change?
How will my status change?

Concern for work

How will the amount of work I do change?
How will my interest in the work change?
How will the importance of my work change?
How will the challenge of the work change?
How will the work pressures change?
How will the skill demands on me change?
How will my physical surroundings change?
How will my hours of work change?

Concern for relationships

How will my relationships with my coworkers change?
How will my relationships with my superior change?
How will my relationships with my subordinates change?
How will what my family thinks of me change?[24]

A supervisor who wanted to use Reddin's theory to overcome your resistance to change would try to identify your concerns and how powerfully you held

---

[24]Ibid.

them. Then in a kind of tug of war, with the supervisor pulling at one end and you pulling at the other, the supervisor would try to change your mind about your concerns.[25] The supervisor would attempt to diminish as many of your concerns as possible by suggesting benefits of changing that outweigh them. Let's say the two most pressing concerns for you are how your informal influence with the faculty will change and the additional amount of work that will be required. The supervisor might try to convince you that teaming provides a better arena for your influence to increase. Further, the supervisor might try to counter your concern about increased work load by helping you to see the possibilities of becoming a team leader. Both of these advantages can increase your chances of ultimately becoming an assistant principal. The supervisor, in other words, seeks to overcome your resistance to change by offering attractions that increase the pull from one side of the tug of war or by removing resisters that decrease the pull from the other side.

Some researchers have focused on the concerns issue in a developmental sense, seeking to find out what are initial concerns of teachers and what concerns comes later. They reason that depending upon level of concern, teachers are likely to focus on one set of limited issues as opposed to another. A good change strategy, therefore, calculates carefully what the level of concern is and gives attention to the correct corresponding issues. This work has led to the development of the "concerns-based adoption model" of change. This model charts the changing feelings of teachers as they learn about a proposed change, prepare to use it, then use it, and finally make it a part of their everyday repertoire. The model proposes seven stages of concern as follows:[26]

1	Awareness	I am not concerned about it.
2	Informational	I would like to know more about it.
3	Personal	How will using it affect me?
4	Management	I seem to be spending all my time getting material ready.
5	Consequence	How is my use affecting kids?
6	Collaboration	I am concerned about relating what I am doing to what other teachers are doing.
7	Refocusing	I have some ideas about something that would work even better.

The developers of the model do not assume that every teacher marches through all the stages beginning with awareness and ending with refocusing. Nor do they assume that the stages are mutually exclusive, with only one being

---

[25]In the parlance of social science this tug of war is called *force field theory and analysis*. See, for example, Kurt Lewin, *Field Theory in Social Science*. New York: Harper & Row, 1951.

[26]See, for example, Gene E. Hall and Susan F. Louicks, "Teacher Concerns as a Basis for Facilitating Staff Development," *Teachers College Record*, vol. 80, no. 1, 1978; and Shirley M. Hord, William L. Rutherford, Leslie Huling-Austin, and Gene E. Hall, *Taking Charge of Change*. Alexandria, Va.: ASCD, 1977.

tended to at a time. Instead, the stages represent the general kind of development that takes place as changes are adopted and used.

A typical pattern of progression is as follows. In the early stages teachers are likely to have self concerns that center on learning more about the proposed innovation and how it will affect them personally. This is not unlike the category system proposed by Reddin. Once these concerns are taken care of teachers are then ready to focus on the management problems they are likely to face as they begin to implement the change. Next their attention shifts to the impact the change is likely to have on their students. Once comfortable with answers to this question, teachers address issues of collaboration with other teachers in an effort to implement the change and to improve its effects. Finally, since teachers are different, they make adaptations to the innovation in an effort to improve its fit to their own unique circumstance. In sum, the researchers recommend that supervisors interested in promoting change use the concerns-based model as a framework for evaluating where individuals are and for matching change strategies to these levels.

It seems clear that resistance to change occurs when one's basic needs are threatened. Although teachers have different needs, four seem fairly universal[27]:

1 *The need for clear expectations.* Most people require fairly specific information about their jobs to function effectively. People need to know what is expected of them, how they fit into the total scheme of things, what their responsibilities are, how they will be evaluated, and what their relationships with others will be. Change upsets this equilibrium of role definition and expectations.

2 *The need for future certainty.* Closely related to fit is being able to predict the future. People need to have some reliability and certainty built into their work lives. Change introduces ambiguity and uncertainty, which threaten the need for a relatively stable, balanced, and predictable work environment.

3 *The need for social interaction.* Most people value and need opportunities to interact with others. This interaction helps people to define and build up their own self-concepts and to reduce the anxiety and fear they experience in the work environment. People seek support and acceptance from others at work. Change is often viewed as threatening these important social interaction patterns.

4 *The need for control over the work environment and work events.* Most people want and seek a reasonable degree of control over their work environment. People do not want to be at the mercy of the system but instead want to be origins, making decisions that affect their own work lives. When con-

---

[27]Laird W. Nealiea, "Learned Behavior: The Key to Understanding and Preventing Employee Resistance to Change," *Group and Organizational Studies,* vol. 3, no. 2 (1978), pp. 211–223, as quoted in Thomas J. Sergiovanni, *The Principalship: A Reflective Practice Perspective,* 2d ed., Boston: Allyn & Bacon, 1991, p. 260.

trol is threatened or reduced the effect is not only less job satisfaction but also a loss of meaning in work that results in indifference and even alienation. Change efforts that ignore these four needs are likely not only to be ineffective but also to cause important morale problems.

Overcoming resistance to change by carefully calculating the appropriate level of concern of teachers involved and by helping teachers to feel safe and secure are all helpful. But resistance to change also occurs when proposed changes oppose the existing norm systems of the school. A strong change strategy seeks as well to alter the culture of the school by creating new work norms. Although tending to the psychological needs of individual teachers is important, in the end changing schools requires changing school culture. Such an ambitious goal, we will argue, requires two things: that leadership be redefined and practiced differently, and that collegiality be understood as a form of professional virtue. The topic of leadership is complex enough to warrant special attention, and thus it will become the theme of the next several chapters. Collegiality is discussed in the sections that follow.

COLLEGIALITY AS LINCHPIN

It is now accepted that promoting collegiality is an important way to help schools change for the better. Susan Rosenholtz's research, for example, firmly links collegiality to the amount and quality of learning that takes place among teachers.[28] In summarizing the research on collegiality and school improvement, Michael Fullan writes:

> Since interaction with others influences what one does, relationships with other teachers is a critical variable. The theory of change that we have been evolving clearly points to the importance of peer relationships in the school. Change involves learning to do something new, and interaction is the primary basis for social learning. New meanings, new behaviors, new skills, and new beliefs depend significantly on whether teachers are working as isolated individuals (Goodlad, 1984; Lortie, 1975; Sarason, 1982) or are exchanging ideas, support, and positive feelings about their work (Little, 1982; Mortimore, et al., 1988; Rosenholtz, 1989). The quality of working relationships among teachers is strongly related to implementation. Collegiality, open communication, trust, support and help, learning on the job, getting results, and job satisfaction and morale are closely interrelated.[29]

[28]Susan Rosenholtz, *Teachers' Workplace: The Social Organization of Schools.* New York: Longman, 1989.

[29]Fullan with Stiegelbauer, *The New Meaning of Educational Change,* op. cit., p. 79. The Fullan cites are as follows: John Goodlad, *A Place Called School: Prospects for the Future.* New York: McGraw-Hill, 1984; Dan Lortie, *Schoolteacher: A Sociological Study.* Chicago: University of Chicago Press, 1975; Seymour Sarason, *The Culture of the School and the Problem of Change,* revised ed., Boston: Allyn & Bacon, 1982; Judith Warren Little, "Norms of Collegiality and Experimentation: Workplace Conditions of School Success," *American Educational Research Journal,* vol. 19 (1982), pp. 325–340; P. Mortimore, P. Sammons, L. Stoll, D. Lewis, and R. Ecob, *School Matters: The Junior Years.* Sommerset, U.K.: Open Books, 1988; and Rosenholtz, ibid., 1989.

Judith Warren Little's work is most often quoted on this issue:

School Improvement is most surely and thoroughly achieved when:

Teachers engage in frequent, continuous and increasingly concrete and precise _talk_ about teaching practice (as distinct from teacher characteristics and failings, the social lives of teachers, the foibles and failures of students and their families, and the unfortunate demands of society on the school). By such talk, teachers build up a shared language adequate to the complexity of teaching, capable of distinguishing one practice and its virtue from another. . . .

Teachers are frequently observed and provided with useful (if potentially frightening) critiques of their teaching. Such observation and feedback can provide shared referents for the shared language of teaching at a level of the precision and concreteness which makes the talk about teaching useful.

Teachers [and administrators] plan, design, research, evaluate and prepare teaching materials together. The most astute observations remain academic ("just theory") without the machinery to act on them. By joint work on materials, teachers [and administrators] share the considerable burden of development required by long-term improvement, confirm their emerging understanding of their approach and make rising standards for their work attainable by them and their students.

Teachers teach each other the practice of teaching.[30]

Collegiality bridges both concepts of school climate and school culture. Collegiality speaks not only to the degree of trust, openness, and good feelings that exist among a faculty, but also to the kind of norm system that bonds teachers as a collective unit. The bonding aspect of collegiality is key and is often missing in the policies and practices of Supervision I.

One problem is that too often collegiality is confused with congeniality.[31] _Congeniality_ refers to the friendly human relationships that exist among teachers and is characterized by the loyalty, trust, and easy conversation that results from the development of a closely knit social group. Congeniality is often considered to be a measure of school climate. _Collegiality_, by contrast, refers to the existence of high levels of collaboration among teachers and between teachers and principal and is characterized by mutual respect, shared work values, cooperation, and specific conversations about teaching and learning. When congeniality is high a strong informal culture aligned with social norms emerges in the school. But these norms may or may not be aligned with school purposes. By contrast, when collegiality is high a strong professional culture held together by shared work norms emerges in the school. These norms are aligned with school purposes and contribute to increased commitment and improved performance. We believe that congeniality can contribute to the development of collegiality but in itself is not sufficient.

Another problem is that when collegiality _is_ achieved within Supervision I it is often contrived rather than real, resulting from structural rather than norma-

---

[30]Judith Warren Little, "Norms of Collegiality and Experimentation: Workplace Conditions of School Success," _American Educational Research Journal_, vol. 19, no. 3 (Fall 1982), p. 331.

[31]Roland Barth, _Improving Schools from Within_. San Francisco: Jossey-Bass, 1990.

tive changes. Supervisors push for collegiality by altering structures and introducing such innovations as peer coaching and team teaching without addressing the norm structure of the school. As a result, they superimpose a form of collegiality on an unaccepting culture. When this is the case collegial practices become grafted on to the existing school culture.[32] Andrew Hargreaves describes contrived collegiality as

> [c]haracterized by a set of formal, specific bureaucratic procedures to increase the attention being given to joint teacher planning and consultation. It can be seen in initiatives such as peer coaching, mentor teaching, joint planning in specially provided rooms, formally scheduled meetings, and clear job descriptions and training programs for those in consultive roles. These sorts of initiatives are administrative contrivances designed to get collegiality going in schools where little has existed before.[33]

The receiving culture is key in determining whether administratively induced collegiality is contrived or real. When it is real, collegiality results from the felt interdependence of people at work and from a sense of moral obligation to work together. From a cultural perspective, and with the right set of shared norms in place, collegiality can be considered as a form of professional virtue. When this is the case the fulfillment of certain obligations that stem from the teacher's membership in the school as community and membership in the teaching profession requires teachers to be collegial.

Collegiality as professional virtue is comprised of three dimensions: a conception of the good person who values colleagueship for its own sake, connectedness to a community that provides one with the right to be treated collegially and the obligation to treat others collegially, and interpersonal relationships characterized by mutual respect.[34] The first two dimensions are enhanced by a healthy school culture and the third by a healthy school climate.

THE SUPERVISOR IS KEY

Improving schools by helping teachers to reflect on their practice, to learn more about what they do and why, to strive for self-improvement, to share what they know with others, and to strive to improve their practice is at the heart of what supervision seeks to accomplish. This purpose often leads to a focus on how to provide staff development approaches and, in class, how to provide help that teachers welcome and find beneficial. It leads to a concern with how the talents and resources of individual teachers might be shared with others and how the evaluation process can be improved. These supervising aims and activities in-

---

[32]Peter B. Grimmitt, Olaf P. Rostad, and Blake Ford, "Supervision: A Transformational Perspective," in Carl Glickman (ed.), *Supervision in Transition,* 1992 Yearbook of the Association for Supervision and Curriculum Development. Alexandria, Va.: ASCD, 1992.

[33]Andrew Hargreaves, "Contrived Collegiality and the Culture of Teaching." Annual Meeting of the Canadian Society for the Study of Education, Quebec City, 1989.

[34]Thomas J. Sergiovanni, *Moral Leadership: Getting to the Heart of School Improvement.* San Francisco: Jossey-Bass, 1992.

volve change. Change is difficult under ordinary circumstances but particularly trying unless conditions are right. The right conditions, we have argued in this chapter, are those that support both the psychological and symbolic needs of teachers; needs that are the subject matter of school climate and school culture. No matter how well intentioned the supervisor, and no matter how hard that supervisor tries to improve the individual and collective practice of teaching in a school, little will be accomplished without first developing and nurturing the right school climate and culture. Climate and culture are affected by administrative policies; they are affected even more by close, personal contact with the process of teaching and learning. This is the territory of supervision. For this reason, supervisors have a particularly critical role to play.

CHAPTER 12

MOTIVATION, SATISFACTION, AND THE TEACHERS' WORKPLACE

IMPROVING the teachers' workplace is one important way to improve schools. But a great deal of confusion exists about what is really important to teachers and how best to go about such improvement. As a result, and despite good intentions, regressive school policies and practices are often put into place leading to such unanticipated consequences as job dissatisfaction, lack of work motivation, and even alienation among teachers. This confusion stems in part from four common conditions within school systems:

- Labeling teachers as professionals but viewing the work of teaching as bureaucratic.
- Attributing higher standards of trust and moral responsiveness to administrators and supervisors than to teachers.
- Assuming that teachers are primarily motivated by self-interest and thus less willing to respond to work for altruistic reasons.
- Assuming that teachers make decisions about what is important and what to do alone as rational and objective individuals.

The four conditions have a tendency to reinforce each other, thus creating a cycle that makes matters worse. For example, teachers are given bureaucratic work because they're not trusted with the discretion needed for professional work. That being the case, supervisors are needed to tell teachers what to do and to check up on them. Furthermore, teachers are not deemed capable of accepting responsibility for their own professional development. Thus the need for supervisors to provide directive supervision and formal in-service programs. As a result, teachers wind up being the objects of supervision. As objects, they tend to lose their sense of commitment. They either feel resentful and alienated or they become increasingly dependent upon their supervisors. This reaction then makes it necessary for them to be *motivated* by supervisors.

Given the above realities, the motivational strategies supervisors choose typically are based on the belief that the goals of teachers and those of supervisors are not the same. Teachers, it is assumed, do not care as much about matters of schooling as do supervisors. Thus the basis for motivating teachers becomes a series of trades whereby the supervisors give to teachers things that they want in exchange for compliance with the supervisors' requests and requirements. This, in turn, results in the further bureaucratization of the work of teaching, reinforces the supervisor's superior moral standing, places further emphasis on the use of self-interest-oriented motivational strategies, and so perpetuates this regressive cycle. Breaking this cycle requires serious rethinking about what is important to teachers.

BUREAUCRATIC AND PROFESSIONAL WORK

Rethinking the practice of referring to teachers as professionals yet considering their work as bureaucratic is a good place to begin. In today's schools it is common for teachers to be regulated and controlled by an elaborate work system that specifies what must be done and then seeks to ensure that it is done. When this is the case, the work of teachers becomes increasingly bureaucratic. But bureaucratic and professional work are different. Although both bureaucrats and professionals are part of a rationally conceived work system, bureaucrats are *subordinate* to this system. They are responsible for implementing the system according to the provided specifications, and supervision is designed to monitor this process. The emphasis is on doing things right.

Professionals, by contrast, are *superordinate* to their work system. In teaching, the work system represents a point of reference rather than a script. Teachers use the system in ways that makes sense to them as they practice. Supervision for professionals, while no less demanding, is helpful and facilitating in its orientation. In professional work the emphasis is on writing the script while practicing. In a larger sense professionals create their practice as they practice. Unlike bureaucratic technicians, they are researchers, solvers, and inventors, as well as implementers.

The differences between bureaucratic and professional work and the relationship of teachers to this work are illustrated in Figure 12–1. Bureaucratic work seems to fit Supervision I and professional work seems to fit Supervision II. In Supervision I the purpose is to monitor and control the approved system. In Supervision II the purpose is to empower and expand the teachers' view, enabling them to make better decisions as they create the system in use. Levels of satisfaction, commitment, and efficacy are higher when work is conceived as pro-

Supervision I: A bureaucratic view of teaching and supervision:
Teachers are subordinate to the system

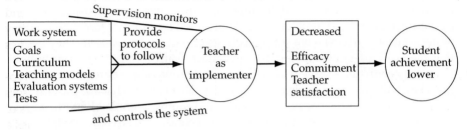

Supervision II: A professional view of teaching and supervision:
Teachers are superordinate to the system

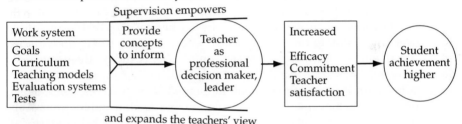

FIGURE 12–1   Supervisions I and II: The characteristics and effects of bureaucratic and professional views of teaching.

fessional and lower when work is conceived as bureaucratic. And, as will be discussed in later sections, these conditions of Supervision II are linked to enhanced feelings of efficacy among teachers and increased student achievement.[1]

TEACHERS AS ORIGINS AND PAWNS

In successful schools teachers tend to be more committed, hardworking, loyal to their school, and satisfied with their jobs. The research on motivation to work reveals that these highly motivating conditions are present when teachers:

Find their work lives to be meaningful, purposeful, sensible, and significant and when they view the work itself as being worthwhile and important.

Have reasonable control over their work activities and affairs and are able to exert reasonable influence over work events and circumstances.

Experience personal responsibility for the work and are personally accountable for outcomes.[2]

---

[1]Patricia T. Ashton and Rodman B. Webb, *Making a Difference: Teachers' Sense of Efficacy and Student Achievement.* New York: Longman, 1986, p. 49.

[2]See, for example, Frederick Herzberg, Bernard Mausner, and Barbara Snyderman, *The Motivation to Work.* New York: Wiley, 1959; Thomas J. Sergiovanni, "Factors Which Affect Satisfaction and Dissatisfaction of Teachers," *Journal of Educational Administration*, vol. 5, no. 1

When teachers experience meaningfulness, control, and personal responsibility at work, they are functioning more as "origins" than as "pawns." An origin believes that behavior is determined by his or her own choosing. A pawn, by contrast, believes that behavior is determined by external forces beyond his or her control.[3] Origins have strong feelings of personal causation. They believe that they can affect events and circumstances that exist in their environment. Pawns, by contrast, believe that forces beyond their control determine what it is that they will do. Pawn feelings, according to Richard DeCharms, provide people with a strong sense of powerlessness and ineffectiveness.[4] Experts such as DeCharms believe that persons under normal conditions strive to be effective in influencing and altering events and situations that comprise their environment. They strive to be causal agents, to be origins of their own behavior. When this is not the case, they experience frustration, powerlessness, and often alienation.

One of the consequences of being an origin rather than a pawn is that one's sense of efficacy is enhanced. An efficacious teacher believes that he or she has the power and ability to produce a desired effect. Efficacy has to do with personal effectiveness, a feeling that one can control events and produce outcomes. Recent research links sense of efficacy not only with motivation and commitment to work but with student achievement. In their study of teachers' sense of efficacy and student achievement, for example, Patricia Ashton and Rodman Webb found that efficacy was related to such teacher behaviors as being warm, accepting, and responsive to students; accepting student initiatives; and giving attention to all the students' individual needs.[5] Efficacy was also related to student enthusiasm and student initiation of interaction with teachers. Finally, teachers' sense of efficacy was related to student achievement. Ashton and Webb studied high school teachers of mathematics and communications. Student achievement was measured by mathematics and language basic skills tests. Their model of the relationship between teachers' sense of efficacy and student achievement is illustrated in Figure 12–2.

The factors contributing to teachers' sense of efficacy and enhanced motivation and commitment are depicted in Figure 12–3. A supportive school climate, the presence of collegial values, shared decision making, and a school culture provide a sense of purpose and define for teachers a shared covenant. These characteristics (discussed in the last chapter) provide for cooperative relationships, strong social identity, a sense of personal causation, origin feelings, high responsibility for work outcomes, and a shared commitment to common goals.

(1967), pp. 66–82; J. R. Hackman and G. Oldham, "Motivation Through Design of Work: Test of a Theory," *Organizational Behavior and Human Performance*, vol. 16, no. 2 (1976), pp. 250–279; and Edward L. Deci, *Why We Do What We Do: The Dynamics of Personal Autonomy*. New York: Putnam, 1995.

[3]Richard DeCharms, *Personal Causation: The Internal Affective Determinants of Behavior*. New York: Academic Press, 1968.

[4]Ibid.

[5]Ashton and Webb, op. cit.

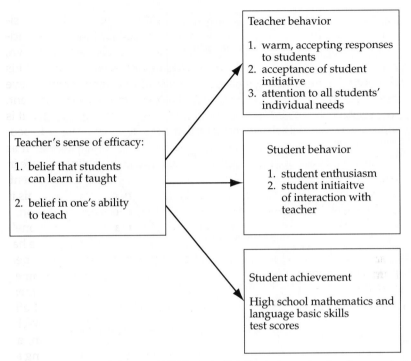

FIGURE 12–2   The Ashton and Webb study: Relation between teachers' sense of efficacy, teaching and learning behaviors, and student achievement.

Figures 12–2 and 12–3 provide glimpses of how the story of teacher motivation to work can end. It is a story quite different from what currently takes place in most schools. To understand this story, it is important to go back to the beginning and examine some basic assumptions that can provide a basis for practicing work motivation differently.

A FRAMEWORK FOR UNDERSTANDING TEACHER MOTIVATION

Motivation is in part an expression of psychological needs and in part a function of moral judgments. The motivational policies and practices of Supervision I overemphasize the former and neglect the latter. Supervision II, by contrast, seeks to join the two into an expanded theory of motivation that better reflects the full nature of human potential.

Theories of motivation can be grouped into three categories: those that emphasize the exchange of rewards or punishment for compliance; those that seek compliance by emphasizing opportunities to experience satisfaction from the work itself; and those that are based on the idea that compliance results from moral judgment. The first category relies heavily on rewards and punishments and on the promise of extrinsic gain. The second category also relies on rewards,

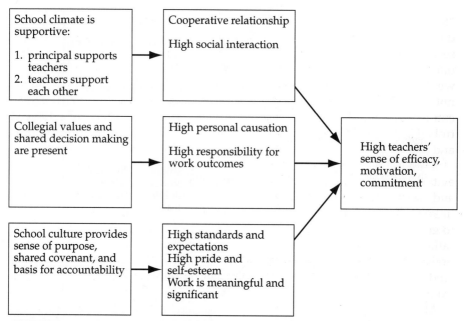

FIGURE 12–3   Factors contributing to teachers' sense of efficacy, motivation, and commitment.

but the rewards depend less on gains made from trades with supervisors and more on teachers finding intrinsic satisfaction in work. The third category, moral judgment, relies on the connection of teachers to professional and community norms that represent a form of moral authority, a theme discussed in chapters 3 and 6. The categories can be expressed in the form of three motivational rules:

1 What gets rewarded gets done.
2 What is rewarding gets done.
3 What is good gets done.[6]

Although all three motivational rules are true, the consequences of their prime use in practice differs. The three rules are examined in the sections below.

WHAT GETS REWARDED GETS DONE

The motivational practices of Supervision I are based largely on the rule "What gets rewarded gets done." This rule works very effectively in the short term. The consequences of using the rule over time, however, are different. The famous

[6]The discussion of motivational rules that follows is drawn from chap. 2, "What Motivates? What Inspires?" and chap. 5, "Creating a State of Flow at Work," in Thomas J. Sergiovanni, *Moral Leadership: Getting to the Heart of School Improvement*. San Francisco: Jossey-Bass, 1992.

"felt-tipped" research of David Greene and Mark Lepper is often cited as evidence that the rule can backfire when trying to motivate children.[7] In that research, preschoolers who were motivated to draw with felt-tipped markers without extrinsic rewards became less interested in this activity once such rewards were introduced. In a separate study Edward Deci and Richard Ryan found that not only does the motivational capacity of adults lessen with the introduction of extrinsic rewards for work, but such rewards resulted in feelings of being controlled by them.[8] These feelings had negative effects on subsequent performance and creativity.

James G. March points out that providing rewards for a performance inevitably leads to an emphasis on measuring performance. This linking of rewards and measurement typically causes problems. In his words, "A system of rewards linked to precise measure is not an incentive to perform well; it is an incentive to get a good score."[9] Given March's view, teachers will work for the rewards rather than the job itself. This circumstance raises a number of important questions. What happens when extrinsic rewards are no longer available to teachers? And what happens to other sources of motivation once extrinsic rewards are introduced?

Although "What gets rewarded gets done" may be true, it seems equally true that what does not get rewarded does not get done. The rule has a tendency to focus one's attention and narrow one's responses to work. For example, teachers who are being rewarded to teach in a certain way are not teaching in other ways. Although in some instances it might be a good idea to encourage teachers to teach in a particular way, as a general rule a policy of this sort is not a good idea. Because of the complex nature of teaching and because of the diversity that exists in student needs and teaching situations, how a teacher ought to teach at any given time cannot be validly determined beforehand. It is a decision that must be made on the spot.

In the 1970s teaching effectiveness research, for example, tended to emphasize direct instructional methods of teaching. Using this research as the basis for developing teacher evaluation systems is in effect a de facto adoption of direct instruction as a one best way to teach. The evaluation system then becomes a source of rewards and punishment for displaying the right or wrong teaching behaviors. True, direct instruction methods seem to work for lower-level learning outcomes and for students whose backgrounds and experiences are very limited. But for higher-level learning outcomes and for students who have a richer base of personal and other experience to draw upon, direct instructional meth-

---

[7]David Greene and Mark R. Lepper, "How to Turn Work into Play," *Psychology Today,* vol. 8, no. 4 (1974), pp. 49–52.

[8]Edward L. Deci and Richard M. Ryan, *Intrinsic Motivation and Self-Determination in Behavior.* New York: Plenum, 1985.

[9]James G. March, "How We Talk and How We Act: Administrative Theory and Administrative Life," in Thomas J. Sergiovanni and John E. Corbally (eds.), *Leadership and Organizational Culture.* Urbana: University of Illinois Press, 1984, pp. 27–28.

ods do not work as well. Cooperative learning strategies, for example, are likely to be better choices. Rewarding the former means you do not get the latter regardless of which of the two might be appropriate.

Another problem with the motivational rule "What gets rewarded gets done" is that for it to be sustained, a busy kind of supervision is required. For example, supervisors must constantly monitor the exchange of rewards for work, must become expert at guessing which rewards are of interest to which teachers and which rewards are not, and must figure out other ways to keep this exchange going. As a result, teachers become increasingly dependent upon the rewards themselves and upon their supervisors to motivate them.

The question of what happens to other sources of motivation once extrinsic rewards are introduced poses additional difficulties. Using the rule "What gets rewarded gets done" often changes a teacher's attachment to an activity from intrinsic or moral to extrinsic. For example, teachers who spend after-school hours with students in clubs or other informal activities because they enjoy it or because they think it's important often change their minds once extrinsic rewards are introduced. Deciding to pay teachers $8 per hour for up to four hours of service a week, for example, is likely to result in very few teachers working more than four hours. Furthermore, if the $8 rate is not increased after two or three years it is very likely that teachers will begin to give less and less during the four hours that they are required to spend after school.

What may be happening in the example above is that the teachers' attachment to their work has changed. Once involved for intrinsic and moral reasons, they now seem to be involved for calculated reasons. A fair day's work for a fair day's pay has been defined for them by the school, and a reward system has been put into place based on this definition. Teachers begin to calculate very carefully the proper equation of investments in work that matches the payoff they receive in return. Their involvement in work changes from intrinsic and moral to extrinsic reasons.

MASLOW'S THEORY AS AN EXAMPLE

One of the most popular constructs used to guide the practice of "What gets rewarded gets done" is Abraham Maslow's theory of motivation.[10] Maslow proposed that all human needs could be grouped into five categories arranged in levels of proficiency from basic to high. The most basic level is physical needs followed by security, social, esteem, and self-actualization. Basic needs, according to the theory, must be met first before a person is motivated by needs at higher levels. Lyman Porter suggested that physical needs cannot be realistically considered to have motivational potential in most work settings and thus substituted

---

[10]Abraham Maslow, *Motivation and Personality*. New York: Harper & Row, 1954.

Security	Affiliation	Self-esteem	Autonomy	Self-actualization
		Self-respect	Control	Working at top potential
	Acceptance	Respected by others as a person and as a professional	Influence	Giving all
Money	Belonging			
	Friendship			Peak satisfaction
			Participant	
Benefits	School membership	Competence		
				Achievement
Tenure	Formal work group	Confidence	Shareholder	
				Personal and professional success
Role consolidation	Informal work group	Recognition	Authority	

FIGURE 12–4   The needs hierarchy.

autonomy for physical as a new category.[11] The levels are often depicted in the form of a "needs hierarchy," as illustrated in Figure 12–4.

Here is how Maslow's theory is used in practicing "What gets rewarded gets done." It is assumed that teachers have needs that can be met at work. At the security level, for example, they have needs for money, benefits, tenure, and clear role expectations. At the autonomy level they have needs to influence, to become shareholders, to have authority, and so on. Supervisors, on the other hand, control the events and circumstances that allow these needs to be met. They can provide teachers with the desired need fulfillment if teachers in turn comply with required role expectations. For example, if teachers teach the right way, take on extracurricular responsibilities, volunteer for committee work, and cheerfully attend the required workshops, they can advance up the school's career ladder. Such advancement entitles them to have more control over what they do, to influence more school decisions, and to receive other benefits that help meet their needs for autonomy. If teachers don't conform to expectations, by contrast, they are likely to have less to say about what is going on in the school and are likely to be more closely watched.

The traditional motivational rule "What gets rewarded gets done" has its place. But by itself, it is neither powerful enough nor expansive enough to provide the kind of motivational climate needed in schools. Furthermore, overuse of the rule in motivating teachers (or, for that matter, students) can lead to many

[11]Lyman Porter, "Job Attitudes in Management: I. Perceived Deficiencies and Need Fulfillment as a Function of Job Level," *Journal of Applied Psychology,* vol. 4 (December 1963), pp. 386–397.

negative consequences. Some of these consequences are summed up by W. Edwards Demming, the famous quality-control expert, as follows:

> People are born with intrinsic motivation, dignity, curiosity to learn, joy in learning. The forces of destruction begin with toddlers—a prize for the best Halloween costume, grades in school, gold stars and honor to the university. On the job, people, teams, divisions are ranked—rewards for the one at the top, punishments at the bottom. MBO, quotas, incentive pay, business plans, put together separately, division by division, cause further loss, unknown and unknowable.[12]

In commenting on Demming's observations, Peter M. Senge notes, "Ironically, by focusing on performing for someone else's approval, corporations create the very conditions that predestine them to mediocre performance."[13] These comments, leveled at corporate America, seem even more appropriate when applied to schooling America.

WHAT IS REWARDING GETS DONE

As Alfie Kohn,[14] Barry Schwartz,[15] and Edward L. Deci[16] have recently pointed out.

"What is rewarding gets done" as a motivational rule has certain advantages over "What gets rewarded gets done." Since the basis of this rule is internal to the work itself, motivation does not depend directly on what the supervisor does or on other external forces. Second, being compelled from within implies a kind of self-management that does not require direct supervision or other kinds of monitoring to be sustained.

The motivational psychologist Frederick Herzberg pointed out that jobs that provide opportunities for experiencing achievement and responsibility, interesting and challenging work, and opportunity for advancement have the greatest capacity to motivate from within.[17] These are not factors that supervisors give to others in return for desired behavior but are instead factors integral to the work of teaching itself. Herzberg's research, and that of others, suggests that the following job characteristics enhance this intrinsic motivation:

> Allow for discovery, exploration, variety and challenge. Provide high involvement with the task and high identity with the task enabling work to be considered important and significant. Allow for active participation. Emphasize agreement with respect to broad purposes and values that bond people together at work. Permit outcomes within broad purposes to be determined by the worker. Encourage autonomy and self-

---

[12]Demming quoted in Peter M. Senge, "The Leader's New Work: Building a Learning Organization," *Sloan Management Review*, vol. 22, no. 1 (1990), p. 7.

[13]Ibid.

[14]Alfie Kohn, *Punished by Rewards*. Boston: Houghton Mifflin, 1993.

[15]Barry Schwartz, *The Costs of Living: How Market Theories Erode the Basic Things in Life*. New York: Norton, 1994.

[16]Deci, *Why We Do What We Do*, op. cit.

[17]Frederick Herzberg, *Work and Nature of Man*. New York: World Publishing, 1966.

determination. Allow persons to feel like "origins" of their own behavior rather than "pawns" manipulated from the outside. Encourage feelings of competence and control and enhance feelings of efficacy.[18]

Herzberg and his colleagues Bernard Mausner and Barbara Snyderman identified two fairly independent sets of job factors that seem to be important to workers. These factors comprise the basic constructs for their motivation-hygiene theory.[19] One set of factors, called *hygienic,* affect whether people are dissatisfied with their jobs and seem to be related to poor performance. The researchers concluded that if supervisors take care of these factors to the extent that they are no longer sources of dissatisfaction, performance will improve to a level of a "fair day's work for a fair day's pay." The workers will rarely, however, be motivated to go beyond this minimum level. The word "hygiene" was used to suggest that though the factors can cause dissatisfaction if neglected, they are not sources of motivation.

The hygiene factors are related to the conditions of work but not the work itself. They include salary, interpersonal relationships with subordinates, superiors, and peers; the quality of supervision received; administrative policies; general working conditions; status; and job security. Herzberg concluded that these factors are not strong enough to motivate people for very long and certainly not without lots of effort from supervisors.

A second set of factors identified, called *motivators,* seem not to result in dissatisfaction or poor performance in work when neglected. But when the motivation factors are present the result is motivation to go beyond "a fair day's work for a fair day's pay." The motivation factors are related to the work and include achievement, recognition, the work itself, responsibility, and advancement. It is the work itself, Herzberg concluded, that provides the sources for intrinsic motivation, and this kind of motivation seems to make the difference.

The motivation-hygiene theory has its critics. Many feel that the findings may well be artifacts of the methods used by researchers, thus portraying an oversimplified version of reality. For example, Herzberg and his colleagues relied heavily on the critical-incident method and on in-depth interview methods. When their research is replicated using rating scales and other kinds of questionnaires the results are not so easily confirmed. But still, few dispute the overall conclusion from the motivation-hygiene theory that for most people the work itself counts as an important motivator of work commitment, persistence, and performance.

The work of Herzberg and his colleagues represents a pioneering effort to establish a tradition known as *job enrichment research.* Job enrichment research seeks to identify ways in which jobs can be restructured to allow for workers to experience for themselves greater intrinsic satisfaction. The best known is the

---

[18]Thomas J. Sergiovanni, *Value-Added Leadership: How to Get Extraordinary Performance in Schools.* San Diego: Harcourt Brace Jovanovich, 1990, p. 129.
[19]Herzberg et al., op. cit.

work of J. R. Hackman and G. Oldham.[20] These researchers identified three psychological states believed to be critical in determining whether a person will be motivated at work.

Experienced meaningfulness. The individual must perceive his or her work as worthwhile or important by some system of values held.

Experienced responsibility. The individual must believe that he or she personally is accountable for the outcomes of efforts.

Knowledge of results. The individual must be able to determine, on some fairly regular basis, whether or not the outcomes of his or her work are satisfactory.[21]

When the three psychological states are present, according to this job enrichment theory, teachers can be expected to feel good, perform well, and continue to want to perform well in an effort to earn more of these feelings in the future. The three states become the basis for internal motivation, since teachers do not have to depend upon someone outside of themselves to motivate them or lead them.

What can supervisors do to increase the likelihood that teachers will experience meaningfulness, responsibility, and knowledge of results? The answer, according to Hackman and Oldham, is to build into teaching jobs opportunities for teachers to use more of their talents and skills; to allow teachers to engage in activities that allow them to see the whole, and to understand how their contributions fit into the overall purpose and mission (task identity); to view their work as having a significant impact on the lives of their students (task significance); to experience discretion in scheduling work and in deciding classroom arrangements and teaching methods and procedures (autonomy); and to get firsthand and from others clear information about the effects of their performance (feedback). The job enrichment model proposed by Hackman and his colleagues is depicted in Figure 12–5.

Note that in addition to job dimensions, psychological states, and outcomes, an "implementing concepts" panel is provided. These are the suggestions the researchers offer to supervisors interested in building more of the job dimensions into work.

The principle of "combining tasks" suggests that fractionalized aspects of teaching should be put together in larger, more holistic, modules. Comprehensive curriculum development strategies, interdisciplinary approaches, and team-group teaching modes all contribute to the combining of teaching and curriculum tasks. Combining tasks increases not only skill variety, for teachers but their identification with the work as well.

Establishing "client relationships" should be easy to promote, since teachers and students already work in close contact with each other. Some patterns of organization and teaching, however, seem not to encourage close personal rela-

---

[20]Hackman and Oldham, op. cit.

[21]J. R. Hackman, G. Oldham, R. Johnson, and K. Purdy, "A New Strategy for Job Enrichment," *California Management Review,* vol. 17, no. 4, (1975), p. 57.

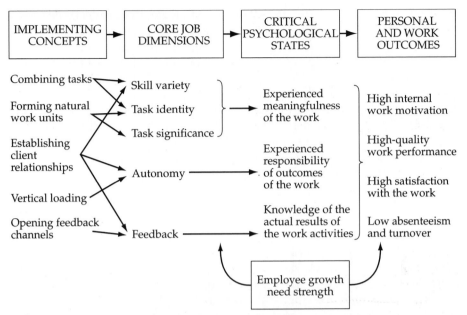

FIGURE 12–5   Job enrichment concepts and practices. *(From J. R. Hackman, G. Oldham, R. Johnson, and K. Purdy, "A New Strategy for Job Enrichment," © 1975 by The Regents of the University of California. Reprinted from* California Management Review, *vol. XVII, no. 4, p. 64, by permission of the Regents.)*

tionships between teachers and students. For example, in junior and senior high schools with 50-minute, six-period days, teachers often view students as "cases" rather than persons. This impersonality is one way teachers protect themselves from the unrelenting pace of being forced to batch-process students.

Forming "natural work units" has some interesting implications for supervision and teaching. The intent of this approach is to increase sense of ownership and continuing responsibility for identifiable aspects of the work. The self-contained elementary school classroom comes closer to this concept than does the departmentalized and quick-moving secondary teaching schedule. But even in the elementary school setting the building of teaching teams that plan and work together and whose members share a common responsibility for students is often lacking.

"Vertical loading" refers to the development of strategies that combine teaching and planning. Providing teachers with more control over schedules, work methods, evaluation, and even the training of less experienced teachers is an example of vertical loading. Giving teachers some budgetary control that allows them discretion in allocating available funds is another example.

"Opening feedback channels" describes what happens when supervisors motivate teachers not only by letting them know how well they are doing but also by promoting working relationships and arrangements that help teachers get feedback from each other. Teacher-evaluation strategies that are designed to provide teachers with formative feedback can be helpful. Clinical supervision, peer supervision, target setting, and other approaches with similar formats are examples. However, although providing teachers with feedback is important, it is best to create ways in which feedback occurs naturally from teachers' day-to-day activities and from working closely with colleagues.

Since virtually every decision supervisors make about school and classroom organization, curriculum development and implementation, materials selection, and teaching itself has implications for job enrichment, every decision has implications as well for either enhancing or diminishing motivation and commitment levels of teachers.

WHAT IS GOOD GETS DONE

Supervision I is based on the assumption that people are by their nature selfish. It is thought that for teachers the guiding motivational force is a desire to maximize self-interest by continually calculating the costs and benefits of options, choosing those that either make them winners or keep them from losing. Supervision I also is based on the assumption that people act rationally, seeking the most efficient means to their goals. They are capable of cold calculation and thus their emotions do not count. Finally, people make decisions as isolated individuals. Each person "keeps score" separate from others. Connections to other people and particularly the social bonds that emerge from such connections do not count very much.

Amitai Etzioni challenges the motivational assumptions of Supervision I by asking this question:

> Are men and women akin to single minded, "cold" calculators, each out to "maximize" his or her well being? Are human beings able to figure out rationally the most efficient way to realize their goals? Is society mainly a marketplace, in which self-serving individuals compete with one another—at work, in politics, and in courtship . . . enhancing the general welfare in the process? Or do we typically seek to do both what is right *and* what is pleasurable, and find ourselves frequently in conflict when moral values and happiness are incompatible?[22]

Etzioni acknowledges the importance of self-interest but suggests that people are perfectly capable of sacrificing self-interest and indeed regularly sacrifice self-interest for other interests. He provides compelling evidence that people are just as likely, if not more likely, to be motivated by what they think is right and good, by obligations they feel, and by the norms and values they consider important and just. Most supervisors agree with Etzioni when it comes to describing themselves. For example, supervisors put in demanding hours at work, often putting the job "ahead" of leisure time and family matters. Etzioni believes that the capacity to sacrifice self-interest is not limited to supervisors but is wide-

---

[22]Amitai Etzioni, *The Moral Dimension Toward a New Economics.* New York: Free Press, 1988, p. ix.

spread. There is no reason to believe, in other words, that parents and teachers, cafeteria workers, and custodians are less likely than supervisors to sacrifice their self-interest for the common good.

The belief that teachers are rational and cold calculators who are routinely capable of controlling their emotions, biases, and preferences by putting reason and logic first is also suspect. Anyone who has bought a new car understands this. Despite the best rational planning to ensure that the car chosen is both practical and within budget, in the end most people are swayed by less objective factors. Having completed the purchase, they desperately attempt to rationalize buying that "spiffy two-door with the small trunk." People strive to appear rational in an effort to cover up the fact that they are not.

Etzioni challenges as well the idea that people make decisions as isolated individuals. He provides compelling evidence that "social collectivities (such as ethnic and racial groups, peer groups at work, and neighborhood groups) are the prime decisionmaking units.[23] He acknowledges that individual decision making exists but it typically reflects collective attributes and processes, having been made within the context created by one's memberships in various groups. For teachers, membership in the profession of teaching and membership in the school as community provide the kind of collective attributes that hinder individual decision making. For example, a teacher may want to take a teaching shortcut but feels compelled to do otherwise by group norms or by having been socialized in what it means to be a teacher. Or equally likely, a teacher who wants to stay after school to help students decides otherwise as a result of pressure from other teachers who have implicitly agreed that everyone should leave early. Connections are so important and the process of socialization as a result of memberships is so complete that the concept of individual decision maker appears to be more myth than reality.

The literature on community building in schools discussed in chapters 4 and 5 points also to the primacy of morality, emotions, and social bonds in motivating teachers *and* students. In communities members are bonded together in special ways because they are together bound to shared ideas and ideals that represent moral commitments. At root in an authentic community is a community of mind that speaks to members in a moral voice, a voice that lays claim on them. This claim is understood as an obligation that must be met. Motivation, under these circumstances, is neither rules-based nor rewards-based but norms-based.

Motivation in Supervision I and in Supervision II differs because of the importance the latter gives to morality, emotions, and social bonds. These differences are summarized in Table 12–1. In Supervision II, teachers regularly pass moral judgments over their urges, routinely sacrificing self-interest and pleasure for other reasons. Furthermore, actions and decisions that teachers make are influenced by what they value and believe as well as by self-interest, and when the two are in conflict it is the former that typically takes precedence over the

---

[23]Ibid., p. 4.

TABLE 12–1
MORALITY, EMOTION, AND SOCIAL BONDS IN SUPERVISIONS I AND II

Supervision I	Supervision II
Morality	**Morality**
Self-interest is the driving force. People seek to maximize their gains and cut their losses. Morality is defined in terms of self-interest.	People pass moral judgments over their urges and as a result often sacrifice self-interest for other causes and reasons.
Emotions	**Emotions**
People rationally seek the most efficient means to their goals. Emotions don't count.	People choose largely on the basis of preference and emotions.
Social bonds	**Social bonds**
People are isolated individuals who reason and calculate individually, thus making decisions on their own. Social bonds don't count.	People are members of groups, and the social bonds that emerge from this membership shape their individual decisions.

latter. Presently teachers represent an underutilized resource. They will remain underutilized as long as "What gets rewarded gets done" dominates the motivational scene by continuing to be the prime basis for supervisory practice. Teachers deserve more than this and schools need more than this. Changing supervision practices in a way that acknowledges the importance of "What is rewarding gets done" and "What is good gets done," we believe, is a step in the right direction.

CHAPTER 13

CLASSROOM SUPERVISION AND TEACHER EVALUATION

TOO often teacher evaluation means the rating, grading, and classifying of teachers using some locally standardized instrument as a yardstick. Generally the instrument lists traits of teachers assumed to be important, such as "The teacher has a pleasant voice," and certain tasks of teaching considered to be critical, such as "The teacher plans well." The evaluator usually writes in comments as, increasingly, does the teacher.

This evaluation instrument is filled out after a classroom observation of the teacher, often lasting from a half hour to one hour. The observation visit is usually preceded by a conference, which varies from a brief encounter to a session where lesson plans, objectives, and teaching strategies are discussed. Sometimes a postobservation conference follows, wherein comments and ratings are discussed and negotiated. Usually, the teacher-evaluation procedure is concluded when both parties sign the instrument. The instrument is then forwarded to the district archives. This teacher-evaluation procedure may occur once or twice a year for the tenured teacher and two to four times a year for novices. Many teachers report having been observed in the classroom only a handful of times, and some report almost never being observed after achieving tenure.

In an effort to correct this problem, some states have passed laws that require a much more intensive evaluation, often using state-provided standardized instruments. The instruments are comprised of teaching behaviors claimed to be linked to the "teaching effectiveness" research or to other models of effective

se of this link to research, the instruments are considered to be "objective." As we point out later, the systems turn out to be nei-nor objective and the teaching-effectiveness research upon which be based is often misrepresented.

ge neither teachers nor administrators and supervisors are satisfied with pr. t procedures. More damaging, many supervisors privately view the procedures as lacking in credibility. What are the likely effects of participating in a system characterized by such doubts? The system takes on a certain artificial or mechanical quality, a routine functioning that becomes an end in itself.

Some schools practice classroom supervision by remote control. This scientific-management view assumes that if the focus is on educational program administration and supervision through development of a materials-intensive curriculum, usually linked to a detailed curriculum syllabus or detailed predetermined objectives, then teachers can be supervised from a distance. Teaching behavior becomes more predictable and reliable as teaching objectives and materials become more detailed, structured, and standardized. Thus, what teachers do is controlled by governing the objectives they pursue, the materials they use, the curricula they follow, the assignments and tests they give, and the schedules they follow. Alternatively, teachers might be free to make curricular and teaching decisions but are held accountable for the scores of their students on standardized criterion reference tests. In this scheme they wind up making predictable decisions about curricula and teaching that are aligned with test objectives. The testing program itself becomes a system of supervision that winds up controlling teachers.

Seeking to control classroom practices by remote control raises nagging questions. How can supervisors be sure that teachers are indeed performing prescribed duties up to standard? What evaluation technologies can be used to answer this question? The problem is that technologies of classroom observation and evaluation are too often shrouded in scientism not found even in the more legitimate sciences. Yet most teachers and supervisors privately believe that *teaching is far more an artistic enterprise than a scientific one.*

In the next several chapters we propose artistic and reflective approaches to supervision and evaluation that are more consistent with how teachers think and what they do and with the complexities involved in the work of teaching and learning. Basic to the discussion is the view that supervision should be less connected to roles. It should be a process and sometimes a set of skills available to teachers and principals alike. Indeed, the future we advocate is a supervision based less and less on bureaucratic authority and more and more on professional and moral authority—a supervision firmly in the hands of both teachers and principals and sensitive to the needs of the local school community.

The discussion begins by examining some critical issues that will affect how supervision is received and practiced. Among them are how to avoid a rational bias, how to differentiate between measurement and evaluation, how to ensure comprehensiveness, and how to measure up to standards of credibility.

AVOIDING A RATIONAL BIAS

Practices of classroom supervision and evaluation need to reflect the realities of our human nature and the realities of teaching. This may seem like an obvious thought, but these realities are typically overlooked. Instead of being sensitive to human nature and teaching, classroom supervision and evaluation typically plays to images of scientism. Many educators, for example, dream of building a body of knowledge, a method of inquiry, and patterns of practice that will provide the basis for a true profession of teaching and clinically oriented supervision comparable with that of architecture and medicine or perhaps the performing arts professions.[1] We believe that it is possible for supervision and teaching to become established and recognized fields of inquiry and professional practice. The question is: Are educators going about this process the right way? Presently, theorizing and model building is patterned too closely after the physical sciences. Unfortunately, this patterning is simplistic. The problems addressed, the theorizing, how research is conducted, the conclusions drawn, and the building of practice models based on this inquiry are not sufficiently complex or comprehensive to be considered scientific by the established scientific community. Nor do they meet the standards of scientific and professional rigor that characterize the established professions. Persistence in spite of these obstacles leads to the development of *rationalistic* theories and practices.

According to Terry Winograd and Fernando Flores, "The rationalistic tradition is distinguished by its narrow focus on certain aspects of rationality which . . . often leads to attitudes and activities that are not rational in a broader perspective.[2] Further, as the philosopher Charles Taylor suggests, rationalistic theories and models are typically implausible given the realities of practice and tend to lead to bad science by being either wordy elaborations of the obvious or by dealing with trivial questions.[3] Stated in our context, rationalistic theories and models do not fit the real world of teaching and supervision. When such models are used anyway, teaching typically suffers and teachers and supervisors experience frustration, combined with a loss of confidence in what sound theory and research can provide.

[1]For a more in-depth analysis of the point of view provided in the chapter see Thomas J. Sergiovanni, "Expanding Conceptions of Inquiry and Practice in Supervision and Evaluation," *Educational Evaluation and Policy Analysis*, vol. 6, no. 3 (1984), pp. 355–363; "Landscapes, Mindscapes and Reflective Practice in Supervision," *Journal of Curriculum and Supervision*, vol. 1, no. 1 (1985), pp. 5–17; "Understanding Reflective Practice," *Journal of Curriculum and Supervision*, vol. 6, no. 4 (1986), pp. 355–363; "The Metaphorical Use of Theories and Models in Supervision: Building a Science," *Journal of Curriculum and Supervision*, vol. 2, no. 3 (1987), pp. 221–232; "We Need a TRUE Profession!" *Educational Leadership*, vol. 44, no. 8, 1987; and "Science and Scientism in Supervision and Teaching," *Journal of Curriculum and Supervision*, vol. 4, no. 2 (1989), pp. 93–102.

[2]Terry Winograd and Fernando Flores, *Understanding Computers and Cognition*. Norwood, N.J.: Ablex, 1986, p. 8.

[3]Charles Taylor, *Philosophy and the Human Sciences Philosophical Papers*, vol. 2. London: Cambridge University Press, 1985.

Building generic models of teaching and supervisory practice based on the "process-product teaching-effectiveness" research is an example of rationalistic rather than rational thinking. This research reveals that the explicit or direct teaching model is an effective way to teach basic reading and computational skills and simple subject-matter mastery to elementary school children. Assuming that this method represents "effective teaching" and thus prescribing this teaching as a means by which all learning should take place is hardly a rational approach to model building and to teaching practice. Yet consultants, workshop specialists, contributors to widely circulated professional publications, and others have been quite successful in convincing many policymakers and professionals that explicit teaching is indeed the same as effective teaching. One popular example at this writing is the adoption by school districts and in some cases by entire states of teacher-evaluation checklists and other instruments composed of items primarily or exclusively based on this research. This results in uniform use of an instrument that might be appropriate for a limited range of teaching and learning outcomes but is invalid for other teaching and learning outcomes.

Whether we are talking about the process-product teaching-effectiveness research or some other body of scientific knowledge, the indicators of effectiveness commonly cited are an artifact of how the researchers decided to define effectiveness. Had they defined effectiveness differently, different indicators would have been discovered. The indicators, therefore, are not entirely independent or objective but a function of human decisions. Imagine what the consequences of redefining effectiveness would be in schools and indeed states that use evaluation instruments based on the original teaching-effectiveness research? Since the instrument behaviors would no longer be "valid," teachers thought to be "winners" might well be "losers" and vice versa. Winning and losing in teacher evaluation is never entirely objective but always in part an artifact of the evaluation system used.

What changes are needed in the ways in which educators think about, inquire, and practice if teaching and supervision are to become less rationalistic and more rational? First, mindscapes of how schools work and how life in classrooms unfolds need to change. Mindscapes help people construct their reality. Different realities lead to different supervisory and teaching practices. Teaching, for example, is often thought of as a tightly connected process that resembles the throwing of teaching pitches into a learning outcome zone. There is always the danger that some pitches will miss the zone and thus be declared balls. Therefore, supervision, within this mindscape, focuses on increasing the likelihood of teaching strikes being thrown. The emphasis is on programming and monitoring the practice of teaching to ensure that the process unfolds in a reliable and predictable manner. The problem with this mindscape is that it does not reflect the realities of practice, provides a limited and unsophisticated view of the nature of teaching and learning, and offers a regressive view of the role of the teacher.

PATTERNED RATIONALITY

When teaching is conceived as pitching, detailed goals and objectives are considered critical. But teachers typically do not think and act in accord with discrete goals and objectives as much as they do in value patterns. Reading teachers, for example, are as concerned with the students' ability to synthesize and extend as they are with the mastery of reading fundamentals. They recognize that both goals need to be pursued in a manner that makes the experience of reading a joyful activity. But the three goals are often in competition. Too much emphasis on one can negatively affect each of the other two. The issue for the teacher is how to achieve a balance between and among competing values; the rationality that is appropriate is not linear or bureaucratic but pursues a pattern of outcomes. Some experts refer to this as *patterned rationality.*[4] Since teachers are concerned with outcomes that produce a sensible pattern, it is difficult to ask them to think specifically in terms of this outcome or that or even several outcomes discretely.

The surfing metaphor is much more descriptive of how teachers think and act. Teachers ride the wave of the teaching pattern as it uncurls. In riding the wave, they use various models of teaching and learning not rationalistically to prescribe practice but rationally to inform intuition and enhance professional judgment. A rational science of supervision and teaching places more emphasis on developing strategies that reflect a higher concern for values than goals, for patterns than discrete outcomes, and for learning how to ride the pattern of the wave of teaching.

Craft knowledge reveals that when teachers do think about goals and objectives, they're just as likely to think about discovering them in the act of teaching as they are in setting them beforehand. Teachers adopt a more strategic than tactical view of goals and objectives. When "surfing," they gear their practice toward broad and often changing goals and rely heavily on assessing what was worthwhile after learning encounters have been concluded. Teachers are not likely to declare that something worthwhile did not count simply because they did not anticipate it beforehand. This reality is not sufficiently accounted for in rationalistic models of teaching and supervision.

CONFUSING EVALUATION AND MEASUREMENT

Rationalistic thinking is encouraged by the confusion that exists between measurement and evaluation. For example, much of what passes as evaluation isn't evaluation at all but measurement. Suppose you are interested in buying blinds for a window in your home. You would first need to know the size of the window. The window is 22 inches wide by 60 inches long. This set of figures is now your

---

[4]Jean Hills, "The Preparation of Educational Leaders: What's Needed and What's Next?" UCEA Occasional Paper 8303, Columbus, Ohio: University Council for Educational Administration, 1982.

standard. You find some extra blinds in the attic. Using a ruler, you carefully measure the blinds and learn that none "measures up" to your standard. Though you had a role to play in this process it was really the ruler that counted. Someone else using the same ruler would very likely have reached the same conclusion.

Though measurements need to be accurate and some skill is involved in the process, the standard against which measurements are weighed and the measuring device are more important than the person doing the measuring. Ideally, measurement should be "person-proof" in the sense that each person measuring should reach the same conclusion. Interrater reliability is highly valued. Thus in measurement-oriented evaluation systems the role of the evaluator is *diminished*. Principals and supervisors are *less important* than the instruments and procedures they use. Further, when a measurement-oriented evaluation system is imported to a school or state, principals, supervisors, teachers, and the public forfeit the right to decide for themselves what is good teaching—what is the kind of teaching that makes sense to them given their goals, aspirations, the characteristics of their community, and so forth. Measurement-oriented evaluation systems, therefore, not only frequently result in rationalistic practices; they can threaten one of the fundamental values undergirding schooling in America—the right to choose.

Evaluation, by contrast, is a distinctly human process that involves discernment and making informed judgments. Evaluation is never value-free or context-free. In our example above, having decided on the size of blinds needed, all subsequent decisions are a matter of preference, taste, and purpose. What effect do you want to create in the room you are decorating? Do you prefer wooden or metal blinds, a soft or bold look, warm or cool colors? How will the available options fit into the broader decorating scheme of the room? In matters of evaluation "interrater reliability" is not highly valued. Instead the evaluator's judgment given desired effects is what counts. Evaluation is a distinctly human rather than mechanical process.

ISSUES OF COMPREHENSIVENESS

A good supervisory and evaluation system is one that is sufficiently comprehensive to serve a variety of purposes. As suggested earlier, the typical system now in place in most schools is measurement-oriented, seeking to establish the extent to which each teacher measures up to some preexisting standard. This standard is presumed to represent some minimum level of basic competence in teaching and is presumed to provide a yardstick for comparing one teacher or group of teachers to others who are being held to the same standard.

This *standards-referenced teacher evaluation* may have an important role to play in school district evaluation systems, but it is always a limited one.[5] For legal and

---

[5]The discussion of standards-referenced, criterion-referenced, and personally referenced teacher evaluation approaches parallels Elliot Eisner's discussion of norm-, criterion-, and personally refer-

other reasons school districts use standards-referenced teacher evaluation to establish for the record that teachers have met minimum requirements. But once teachers have proved themselves by passing this test, it no longer makes sense to continue to require them to pass the test again and again, year after year. Repeated use of standards-referenced teacher evaluation for the same people not only is a poor use of supervisory time, but also focuses the evaluation on minimum rather than on discovery, experimentation, and growth. Further, continued use makes evaluation ritualistic rather than something that teachers consider meaningful and useful.

Standards-referenced teacher evaluation is typically conducted using an instrument that records the presence or absence of teaching behaviors and teaching characteristics. The instrument is designed to track whether teachers are following accepted basic protocols. Reliability is very important to the success of standards-referenced teacher evaluation. Each evaluation should be duplicated exactly by another evaluator. To achieve this reliability, architects of standards-referenced teacher evaluation systems work hard to rule out judgments of goodness. Recording the presence or absence of behaviors, characteristics, or protocols, for example, requires little judgment. It is a measurement task rather than an evaluation one. Ideally, standards-referenced teacher evaluation should be "supervisor-proof."

In a comprehensive supervisory and evaluation system the emphasis should be on two other types of evaluation: *criterion-referenced teacher evaluation* and *personally referenced teacher evaluation.*[6] Criterion-referenced teacher evaluation seeks to establish the extent to which a teacher's practice embodies certain goals and purposes and values considered important to the school. Assuming that the following questions reflect a particular school's shared purposes and values, such an evaluation might ask: Does the teacher provide a classroom climate that encourages openness and inquiry? Do teachers accept students without question as individuals? Do teachers teach for understanding? Are students enrolled as "workers" and teachers as facilitators or managers of the teaching and learning environment? Do students have responsibility for setting learning goals and deciding on learning strategies? Is cooperation emphasized over competition? Is diversity respected? Different values lead to different norms, and different norms lead to different questions for guiding the evaluation.

Criterion-referenced evaluation is in many respects a form of inquiry that is constructed around the issues deemed important by teacher and supervisor. For this reason evaluation extends throughout the teacher's career. As time goes on the nature of the questions that guide the evaluation should evolve from Does

---

enced student evaluation. See Elliot W. Eisner, *The Enlightened Eye: Qualitative Inquiry and the Enhancement of Educational Practice,* New York: Macmillan, 1991, pp. 101–103.

[6]See, for example, ibid., p. 102, for a discussion of these concepts as applied to student evaluation.

the teacher's practice reflect a given value? to Are there better ways to do it? and What is the worth of the value in the first place? Criterion-referenced teacher evaluation does not lend itself to instruments very well. Other forms of supervision such as clinical supervision, peer supervision, action research, and portfolio development are better options.

Personally referenced teacher evaluation emphasizes the teacher's personal goals and comparisons between past and present performance given these goals. No external standards or norms are used to fix baselines for making such comparisons. Instead the purpose of personally referenced teacher evaluation is to help teachers understand and critically appraise their practice in light of their preferences, purposes, and beliefs. Personally referenced teacher evaluation also helps teachers to gauge the progress they are making in achieving their goals.

ISSUES OF CREDIBILITY

Credibility is an important issue in teacher evaluation, particularly if the evaluator goes beyond description to interpretation, identification of themes, and appraisal of worth. In using case study methods to develop portraits of classrooms that lend themselves to evaluation, Elliot Eisner identifies three standards of credibility: structural collaboration, consensual validation, and referential adequacy.[7] The three sources of credibility apply as well to the evaluation of teaching.

The collaboration standard asks if multiple sources of information are used in providing descriptions, forming judgments, and reaching conclusions about a particular teacher's teaching. Is classroom observation backed up with other sources of information? Such sources might include interviews with teachers, examples of student work, photo essays, data descriptions of teacher-student interaction patterns, movement flowcharts, case studies of students, an analysis of books read by students, student performance exhibits, a folio of tests, and homework assignments and other assignments given by the teacher. In supplying multiple sources of information about his or her teaching, the teacher must become a partner in the process. The teacher, after all, is in the best position to decide what sources of evidence are most appropriate to the particular form of evaluation.

The consensus standard seeks agreement among competent others that sources of evaluation information make sense, that descriptions are sound, that interpretations are compelling, and that the conclusions drawn are plausible. The key partners to any agreement are, again, the teacher whose work is the focus of the evaluation and the person or persons (principal, other teachers, teams of teachers) assuming the supervisory role. Failing agreement at this level, third-party agreement may be necessary if conclusions need to be reached to resolve certain personnel matters such as retention or tenure. The consensus standard

---

[7]Ibid., pp. 110–114. See also Elliot W. Eisner, *The Educational Imagination,* 2d ed. New York: Macmillan, 1985.

should not be confused with interrater reliability as understood in standards-referenced evaluation. The consensus standard seeks more holistic agreement about the adequacy of the evaluation process itself and about what it means for the teacher in question. For less contentious evaluation, all that is needed is a serious study of the evidence and the rendering of an opinion backed up by a simple statement of a paragraph or two. The art, drama, or film critic might serve as a helpful metaphor: The critic rates the subject and then provides a vivid assessment of that subject to validate that rating.

When teacher and supervisor disagree and the consequences for employment or reputation or both are significant, the consensus standard may require two or more independent evaluations complete with detailed writeups in the form of case studies. The studies are then compared. Each critic's opinion is considered, and the reasoning provided is assessed. The specifics of the case studies, the evidence gathered, the interpretations made, and other details need not overlap. In fact, they can be quite different. But for consensus to be judged to exist the evidence needs to lead to the same conclusion. If consensus is not reached, a further step may be necessary. Different critics may be focusing on different aspects of the teacher studied and may bring different perspectives that lead to different conclusions. For this reason, evaluators or critics need to be brought together in conversation to discuss this possibility. If, as may happen in rare instances, differences cannot be reconciled by negotiation, the evaluation may have to be invalidated and the process repeated with different evaluators.

The standard of referential adequacy can be met by examining the nature of the evaluation writeup itself. In assessing referential adequacy, Eisner asks if the description of events is rich enough and detailed enough so that others are able to see things and understand things that would be missed without the benefit of the writeup. According to Eisner, an evaluation writeup "is referentially adequate to the extent to which a reader is able to locate in its subject matter the qualities the critic addresses and the meanings he or she ascribed to them."[8] The evaluation, in other words, speaks for itself.

THE FOCUS OF CLINICAL SUPERVISION

In the interest of focusing attention on classroom supervision, some experts distinguish between classroom supervision and out-of-class supervision, with the former being clinical and the latter general. Morris Cogan, for example, cites two purposes of clinical supervision in his popular book entitled *Clinical Supervision:* "The first is to develop and explicate a system of in-class supervision that, in competent hands, will prove powerful enough to give supervisors a reasonable hope of accomplishing significant improvements in the teacher's classroom instruction. The second purpose is to help correct the neglect of in-class or clinical su-

[8]Ibid., p. 114.

pervision and to establish it as a necessary complement to out-of-class ('general') supervision."[9]

In a similar vein, Robert Goldhammer refers to clinical supervision as follows:

> First of all, I mean to convey an image of face-to-face relationships between supervisors and teachers. History provides the principal reason for this emphasis, namely, that in many situations presently and during various periods in its development, supervision has been conducted as supervision from a distance, as, for example, supervision of curriculum development or of instructional policies framed by committees of teachers. "Clinical" supervision is meant to imply supervision up close.[10]

General and clinical supervision are, of course, interdependent. Meaningful classroom interventions are built upon healthy organizational climates, facilitated by credible leadership, and premised on a reasoned educational program. Although general supervision is an important and necessary component of effective supervision, without clinical supervision it is not sufficient.

Clinical supervision refers to face-to-face contact with teachers with the intent of improving instruction and increasing professional growth. In many respects, a one-to-one correspondence exists between improving classroom instruction and increasing professional growth, and for this reason staff development and clinical supervision are inseparable concepts and activities. How does evaluation fit into this picture? Evaluation is a natural part of one's professional life and occurs continuously. Every decision that teachers, administrators, and supervisors make is preceded by evaluation (often implicit) of some sort. Evaluation is valuing, and valuing is judging. These are natural events in the lives of educational professionals and, of course, are critical aspects of clinical supervision and staff development.

SUPERVISORY PURPOSES

Evaluation can have a number of focuses, some of which are more compatible with events, purposes, and characteristics of supervision than others. Evaluation experts, for example, make an important distinction between *formative* and *summative* evaluation.[11] Teacher-evaluation procedures typically found in school can be classified as summative. Evaluation that emphasizes ongoing growth and development would be considered formative. Consider the following distinctions:

1 Summative evaluation of teachers has a certain finality to it—it is terminal in the sense that it occurs at the conclusion of an educational activity.

---

[9]Morris L. Cogan, *Clinical Supervision.* Boston: Houghton Mifflin, 1973, p. xi.

[10]Robert Goldhammer, *Clinical Supervision: Special Methods for the Supervision of Teachers.* New York: Holt, 1969, p. 54.

[11]Michael Scriven, "The Methodology of Evaluation," in Robert Stake (ed.), *AERA Monograph on Curriculum Evaluation,* no. 1. Chicago: Rand McNally, 1965. See also Benjamin Bloom, Thomas Hastings, and G. F. Madaus, *Handbook on Formative and Summative Evaluation of Student Learning.* New York: McGraw-Hill, 1971.

In evaluating a teacher's performance, summative evaluation suggests a statement of worth. A judgment is made about the quality of one's teaching.

2 Summative evaluation is a legitimate and important activity that, if done carefully, can play a constructive role in a school's total evaluation strategy.

3 Formative evaluation of teachers is intended to increase the effectiveness of ongoing educational programs and activity. Evaluation information is collected and used to understand, correct, and improve ongoing activity.

4 With respect to teaching, formative evaluation is concerned less with judging and rating the teacher than with providing information which helps improve teacher performance.

5 In the strictest sense formative and summative evaluation cannot be separated, for each contains aspects of the other, but it is useful nevertheless to speak of a formative focus and a summative focus to evaluation.[12]

The focus of clinical supervision should be on formative evaluation. The supervisor is first and foremost interested in improving teaching and increasing teachers' personal development. Does this emphasis conflict with demands that teachers be held accountable for their actions? We think not. A formative evaluation emphasis is entirely consistent with holding teachers accountable in a professional, not bureaucratic, sense. Professional accountability is growth-oriented and implies a commitment to consistent improvement. Bureaucratic accountability is not growth-oriented at all but merely seeks to ensure that teachers measure up to some predetermined standard.

From time to time supervisors will indeed be engaged in a more summatively focused evaluation. Though the supervisor's major commitment is to formative evaluation, occasional problems occur and incompetent teachers or teachers whose philosophy and orientation differ markedly from that of the school will be discovered. As a result, withholding tenure or dismissal of a tenured teacher may well be considered. Personnel actions of this sort are so intertwined with existing local administrative policies and state statutory restrictions and requirements that a totally different mind-set is needed. Such a procedure is best placed in the hands of a line administrative officer of the district. In the case of a principal who assumes both supervisory and administrative roles, the teacher should be informed of the focus and the tone of the evaluation procedure that is to follow. The school attorney would most likely be consulted regarding due process if administrative guidelines on this question are wanting. In Toledo and other school districts the teachers' union is involved in the process, working cooperatively with "management" to ensure due process on the one hand and *warranted* dismissal on the other. Many state education agencies and state school

---

[12]Thomas J. Sergiovanni, *Handbook for Effective Department Leadership Concepts and Practices in Today's Secondary Schools.* Boston: Allyn & Bacon, 1977, p. 372.

board associations publish pamphlets and other guidelines on this controversial and increasingly legalistic problem.

Practically speaking, improving classroom instruction must start with the teacher. Sustained changes in teacher behavior and sustained improvements in classroom functioning occur when teachers are committed to these changes. That being the case, supervisors are forced to depend upon the cooperation of teachers. Indeed, supervisors rarely change teachers but help them to change, a condition more suited to formative evaluation.

Different teacher-evaluation purposes require different teacher-evaluation standards, criteria, and practices. When the purpose is quality control to ensure that teachers measure up, standards, criteria, expectations, and procedures should take one form. When the purpose is professional improvement to help increase teachers' understanding and enhance teaching practice, standards, criteria, expectations, and procedures should take a different form. In an evaluation for quality control the process should be formal and documented; criteria should be explicit and standards should be uniform for all teachers; criteria should be legally defensible as being central to basic teaching competence; the emphasis should be on teachers meeting requirements of minimum acceptability; and responsibility for evaluation should be in the hands of administrators and other designated officials. When the purpose of teacher evaluation is professional improvement, the process should be informal; criteria should be tailored to the needs and capabilities of individual teachers; criteria should be considered to be appropriate and useful to teachers before they are included in the evaluation; the emphasis should be on helping teachers reach agreed-upon professional development goals; and teachers should assume major responsibility for the process by engaging in self-evaluation and collegial evaluation, and by obtaining evaluation information from students.

The outcome of evaluation for quality control should be the protection of students and the public from incompetent teaching. Unquestionably this is an important outcome and a highly significant responsibility for principals and other supervisors, as well as teachers. The outcome of evaluation for professional improvement is quite different. Rather than ensuring minimum acceptability in teaching, professional improvement guarantees quality teaching and schooling for the students and the public.

The 80/20 quality rule spells out quite clearly what the balance of emphasis should be as schools, school districts, and states engage in teacher evaluation. *When more than 20 percent of supervisory time and money is expended in evaluation for quality control or less than 80 percent of supervisory time and money is spent in professional improvement, quality schooling suffers.* The 80/20 quality rule provides a framework for those responsible for evaluation of teachers to evaluate whether their efforts are indeed directed toward quality schooling. In making this assessment, less attention should be given to the rhetoric (what those responsible for teacher evaluation say their purposes are) and more to the standards and procedures that are used. The standards and procedures associated with each of the two purposes of evaluation are outlined in Table 13–1. For example, if the stan-

TABLE 13–1
DIFFERENT PURPOSES, DIFFERENT STANDARDS FOR EVALUATION

Purposes	
Quality control (ensuring that teachers meet acceptable levels of performance)	Professional improvement (increasing understanding of teaching and enhancing practice)

Standards	
The process is formal and documented.	The process is informal.
Criteria are explicit, standard, and uniform for all teachers.	Criteria are tailored to needs and capabilities of individual teachers.
Criteria are legally defensible as being central to basic teaching competence.	Criteria are considered appropriate and useful to teachers.
Emphasis is on meeting minimum requirements of acceptability.	Emphasis is on helping teachers reach agreed-upon professional development goals.
Evaluation by administrators and other designated officials counts the most.	Self-evaluation, collegial evaluation, and evaluation information for students count the most.

Outcome	
Protects students and the public from incompetent teaching.	Guarantees quality teaching and schooling for students and the public.

The 80/20 Quality Rule: When more than 20 percent of supervisory time and money is expended in evaluation for quality control *or* less than 80 percent of supervisory time and money is expended in professional improvement, quality schooling suffers.

dards in the left-hand column are emphasized, quality control is the purpose of the evaluation regardless of what is said about the purposes.

CLINICAL SUPERVISION IN PRACTICE

Emerging from the real world of professional practice, clinical supervision evolved from a series of problems faced by supervisors as they worked with teachers and would-be teachers. The essential ingredients of clinical supervision include the establishment of a healthy general supervisory climate, a mutual support system called "colleagueship," and a cycle of supervision comprising conferences, observation of teachers at work, and pattern analysis.

Clinical supervision is based on a number of assumptions that differ from those of traditional rating and evaluating and prescribes a pattern of action that departs substantially from present practice. In clinical supervision it is assumed that the school curriculum is, in reality, what teachers do day by day, that changes in curriculum and in teaching formats require changes in how teachers think about and understand their teaching and how they behave in classrooms; that supervision is a process for which both supervisors and teachers are responsible; that the focus of supervision is on teacher strengths; that given the right conditions teachers are willing and able to improve; that teachers have large reservoirs of talent, often unused; and that teachers derive satisfaction from challenging work.

Clinical supervision is a partnership in inquiry. The person assuming the role of supervisor functions more as an individual with experience and insight (or, in the case of equals, with a better vantage point in analyzing another colleague's teaching) than as an expert who determines what is right and wrong. The issue of authority is very important in the process. The clinical supervisor derives his or her authority from being able to collect and provide information desired by the teacher and from being able to help the teacher to use this information in the most effective way. This authority is functional, as compared with formal authority derived from one's hierarchical position. Functional authority is associated with higher levels of teacher satisfaction and performance.

The purpose of clinical supervision is to help teachers to modify existing patterns of teaching in ways that make sense to them. Evaluation is, therefore, responsive to the needs and desires of the teacher. It is the teacher who decides the course of a clinical and supervisory cycle, the issues to be discussed, and for what purpose. Obviously, those who serve as clinical supervisors will bring to this interaction a considerable amount of influence; but, ideally, this influence should stem from their being in a position to provide the help and clarification needed by teachers. The supervisor's job, therefore, is to help the teacher select goals to be improved and teaching issues to be illuminated, and to understand better his or her practice. This emphasis on understanding provides the avenue by which more technical assistance can be given to the teacher; thus, clinical supervision involves the systematic analysis of classroom events.

Clinical supervision typically is viewed as an overall pattern of working with teachers that can take a number of forms and follow a number of paths. Consistency is needed, of course, at the strategy level where assumptions and the overall framework come into play. But diversity is needed in developing operational tactics if clinical supervision is to accommodate itself to the array of needs of supervisors and teachers and to the particular characteristics of teaching situations. Clinical supervision, therefore, is basically a design for working with teachers within which a number of technologies, perspectives, and approaches can be used.

THE CYCLE OF CLINICAL SUPERVISION

In a few pages we are not able to provide all the techniques associated with clinical supervision. Competency will come with practice as supervisors team together in learning the skills of clinical supervision. The intent here is to describe the cycle of supervision, to provide some basic principles and concepts underlying clinical supervisory practice, and to suggest some techniques and tools that supervisors might find useful as they begin to develop competencies as clinical supervisors.

Cogan identifies eight phases in the cycle of supervision.[13]

1 *Phase 1 requires establishing the teacher-supervisor relationship.* This first phase is of particular importance, for upon its success rests the whole concept of clinical supervision. Teachers are suspicious of evaluation in general, and the intense sort of supervision prescribed by Cogan can be even more alarming. Furthermore, the success of clinical supervision requires that teachers share with supervisors responsibility for all steps and activities. The supervisor has two tasks in phase 1: building a relationship based on mutual trust and support and inducting the teacher into the role of cosupervisor. Cogan believes that both tasks should be well advanced before the supervisor enters the teacher's classroom to observe teaching. Phase 1 establishes the colleagueship relationships deemed critically important by Cogan.

2 *Phase 2 requires intensive planning of lessons and units with the teacher.* In phase 2 teacher and supervisor plan, together, a lesson, a series of lessons, or a unit. Planning includes estimates of objectives or outcomes, subject-matter concepts, teaching strategies, materials to be used, learning contexts, anticipated problems, and provisions for feedback and evaluation.

3 *Phase 3 requires planning of the classroom observation strategy by teacher and supervisor.* Together teacher and supervisor plan and discuss the kind and amount of information to be gathered during the observation period and the methods to be used to gather this information.

4 *Phase 4 requires the supervisor to observe in-class instruction.* Cogan emphasizes that only after careful establishment of the supervisory relationship and the subsequent planning of both the lesson or unit and the observation strategy does the observation take place.

5 *Phase 5 requires careful analysis of the teaching-learning process,* As cosupervisors, teachers, and supervisors analyze the events of the class. They may work separately at first or together from the beginning. Outcomes of the analysis are identification of patterns of teacher behavior that exist over time and critical incidents that occurred that seemed to affect classroom activity, and extensive descriptions of teacher behavior and evidence of that behavior. It is believed that teachers have established persistent patterns of teaching that are evidenced and can be identified as a pattern after several carefully documented observations and analysis.

6 *Phase 6 requires planning the conference strategy.* Supervisors prepare for the conference by setting tentative objectives and planning tentative processes, but in a manner that does not program the course of the conference too much. They plan also the physical settings and arrange for materials, tapes, or other aids. Preferably, the conference should be unhurried and on school time. Cogan notes that it may well be necessary to arrange for coverage of a teacher's classroom responsibilities from time to time.

---

[13]Cogan, op. cit.

7 *Phase 7 is the conference.* The conference is an opportunity and setting for teacher and supervisor to exchange information about what was intended in a given lesson or unit and what actually happened. The success of the conference depends upon the extent to which the process of clinical supervision is viewed as formative, focused evaluation intended to help in understanding and improving professional practice.

8 *Phase 8 requires the resumption of planning.* A common outcome of the first seven phases of clinical supervision is agreement on the kinds of changes sought in the teacher's classroom behavior. As this agreement materializes, the eighth phase begins. Teacher and supervisor begin planning the next lesson or unit and the new targets, approaches, and techniques to be attempted.

It appears as though the clinical supervision cycle describes that which many supervisors have been doing all along. But a quick review of the assumptions, particularly the concept of cosupervisor, suggests that the resemblance may be superficial. The supervisor works at two levels with teachers during the cycle: helping them to understand and improve their professional practice and helping them to learn more about the skills of classroom analysis needed in supervision. Furthermore, while traditional classroom observation tends to be sporadic and requires little time investment, clinical supervision asks that supervisors give 2 to 3 hours a week to each teacher. Supervisors can better manage their time by involving only part of the faculty at a time—perhaps one-third for 3 months in rotation. As teachers themselves become competent in clinical supervision and assume increased responsibility for all phases, they should participate in clinical supervision as a form of collegial supervision. Indeed, for clinical supervision and its hybrids that emphasize other forms of shared and serious inquiry into teaching to become widespread, teachers will have to become key players by engaging in collegial supervision. No hard-and-fast rules exist that exclude teachers from assuming roles as clinical supervisors. Collegial supervision and clinical supervision are quite compatible.

EDUCATIONAL PLATFORM

Most supervisors and teachers know that teaching is not nearly as objective and explicit as one might think. Indeed, teachers, supervisors, and others bring to the classroom a variety of agendas, some public, many hidden, and probably most unknown, each of which influences the decisions they make. The agendas tend to fall into three major categories: what one believes is possible, what one believes is true, and what one believes is desirable. Together the three are the essential ingredients of one's *educational platform*.[14] A platform implies something that supports one's action and by which one justifies or validates one's own actions.

---

[14]Decker Walker, "A Naturalistic Model for Curriculum Development," *The School Review*, vol. 80, no. 1 (1971), pp. 51–65.

An approximate analogy would be that of a political platform. This platform states the basic values, critical policy statements, and key positions of an individual or group. Once known, the political platform can be used to predict responses that a politician or political party is likely to make to questions on various campaign issues. The concept of education platform, particularly as it affects curriculum and educational program matters, is discussed at length in Chapter 10. Here our attention is focused on platform as it relates to clinical supervision.

Assumptions, Theories, and Beliefs

The components of one's educational platform are the assumptions, theories, and beliefs one has formed concerning key aspects of effective teaching, such as the purpose of schooling, perceptions of students, what knowledge is of most worth, and the value of certain teaching techniques and pedagogical principles. For purposes of illustration, consider each component below, recognizing that operationally they are inseparable.

Assumptions that teachers hold help answer the question What is possible? Assumptions are composed of one's beliefs, the concepts one takes for granted, and the ideas one accepts without question about schools, classrooms, students, teaching, learning, and knowledge. They help the teacher to define what classrooms are actually like and what is possible to accomplish within them. They also are important to the decisions that teachers make, because they set the boundaries for what information will or will not be considered and for other possibilities and actions at the onset of instruction.

Theories help answer the question What is true? They are beliefs about relationships between and among assumptions one considers to be true. Theories form the basis for developing teaching strategies and patterns of classroom organizations.

Beliefs about what is desirable in classrooms are derived from assumptions and theories that one holds regarding knowledge, learning, classrooms, and students. What is desirable is expressed in the form of intents, aims, objectives, or purposes.

Consider, for example, a teacher whose educational platform includes the assumptions "Little or no knowledge exists that is essential for everyone to learn" and "Youngsters can be trusted to make important decisions." The two assumptions might lead to the theory "Students who are allowed to influence classroom decisions will make wise choices and will become more committed learners." That being the case, a corresponding aim for that teacher might be "to involve students in shared decision making," or perhaps "to have students interact with subject matter in a manner that emphasizes its concepts and structure rather than just its information."

Contrast this with a teacher whose educational platform includes the assumption "The only justifiable evidence of good teaching is student acquisition of subject matter as specified by the teacher or as measured by the test" and the assumption "Motivation of students should reflect the realities of the world outside the school, where good behavior and performance are publicly rewarded and poor behavior and performance are publicly punished." The two assumptions might well lead to the theory "Students need to be motivated, on the one hand, and disciplined, on the other, to get the behavior and performance that leads to acquiring the most subject matter in the least amount of time." In this case, a corresponding aim might be "to provide rewards and privileges to students who behave and perform to the teacher's expectations and punishment to those who do not."

Educational platforms are powerful determinants of the nature and quality of life in classrooms. For example, imagine the fate of students in the classrooms of people who consider themselves teachers of French or biology and not of students, as compared with teachers who view instruction in a more holistic and integrated way. Consider next the fate of the supervisor who wants the first type of teacher to be more sensitive to individual differences of students and to emphasize the joy of learning French or biology as well as mastery of subject matter, but does not take into account the teacher's educational platform. Unless the supervisor is a master at behavior modification and the teacher witless enough to respond passively to stimuli from the supervisor, change in teaching behavior will require some altering of educational platforms.

Known and Unknown Platform Dimensions

In the world of the classroom the components of educational platforms are generally not well known. That is, teachers tend to be unaware of their assumptions, theories, or objectives. Sometimes they adopt components of a platform that seem right, that have the ring of fashionable rhetoric, or that coincide with the expectation of important others, such as teachers whom they admire, or of groups with which they wish to affiliate. Although teachers may overtly adopt aspects of educational platforms in this manner, covertly, or unknowingly, they are often likely to hang onto contradictory assumptions, beliefs, and theories. Publicly they may say (or espouse) one thing and assume that their classroom behavior is governed by this statement, but privately, or even unknowingly, they may believe something else that actually governs their classroom behavior. Indeed, teachers are not aware that often their classroom decisions and behavior contradict their espoused platform.

THEORIES GOVERNING TEACHER BEHAVIOR

The clinical supervisor needs to be concerned with two theories that the teacher brings to the classroom—an *espoused theory* and a *theory in use*. As Chris Argyris and David Schön suggest:

> When someone is asked how he would behave under certain circumstances, the answer he usually gives is his espoused theory of action for that situation. This is the theory of action to which he gives allegiance, and which, upon request, he communicates to others. However, the theory that actually governs his action is his theory in use. This

theory may or may not be compatible with his espoused theory; furthermore, the individual may or may not be aware of the incompatibility of the two theories.[15]

When one's espoused theory matches one's theory in use, they are considered congruent. Congruence exists, for example, for the teacher who believes that self-image development in youngsters is desirable in its own right and is related to student achievement and whose teaching behavior and artifacts of that behavior confirm this espoused theory. Lack of congruence between a person's espoused theory and the theory in use, *when known,* proposes a dilemma to that individual. A second teacher, for example, shares the same espoused theory regarding self-concept, but his or her pattern of questioning, use of negative feedback, use of the bell curve, and insistence on standard requirements may reveal a theory in use incongruent with the espoused theory. The social studies teacher who believes in and teaches a course in American democracy in a "totalitarian" manner represents another example of incongruency between espoused theory and theory in use.

THE JOHARI WINDOW

A useful way of understanding how known and unknown platform dimensions of teachers fit into clinical supervision is by examining the *Johari window* as it relates to espoused theories and theories in use.[16] This relationship is illustrated in Figure 13–1.

The Johari window in this case depicts the relationship between two parties, teacher and clinical supervisor. The relationship revolves around aspects of the teacher's educational platform known to self and others, known to self but not others, not known to self but known to others, and not known to self or others. Four cells are depicted in the Johari window, each representing a different combination of what the teacher knows or does not know about his or her teaching as contrasted with what the supervisor knows and does not know about that teacher's teaching.

In the first cell, *the public or open self,* the teacher's knowledge of his or her teaching behavior and other aspects of his or her professional practices corresponds with the supervisor's knowledge. This is the area in which communication occurs most effectively and in which the need for the teacher to be defensive, to assume threat, is minimal. The clinical supervisor works to broaden, or enlarge, this cell with the teacher.

In the second cell, *the hidden or secret self,* the teacher knows about aspects of his or her teaching behavior and professional practice that the supervisor does not know. Often the teacher conceals these aspects from the supervisor for fear

---

[15]Chris Argyris and David A. Schön, *Theory in Practice: Increasing Professional Effectiveness.* San Francisco: Jossey-Bass, 1974, p. 7.

[16]Joseph Luft, *Of Human Interaction.* New York: National Press Books, 1969. The Johari window was developed by Joseph Luft and Harry Ingham and gets its name from the first names of its authors.

	What the supervisor knows about the teacher	What the supervisor does not know about the teacher
What the teacher knows about himself	Public or open self 1	Hidden or secret self 2
What the teacher does not know about himself	Blind self 3	Undiscovered or subconscious self 4

FIGURE 13-1   The Johari Window and the educational platform. *(From Thomas J. Sergiovanni,* Handbook for Department Leadership Concepts and Practices in Today's Secondary Schools. *Boston: Allyn & Bacon, 1977.)*

that the supervisor might use this knowledge to punish, hurt, or exploit the teacher. The second cell suggests how important a supervisory climate characterized by trust and credibility is to the success of clinical supervision. In clinical supervision the teacher is encouraged to reduce the size of this cell.

In the third cell, *the blind self,* the supervisor knows about aspects of the teacher's behavior and professional practice of which the teacher is unaware. This cell, though large initially, is reduced considerably as clinical supervision for a given teacher develops and matures. This is the cell most often neglected by traditional teacher-evaluation methods. Indeed, clinical supervision is superior to most other supervising strategies in helping teachers understand dimensions of teaching found in the "blind self."

In the fourth cell, *the undiscovered self,* one finds aspects of teacher behavior and professional practice not known to either teacher or supervisor. The size of this cell is reduced as clinical supervision progresses. Teachers and supervisors discover and understand more and more about their beliefs, capabilities, strengths and weaknesses, and potential.

HELPING TEACHERS CHANGE

Creating a condition for change greatly facilitates the change itself. For example, if individual teachers are unaware of inconsistencies between their espoused theories and their theories in use, they are not likely to search for alternatives to their present teaching patterns. One way in which search behavior can be evoked is by identifying dilemmas. Dilemmas become apparent when teachers learn that their theories in use are not consistent with their espoused theory.

Dilemmas promote an unsettled feeling in a person. Their espoused educational platforms mean a great deal, and what they stand for and believe is linked to their concept of self and sense of well-being. Dilemmas that emerge from inconsistencies between these images and actual behavior are upsetting and need to be resolved. Indeed, they are likely to lead to a search for changes either in one's espoused theory or in one's theory in use.[17]

Readiness for change is a critical point in the process of clinical supervision. It is at this point that an appropriate support system needs to be provided. Part of this support system will be psychological and will be geared toward accepting and encouraging the teacher. But part must also be technical and will be geared toward making available teaching and professional practice alternatives to the teacher.

Argyris and Schön point out that congruence is not a virtue in itself. A "bad" espoused theory matched to a theory in use may be far less desirable, from the supervisor's point of view, than a "good" espoused theory insufficiently matched.[18]

SOME EVIDENCE

To this point in our discussion of developing a theory of clinical supervision we have suggested that:

A teacher's classroom behavior and the artifacts of that behavior are a function of assumptions, theories, and intents the teacher brings to the classroom. Together these compose the teacher's educational platform.

Educational platforms exist at two levels: what teachers say they assume, believe, and intend (their espoused theory), and the assumptions, beliefs, and intents inferred from their behavior and artifacts of their behavior (their theory in use).

Espoused theories are generally known to the teacher.

Theories in use are generally not known to the teacher and must be constructed from observation of teacher behavior and artifacts of that behavior.

Lack of congruence between a teacher's espoused theory and the teacher's theory in use proposes a dilemma to the teacher.

Faced with a dilemma, a teacher becomes uncomfortable, and search behavior is evoked.

---

[17]Leon Festinger, *Theory of Cognitive Dissonance.* Evanston, Ill.: Row, Peterson, 1975; and Milton Rokeach, "A Theory of Organizational Change within Value-Attitude Systems," *Journal of Social Sciences,* vol. 24, no. 21 (1968).

[18]Argyris and Schön, op. cit.

Dilemmas are resolved by teachers modifying their theory in use to match their espoused theory. It is possible that espoused theory will be modified to match theory in use, but because of the link between espoused theory and self-esteem, and self-esteem with the esteem received from others, the more common pattern will be the former.

Although a number of studies suggest that indeed teachers are likely to respond as suggested,[19] several caveats are in order. For example, in reviewing the literature on consistency theory, William McGuire notes that search behavior is only one of several possible reactions to dissonance. Additional examples of dissonance reduction, he notes, are *avoidance,* whereby one represses the matter by putting the inconsistency out of mind; *bolstering,* whereby the inconsistency is submerged into a larger body of consistencies so as to seem relatively less important; *differentiation,* whereby one sees the situation causing dissonance to be different in a particular case ("I wasn't actually putting down the youngster but just giving her a taste of her own medicine"); *substitution,* whereby one changes the object about which he or she has an opinion rather than the opinion itself ("It is true that I said all school administrators are petty bureaucrats, and they are, but he is a statesman, not a bureaucrat"); and *devaluation,* whereby one downgrades the importance of the inconsistency in question, thus making it more tolerable.[20] The extent to which a teacher faces up to inconsistencies between espoused platform dimensions and those actually in use may well depend, as suggested earlier, upon the quality of climate and setting the supervisor provides—colleagueship, in Morris Cogan's language.[21]

Many forms of clinical supervision resemble artistic approaches. Such forms are artistic when they rely on developing a complete representation of a teaching episode and when they use this representation as a basis for making inferences and building understanding of events. Videotaping is the most common method of representation associated with clinical supervision. Clinical supervision uses the data at hand (actually generated from the environment and activities being evaluated) rather than data that fit a preconceived rating form or a set of instrument specifications, and it places the teacher in a key role as generator, interpreter, and analyst of events described.

Sometimes clinical supervisors take too seriously the need to "scientifically" and "objectively" document events. Sometimes they focus too intensely on the

---

[19]Using Flanders's interaction-analysis techniques as a means of collecting information and as a basis for producing verbal feedback, Tuckman, McCall, and Hyman conclude that "behavior and self-perception of experienced, in-service teachers *can* be changed by involving a discrepancy between a teacher's observed behavior and his own self-perception of his behavior, and then making him aware of this discrepancy via verbal feedback." See Bruce W. Tuckman, Kendrick M. McCall, and Ronald T. Hyman, "The Modification of Teacher Behavior: Effects of Dissonance and Feedback," *American Educational Research Journal,* vol. 6, no. 4 (1969), pp. 607–619.

[20]William J. McGuire, "The Current Status of Cognitive Consistency Theories," in Shel Feldman (ed.), *Cognitive Consistency, Motivational Antecedents, and Behavioral Consequents.* New York: Academic, 1966, pp. 10–14.

[21]Cogan, op. cit., p. 67.

stepwise or work-flow aspects of clinical supervision. Sometimes they rely too heavily on predetermined objectives or on specifying detailed blueprints and plans that subsequently determine the direction of the evaluation. But clinical supervision can be geared to discovering and understanding rather than determining, and in that sense it has artistic potential. Additional artistic strategies that can be used either separate from clinical supervision or as a part of clinical supervision are described in the sections that follow. These techniques are powerful means for providing rich descriptions of classroom activity from which theories in use might be inferred.

CONNOISSEURSHIP AND CRITICISM

It is difficult to discuss artistic alternatives to present teacher-evaluation practices without reference to the work of Elliot Eisner.[22] Eisner is concerned with developing in supervisor and teacher the qualities and skills of appreciation, inference, disclosure, and description. He refers to these qualities as the cultivation of educational connoisseurship and criticism. It is through the art of connoisseurship that one is able to appreciate and internalize meanings in classrooms and through the skill of criticism that one is able to share or disclose this meaning to others. Eisner uses references to wine connoisseurship and art criticism as illustrations of these concepts. The art of appreciation is the tool of the connoisseur and the art of disclosure the tool of the critic. James Cross uses the example of sports commentators and writers to illustrate the combined application of connoisseurship and criticism.

> Most of us are familiar with some of the techniques employed by commentators in describing and remarking on well-executed plays or potentially victorious strategies. Plays executed with finesse are often seen in stop action, instant replay, slow motion or are recounted in stirring detail on sports pages. One of the major contributions of these commentators is their great knowledge of sports, familiarizing them with possibilities so they know whether a flanker reverse, off tackle run, screen pass or draw-play was used or has potential for gaining yardage in a given situation, or when the bump and run, blitz, or single coverage was used or likely to prevent gain. Knowledge about educational potentials is also necessary. The potentially worthwhile tactics of

---

[22]Elliot Eisner, "Applying Educational Connoisseurship and Criticism to Education Settings." Stanford, Calif.: Stanford University, Department of Education, undated, mimeo; see also his "Emerging Models for Educational Evaluation," op. cit.; and "The Perceptive Eye: Toward the Reformation of Educational Evaluation," op. cit. Eisner notes that, unfortunately, to many the word "connoisseurship" has snobbish or elitist connotations, and criticism implies a *hacking* or negativistic attitude. In his words, "Connoisseurship, as I use the term, relates to any form of expertise in any area of human endeavor and is as germane to the problem involved in purse snatching as it is to the appreciation of fine needle point." And "criticism is conceived of as a generic process aimed at revealing the characteristics and qualities that constitute any human product. Its major aim is to enable individuals to recognize qualities and characteristics of a work or event which might have gone unnoticed and therefore unappreciated." Quoted from "The Perceptive Eye: Toward the Performance of Educational Evaluation," footnote 2.

teaching or those in use—the bump and runs or flanker reverses of schooling—need to be described and conveyed.[23]

The commentator's ability to render play-by-play action in a fashion that permits an audience to see and feel the game as he or she does depends upon a feel of intimacy with the phenomena under study not permitted by mere attention to game statistics and other objective information and upon a quality of disclosure more vivid than a box score. And in education, the evaluator's ability to describe classroom life in a fashion that permits other educators to see and feel this environment as he or she does depends upon a similar intimacy with classroom phenomena (educational connoisseurship) and a rendering of this intimacy (educational criticism) well beyond that provided by a brief observation or two accompanied by a series of ratings or a teacher-evaluation checklist. Eisner maintains that educational connoisseurship is to some degree practiced daily by teachers and supervisors:

> The teacher's ability, for example, to judge when children have had enough of art, math, reading or "free time" is a judgment made not by applying a theory of motivation or attention, but by recognizing the wide range of qualities that the children themselves display to those who have learned to see. Walk down any school corridor and peek through the window; an educational connoisseur can quickly discern important things about life in that classroom. Of course judgments, especially those made through windows from hallways, can be faulty. Yet the point remains. If one knows how to see what one looks at, a great deal of information . . . can be secured. The teacher who cannot distinguish between the noise of children working and just plain noise has not yet developed a basic level of educational connoisseurship.[24]

Eisner believes that the existing level of connoisseurship found in teachers and supervisors can and should be refined, that perceptions can be enhanced and sharpened, and that understanding can be increased. He further points out that

> . . . connoisseurship when developed to a high degree provides a level of consciousness that makes intellectual clarity possible. Many teachers are confronted daily with prescriptions and demands from individuals outside the teaching profession that are intended to improve the quality of education within the schools. Many of these demands the teachers feel in their gut to be misguided or wrong-headed; the demands somehow fly in the face of what they feel to be possible in a classroom or in the best interests of children.[25]

In this context he notes: "Many teachers, if you ask them, are unable to state why they feel uneasy. They have a difficult time articulating what the flaws are in the often glib prescriptions that issue from state capitols and from major universities. Yet, the uneasiness is not always, but often justified." And further: "Many teachers have developed sufficient connoisseurship to feel that something

[23]James Cross, "Applying Editorial Connoisseurship and Criticism to Supervisory Practices. Doctoral dissertation. Urbana: University of Illinois, Educational Administration and Supervision, 1977.
[24]Eisner, "The Perceptive Eye," p. 9.
[25]Ibid., pp. 10–11.

is awry but have insufficient connoisseurship to provide a more adequate conceptualization of just what it is."[26]

When applied to supervision, educational connoisseurship is a necessary but insufficient art. Classroom understanding needs to be described and communicated, and this aspect of the process, the art of disclosure, is what Eisner refers to as educational criticism. There is much to learn about cultivating the art of connoisseurship and the skills of disclosure. Much will depend upon the ability of educators to regain confidence in themselves, in their ability to analyze and judge, in their willingness to rely on intuition and perception—all today often considered dubious skills, ones to be discounted in the face of objective and scientific demands for accountability.

MORE THAN DESCRIBING

Unique to artistic approaches to supervision and evaluation is the emphasis on identifying meanings in teaching activity and classroom life rather than *only* describing teaching and classroom events. For example, many advocates of clinical supervision recommend that the supervisor develop an accurate and objective record of teaching. Often videotapes of teaching, exact transcripts of teacher-student talk, or tally sheets of some sort that record data of interest to the teacher and the supervisor are recommended. Typically, the supervisor is expected to avoid interpretation, leaving the extraction of the meaning behind events to the teacher or, when a particularly good relationship exists between teacher and supervisor, to both parties during the conference phase of a clinical supervision cycle.

When using more artistic approaches to clinical supervision, supervisors try to go beyond description to the interpretation of teaching events. Following Ian Ramsey,[27] John Mann distinguishes between *picturing* and *disclosure* models.[28] Picturing models of evaluation try to be much like the teaching activity and classroom life under study. Disclosure models, on the other hand, contain key characteristics of the teaching activity in classroom life under study but move beyond to interpreting meaning, raising issues, and testing propositions about this phenomenon. Some of these distinctions are suggested in Table 13–2. As you examine the disclosure side of the ledger in Table 13–2, notice the emphasis given to going beyond the data in the strictest sense, to telling a story represented by the data. For example, consider the following excerpt from the "disclosure" of a classroom by Robert Donmoyer:

> All these forces combined to produce a profound effect upon the teacher and to profoundly influence her behavior in the classroom. She becomes, as she herself has said, an accountant. Most of her day is spent checking and recording what students have

[26]Ibid., p. 11.
[27]Ian Ramsey, *Models and Mystery*. London: Oxford University Press, 1964.
[28]John S. Mann, "Curriculum Criticism," *The Teachers College Record*, vol. 71, no. 1, pp. 27–40, 1967.

TABLE 13–2
COMPARING PICTURING AND DISCLOSURE MODELS OF TEACHER EVALUATION

Picturing	Disclosure
1. Intent	
To describe the teaching phenomenon under study as exactly as possible. To develop a replica, photo image, or a carbon copy of reality. Agendas and issues are those embedded in the data.	To interpret the teaching phenomenon under study. To illuminate issues, disclose meetings, and raise hypotheses or propositions. Agendas and issues are those that emerge from the data.
2. Analogies	
Legal transcript, videotape, photo-replica, interaction-analysis, electronic portrait, music or dance score, play script, historical chronology.	Impressionistic painting, collage, book review, interpretive photo, music, dance or play performance, story.
3. Key Questions	
What exactly happened in this class? How can I describe events objectively?	What issues emerge from the study of this class? How can I represent or illuminate these issues in a meaningful way?
4. Validity Check	
Are events described accurately?	When actual events are observed, do they reasonably lead to the inferences and interpretations?

and haven't done. Math, spelling, and language assignments must be checked, and if there are mistakes (and there usually are) they must be rechecked and, sometimes, rechecked again. Then checked assignments must be checked off on each student's math, spelling, or language contract. When each contract is completed, each contract must be checked out. After this is done, the student must take home the work included on this contract and bring back a note signed by his parents indicating they saw the work. This note, of course, must be checked in.

This checking and rechecking and checking out and checking in is all performed with mechanized precision. The teacher's face remains immobile except for an occasional upward turn at the corners of her mouth, the eyes never smile.

The teacher exhibits great economy of movement and gesture. It's almost as if Ms. Hill were a marionette whose strings are too tight, hence her gestures must be tight and close to her body.[29]

Notice that Donmoyer does not provide a detailed description of the number of times the teacher checks this or that, but offers instead the word "accountant" not only to suggest the actual checking of student work but to communicate a meaning that transcends the particular issues of checking and rechecking and to

[29]Robert Donmoyer, "School and Society Revisited: An Educational Criticism of Ms. Hill's Fourth-Grade Classroom," as quoted in Eisner, *The Educational Imagination*, op. cit., p. 231.

comment on an important dimension of the climate and quality of life in this particular classroom.

The concepts of picturing and disclosure might be viewed as range parameters within which a supervisor can work. At times picturing events as accurately as possible might make sense, and at other times moving toward the disclosure end of the range might be more appropriate. One can catalog approaches to supervision and evaluation used by a particular school or a particular supervisor on such a range scale as a way of identifying the array of possibilities that exist in the school. It should be noted, however, that the more a supervisory and evaluation strategy approaches the disclosure end of this range, the more important is the quality of the relationship between teacher and supervisor to the success in this approach. Disclosure strategies of supervision and evaluation require a particularly strong climate of trust and understanding among those involved in the process of supervision and evaluation. The relatively safer picturing end of this continuum may be appropriate initially, and as the supervisory relationship matures, movement could then progress toward the disclosure end.

CRITICISMS OF ARTISTIC APPROACHES

Artistic approaches to supervision and evaluation are often criticized for lacking precision and for being subjective. These criticisms are undeniable, but the alternative, to limit analysis of teaching and supervisory practice to only what is precise and objective, is neither scientific nor helpful and thus is unacceptable. A helpful and effective system of supervision must give prime attention to data that make sense to teachers. "Brute" data become sensible when interpreted and as meanings are established. But can such a subjective system of supervision be fair? How can the validity of the system be verified? The key to solving these problems rests in the person who assumes responsibility for establishing meanings. Some protections are offered, for example, if proposed meanings are offered as hypotheses and if accepted meanings are arrived at cooperatively by teacher and supervisor.

The precision issue remains important. Some argue that only data that can be accurately and precisely observed and recorded should be part of the evaluation process. Unfortunately, evaluation issues that can meet this rigorous, albeit artificial, standard are often less important than those that cannot. Limiting the evaluation to issues that lend themselves to precision can lead to a serious measurement error, often referred to as an "error of the third type." In this type of error, statistical confidence limits are correctly set and precise measurements standards are applied but the *wrong problem* is addressed. This misplaced cogency might best be summed up by John Tukey's admonition: "Far better an approximate answer to the right question, which is often vague, than an exact answer to the wrong question, which can always be made precise."[30] A more helpful

---

[30]Quoted by R. Rose, "Disciplined Research and Undisciplined Problems," in C. Carol H. Weiss (ed.), *Using Social Research and Public Policy Making.* Lexington, Mass.: Heath, 1977, p. 23.

approach in sorting out the extent to which artistic approaches to clinical supervision are useful and the circumstances under which they are useful is to understand their limitations as well as their strengths.

THE EVALUATION PORTFOLIO

Videotaping is a common technique associated with clinical supervision and with the arts of educational connoisseurship and criticism. Indeed, videotaping can provide a useful and readily accessible representation of teaching episodes and classroom activities. But because of the selective nature of lens and screen, this technique can also frame perception and evoke slanted meanings. Furthermore, what the screen shows always represents a choice among possibilities and therefore provides an incomplete picture. And finally, some aspects of classroom life do not lend themselves very well to lens and screen and could be neglected.[31]

Artifacts analysis and/or portfolio development, when used in conjunction with videotaping, can help provide a more complete representation of classroom life and therefore can increase meaning.[32] These approaches, however, can stand apart from videotaping and indeed can stand apart from each other.

Imagine a classroom or school deserted suddenly 20 years ago by its teacher and students and immediately being sealed. Everything there remains exactly as it was at the moment of desertion—desks, chairs, interest centers, work materials, test files, homework assignments, reading center sign-up lists, star reward charts and other "motivational devices," bulletin boards, workbooks, student notebooks, grade books, plan books, library displays, teacher workroom arrangements, student lounge-area arrangements, and so on.

Twenty years later you arrive on the scene as an amateur anthropologist intent on learning about the culture, way of life, and meaning of this class (its goals, values, beliefs, activities, norms, etc.). As you dig through the classroom, what artifacts might you collect and how might you use them to help you learn about life in this school? Suppose, for example, you were interested in discovering what was important to teachers, how teachers viewed their roles in contrast to that of students, what youngsters seemed to be learning and/or enjoying, and how time was spent. In each case what might you collect? What inferences might you make, for example, if you were to find most of the work of students to be in the form of short-answer responses in workbooks or on ditto sheets, no student work displayed in the class, all student desks containing identical materials, and a teacher test file with most questions geared to the knowledge level of the taxonomy of educational objectives?

Portfolio development represents a teacher-evaluation strategy similar to that of artifacts analysis but with some important differences. The intent of portfolio

---

[31]This discussion follows Sergiovanni, "Reforming Teacher Evaluation," op. cit.

[32]See Patricia Scheyer and Robert Stake, "A Program's Self-Evaluation Portfolio." Urbana: University of Illinois at Urbana-Champaign, Center for Instructional Research and Curriculum Evaluation, undated mimeo, for a discussion and application of this concept for program evaluation.

development is to establish a file or collection of artifacts, records, photo essays, cassettes, and other materials designed to represent some aspect of the classroom program and teaching activities. Although the materials in the portfolio should be loosely collected and therefore suitable for rearrangement from time to time to reflect different aspects of the class, the portfolio should be designed with a sense of purpose. The teacher or teaching team being evaluated is responsible for assembling the portfolio and should do it in a fashion that highlights their perception of key issues and important concerns they wish to represent.

Like the artist who prepares a portfolio of his or her work to reflect a point of view, the teacher prepares a similar representation of his or her work. Together supervisor and teacher use the collected artifacts to identify key issues, to identify the dimensions of the teacher's educational platform, as evidence that targets have been met, and to identify serendipitous but worthwhile outcomes. A portfolio collection could be used, for example, to examine such issues as:

Are classroom activities compatible with the teacher's espoused educational platform and/or that of the school?

Do supervisor and teacher have compatible goals?

Are youngsters engaging in activities that require advanced cognitive thinking or is the emphasis on lower-level learning?

Do youngsters have an opportunity to influence classroom decisions?

Is the classroom program challenging all the students regardless of academic potential or are some youngsters taught too little and others too much?

Are the youngsters assuming passive or active roles in the classroom?

Is the teacher working hard? That is, is there evidence of planning, care in preparation of materials, and reflective and conscientious feedback on students' work, or are shortcuts evident?

Does the teacher understand the subject matter?

What is the nature and character of the hidden curriculum in this class?

Although portfolio development and artifacts analysis share common features, the most notable of which is the collection of artifacts, portfolio development is the responsibility of the teacher. The teacher decides what will be represented by the portfolio and the items to be included in its collection. Together the teacher and supervisor use this representation to identify issues for discussion and analysis.

A CAVEAT ON THE USE OF PORTFOLIOS

The evaluation portfolio is a good idea. But, as is the case with many other good ideas, when portfolio use is uniformly mandated or linked to a bureaucratic and measurement-oriented system of evaluation it becomes both ritualistic and burdensome. Items are collected and filed not because of reasons that make sense to teachers and supervisors but because of the characteristics of the evaluation system. In a worst-case scenario, supervisors wind up using portfolio items as a way to play "gotcha" with teachers, and teachers develop padded portfolios to cover all the bases or to logjam the evaluation system.

The best protection against misuse of the portfolio is to take to heart the basic meanings and intentions behind clinical supervision. Basic to understanding supervision is the view that teaching practices are governed by the interplay of two theories: an espoused theory, which represents the teacher's public educational platform, and a theory in use, which represents the teacher's actual educational platform or platform in use. Often this actual platform is tacitly held. Clinical supervision seeks to infer the teacher's actual platform by examining what is going on in the classroom and assessing its meaning. This is done through observation in the classroom, analysis of videotapes, collection of artifacts and portfolios, and other techniques. When a supervisor confronts a teacher with the fact that the teacher's theory in use is not consistent with his or her espoused theory, dilemmas can be identified. Once these dilemmas are discovered, the teacher can attempt to resolve them. This process of resolution acts as a stimulus to change.

The portfolio is an artistic metaphor entirely compatible with conceptions of supervision and evaluation as forms of connoisseurship and criticism. Taken together, these ideas place clinical supervision in the realm of discovery, reflection, self-understanding, and professional improvement. As described in this chapter both clinical supervision and its conceptual underpinnings, when applied to other models of supervision aimed at professional development, should be at the center of supervisory practice.

CHAPTER 14

PROVIDING OPTIONS
TO TEACHERS

$\mathbf{T}$HE capacity for students to learn and perform as well as their social and moral development improves as classrooms become learning communities and teaching becomes learner centered. This basic principle of Supervision II is shared by many school districts and even states. Texas, for example, recently adopted a set of proficiencies teachers are expected to display based on the following vision:

> The teacher is a leader of a learner-centered community, in which an atmosphere of trust and openness produces a stimulating exchange of ideas and mutual respect. The teacher is a critical thinker and problem solver who plays a variety of roles when teaching. As a coach, the teacher observes, evaluates, and changes direction and strategies whenever necessary. As a facilitator, the teacher helps students link ideas in the content areas to familiar ideas, to prior experiences, and to relevant problems. As a manager, the teacher effectively acquires, allocates, and conserves resources. By encouraging self-directed learning, and by modeling respectful behavior, the teacher effectively manages the learning environment so that optimal learning occurs.[1]

Any serious attempt to make this vision a reality must include as its strategy the transformation of classrooms and schools into:

---

[1]Texas Education Agency, "Learner-Centered Schools for Texas: Vision of Texas Educators." State Adopted Proficiencies for Texas, 1994, p. 4.

Reflective communities within which not only students but teachers develop insights into their own strength and weaknesses as learners and use this information to call upon different strategies for learning.

Developmental communities within which it is acknowledged that not only students but teachers develop at different rates and at any given time are more ready to learn some things than others.

Diverse communities within which different talents and interests of not only students but teachers are recognized and acknowledged by decisions that are made about curriculum, teaching, and assessment.

Conversational communities within which high priority is given to creating an active discourse that involves the exchange of values and ideas not only among students but among teachers and between students and teachers as everyone learns together.

Caring communities within which not only students but teachers learn to be kind to each other, to respect each other, and to help each other to grow as learners and as persons.

Responsible communities within which not only students but teachers come to view themselves as part of a social web of meanings and responsibilities to which they feel a moral obligation to embody as members of the same school community.[2]

Few axioms are more fundamental than the one that acknowledges the link between what happens to teachers and what happens to students. Inquiring classrooms, for example, are not likely to flourish in schools where inquiry among teachers is discouraged. A commitment to problem solving is difficult to instill in students who are taught by teachers for whom problem solving is not allowed. Where there is little discourse among teachers, discourse among students will be harder to promote and maintain. And the idea of making classrooms into learning communities for students will remain more rhetoric than real unless schools become learning communities for teachers too. Thus, for classrooms to be transformed, schools themselves must be transformed into:

Professional communities within which teachers depend on each other not only for caring and support but to learn and inquire together as members of a shared practice.

Vito Perrone believes that the teacher's role is central to improving the quality of learning for students. For him, teacher development is key because "the quality of teachers' understandings influences to a large degree what teachers do in classrooms."[3] Good teacher-development programs and efforts, he reasoned, should be based on the assumption that "the best source for teachers to

---

[2]Thomas J. Sergiovanni, *Leadership for the School House*. San Francisco: Jossey-Bass, 1996, pp. 138–140.

[3]Vito Perrone, "Supporting Teacher Growth," *Childhood Education*, vol. 54, no. 6 (1978), p. 298.

learn more about teaching and learning, child growth and development, materials and methods is through an examination of one's own practice."[4]

This new vision of teacher development as being driven by teacher-identified needs and as being situated in the practice of teachers rubs against the grain of our "one best way" of providing in-service to teachers. Schools are easier to run when things are uniform, not varied. Same workshop themes for all are easier to plan, provide, and evaluate than more individualized and less formal approaches to improvements. Challenging this habit with a new vision can be unsettling. Principals and other supervisors, for example, are constantly struggling to sort out those aspects of schooling that need to be kept more or less uniform and those aspects that call for diversity. What is the right balance between uniform school rules and the different rules that teachers and teams work out with their students? What parts of the school schedule must be considered fixed and what parts can teachers create in use as they plan and teach? What content should be considered as curriculum imperatives and what content should emerge from teacher and student preferences, needs, and interests?

Resolving the tugs between the needs for uniformity and diversity requires a great deal of time and skill. The task is made a little easier if supervisors are able to develop a framework for making decisions. Understanding schools as learning communities can help. The bias in learning communities should be in favor of diversity for both moral and practical reasons. From a moral perspective, democratic values include respect for individual differences and the rights of teachers to be involved in matters that affect them, including how they will work together, what they will do, and how they will be evaluated. From a practical perspective, when individual differences in preferences, style, and temperament are honored teachers respond with greater commitment, better performance, and increased satisfaction. Furthermore, diversity in teaching styles, patterns of classroom organization, and interpretations of curriculum increases the range of possibilities and encourages learning among teachers.

In this chapter we are concerned about differences that teachers bring to their work. Accommodating these differences, we reason, requires abandoning commitment to a one best supervisory and evaluation system. In its place we propose a range of options and suggest that teacher preferences and needs should be primary in deciding which options make the most sense.

EXAMPLES OF OPTIONS

We propose that in every school a plan for supervision should be developed that includes at least five options: clinical supervision, collegial supervision, self-directed supervision, informal supervision, and inquiry-based supervision.[5] Ad-

---

[4]Ibid.

[5]The discussion of options for supervision presented in this chapter follows the views of Allan A. Glatthorn, *Differentiated Supervision*. Alexandria, Va.: Association for Supervision and Curriculum Development, 1984; and the discussion of options for supervision that appears in T. J. Sergiovanni, *The Principalship: A Reflective Practice Perspective*, 3d ed. Boston: Allyn & Bacon, 1995, pp. 244–248.

ditionally, we propose that teachers play key roles in deciding which of the options make most sense to them given their needs at the time. And finally, we propose that in implementing the options, supervision should be viewed as a process that is equally accessible to teachers and administrators. Equal access does not mean that principals and supervisors should be excluded from the process of supervision. They have important roles to play. But we do not believe that it is right or sensible for supervisors to monopolize the process by excluding teachers from roles as supervisors or by relegating them to token roles.

Excluding teachers denies the reality that although formal supervisors bring expertise to the process, teachers as a group command the largest share of expertise in subject matter, knowledge about the particular students being taught, and the pedagogical knowledge needed to teach those students effectively. One problem with traditional conceptions of supervision is that they equate hierarchy with expertise by assuming that supervisors as a group know more about teaching than do teachers as a group.

In Chapter 3 we proposed that professional authority be taken seriously as a basis for what is done in schools. The viability of professional authority depends on whether the virtuous side of professionalism can be adequately defined and accepted as legitimate. The dimensions of virtue proposed included commitment to the following: exemplary practice, practice toward valued social ends, a concern for the practice of teaching itself rather than one's own practice solely, and the caring ethic. All four commitments provide compelling reasons for teachers to be involved in the process of supervision as equal partners. Together the four redefine teaching from a singular practice to a collective one. In a collective practice the supervisory process becomes a natural and informal part of the everyday lives of teachers at work.

From a practical perspective, disconnecting the process of supervision from hierarchic roles reflects what goes on in schools anyway. The research by both Emil Haller and Charles Keenan, for example, reveals that both the Canadian and American teachers they studied were very much inclined to depend upon each other when seeking help in solving problems, when searching for sources of new ideas about teaching, and when seeking other kinds of assistance.[6] Formal supervisors counted, but not nearly as much as other teachers. Teachers held the advice of other teachers in higher regard than advice from other sources. Although not officially acknowledged, there appears to be an informal system of supervision in place in schools; the evidence suggests that this informal system is more important and useful to teachers than is the formal system. By disconnecting supervision from hierarchic roles and viewing it instead as a process accessible to both teachers and supervisors, educators can legitimize this informal system of supervision.

---

[6]Emil J. Haller, *Strategies for Change.* Toronto: Ontario Institute for Studies in Education, Department of Educational Administration, 1968; and Charles Keenan, "Channels for Change: A Survey of Teachers in Chicago Elementary Schools." Ph.D. dissertation. Urbana: University of Illinois, Department of Educational Administration, 1974.

In the sections below an overview of the proposed options for supervision is provided. Attention is then given to the topic of individual differences among teachers, and ideas are presented that can help supervisors navigate through these differences in seeking to match options to teacher inclinations and need.

CLINICAL SUPERVISION AS AN OPTION

In Chapter 13 we proposed that clinical supervision be viewed as a partnership in inquiry shared by teacher and supervisor that is intended to help teachers modify existing patterns of teaching in ways that make sense to them. Clinical supervision is not for everyone, nor is it a strategy that can sustain itself over a long period of time. The process is demanding in the time it requires from both teacher and supervisor. There is a danger that continuous use of this approach can result in a certain ritualism as each of the steps are followed. Clinical supervision may be too much supervision for some teachers. That is, not all teachers will need such an intensive look at their teaching. And finally, teachers' needs and dispositions as well as learning styles vary. Clinical supervision may be suitable for some teachers but not for others when these differences are taken into consideration.

COLLEGIAL SUPERVISION

In collegial supervision teachers agree to work together for their own professional development.[7] Allan Glatthorn defines this approach as a "moderately formalized process by which two or more teachers agree to work together for their own professional growth, usually by observing each other's classroom, giving each other feedback about the observations, and discussing shared professional concerns.[8]

Collegial supervision can take many different forms. In some schools teachers may organize themselves into teams of two or three. It might be a good idea in some cases for at least one member of the team to be selected by the principal or supervisor, but there are no rigid rules for composing collegial supervision teams. Once formed, the teams may choose to work together in a number of ways ranging from clinical supervision to less intensive and more informal processes.

Team members may, for example, simply agree to observe each other's classes and provide help according to the desires of the teacher being observed. The teachers might then confer, giving one another informal feedback and discussing issues of teaching that they consider important. An approach that relies on Madeline Hunter's teaching steps and elements of lesson design or on cooperative learning might be used.[9] In this case, the emphasis on teaching might be narrowly

---

[7]Glatthorn, op. cit.
[8]Ibid., p. 39.
[9]See, for example, Madeline Hunter, "Knowing, Teaching and Supervision," in Philip Hosford (ed.), *Using What We Know About Teaching*. Alexandria, Va.: Association for Supervision and

focused on specific issues inherent in the model that the teacher deems important. On still another occasion the emphasis might be quite unfocused in order to provide a general feel or rendition of teaching. All that is needed is for team members to meet beforehand to decide "the rules and issues" for the observation and for any subsequent conversations or conferences.

Glatthorn describes five different forms collegial supervision might take:

> Professional dialogue among teachers featuring guided discussion and focusing on teaching as a process of thinking. The purpose of professional dialogue is to enhance reflective practice.
>
> Curriculum development featuring teachers working together on such themes as how to operationalize the existing curriculum, adapt the curriculum to the wide variety of students and situations faced in the classroom, and enriching the existing curriculum by inventing and developing new curriculum units and materials.
>
> Peer supervision featuring observations of each other's teaching followed by analysis and discussion.
>
> Peer coaching featuring collaborative development and practice of new teaching methods and skills in both "workshop" settings and under actual teaching conditions.
>
> Action research featuring the study of problems being faced and the development of feasible solutions that result in changes in one's teaching practice.[10]

Traditionally supervision has come to mean some form of classroom observation. But collegial supervision extends well beyond classroom observation. It provides a setting in which teachers can informally discuss problems they face, share ideas, help one another in preparing lessons, exchange tips, and provide other support to one another. Some suggestions for implementing collegial supervision are provided in Table 14–1.

At issue in considering collegial supervision as an option is the nature of collegiality that emerges. For example, collegiality might be contrived if it is only an artifact of administrative arrangements. Andrew Hargreaves and R. Dawe describe contrived collegiality as bureaucratic procedures and administrative arrangements that are designed to encourage teachers to engage in joint teacher planning and consultation. Examples include peer coaching, mentor teaching, and training programs for those in consultative roles. To Hargreaves, such initiatives are administrative contrivances designed to create collegiality in schools.[11] The receiving school culture is key in determining whether adminis-

---

Curriculum Development, 1984; and Robert E. Salvin, "Cooperative Learning," *Review of Educational Research,* vol. 50, no. 2 (1988), pp. 315–342.

[10]Allan A. Glatthorn, "Cooperative Professional Development: Peer-Centered Options for Teacher Growth," *Educational Leadership,* vol. 45, no. 3 (1987), p. 32. Action research and peer supervision in the form of clinical supervision are treated in this discussion as separate options. Both might involve collaboration with other teachers, a closer, more private relationship between formal supervisor and teacher, or, as in the case of action research, an individual initiative.

[11]See, for example, "Contrived Collegiality and the Culture of Teaching." Annual Meeting of the Canadian Society for the Study of Education, Quebec City, 1989; and Andrew Hargreaves and R. Dawe, "Paths of Professional Development: Contrived Collegiality, Collaborative Culture, and the Case of Peer Coaching," *Teaching and Teacher Education,* vol. 4, no. 3 (1990). See also Peter P. Grummet, Olaf P. Rostad, and Blake Ford. "The Transformation of Supervision," in Clark Glickman

TABLE 14–1

GUIDELINES FOR IMPLEMENTING COOPERATIVE PROFESSIONAL DEVELOPMENT

1. Teachers should have a voice in deciding with whom they work.

2. Principals should retain final responsibility for the makeup of collegial supervision teams.

3. The structure for supervision should be formal enough for the teams to keep records of how and in what ways time has been used and to provide a general *nonevaluative* description of activities. This record should be sent annually to the principal.

4. The principal should provide the necessary resources and administrative support enabling teams to function during the normal range of the school day. The principal might, for example, volunteer to cover classes as needed, or to arrange for substitutes as needed, or to provide for innovative schedule adjustments enabling team members to work together readily.

5. If information generated within the team about teaching and learning might be considered even mildly evaluative, it should stay with the team and not be shared with the principal.

6. Under no circumstances should the principal seek evaluation data from one teacher about another.

7. Each teacher should be expected to keep a professional growth log that demonstrates that he or she is reflecting on practice and growing professionally as a result of activities.

8. The principal should meet with the team at least once a year for purposes of general assessment and for sharing of impressions and information about the process.

9. The principal should meet individually at least once a year with each team member to discuss his or her professional growth log and to provide any encouragement and assistance that may be required.

10. Generally, new teams should be formed every second or third year.

Source: Thomas J. Sergiovanni, *The Principalship: A Reflective Practice Perspective,* 2d ed. Boston: Allyn & Bacon. 1991. p. 304.

tratively induced collegiality becomes contrived or real. Grafted onto the existing school culture, collegiality is very likely to remain contrived. Collegiality becomes real when it emerges as a result of felt interdependence among teachers, and when teachers view it as an integral part of their professional responsibility to help others and to seek help from others when needed.

Mentoring as a Special Case

Mentoring is a form of collegial supervision. A mentor is a person entrusted with the tutoring, education, and guidance of another person who is typically new to teaching or new to a given school. The mentoring relationship is special because of its entrusting nature. Those being mentored are dependent upon their mentors to help them, protect them, show them the way, and develop more fully their skills and insights. The mentor is presumed to know more not only about mat-

---

(ed.), *Supervision in Transition: The 1992 ASCD Yearbook.* Alexandria, Va.: Association for Supervision and Curriculum Development, 1992, pp. 185–202.

ters of teaching but also about the school's culture so that the novice can navigate through this culture successfully. The unequal nature of the relationship makes it a moral one.

In some respects the tutorial, educational, and advisory aspects of the mentoring relationship are developmental. Initially most novices seek assistance. They want to know what they are supposed to do, where things are, how to make requests, and what are accepted practices. They want concrete help in setting up their classrooms, establishing routines, and getting started. They want, in other words, to be tutored by an individual they trust without worrying too much about having to make an impression.

Because of its dependent nature, the tutorial relationship often represents a source of great satisfaction for the mentor. In many respects the mentor becomes the center of the novice's life. But the purpose of mentoring is to help a novice become independent. For this to happen the mentoring relationship needs to evolve quickly from one of tutelage to one of mutual edification. This happens when novices ask less and mentors tell less and when both settle down to solving problems together. "How might I best do this?" is answered with, "What ideas do you have? That one sounds promising. Let's try it out." and eventually, "How do you think it's going?"

The mentoring relationship matures when it becomes reciprocal. The novice seeks advice from the mentor and the mentor seeks to transform the relationship from mentoring to colleagueship by soliciting advice in return, by sharing problems, and by valuing the perspectives of the newcomer. Given what is known about the importance of the school's inside culture, the informal norm system that exists among teachers, and the potential that exists for teachers to share talents, mentoring makes sense as a natural way to orient new teachers, give them a successful start, and invite them to become full colleagues.

SELF-DIRECTED SUPERVISION

In self-directed supervision teachers work alone by assuming responsibility for their own professional development. They might, for example, develop a yearly plan that includes targets or goals derived from an assessment of their own needs. This plan then might be shared with supervisors or other designated individuals. As the process unfolds, teachers should be allowed a great deal of leeway in developing the plan, but supervisors should be responsible for ensuring that the plan and selected improvement targets are both realistic and attainable. At the end of a specific period, normally a year, supervisor and teacher meet to discuss the teacher's progress in meeting professional development targets. Teachers would be expected to provide some sort of documentation, perhaps in the form of a portfolio that includes such things as time logs, reflective practice diaries, schedules, photo essays, tapes, samples of students' work, and other artifacts that illustrate progress toward goals. The yearly

TABLE 14–2
GUIDELINES FOR IMPLEMENTING SELF-DIRECTED SUPERVISION

1. *Target setting.* Based on last year's observations, conferences, summary reports, clinical supervision episodes, or other means of personal assessment, teachers develop targets or goals that they would like to reach in improving their teaching. Targets should be few, rarely exceeding five or six and preferably limited to two or three. Estimated time frames should be provided for each target, which are then shared with the supervisor, along with an informal plan providing suggested activities for teacher engagement.

2. *Target-setting review.* After reviewing each target and estimated time frame, the supervisor provides the teacher with a written reaction. Further, a conference is scheduled to discuss targets and plans.

3. *Target-setting conference.* Meeting to discuss targets, time frames, and reactions, the teacher and supervisor revise targets if appropriate. It may be a good idea for the supervisor to provide a written summary of the conference to the teacher. Teacher and supervisor might well prepare this written summary together.

4. *Appraisal process.* Appraisal begins at the conclusion of the target-setting conference and continues in accordance with the agreed-upon time frame. The specific nature of the appraisal process depends on each of the targets and could include formal and informal classroom observations, an analysis of classroom artifacts, videotaping, student evaluation, interaction analysis, and other information. The teacher is responsible for collecting appraisal information and arranges this material in a portfolio for subsequent discussion with the supervisor.

5. *Summary appraisal.* The supervisor visits with the teacher to review the appraisal portfolio. As part of this process, the supervisor comments on each target, and together the teacher and supervisor plan for the next cycle of self-directed supervision.

Note: The supervisor may be the principal, a mentor teacher, or a team of teachers with whom the teacher is working.
Source: Thomas J. Sergiovanni, *The Principalship: A Reflective Practice Perspective,* 2d ed. Boston: Allyn & Bacon, 1991, p. 305.

conference would then lead to the setting of new targets for future self-directed supervisory cycles.

There are a number of problems with approaches to supervision that rely heavily on target setting. For example, supervisors might be inclined to adhere rigidly to prespecified targets and to sometimes unnecessarily impose their own targets on teachers. Rigidly applying a target-setting format to supervision unduly focuses on the process. Teachers tend to direct their attention to prestated targets, and as a result other areas of importance not targeted can be overlooked or neglected. Target setting is meant to help and facilitate, not to hinder the self-improvement process.

Self-directed approaches to supervision are ideal for teachers who prefer to work alone or who, because of scheduling or other difficulties, are unable to work cooperatively with other teachers. This option is efficient in use of time, less costly, and less demanding in its reliance on others than is the case with other options. Furthermore, this option is particularly suited to competent teachers who are able to manage their time well. Some guidelines for implementing self-directed supervision are provided in Table 14–2.

INFORMAL SUPERVISION

Included in any array of options should be a provision for informal supervision. Informal supervision is comprised of the casual encounters that occur between supervisors and teachers and is characterized by frequent informal visits to teachers' classrooms, conversations with teachers about their work, and other informal activities.

Successful informal supervision requires that certain expectations be accepted by teachers. Otherwise it will likely be viewed as a system of informal surveillance. Principals and other supervisors need to be viewed as principal teachers who have a responsibility to be a part of all the teaching that takes place in the school. They need to be viewed as instructional partners to every teacher in every classroom for every teaching and learning situation. When informal supervision is in place, principals and supervisors become common fixtures in classrooms, coming and going as part of the natural flow of the school's daily work. But this kind of relationship is not likely to flourish unless it is reciprocal. If teachers are to invite supervisors into their classrooms as equal partners in teaching and learning, teachers must in turn be invited into the process of supervision as equal partners.

Although we list informal supervision as an option, it should perhaps be understood as one kind of supervision that is included in any range of options that a school might provide.[12] In addition to informal supervision, teachers should be involved in at least one other approach such as clinical, collegial, self-directed, or inquiry-based supervision. In selecting additional options, supervisors should accommodate teacher preferences and honor them in nearly every case. Nonetheless, final responsibility for deciding the appropriateness of a selected option should probably be reserved for the supervisor.

INQUIRY-BASED SUPERVISION

Inquiry-based supervision in the form of action research is an option that can represent an individual initiative or a collaborative effort as pairs or teams of teachers work together to solve problems. In action research the emphasis is on the problem-solving nature of the supervisory experience. Mixing the word "research" with such words as "action" or "supervision" may cause some initial confusion. Research, after all, is generally thought to be something mysterious, remote, statistical, and theoretical. And further, teachers and researchers have been thought to occupy two separate ends of a continuum. What is a teacher-researcher anyway? Glenda Bissex responds as follows:

> To dispel some traditional associations with the word *research,* I'll begin by saying what a teacher-researcher *isn't.*
>
> A teacher-researcher doesn't have to study hundreds of students, establish control groups, and perform complex statistical analyses.

[12]Glatthorn, *Differentiated Supervision,* op. cit., p. 59.

A teacher-researcher may start out not with a hypothesis to test but with a "wondering" to pursue: "I wonder how much my students think about their writing outside of class. Vicky mentioned today that she mentally revises compositions on the bus coming to school. What about the others now that they're writing on their own topics?"

A teacher-researcher does not have to be antiseptically detached. He knows that knowledge comes through closeness as well as through distance, through intuition as well as through logic.

When a teacher-researcher writes about what she's discovered, she need not try to make her writing sound like a psychology textbook. Her audience is herself, other teachers, her students, their parents, her principal, maybe even the school board—none of whom is likely to be upset by plain English and a personal style.

A teacher-researcher is not a split personality with a poem in one hand and a microscope in the other.

So what is a teacher-researcher?

A teacher-researcher is an observer

a questioner

a learner

and a more complete teacher.[13]

When action research is undertaken as an individual initiative, a teacher works closely with the supervisor in sorting out a problem and developing a strategy for its resolution and in sharing findings and conclusions. Implications for practice are then identified, and strategies for implementing these changes are then developed. When action research involves collaboration with other teachers, problems are "coresearched," findings are shared, and together teachers ferret out implications for changing in their teaching practice. Among all the options, action research requires the highest level of reflection and promises a great deal with respect to discovering new insights and practices.

Basic to action research is the belief that individual teachers and groups of teachers can undertake research to improve their own practice. Although increasing understanding and building one's store of conceptual knowledge is an important outcome of action research, its prime purpose is to alter the teaching practices of the researchers themselves. Florence Stratemeyer and her colleagues describe action research as "a process aimed at discovering new ideas or practices as well as testing old ones, exploring or establishing relationships between causes and effects, or of systematically gaining evidence about the nature of a particular problem.[14]

Although usually articulated as steps, action research proceeds as a process that more accurately involves phases that are less clearly defined. Stratemeyer and her colleagues explain:

> For convenience, the phases of this process are frequently described in terms of steps although in reality they are neither neat nor discrete. Instead, there is usually a flow

---

[13]Glenda L. Bissex, "What is a Teacher-Researcher?" *Language Arts,* September 1986. Copyright 1986 by The National Council of Teaching of English. Reprinted with permission.

[14]Florence B. Stratemeyer, Handen L. Forkner, Margaret G. McKim, and A. Harry Passow, *Developing a Curriculum for Modern Living,* 2d ed. New York: Teachers College, 1957, p. 708.

from one to another, sometimes back and forth, without clear demarcations. These phases are quite similar to the sequence of the problem solving process: the problem is identified and refined; hypotheses are formulated or hunches are advanced about its solution; the hypotheses are tested and evidence is collected, organized, and analyzed; and generalizations are drawn from the data and are retested for further validation of conclusions. In a controlled laboratory situation, the research process may closely parallel these so called problem solving steps. In the classroom situation, the process flow is usually quite different.[15]

Millie Almy and Celia Genishi propose the following as the basic steps for action research:

Step 1   Identify the problem
Step 2   Develop hunches about its cause and how it can be solved
Step 3   Test one or more of the hunches
   (a)   Collect data, evidence about the situation.
         Some hunches held initially or tentatively may have to be rejected when more of the facts of the situation are known. Hunches that seem reasonable after careful consideration become the hypotheses of scientific investigations.
   (b)   Try out the hunches in action (the tryout may be in a test tube or in a classroom).
   (c)   See what happens (collect more data or evidence).
   (d)   Evaluate or generalize on the basis of evidence.[16]

For many teachers, action research works best when they engage in the process cooperatively. Problems that emerge might be of concern schoolwide or might be of concern to only two teachers whose classrooms are located across from each other. Action research as a collegial process often can result from other forms of supervision. For example, a cycle of clinical supervision might reveal pressing problems that are beyond the scope of understanding at the time. Adopting an action research stance, under this circumstance, may well be an attractive option. Examples of action research conceived as an individual activity and as a collegial undertaking are presented in Appendixes 14–1 and 14–2.

RENEWING INTEREST IN THE ADVISORY

During the 1960s and 1970s a great deal of interest was expressed in the concept of an *advisory system* as an alternative to traditional supervision. Writing in 1975, Theodore Manolakes noted:

> Possibly no other vehicle for improving instruction and the practice of teachers in the past decade has received more attention and effort than what has come to be known as the advisory system. The efforts to humanize and open up the schools that began in the late 60s have resulted in the appearance of a large number of professionals who

[15]Ibid.
[16]Millie Almy and Celia Genishi, *Ways of Studying Children: An Observation Manual for Early Childhood Teachers*, rev. ed. New York: Teachers College Press, 1979, pp. 3–4.

do not view themselves as supervisors in the usual sense, but who are committed to aiding teachers to develop more effective educational programs for children. Some of these advisors are employees of school districts who have been relieved of teaching duties to carry on advisory functions, while others work in schools but are employed by private agencies or universities.[17]

Borrowed from the wave of professionalism that swept both Great Britain and the United States during the period, the advisory was a nonevaluative system of support and help made available directly to teachers.

According to Maja Apelman, an advisor:

1 provides assistance only upon request of the teacher
2 has no evaluative [traditional] or supervisory function
3 has no predetermined agenda and does not impose or implement mandated programs
4 provides assistance in terms of teachers' needs, goals and objectives
5 acts as a support and resource person for the professional growth of teachers and helps them develop more effective educational programs for children
6 respects teachers' autonomy and works towards strengthening teachers' independence
7 develops long-term collegial relationships based on mutual trust and respect[18]

The modern-day version of an advisor is often called as instructional guide or lead teacher. Adding the advisory as another option for supervision makes sense. Because of its confidential nature, the advisory option may be attractive to teachers who are experiencing classroom problems and want to deal with them systematically but privately. Similarly, many teachers may be ready for significant changes in their teaching practice and will feel more comfortable working with someone on a more "off the record" basis.

A CONTINGENCY PERSPECTIVE

A contingency view of supervision is based on the premise that teachers are different and that matching supervisory options to these differences is important. In recent years developmental theorists such as Carl Glickman[19] and Art Costa[20]

[17] Theodore Manolakes, "The Advisory System and Supervision," in Thomas J. Sergiovanni (ed.), *Professional Supervision for Professional Teachers*, Washington, D.C.: Association for Supervision and Curriculum Development, 1975, pp. 51–64.

[18] Maja Apelman, "Working with Teachers: The Advisory Approach," in Karen K. Zumwalt (ed.), *Improving Teaching*, 1969 ASCD Yearbook, Alexandria, Va.: Association for Supervision and Curriculum Development, 1986, p. 116.

[19] Carl D. Glickman, *Supervision and Instruction: A Developmental Approach*. Boston: Allyn & Bacon, 1985.

[20] Art L. Costa, *Supervision for Intelligent Teaching: A Course Syllabus*. Orangevale, Calif.: Search Models Unlimited, 1982.

have made considerable progress in suggesting how this matching might be done. These experts examine such dimensions as levels of professional maturity and cognitive complexity and suggest that as levels vary among teachers so should supervisory approaches and styles. Another group of theorists, such as R. S. Dunn and K. J. Dunn[21] and David Kolb, Irwin Rubin, and James McIntyre,[22] have been interested in the concept of learning styles and how, as these styles vary, opportunities for learning, problem solving, and personal growth should also vary. Accounting for motives of teachers provides still a third dimension to the matching of individual teachers with supervisory options. Social motives theories such as those of David McClelland and his colleagues find that as important work motives such as the need for achievement, power, and affiliation vary among workers, the work conditions and settings they find motivating vary as well.[23]

Matching supervisory options to individual needs, therefore, has great potential for increasing the motivation and commitment of teachers at work. The section that follows *explores* these important individual dimensions and *suggests* compatible supervisory options.[24] Readers should not be under the illusion that tight and concise matching of supervisory options to individual needs and preferences is possible. It isn't. But more informed matching decisions can be made by considering the possibilities discussed.

PSYCHOLOGICAL TYPES AS METAPHOR FOR DIFFERENCE

Given the complexity of human nature, no discussion of individual differences can be exhaustive. Thus any set of ideas that seeks to chart and simplify individual differences can be viewed only as a metaphor. Carl Jung's theory of psychological types represents a preeminent metaphor for the range of individual differences in temperament that are likely to be found in any faculty and among any group of supervisors.[25] These types can provide supervisors with helpful constructs and frames for understanding their own character and temperament and for sorting and understanding the differences among teacher-colleagues. Jung's theory is complicated, however, and thus this discussion will not be exhaustive. We are interested in only the essential elements of the theory and their application to the issue of providing options in supervision. For interpretations of Jung's

---

[21]R. S. Dunn and K. J. Dunn, "Learning Styles Teaching Styles: Should They . . . Can They . . . Be Matched?" *Educational Leadership,* vol. 36, no. 4 (1979).

[22]David A. Kolb, Irwin M. Rubin, and James M. McIntyre, *Organization Psychology: An Effective Approach to Organizational Behavior.* 4th ed. Englewood Cliffs, N.J.: Prentice-Hall, 1984.

[23]See, for example, David C. McClelland, J. W. Atkinson, R. A. Clark, and E. L. Lowell, *The Achievement Motive.* New York: Appleton-Century-Crofts, 1953; David C. McClelland and D. Burnham, "Power Is the Great Motivator," *Harvard Business Review,* vol. 54, no. 2 (1976), pp. 110–111.

[24]This section follows closely Sergiovanni, *The Principalship,* op. cit., pp. 306–315.

[25]C. S. Jung, *Psychological Types.* New York: Harcourt Brace & World, 1923.

theory we rely on the work of Isabel Myers,[26] David Keirsey and Marilyn Bates,[27] and Robert Benfari.[28]

According to the theory, psychological types are comprised of different combinations of preferences and temperaments that define each individual as a distinct personality. Four pairs of preferences are important: extroversion (E) versus introversion (I), intuition (N) versus sensation (S), thinking (T) versus feeling (F), and judging (J) versus perceiving (P). From the four pairs 16 different psychological types are thought to exist.[29]

According to Keirsey and Bates[30] the key words that differentiate each of the four preference sets are as follows:

- Extroversion from introversion; sociability over territoriality, breadth over depth, external over internal, and interaction over concentrating
- Sensation from intuition; experience over hunches, realistic over speculative, past over future, actual over possible, fact over fiction, practicality over ingenuity
- Thinking from feeling; objective over subjective, principles over values, laws over circumstances, impersonal over personal, criteria over intimacy
- Judging from perceiving; settled over pending, decided over gathering more data; fixed over flexible, plan ahead over adapt as you go, decided over tentative

Different combinations of preferences lead to very different realities for teachers and supervisors. Keirsey and Bates conclude that both introverted and extroverted teachers who also prefer sensation over intuition and judging over perceiving (known as "SJs," in the language of theory) are likely to be more structured in their teaching, favoring recitation, drill, composition, tests, quizzes, and demonstrations. They are likely as well to prefer well-established classroom routines, have well laid out and sequential plans, and to be "firm and fair disciplinarians who expect students to obey the rules of the classroom and institution.[31] Since these preferences are presumed to emerge from deep-rooted psychological temperaments, they are not too easily changed. A supervisor with a different bent will be hard pressed in trying to change the behavior and outlook of SJ teachers. Keirsey and Bates report that about 56 percent of teachers can be characterized as SJ.[32]

---

[26]Isabel Myers, *Manual: The Myers-Briggs Type Indicator*. Palo Alto, Calif.: Consulting Psychologists Press, 1962.

[27]David Keirsey and Marilyn Bates, *Please Understand Me: Character and Temperament Types*. Del Mar, Calif.: Prometheus Nemesis Book Company, 1978.

[28]Robert Benfari, *Understanding Your Management Style Beyond the Meyers-Briggs Type Indicators*. Lexington, Mass.: Heath, 1991.

[29]The 16 types are labeled according to the letters of preferences in each of the four pairs: ENTJ, INFJ, ESFP, ISTJ, etc.

[30]Keirsey and Bates, op. cit., p. 25.

[31]Ibid., p. 159.

[32]Ibid., p. 166.

In contrast, introverted and extroverted teachers who prefer intuition over sensation and feeling over thinking (called "NFs") represent 32 percent of teachers according to Keirsey and Bates.[33] As a group, these teachers prefer teaching styles characterized by group projects, lessons that feature lots of interaction and discussion, exhibitions, simulations, and games. NFs are also likely to be more concerned with teaching the "whole child," to be in touch with the climate and temper of their classrooms, changing teaching topics and strategies accordingly, creating their own curriculum materials, giving more attention to values, allowing students more input, and teaching in more personalized ways.

IMPLICATIONS FOR SUPERVISION

From a psychological types perspective, preferences for particular styles of teaching, classroom climate, and curriculum arrangements may be as much a function of temperament as of reason or philosophy; this stance raises important and interesting questions. Just how far, for example, should supervisors go in trying to change the way teachers teach? How fruitful is deciding on a particular approach to teaching (i.e., the lesson cycle, direct instruction, or cooperative learning), then insisting that all teachers use this approach? Does it make sense to require all teachers to work together in teams? Should all teachers be required to use a structured and sequential curriculum or, inversely, to create their own materials in use as needs and circumstances dictate? Or does it make more sense to encourage diversity in these matters and to invite teachers to work in ways that make sense to them? Depending on how one answers these questions, one has two alternatives: continue the present practice of developing singular and standardized supervisory systems, putting them into place, and evaluating everyone on the same terms or providing options for supervision and inviting teachers to play key roles in deciding which options make sense and in sharing responsibility for implementing the options.

Cynthia Norris believes that respecting differences and encouraging diversity are key in providing a supervision that enhances both leader development and student learning. In her words, "What can supervisors do to promote teacher development and enhance student learning? One answer lies with a renewed respect for those they supervise. Central to that respect must be an appreciation of each teacher's uniqueness and an understanding of how diversity enhances rather than limits the educational process. Supervisors must also become acquainted with their own unique style and understand how their behavior impacts those they supervise.[34]

Building on Jung's theories[35] and the work of N. Herrmann[36], Norris identifies four different temperament styles that shape not only how teachers teach but

---

[33]Ibid.
[34]Cynthia Norris, "Supervising with Style," *Theory into Practice,* vol. 30, no. 2 (1991), p. 128.
[35]Jung, op. cit.
[36]N. Herrmann, *The Creative Brain.* Lake Lure, N.C.: Brain Books, 1988.

how supervisors supervise as well. Two of the styles—facts and form—stem from a decided preference for rationality, and two—futures and feelings—a decided preference for intuition. According to Norris's framework:

> Teachers with Fact styles rely heavily on data, focus on the realities of the present, generalize from specific situations, conceptually view lessons as being comprised of segmented components, emphasize precision and efficiency, and value fairness and consistency. As teachers they are likely to be subject matter oriented and to rely on sequential thinking.
>
> Teachers with Form styles adhere closely to policies and guidelines, value control and predictability, stick to the tried and true, are methodical and detailed, focus on the immediate situation, and concentrate on verifiable facts. Their classrooms are likely to be highly organized and structured and they feel most comfortable when they know exactly what is expected of them and have a fairly structured model of teaching to follow.
>
> Teachers with Futures styles place much less emphasis on policies and procedures, look beyond what is to possibilities, avoid details, view situations holistically, and seek many sources of information. In teaching they give prime emphasis to student abilities, interests and needs and seek to develop open learning climates that provide support and encourage creativity. They are particularly good at self-concept development.
>
> Teachers with Feeling styles place concern for others above all other concerns, encourage student centered activities, focus on feelings and emotional tone in developing classroom climates, and try to understand why students feel and behave the way they do. In teaching they encourage originality and problem solving, push students beyond factual knowledge, emphasize discovery and pose "why" questions.[37]

Norris believes that "if supervisors seek to change a teacher's basic style and impose their own view of teaching, they fail to foster the development of that teacher's potential. Although growth should be expected of all teachers, that growth should not be measured against someone else's style (even the supervisor's). It is the supervisor's task to help develop the teacher's uniqueness."[38] Once again we are forced to conclude that accommodating diversity in styles and needs requires the abandoning of single-minded supervisory systems that treat everyone the same in favor of options.

THE QUESTION OF SUPERVISORY STYLE

Does honoring the differences among teachers and working with them to identify supervisory options that have appeal mean that diversity in supervisory styles should also be respected and encouraged? Following Norris's conceptual framework, supervisors too can be grouped into fact, form, futures, and feelings categories. And each category spells a different supervision and a different way of working with teachers. Are they all equal? We suggest that they are not.

---

[37]Norris, op. cit., pp. 128–133.
[38]Ibid., p. 132.

Facts supervisors, for example, are characterized by logical, detailed, and sequential thought. They are likely to be directive in approach, feeling compelled to structure the supervisory relationship, break down lessons into components, analyze lessons for the teacher, and point out shortcomings. They then are likely to place emphasis on developing verbal or written school improvement plans that include problems to be resolved, improvement objectives, and a schedule for implementation. Facts supervisors tend to use such phrases as:

- Your lesson concepts were not clearly defined.
- You should have included these key points.
- Many details, such as dates, were inaccurately presented.
- You will strengthen your lesson by elaborating on specific relationships, such as. . . .
- Let me outline some approaches you should use.
- If you plan to finish the course content, you cannot afford to waste time with a few students having difficulty.
- I'd like to list specific goals and targets for your improvement plan.[39]

Form supervisors are likely to emphasize the "correct methods" of teaching and to expect teachers to use these methods with precision and exactness. They are attracted to packaged teaching models and packaged evaluation systems that spell out lesson cycles, specific steps to follow, and lists of teaching behaviors to emulate. Their approach is likely to be conservative, detached, and impersonal as they take a judicial stance. They define good teaching by the accepted model, and their job is to note whether the model is being implemented or not and to follow up by giving suggestions to teachers that better align what they do with what they are supposed to do. Form supervisors tend to use such phrases as:

- You should better organize your teaching materials. Much time was wasted during the lesson.
- Students need established rules and procedures for classroom behavior.
- I observed inconsistency in your classroom discipline.
- Many students were off-task during the lesson.
- I suggest that you arrange the group according to a planned seating arrangement.
- Your lesson plan did not work for you.
- Follow the basic components of the lesson cycle.
- Your improvement plan should include the following objectives.[40]

Feeling supervisors are likely to rely more on their own intuition in deciding what to do and how. They expect teachers to be child-centered and believe that not much progress will be made academically unless the focus teaching is broad enough to include student developmental needs, the home situation, basic health concerns, and other characteristics that comprise "the whole child." They believe

[39]Ibid., p. 130.
[40]Ibid.

that in practice, cognitive and affective domains must be brought together. Thus they are likely to encourage teachers to individualize teaching and to encourage self-esteem building. Feeling supervisors seek to involve the teaching process in lesson analysis and in deciding other supervisory issues. They tend to use the following phrases:

- I get a special feeling when I walk into your classroom. The climate is conducive to learning.
- Discussion groups were a major feature of your lesson.
- What has made these groups effective?
- You seem to recognize that Billy was having difficulty in showing support. Explain some strategies you have used with him.
- The group project encouraged creative expression among the students.
- Do you have ideas for enlarging today's lesson through this method?
- Let's plan together some ideas for your continued development; what is especially important to you?[41]

Futures supervisors are likely to expect teachers to go beyond the factual by placing emphasis on higher-order thinking and by searching for questions as well as answers. They have little patience with unimaginative rote learning and recitation. They welcome input from teachers and try hard not to assume roles as experts with all the answers. As Norris explains, futures supervisors work to "build partnerships. Teachers are encouraged to search for their own solutions and to investigate a wide variety of possibilities. Emphasis is on 'why' rather than 'how.' "[42]

Futures supervisors tend to use the following phrases:

- Let's restructure today's lesson.
- I like your ideas on components you feel especially good about.
- If there are areas of discomfort, please address those, too.
- Together we'll explore some techniques that might work for you.
- Do you perceive some possibilities for further exploration in the comment made by Jim?
- How might you add to this concept?
- Have you considered focus areas for increased development?
- How may I assist you with your plan?[43]

The merit in Norris's framework is less in the particulars and more in the issues she frames and the general orientation to differences she provides. Few supervisors, for example, are likely to fit neatly into one or another category, and none of the categories captures completely the complexities involved. With this caveat in mind it is our position that some supervisory styles are more likely to be effective than others. For example, supervisors who bring to their practice fea-

---

[41]Ibid., pp. 130–131.
[42]Ibid., p. 131.
[43]Ibid.

tures of the feeling and futures styles are likely to be more effective than those who emphasize the facts and form style. Norris points out that as a group, teachers prefer supervisors to be collaborative and nondirective, flexible in problem solving, and warm and accepting.[44]

Despite the reality that feeling and futures supervisors have distinct views about what is good teaching, their basically cooperative and problem-oriented style of supervision allows them to function successfully not only with the feeling- and futures-oriented teachers but also with the facts and form teachers. In contrast, the rigid and directive style of feeling and form supervisors seems not to be inclusive enough to accommodate feeling and futures teachers very well. Facts and form supervisors expect teachers to measure up to some preconceived standard and to adjust their teaching to fit the form of this standard.

SUPERVISORY STYLES AND COGNITIVE COMPLEXITY

Carl Glickman,[45] Art Costa,[46] and other developmental theorists believe that cognitive complexity levels of teachers should be an important consideration in matching supervisory options to teacher needs.

Cognitive complexity is concerned with both the content and the structure of teachers' thoughts, with particular emphasis on the structure.[47] For example, two teachers may share the same beliefs about the value of cooperative learning but may differ markedly in the complexity with which they view these beliefs. The content of the beliefs is similar but the structure is different. The first teacher views cooperative learning as being universally applicable rather than as one of many available strategies. The second teacher views cooperative learning as a strategy more appropriate in some instances but less appropriate in others. Although both teachers share common beliefs about cooperative learning, they differ as to the structure of those beliefs. The second teacher's thinking is characterized by higher levels of cognitive complexity than is the first. Teachers with higher levels of cognitive complexity are able to give attention to a number of different concepts relating to a particular issue and to see interconnections among these concepts. They are able to be more reflective in their practice, to understand better the subtleties of teaching, and to make more complex decisions about teaching.

Lower levels of cognitive complexity are characterized by simple and concrete thinking and practice. Higher levels of cognitive complexity are characterized by more complex abstract thinking and practice. One important finding from the research on teaching is that teachers with higher levels of cognitive complexity

[44]Norris cites authorities such as Arthur Blumberg and W. A. Weber, "Teacher Morale as a Function of Perceived Behavioral Style," *Journal of Educational Research*, vol. 62, no. 3 (1968), pp. 109–113; and N. L. Whistler and N. E. Wallace, "How Teachers View Their Supervision," *Catalyst for Change*, vol. 14, no. 1 (1984), pp. 26–29.

[45]Glickman, op. cit.

[46]Costa, op. cit.

[47]O. J. Harvey, "System Structure, Flexibility and Creativity," in O. J. Harvey (ed.), *Experience, Structure, and Adaptability*. New York: Springer, 1966.

provide a greater range of teaching environments to students. Their practice is characterized by a wider variety of teaching strategies and methods.[48] Additionally, it appears that students of teachers with higher levels of cognitive complexity tend to achieve more than do students of teachers with lower levels.[49]

N. A. Sprinthall and L. Theis-Sprinthall believe that cognitive complexity increases as teachers are exposed to more stimulating teaching environments.[50] For example, teachers who have more opportunities to interact with their supervisors and with other teachers about their teaching, who have greater opportunities for obtaining feedback about their teaching, and who have greater opportunities for experimenting in a supportive environment can all be expected to develop higher levels of cognitive complexity. One benefit of providing options for supervision is that opportunities for teachers to experience more stimulating teacher environments are increased.

MATCHING SUPERVISORY STYLES TO SITUATIONS

As suggested earlier, how supervisors decide to work with teachers can be referred to as their supervisory *style*. Styles are different from supervisory options. Within any particular option, supervisors might choose to behave differently. For example, when working with different teachers within the self-directed supervisory option it might make sense to be directive with one teacher, collaborative with another teacher, and nondirective with a third. The directive supervisory style emphasizes structure and more frequent interaction with the teacher; the collaborative emphasizes shared responsibility, joint decision making, and collegiality; and the nondirective emphasizes facilitating the teacher's plans and efforts in providing necessary support.[51] In Figure 14–1 Costa describes each of the three styles and gives examples of how they might look in practice. The matching of supervisory styles to situations sounds deceptively simple in theory but is complex in practice.

PRESCRIPTIONS OR FRAMES?

Striking the right balance between uniformity and diversity may in the end be easier than dealing with the diversity side of this balance once it is acknowledged. For example, providing supervisory options will not in itself be an effective strategy unless teachers become involved in options that make sense. Matching A with B has a certain logic that can be misleading. As we've pointed out throughout the chapter, our speculations and recommendations are not prescriptions to be applied literally. They represent thought frames that help both supervisors and teachers make better decisions about options. In the end, we believe that once options are provided, teachers should be allowed to choose to participate in those

---

[48]David E. Hunt and Bruce R. Joyce, "Teacher Trainee Personality and Initial Teaching Style," *American Educational Research Journal*, vol. 4, no. 3 (1967), pp. 253–255.

[49]Harvey, op. cit.

[50]N. A. Sprinthall and L. Theis-Sprinthall, "Career Development of Teachers: A Cognitive Perspective." *Encyclopedia of Educational Research*, 5th edition, NY: Free Press, 1982.

[51]Glickman, op. cit.

	More directive style	More collaborative style
Direction	High ◄───►	
Behavior	The supervisor recalls and analyzes the data, proposes alternative strategies, and chooses one to implement.	The supervisor presents the data, invites the teacher to consider alternatives, suggests alternatives. Together they choose alternatives. The initiating supervisor presents the data, invites the teacher to analyze the data, proposes alternatives, and selects those to implement.
Example	Supervisor: "One reason why the class was shouting out answers is that you did not lay out the ground rules as to how they should respond. Also, your classroom was arranged so that they could interact more with you than with each other. You should arrange your class in a circle so they could see each other. Also, you must start the lesson by stating that you want them to take turns and listen to each other's ideas. In the future, I'd like to begin each lesson by setting some ground rules for how they should interact. Then you should plan to spend a few minutes at the end of the lesson evaluating how well they followed those rules. When we meet next Tuesday, I'd like you to share with me just how you intend to structure the lesson and the classroom that day."	Supervisor: "I noted today that several students were not taking turns as you hoped they would. Why is that, do you think?" Teacher: "I don't know. It's always a few kids who interrupt. They just don't seem to know how to listen to each other and wait. I scold them when they do it but they just keep right on." Supervisor: "Would it help, do you think, to lay down some ground rules at the beginning of the lesson?" Teacher: "It might. What do you suggest?" Supervisor: "I think you might tell them what you expect them to do. Take turns, listen to each other, raise their hands." Teacher: "You'd think they'd know that by now. You mean I should be more specific about my expectancies." Supervisor: "Yes. Perhaps, when the lesson is finished, you might take some time to evaluate how well they followed those rules." Teacher: "I can do that. That way the students will evaluate their own behavior rather than making me do it." Supervisor: "Do you think the way you have the classroom arranged is conducive to total group listening and sharing?

FIGURE 14–1 Levels and examples of directiveness in supervisory style. (*Source: Art Costa, Supervision for Intelligent Teaching. Orangevale, Calif.: Search Models Unlimited, 1982, p. 114.*)

that make sense to them. When they do choose an option, however, they should be able to demonstrate that it is indeed an effective one for them. If after implementing an option for a period of time they cannot compellingly argue for continuing in that direction, then supervisors may need to be more aggressive in advising, coaching, and, if need be, steering teachers into more promising options.

More nondirective style

→ Low

The supervisor invites the teacher to share the data, to analyze the data, to propose alternatives for himself or herself.

Supervisor: "How do you feel the lesson went today?"
Teacher: "Pretty well. However, I'm disappointed that so many students are still not taking turns. Did I make my directions clear, do you think?"
Supervisor: "I understand them."
Teacher: "I wonder if I changed the arrangement of the classroom, would that help, do you think?
Supervisor: "When students sit in a circle, that is the position in which most students can see most other students. They can read each other's body language and facial expressions."
Teacher: "Mmm. That's what I'm trying to get them to do; to listen to one another. Next time, I'll try that. Is there anything else I could do to get them to take charge of their own behavior?"
Supervisor: "Having students evaluate themselves, you mean?"
Teacher: "Yes. When the discussion is over, I could take some time to have them discuss how well they listened to each other and took turns."

The teacher initiates by recalling data, analyzing, and prescribing. The teacher invites the supervisor to perform a role.

Teacher: "Today I noticed that there are still some students who are not taking turns and listening to each other. I've got to do something to help them take charge of their own behavior and to be courteous to each other."
Supervisor: "Like what?"
Teacher: "Well, I've gotten them into a circle where they can face each other, I've tried to model these behaviors in my own interaction, and I've talked privately with those students who have the problem. I guess I'm just going to have to lay down some ground rules for good discussion."
Supervisor: "Have you talked this over with the class?"
Teacher: "No, I haven't. Maybe if we'd have a whole class discussion to develop some criteria for good discussions, they could follow their own rules better than mine."
Supervisor: "That's possible."
Teacher: "Could you come into my classroom Tuesday morning during our class meeting? I'd like you to observe the students and me to see if they are setting their own ground rules and whether I'm helping them become more self-directed. Look for those students who are not taking turns and tell me if I could do anything more to help them learn to listen to each other."
Supervisor: "OK."

FIGURE 14–1 *(continued)*

Appendix 14–1: An Example of Individual Action Research*

A fifth-grade classroom teacher, although concerned over a period of time about individual differences in reading ability among the members in his group, observed that variations among his students this year seemed to be even greater than usual. Aside from the

*From Florence B. Stratemeyer, Hamden L. Forkner, Margaret G. McKim, and A. Harry Passow, *Developing a Curriculum for Modern Living.* New York: Teachers College, 1957, pp. 709–710.

teaching of reading, he noted other problems in planning for and with the youngsters be-cause of these differences in reading achievement, interests, and motivations. He became sufficiently dissatisfied with the situation to search for some way of providing more ad-equately for these individual differences in reading as a first step toward improving the other aspects of the teaching-learning situation. He began by trying to discover what these differences were and how they manifested themselves. He assembled all the information available in the cumulative records, including results of standardized tests and measures of past achievement. He then studied some of the literature concerning reading and its effects upon other aspects of learning. From his examination of the literature, he decided that the picture of the students was incomplete and that he needed additional data in order to be able to define the problem more specifically.

As a next step, the teacher gave a diagnostic reading test to pinpoint some of the dif-ficulties his students were encountering. He asked for reports on the kinds of materials the students read and had them keep a log of their reading over a two-week period. He obtained information from the parents as to the reading materials available in the home and the nature of the children's reading out of school. From these data the teacher iden-tified a specific problem within the broad area of concern so that it could be studied. In addition to securing data about the reading skills and habits of the students, the teacher continued to study the literature about individualizing reading instruction. The evidence he collected about the students and the new insights he developed about individualizing reading instruction provided him with some hunches or hypotheses that he could test in his classroom.

This teacher believed that if he set aside more time for working with students in groups of two or three on reading skills, and discontinued the larger reading groups he had been using, then three benefits could result: the students' reading skills would in-crease, their interests in literature would expand, and their ability to work with similar materials in other class units would grow. He decided to test his hypothesis by provid-ing direct reading instruction to students in very small groups for a two-month period. He continued to collect evidence about their reading skills and interests, and noted their behavior in using printed materials in a study of the community in which they were en-gaged. Then he tried his direct reading instruction plan and, at the end of the test period, gathered data about growth in the areas with which he was concerned.

In analyzing the evidence, he found that the work in small groups did help attain cer-tain desired goals but that it made little difference in other areas of concern. Analysis of the data suggested some leads for other possible means of individualizing instruction. He believed, for example, that the additional use of multi-level reading materials seemed a good way to meet the needs of different individuals. The teacher then planned to test his hypothesis about the value of multi-level materials in reading instruction.

Appendix 14–2: An Example of Cooperative Action Research*

Some of the faculty members of a small rural high school, in examining the performance of their top students on a state-wide scholarship test, found that, although the pupils did reasonably well on certain parts of the examination, they were far below youth from other

*From Florence B. Stratemeyer, Hamden L. Forkner, Margaret G. McKim, and A. Harry Passow, *Developing a Curriculum for Modern Living.* New York: Teachers College, 1957, pp. 710–712.

schools in understanding and appreciation of the arts, in handling concepts and abstractions, and in their breadth of reading. These were areas in which the teachers saw important educational goals.

The discussion of the findings resulted in several possible explanations. Two teachers raised the question as to whether this was a general condition or something which only occurred with these particular students. Some faculty members volunteered to gather comparable data for students who had taken this examination over the previous four or five years. Their report was submitted at the next meeting of the group and indicated that the condition had been essentially the same for previous students. Many guesses were made as to why the students in this school should do so much more poorly in these parts of the test than students from other schools, especially since the scores were comparable in sections requiring factual knowledge, and low only in appreciations, attitudes, and generalizing skills. Another meeting followed in which members reported additional findings about the experience of learners in the areas of art, music, literature, and the assimilation of ideas. Other staff members summarized articles and reports about the achievements of youth in other small rural high schools.

After several sessions, the problem began to be clearer and to take on manageable proportions. The teachers decided that the reason their students did less well in certain parts of the examination probably was that they lacked meaningful experiences in these areas. The group hypothesized that if the students were to participate in a seminar, which offered cultural experiences that now seemed to be missing, their attainments in these areas would rise to a point where their understandings would show up favorably in the annual state-wide scholarship examination in comparison with youth from larger urban schools.

The teachers then set up the machinery for testing their hypothesis. Students whose records would cause one to predict that they would achieve the highest results on the examination were invited to participate in a special three-hour session one afternoon each week. Three teachers with differing interests and specializations volunteered to serve as seminar leaders and shifts were made in their teaching schedules to free them for this assignment. These leaders met for weekly preplanning sessions and reported regularly on their activities and problems to a faculty discussion group. A theme was selected and resources were made available. The students helped plan experiences which consisted of listening to symphonic music; reading more mature literature, poems, and plays; viewing television productions; visiting the nearest art museum which was forty-five miles distant; and listening to special resource persons discuss their areas of expertness. In general they explored cultural areas beyond those normally provided in their regular programs. The teachers compiled anecdotal and behavioral data about growth of individual students during the course of the year.

Eventually, these students took the state-wide examination and their scores, particularly in the areas which had concerned the faculty group earlier, were higher than those received by former students during previous years. The faculty group then examined the validity of this test of their original hypothesis and came up with generalizations for further testing. For example, was the provision of the kind of teaching-learning situation which extended the students' cultural orientation and discussion of ideas and concepts the important thing? Assuming it might be, the faculty group began to explore possible modifications in the curriculum design and adaptations in teaching methods which they might try out the following year to see if the values of the seminar could be extended to other students.

15

SUPERVISION AS
TEACHER DEVELOPMENT
AND RENEWAL

THE overarching purpose of supervision is to help teachers improve. The focus of this improvement may be on what the teacher knows, the development of teaching skills, the teacher's ability to make more informed professional decisions, to problem-solve better, and to inquire into his or her own practice. Traditionally, improvement has been sought by providing formal and informal in-service programs and activities. Well-intentioned supervisors are placed in the driver's seat, taking responsibility for the whats, hows, and whens of improvement as they plan and provide in-service and staff-development programs they think will be best for teachers. The emphasis on in-service programs is on training teachers. In recent years in-service has given way to professional development. Here teachers play key roles in deciding the direction and nature of their professional improvement.

Frances Bolin, Judith McConnel Falk, and their colleagues[1] suggest that although in-service programs and professional development may be legitimate and important in their own right, neither are expansive and penetrating enough to tap the full potential for teachers to grow personally and professionally. For example, Bolin writes,

---

[1]See, for example, the articles that appear in Frances S. Bolin and Judith McConnel Falk (eds.), *Teacher Renewal Professional Issues, Personal Choices.* New York: Teachers College Press, 1987.

What would happen if we set aside the question of how to *improve* the teacher and looked instead at what we can do to encourage the teacher. . . . Asking how to encourage the teacher places the work of improvement in the hands of the teacher. It presupposes that the teacher desires to grow, to be self defining, and to engage in teaching as a vital part of life, rather than as unrelated employment. This leads to looking at teaching as a commitment or calling, a vocation . . . that is not adequately contained in the term *profession* as it has come to be used.[2]

FRAMEWORKS FOR GROWTH

According to Bolin, when supervision shifts away from providing improvement experiences and opportunities to encouraging teachers, in-service and staff development give way to *renewal*. Supervision as renewal is more fully integrated into the everyday life of the school as teachers move from the back seat to the driver's seat by assuming full responsibility for their own growth.

In this chapter we examine in-service programming, professional development, and renewal as alternative frameworks for creating a growth-oriented supervision. All three have a role to play, but the full range of growth opportunities for teachers, we suggest, are available only when renewal is emphasized and supported by professional development as needed. In contrast, in-service programming should play a very limited role. This ordering of the three is in direct contrast to that which now dominates current practice. In-service programming dominates, supported by staff development. Renewal, to the extent that it exists, remains at the periphery.

The three frames are contrasted in Figure 15–1. In-service, for example, is a highly directive and structured process. Responsibility for in-service is usually in the hands of someone other than the teacher, and the emphasis is on the development of job-related skills through the provision of training and practice experiences. The workshop featuring a tell, sell, and practice format is often the vehicle for delivering in-service. When in-service is the sole or primary vehicle for promoting growth, teaching comes to be viewed as a job with teachers as workers who, it is apparently assumed, possess limited capacity or will to figure out things for themselves. Though teacher in-service has a long history, teachers do not always regard the process with enthusiasm. It is often too formal and bureaucratic and characterized by a high degree of administrative planning and scheduling. Too often, in-service serves less to provide growth and more to meet legal requirements of one sort or another. Program activities often are selected and developed for uniform dissemination without giving serious consideration to the purposes of such activities or to the needs of individual teachers. Structure, uniformity, and tight control from above result in a training rather than education emphasis. We are not suggesting that in-service be abandoned, for it can

[2]Frances S. Bolin, "Reassessment and Renewal in Teaching," in Bolin and Falk, ibid., p. 11.

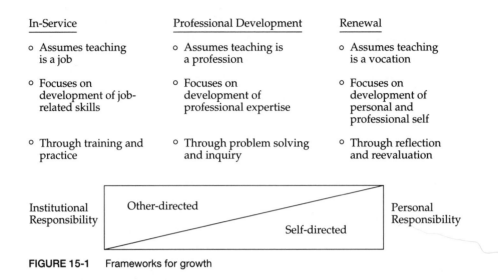

FIGURE 15-1   Frameworks for growth

be useful under proper circumstances. We are suggesting, however, that a commitment to teacher growth requires much more than in-service programming.

Professional development, in contrast, seems more in tune with the view of teaching as a profession. The emphasis is on the development of professional expertise by involving teachers in problem-solving and action research. Teachers and supervisors share responsibility for the planning, development, and provision of staff-development activities, and the focus is much less on training than on puzzling, inquiring, and solving problems.

From the supervisor's standpoint, professional development emphasizes providing teachers with the opportunity and the resources they need to reflect on their practice and to share their practice with others. Herbert Thelen suggests that the most useful professional development programs are characterized by "intensity of personal involvement, immediate consequences for classroom practice, stimulation and ego support by meaningful associates in this situation, and initiating by teacher rather than outside."[3] Anything supervisors can do to help to develop and strengthen professional community among teachers will become an investment in promoting professional development. Supervisors, therefore, help both indirectly, by promoting opportunity and support, and directly, by collaborating with teachers as colleagues.

Judith Warren Little proposes several principles that she believes should guide the thinking of supervisors as they design professional development opportunities and experiences for teachers. Professional development should:

[3]Herbert Thelen, "A Cultural Approach to Inservice Education," in Louis Rubin (ed.), *Improving In-Service Education*. Boston: Allyn & Bacon, 1971, pp. 72–73.

- Offer meaningful intellectual, social and emotional engagement with ideas, with materials and with colleagues.
- Take account of the context of teaching and the experience of teachers.
- Offer support for informed dissent as a means to evaluate alternatives and to scrutinize underline assumptions for what is being proposed or done.
- Place classroom practice in the larger context of purposes and practices of schooling.
- Provide teachers with ways in which they can see and act upon the connections among students' experience, classroom practice, and school wide structures and cultures.
- Prepare teachers to employ the techniques and perspectives of inquiry in an effort to increase their capacity to generate knowledge and to assess the knowledge claimed by others.[4]

Little offers these principles as alternatives to the "one size fits all" in-service training models that when used excessively provide teachers with shallow and fragmented content and subject them to passive roles as they participate in scripted workshops. In professional development the teacher's capacities, needs, and interests are paramount. Teachers are actively involved in contributing data and information, solving problems, analyzing, and so forth. Supervisors are involved as colleagues. Together, principals and teachers work to develop a common purpose themed to the improvement of teaching and learning. Together, principals and teachers work to build a learning and inquiring community.

Milbrey McLaughlin argues that teachers should be empowered in ways that enable them to exercise more control over their classrooms. More control, in her view, is needed for teachers to make the changes in their practices that are necessary for them to teach more effectively.[5] McLaughlin found that teachers' participation in a professional community of like-minded colleagues had a significant effect on their ability to know better what to do in the classroom and to adapt their teaching strategies to more effectively meet student needs.[6]

G. Lichtenstein, M. McLaughlin, and J. Knudsen found that professional knowledge plays a central role in empowering teachers. They point out that the knowledge that counts in empowering teachers is not the stuff of the weekend workshop or the after-school in-service. The knowledge that counts in empowering teachers is the knowledge of the teaching profession in its broadest sense.[7]

[4]Judith Warren Little, "Teacher's Professional Development in a Climate of Educational Reform," *Educational Evaluation and Policy Analysis,* vol. 15, no. 2 (1993), pp. 129–159.

[5]Milbrey McLaughlin, as cited in A. Bradley, "By Asking Teachers About 'Context' of Work, Center Moves to the Cutting Edge of Research," *Education Week,* March 31, 1993.

[6]Milbrey McLaughlin and Joan E. Talbert, *Contexts that Matter for Teaching and Learning.* Stanford, Calif.: Stanford University, Center for Research as the Context of Secondary School Teaching, 1993.

[7]G. Lichtenstein, M. McLaughlin, and J. Knudsen, "Teacher Empowerment and Professional Knowledge," in A. Liberman (ed.), *The Changing Context of Teaching,* Ninety-First Yearbook of the National Society for the Study of Education. Chicago: University of Chicago Press, 1992.

Renewal as still another growth frame focuses on the development of the personal and professional self through reflection and reevaluation. Renewal is not driven so much by professional problems as by one's commitment to teaching as a vocation. As Francis Bolin suggests, renewal implies doing over again, revising, making new yet restoring, reestablishing, and revaluing.[8] In renewal the emphasis is on the individual teacher and his or her personal and professional development.

Neither professional development nor renewal is imposed by the school upon the teacher; the teacher engages in these processes for himself or herself. In-service, on the other hand, typically assumes a deficiency in the teacher and presupposes a set of appropriate ideas, skills, and methods that need to be developed. In-service works to reduce the teacher's range of alternatives—indeed, to bring about conformity. Professional development and renewal assume a need for teachers to grow and develop on the job. Rather than reducing the range of alternatives they seek to increase this range. Teacher growth is less a function of polishing existing skills or of keeping up with the latest developments and more a function of solving problems and of changing as individuals. Growth occurs when teachers see themselves, the school, the curriculum, and the students they teach in a new light. The assumptions, roles, and practices associated with in-service training, professional development, and renewal as models of teacher development are summarized in Table 15–1.

We propose in this chapter that supervisory practice be based on the professional development and renewal models of teacher development. We begin this examination of supervision as development and renewal by first considering various dimensions of teaching competence. A design for professional development and renewal composed of five critical components is then provided. Next, we focus attention on the issue of who should assume responsibility for the provision of growth opportunities, pointing out that responsibility is in part a function of the approach one uses. Three approaches—traditional, informal, and intermediate—are discussed. Characteristics of effective staff-development programs are then considered, and we conclude our discussion by revisiting the question of purpose. Throughout this chapter we build a design that not only addresses issues and synthesizes basic concepts but can serve as a framework for planning, developing, and providing teacher growth programs and opportunities.

TECHNICAL COMPETENCE IN TEACHING

Teaching as an expression of technical competence, the most basic of the four competency types that will be discussed in this section, is the driving force behind most models of supervision and evaluation in use today. It is as well the

---

[8]Francis S. Bolin, *Reassessment and Renewal in Teaching* in Bolin and Judith Falk (eds.), *Teacher Renewal Professional Issues, Personal Choices*, N.Y.: Teachers College Press, 1987.

TABLE 15–1
MODELS OF TEACHER DEVELOPMENT

	Training	Professional	Renewal
Assumptions	Knowledge stands above the teacher.	The teacher stands above knowledge.	Knowledge is in the teacher.
	Knowledge, therefore, is instrumental. It tells the teacher what to do.	Knowledge is, therefore, conceptual. It informs the teacher's decisions.	Knowledge, therefore, is personal. It connects teachers to themselves and others.
	Teaching is a job and teachers are technicians.	Teaching is a profession and teachers are experts.	Teaching is a calling and teachers are servants.
	Mastery of skills is important.	Development of expertise is important.	Development of personal and professional self is important.
Roles	Teacher is consumer of knowledge.	Teacher is constructor of knowledge.	Teacher is internalizer of knowledge.
	Supervisor is expert.	Supervisor is colleague.	Supervisor is friend.
Practices	Emphasize technical competence.	Emphasize clinical competence.	Emphasize personal and critical competencies.
	Build individual teacher's skills.	Build professional community.	Build a caring community.
	Through training and practice.	Through problem solving and inquiry.	Through reflection and reevaluation.
	By planning and delivering training.	By emphasizing inquiry, problem solving, and research.	By encouraging reflection, conversation, and discourse.

Source: Thomas J. Sergiovanni, *The Principalship: A Reflective Practice Perspective.* Boston: Allyn & Bacon, 1995, p. 209.

basis for most teacher improvement programs and efforts. An example of an emphasis on technical competence is a focus on a list of teaching behaviors found to be linked to certain dimensions of teaching effectiveness. When technical competence is overemphasized, such teaching behaviors inevitably are found on evaluation checklists and become the basis for developing companion supervisory strategies designed to check for and encourage their use. Completing this picture are workshops and other in-service efforts that teach educators how to use the behaviors and to provide tips to supervisors as to how they might be assessed.

As a general rule, the type of teaching competence being addressed and its resulting view of teaching determine the kind of supervision and the frame for teacher growth that are used. Technical competency is important to successful teaching and learning. But over the long run this type of competency should not be the major concern in teaching or the major focus of growth and development efforts. Once technical competence is assured, primary attention should be given to clinical, personal, and critical teaching competencies.

CLINICAL, PERSONAL, AND CRITICAL TEACHING COMPETENCIES

In a groundbreaking synthesis of a broad range of philosophical, theoretical, and research knowledge on successful teaching practices, Nancy Zimpher and Kenneth Howey describe four major types of teaching competence that they believe can be facilitated by appropriate supervisory and staff-development practices: technical, clinical, personal, and critical.[9] The four are depicted and discussed in Table 15–2. Zimpher and Howey maintain that all four competency types are essential to good teaching and that each should be considered in choosing appropriate supervisory practice, determining appropriate emphasis in teacher growth programs, and deciding on the right mix of service, staff development, and renewal as frames for planning.

When the emphasis is on clinical competence, the teacher functions as a problem solver and expert clinician who frames problems and issues and comes to grips with solutions. The images of teaching as problem solving and decision making are at the heart of clinical competence. Supervisory opportunities and efforts that enhance inquiry, encourage reflection, build problem-solving skills, and help teachers make more informed decisions about their practice address the clinical competence. Building clinical competence is the major goal of professional development.

When the emphasis is on personal competence, the teacher functions as one able to understand and interpret his or her teaching in a manner that provides for meaning and significance. Supervision addresses personal competence by helping increase teacher self-awareness, understanding of teaching practice, and interpretive capacities.

Critical competence deals with issues of value and importance in the hidden meanings that underlie teaching practice. Within the critical competence, teaching is viewed as an ethical science concerned with worth and purpose. Technical competence, for example, emphasizes doing things right. In contrast, critical competence emphasizes what is worth doing and doing right things. Personal and critical competence are the major goals of renewal.

Zimpher and Howey's description of each of the four types of competence can be used by supervisors to evaluate the balance of emphasis that characterizes present school practice. Using Table 15–2, readers might, for example, examine

---

[9]Nancy Z. Zimpher and Kenneth R. Howey, "Adapting Supervisory Practice to Different Orientations of Teaching Competence," *Journal of Curriculum and Supervision*, vol. 2, no. 1 (1987), pp. 101–127.

	Technical Competence	Clinical Competence	Personal Competence	Critical Competence
Conception of the teacher	Determines in advance what is to be learned, how it is to be learned, and criteria by which success is to be measured	Instructional problem solver; clinician frames and solves practical problems; takes reflective action; inquirer	Understanding of self; self-actualized person who uses self as effective and humane instrument	Rational, morally autonomous, socially conscious change agent
Focus of supervision	Mastery of methods of instruction: specific skills (how to ask good questions); how to apply teaching strategies; how to select and organize curriculum content; how to structure the classroom for learning what techniques to use to maintain control	Reflective decision making and action to solve practical problems (what should be done about disruptive behavior) as well as reconsideration of intents and practices to take action to solve practical problems	Increase self-awareness, identity formation, and interpretive capacities, e.g., self-confrontation; values clarification; interpersonal involvement; small-group processes; develop personal style in teaching roles	Reflective decision making and action to form more rational and just schools, critique of stereotypes/ideology, hidden curriculum, authoritarian/permissive relationships, equality of access, responsibilities, and forms of repressive social control
Conception of the supervisor	Technical expert/master provides for skill development and efficient/effective use of resources in classroom; translator of research theory into technical rules for application in classrooms	Fosters inquiry regarding the relationship of theory and practice; fosters reflection about the relationship of intents and practice and reconsideration/modification of intent/practice in light of evaluation of their conscience	Expert in interpersonal competence and theories of human development; nondirective participant: warm and supportive learning environment, responsiveness to teacher-defined needs and concerns, wisdom in guiding free exploration of teaching episodes, diagnosing theories-in-use	Collaborator in self-reflective communities of practitioner-theorists committed to examining critically their own/institutional practices and improving them in interests of rationality and social justice; provides challenges and support as do other participants in dialogue

TABLE 15-2 (continued)

Type of theoretical knowledge	Technical guidelines from explanatory theory; analytic craft knowledge about what constitutes "good" practice	Synthesis of normative, interpretive, and explanatory knowledge to form intellectually and morally defensible practical judgments about what to do in a particular situation	Analytic and interpretive theory to understand and make explicit reasons underlying symbolic interaction—essentially those which occur in the class	Critical theory of education; unite philosophical analysis and criticism and causal and interpretive science
Mode of inquiry	Applied science, functional and task analysis, linear problem solving to determine how to accomplish given ends	Practical action research to articulate concerns, plan action, monitor action, and reflect on processes and consequences to improve our teaching practices; rationale building	Phenomenological, ethnographic, hermeneutic analysis and interpretation; analyze elements of teaching episodes	Collaborative action and reflection to transform the organization and practice of education; group inquiry regarding conditions of communicative interaction and social control
Level of reflectivity	Specific techniques needed to reach stated objectives involve instrumental reasoning; means-end (if, then) relative to efficiency/effectiveness	Practical reasoning and judgment relative to what should be done (best course of action under the circumstances)	Interpretation of intended meaning of verbal and nonverbal symbols and acts; introspection relative to self-awareness/identity	Critical self-reflection; reflexivity and social critique to uncover contradictions/inadequacies and different conceptions of educational practice as values with society

TABLE 15–2 *(continued)*

Range of complexity	From: Learning/using specific skills To: Learning/using complex curricular and instructional systems	From: Examining what one is doing in the classroom and making needed changes (inquiry and reflection about one's teaching) To: Action research and practical deliberation among colleagues in school/district to solve common educational concerns	From: Self-awareness and survival concerns To: Using knowledge of adult moral and cognitive development to inform teacher practice	From: Consciousness raising about school practices that are self-defeating in terms of learning and teaching, such as exposing hidden curriculum To: Collaboration of critical inquirers to reconstruct/transform schooling/society

Source: Nancy L. Zimpher and Kenneth R. Howey, "Adapting Supervisory Practices to Different Orientations of Teaching." *Journal of Curriculum and Supervision,* vol. 2, no. 2 (1987). This table combines tables 1 and 2 from their article. Zimpher and Howey acknowledged the major contribution of Sharon Strom, a doctoral candidate at the University of Minnesota, in the development of tables 1 and 2.

teacher-evaluation practices now in use in their schools, the supervision that accompany these practices, and the content and structure of teacher growth and development programs that have been implemented over the past two years. Then using a total of 100 points, assign points to each of the four critical competencies to reflect the emphasis that characterizes current practice. The following grid might be helpful:

	Technical competence	Clinical competence	Personal competence	Critical competence	Total points
Evaluation practices					100
Supervision practices					100
Teacher growth and development purposes, content, structure					100
Total					300

A best distribution among the four types of teaching competence cannot, of course, be determined separate from the characteristics of the situation at hand. A school with a large proportion of novice teachers might well need to give more attention to the technical competencies of teaching. A school with a large proportion of highly accomplished and experienced teachers might need more attention to other types of teaching competence. Total the points in each of the competency columns; using 300 points as the base, determine the percentage of emphasis across the four competency areas.

A DESIGN FOR TEACHER GROWTH AND DEVELOPMENT

In the sections that follow, a design framework for teacher growth and development composed of five critical components—*intents, substance, performance expectations, approach,* and *responsibility*—is presented. In using this design, supervisors and teachers need to be concerned about program intents and substance and, in turn, to match these with appropriate approaches, competency levels, and responsibility designations.

Intents

Teacher growth and development programs and activities are often designed around such intentions as presenting information, helping teachers understand this information, helping teachers use this understanding in their teaching, and helping teachers to accept, and be committed to, these new approaches. *Presenting* information is a *knowledge*-level intent. For example, a program might be designed to introduce a group of science teachers to the concept and language of inquiry teaching. Promoting *understanding* is a *comprehension*-level intent. The intent here might be to help teachers to understand how inquiry teaching might affect the way they presently plan and organize instruction. *Using* inquiry methods effectively in teaching a particular biology unit is an example of an *applications*-level intent. Although each of these levels is necessary, none is sufficient to gain sustained use of inquiry methods by teachers. Teacher may be able to demonstrate such methods on demand but are not likely to use them once out of the spotlight unless they believe in, and are committed to, such methods. Becoming *committed* to inquiry methods as a useful approach to science teaching is a *value-* and *attitude-integration*-level intent. Knowing what level to aim for and then focusing on this level are important insights and skills.

Substance

Louis Rubin has identified four critical factors in good teaching, each of which he believes can be improved through appropriate teacher growth and development activities:

The teacher's sense of purpose
The teacher's perception of students
The teacher's knowledge of subject matter
The teacher's mastery of technique[10]

Sense of purpose and perception of students are part of a teacher's *educational platform* and as such represent values, beliefs, assumptions, and action theories a teacher holds about the nature of knowledge, how students learn, appropriate relationships between students and teachers, and other factors. One's educational platform becomes the basis for decisions one makes about classroom organization and teaching, and, indeed, once a platform is known, key decisions the teacher will make can be predicted with reliability.

A teacher who considers his or her purpose to impart information is likely to rely heavily on teacher talk and formal classroom arrangements. Likewise, a teacher who perceives youngsters as being basically trustworthy and responsible is likely to share responsibilities for decisions about learning with the class.

---

[10]Louis J. Rubin, "The Case for Staff Development," in Thomas J. Sergiovanni (ed.), *Professional Supervision for Professional Teachers*. Washington, D.C.: Association for Supervision and Curriculum Development, 1975.

If a supervisor were interested in reducing teacher talk and/or increasing student responsibility, he or she would have to contend with the critical factor of purpose and perception of teachers. His or her target is the restructuring of educational platforms of teachers.

In describing the importance of knowledge of subject matter, Rubin notes:

> There is a considerable difference between the kind of teaching that goes on when teachers have an intimate acquaintance with the content of the lesson and when the acquaintance is only peripheral. When teachers are genuinely knowledgeable, when they know their subject well enough to discriminate between the seminal ideas and the secondary matter, when they can go beyond what is in the textbook, the quality of the pedagogy becomes extraordinarily impressive. For it is only when a teacher has a consummate grasp of, say, arithmetic, physics, or history that their meaning can be turned outward and brought to bear upon the learner's personal experience. Relevancy lies less in the inherent nature of a subject than in its relationship to the child's frame of reference. In the hands of a skilled teacher, poetry can be taught with success and profit to ghetto children.[11]

Although content versus process arguments continue from time to time, both aspects of instruction are necessary for effective teaching. Our observation is that the less the teacher knows about a particular subject, the more trivial the teaching and the more defensive the pedagogy. By defensive pedagogy we mean dominance by the teacher and strict adherence to curriculum materials. But a teacher can have a great appreciation for a particular field of study and still not be able to communicate its wonder and excitement effectively. Mastery of technique, classroom organization and management, and other pedagogical skills make up the fourth critical dimension of effective teaching. Each of the critical factors in good teaching can be understood and developed as technical, clinical, personal, or critical teaching competence.

These dimensions are the basis for deciding the substance of staff-development programs. Comprehensive programs are concerned with all four—the teacher's conception of purpose, sensitivity to students, intimacy with subject matter, and basic repertory of teaching techniques. Purpose and sensitivity remain key, for they shape the teacher's reality and become the basis for making teaching decisions about subject matter and technique. This observation raises questions about viewing technical, clinical, personal, and critical competency types as being rigidly developmental. Developmental thinking leads supervisors to reason that they must first provide in-service to build basic technical skills, shifting only later to professional development and renewal frames for "higher" levels of competency. It turns out that personal and critical competency may be so fundamental in shaping the teacher's basic view of teaching that they influence as well the development of basic teaching skills. Following this reasoning, the competency levels might best be viewed as a pattern for defining teaching that can be addressed by the provision of in-service, staff development,

[11]Ibid., p. 47.

or renewal opportunities as appropriate. Multiple frames leads us to conclude that providing options (to be discussed in the next chapter) and encouraging teachers to make informed choices among them should be at the crux of a school's overall teacher growth strategy.

Performance Expectations

What are the major performance expectations for which teachers should be accountable? It is reasonable to expect that teachers *know how* to do their jobs and keep up with major developments. But knowing and understanding are not enough. Teachers also are expected to put their knowledge to work—to demonstrate that they *can do* the job. Still, demonstrating knowledge is a fairly low-level competency. Most teachers are competent enough and clever enough to come up with the right teaching performance when the supervisor is around. The proof of the pudding is whether they *will do* the job of their own free will and on a sustained basis. Finally, as professionals, teachers are expected to engage in a life-long commitment to self-improvement. Self-improvement is the *will-grow* performance expectation. Self-employed professionals (doctors, accountants, etc.) are forced by competition and by visible product evaluation to give major attention to the will-grow dimension. Teachers, as organizational professionals whose "products" are difficult to measure, have not felt this external pressure for continuing professional growth. Increasingly, however, school districts are making the will-grow dimension a contractual obligation, and indeed teachers who are perfectly satisfactory in the know-how, can-do, and will-do performance expectations face sanctions (including dismissal) for less than satisfactory commitment to continuing professional growth.

The relationships between performance expectations, intents, and substance are summarized in Figure 15–2. For example, in the know-how area, teachers are expected to know and understand purposes, students, subject matter, and techniques. In the can-do area, teachers apply this knowledge of substance to their

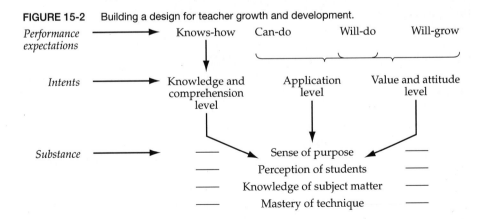

FIGURE 15-2   Building a design for teacher growth and development.

classrooms. Will-do, however, requires not only ability to apply this knowledge but a commitment to its application over time. Teacher growth programs aimed at the will-do dimension must have "value and attitude" as well as application intents. If performance and commitment are to be sustained over time, teachers must see value in what they do and believe it is important to commit themselves. Will-grow is equally dependent upon value and attitude intents. Thus supervisors working with teachers in the will-do and will-grow areas and who choose strategies suited only to knowledge and comprehension are not likely to be successful.

Approach and Responsibility

We have now discussed three of five design components for planning and providing teacher growth and development opportunities: intents, substance, and performance expectations. Two more remain: the *approach* used and the locus of major *responsibility*. Approaches can be grouped into three general categories: traditional, informal, and intermediate. Traditional approaches generally are more formal and structured and designed to meet specific and uniform objectives. They emerge from the in-service frame. Informal approaches, on the other hand, are loosely structured and rely on discovery and exploration techniques. Often objectives are not predetermined but are discovered or assessed after the fact. Intermediate approaches are moderately structured with a predetermined agenda that permits a great deal of flexibility. Both are aligned with the staff-development and renewal frames.

Traditional Approaches and Supervisory Responsibility   Traditional approaches to staff development are well known to supervisors and administrators and need little elaboration. They seem best suited when a problem can be defined as a deficit in knowledge of some kind. Traditional approaches typically are accompanied by clear objectives and rely on conventional, though well-executed, instruction. Teachers generally assume passive roles and are exposed to logically structured programs or activities. Techniques most often used are lecture, illustrated lecture, demonstration, and observation, often followed by guided discussion activities.

Traditional approaches seem well suited to routine information updating of the latest books, techniques, principles, and ideas relating to one's work. It is not assumed that a particular group is considering adopting something new, but that the group is only learning more about it. As intents change from learning to understanding, to applying, to integrating new things into one's repertoire of behavior, approaches will need to change if efforts are to be effective. The widespread use of traditional approaches to the virtual exclusion of other approaches would lead one to conclude that educators have an insatiable appetite for knowledge but are not interested in doing very much with this knowledge.

The locus of responsibility for traditional approaches to teacher growth and development is with the administration as it executes its personnel administration functions. Although traditional approaches have a place and should remain administrative responsibilities, alone they represent a minimum commitment to teacher growth and development.

Informal Approaches and Teacher Responsibility   Perhaps the most innovative and provocative approaches to teacher growth and development are those that rely on exploration and discovery by teachers. It is assumed that by providing teachers with a rich environment loaded with teaching materials, media, books, and devices, and that with generous encouragement and support from principals and supervisors, teachers will interact with this environment and with each other through exploration and discovery. Exploration and discovery can help many teachers to find themselves, to unleash their creativity, to learn more about their own capabilities as people and teachers, and at the same time to pick up new teaching ideas, activities, and methods.

Earlier we noted that in most useful growth and development programs for teachers one finds intensity of personal involvement, immediate consequences for classroom practice, stimulation and ego support by meaningful associates in the situation and initiating by teacher rather than outside.[12] Informal approaches seem best able to meet these criteria, and because of their enormous potential, such approaches should play an important role in school district planning. Major responsibility for informal approaches rests with teachers. They can take a variety of forms: two teachers sharing ideas; a team or family of teachers working and planning together; teacher involvement in an inbuilding resource center; and participation in district or area teacher centers. Informal approaches should be encouraged and supported.

Teacher centers deserve special attention. They represent fledgling, but promising, attempts to elevate and legitimize the role of teacher in accepting some of the responsibility for their own growth and development. In describing such centers Kathleen Devaney notes:

> There is a notion of *teachers centers* which is essentially an image of a place—small, welcoming, hand-built—where teachers come voluntarily to make things for classrooms, to exchange ideas, and to learn in a format of one-shot or short-series workshops rather than semester-long courses based on lectures and texts. Because this place is noninstitutional neutral ground, teachers can let down their hair, drop competitiveness and defensiveness, and thus find starting points for self-improvement and professional growth.[13]

Some centers indeed fit the "noninstitutional neutral ground" pattern, but no hard and fast rules regarding location exist. A teacher center can be developed and operated in a surplus classroom or perhaps in an overlooked or underutilized basement location of a particular school. The center could be limited to only

---

[12]Herbert Thelen, op. cit.

[13]Kathleen Devaney, "What's a Teacher Center For?" *Educational Leadership*, vol. 33, no. 6 (1976), p. 413. This issue of *Educational Leadership* was guest-edited by Vincent Rogers, and its theme is teacher centers.

teachers of that school or perhaps expanded to serve district or area teachers. The closing of schools in many districts is conducive to the establishment of a district or area teacher center in abandoned school buildings. Some centers can be located in storefronts and warehouses. Regardless of scale or location, some common aspects exist, the most notable being that the locus of responsibility for planning and operation is with teachers. Further commonalities are suggested by Devaney:

> The common purpose which stands out as a bond linking widely dissimilar teachers centers is the aim to help teachers enliven, individualize, personalize, enrich, elaborate, reorganize, or re-conceptualize the curriculum within their own classrooms. Study of scores of teachers center program offerings and calendars demonstrates center leaders' belief that help to teachers in the area of curriculum is the most teacher-responsive service they can offer. These centers teach teachers how to use manipulative, real-world, exploratory, frequently individualized curriculum materials and how to gradually reorganize classroom space and time to accommodate greater student activity and interaction. They engage teachers in adapting packaged curriculum materials, making their own materials, or building classroom apparatus, and often they involve teachers in some new study—often math or science—or craft so as to reacquaint them with the experience of being active, problem-solving learners themselves.[14]

Changes of lasting quality in schools depend heavily on grassroots processes. Additionally, it seems clear that teachers look to other teachers as important models for change. In two separate studies with similar themes both Emil Haller and Charles Keenan[15] asked teachers to identify to whom they go for help when they run into curriculum problems and to whom they could go for ideas and insights about teaching and learning. The Canadian and American teachers who responded to these questions also were asked which sources of new ideas were most creditable. Choosing from such categories as principal, supervisor, central office staff, professor, research journals, and so on, the overwhelming choice in response to each question was *other teachers.* Teachers go to other teachers for help and for sources of new ideas, and they believe in each other—potent reasons for supervisors to provide support for informal teacher growth and staff-development approaches.

Intermediate Approaches and Supervisory Responsibility   Informal approaches are low-keyed, classroom-focused, teacher-oriented, and particularistic. Traditional approaches, on the other hand, are high-keyed, more formal, system- or school-oriented, and universal. A supervisory system of teacher growth and development, in contrast, assumes an intermediate position whereby the supervisor enters into a relationship with teachers on an equal footing and assumes

---

[14]Ibid., p. 414.

[15]Emil J. Haller, *Strategies for Change.* Toronto: Ontario Institute for Studies in Education, Department of Educational Administration, 1968; and Charles Keenan, "Channels for Change: A Survey of Teachers in Chicago Elementary Schools." Doctoral dissertation. Urbana: University of Illinois, Department of Educational Administration, 1974.

an active role along with teachers. The teachers' capacities, needs, and interests are paramount, but sufficient planning and structure is introduced to bridge the gap between these interests and school program and instruction needs.

Intermediate staff-development approaches usually have the following characteristics:

1 The teacher is actively involved in contributing data, information, or feelings, solving a problem, or conducting an analysis.
2 The supervisor shares in the contributing, solving, and conducting activities above as a colleague of the teacher.
3 In colleagueship the supervisor and teachers work together as professional associates bound together by a common purpose. The common purpose is improvement of teaching and learning through the professional development of both teacher and supervisor.[16] Neither the teacher's autonomy as a professional nor the supervisor's responsibilities as a professional are compromised in the process, since the relationship is based not on authority but on a commitment to professional improvement.
4 Staff-development activities generally require study of an actual situation or a real problem and use live data, either from self-analysis or from observations of others.
5 Feedback is provided, by the supervisor, by other teachers, or as a result of joint analysis, which permits teachers to compare observations with intents and beliefs, and personal reactions with those of others.
6 The emphasis is on direct improvement of teaching and learning in the classroom.

CHARACTERISTICS OF EFFECTIVE STAFF-DEVELOPMENT PROGRAMS

By way of summary, excerpts from a study of staff-development programs conducted under the auspices of the Florida State Department of Education are provided. The study suggests a number of clear patterns of effectiveness consistent with the recommendations provided above:

School-based programs in which *teachers participate as helpers to each other and planners of in-service activities* tend to have greater success . . . than do programs . . . conducted by college or other outside personnel without the assistance of teachers.

In-service education programs that have *differentiated training experiences for different teachers* (that is, "individualized") are more likely to accomplish their objectives than are programs that have common activities for all participants.

---

[16]Our definition of colleagueship follows Morris Cogan, *Clinical Supervision*. Boston: Houghton Mifflin, 1973, chap. 5. In contrast, the relationship between supervisor and teacher in traditional approaches is more clearly superordinate-subordinate, and in informal approaches the supervisor is more of a helper, facilitator, or passive supporter. In the intermediate approach the supervisor is neither dominating nor passive but is involved, side by side, with the teacher as a colleague.

In-service education programs that *place the teacher in an active role (constructing and generating materials, ideas, and behavior)* are more likely to accomplish their objectives than are programs that place the teacher in a receptive role. . . .

In-service education programs in which *teachers share and provide mutual assistance* to each other are more likely to accomplish their objectives than are programs in which each teacher does separate work.

Teachers are more likely to benefit from in-service programs in which they can *choose goals and activities for themselves,* as contrasted with programs in which the goals and activities are preplanned. [Italics added][17]

In their extensive review of the literature on staff development, experts Dennis Sparks and Susan Loucks-Horsley list the following as "well-known" effective practices:

Programs conducted in school settings and linked to school-wide efforts

Teachers participating as helpers to each other and as planners, with administrators, of inservice activities

Emphasis on self instruction with differentiated training opportunities

Teachers in active roles, choosing goals and activities for themselves

Emphasis on demonstration, supervised trials and feedback; training that is concrete and ongoing over time

Ongoing assistance and support available on request[18]

Notice the importance given to teacher involvement in planning, differentiated experiences for different teachers, active roles, using ideas, materials, and behavior found in the actual teaching situation, teachers working with and helping other teachers, and teacher goals.

INFORMING REFLECTIVE PRACTICE

In most schools and school districts technical teaching competence commands the major share of teacher growth and development attention and resources. The emphasis is on learning the facts, rules, and procedures and applying them to a presumably nonproblematic, relatively uniform, and stable teaching situation. Often these technical teaching skills are considered to be generic and thus universally applied to all situations, and sometimes this is indeed the case. At one level of abstraction, for example, it is true that positive reinforcement is positive reinforcement, wait time is wait time, on task is on task, and monitoring is monitoring regardless of the teaching and learning context. Supervision that re-

[17]Roy A. Edelfelt and Margo Johnson, *Rethinking In-Service Education.* Washington, D.C.: National Education Association, 1975, pp. 18–19, as quoted in Devaney, op. cit., p. 416. The original report is Gordon Lawrence, *Patterns of Effective In-Service Education.* Tallahassee, Fla.: State Department of Education, 1974.

[18]Dennis Sparks and Susan Loucks-Horsley, "Five Models of Staff Development for Teachers," *Journal of Staff Development,* vol. 10, no. 4, p. 40, Fall 1989.

sponds to this focus seeks to train teachers in the appropriate techniques and to provide coaching directed to detecting and correcting errors as the techniques are applied.

In addition to professional knowledge construed as technical facts, rules, and techniques, Donald Schön proposes two other understandings: professional knowledge in the form of "thinking like a teacher" and professional knowledge as "reflection-in-action."[19] In thinking like a teacher one not only masters the appropriate facts and techniques but learns form of inquiry "by which competent practitioners reason their way, in problematic instances, to clear connections between general knowledge and particular cases."[20] In knowledge of this sort it is presumed that a right way exists to match every situation, and the emphasis is on how one analyzes situations and decides what is the appropriate, right way to apply. There is a link between this way of knowing and professional knowledge construed in a technical sense. But the emphasis in thinking like a teacher is on learning how to decide when to use what. Supervision that emphasizes thinking like a teacher relies less on training and more on coaching, apprenticing, and other forms of mentoring.

In earlier chapters we pointed out that one problem with overemphasizing technical aspects of supervision that may be suitable for specific problems, stable environments, and deterministic teaching is that the real world is for the most part ambiguous, complex, and fluid. Teachers, for example, are often unsure of what their goals and objectives are, sometimes discover goals and objectives while they are teaching, and invariably pursue multiple goals and objectives that from time to time even conflict with each other. In the real world of teaching, plans rarely unfold as planned. Circumstances are typically not quite like those anticipated. Student reactions are difficult to predict. Subject matter, content, and concepts connect themselves in ways not expected, and so on. Teaching, then, is somewhat like surfing, and teachers ride the pattern of the wave of teaching as it uncurls. Teachers, therefore, need to learn to make new sense of uncertain unique and conflicting situations that they face in their practice. To do this, Schön suggests that professional knowledge be construed as "reflection in action." From this stance one does not assume that existing professional knowledge fits every case or that every problem has a right answer. Instead teachers will need to "learn a kind of reflection-in-action that goes beyond stable rules—not only by devising new methods of reasoning . . . but also by constructing and testing new categories of understanding, strategies of action, and new ways of framing problems."[21]

When professional knowledge is understood as reflection in action, staff development and supervision are drawn together. The context for reflection in action is the teacher's practice, and this practice takes place in the classroom, not

---

[19]Donald A. Schön, *Educating the Reflective Practitioner*. San Francisco: Jossey-Bass, 1987.
[20]Ibid., p. 39.
[21]Ibid.

in the school auditorium, during institute day, the cafeteria as setting for an after-school workshop. Staff development designed to inform reflective practice, therefore, needs to be largely classroom-based. In this sense, staff development, supervision, mentoring, and coaching should not be viewed as separate and distinct roles but as dimensions of the role of supervisor as he or she works to enhance the technical, clinical, personal, and critical competencies of teaching and to promote professional knowledge in its technical sense in the form of thinking like a teacher and in the form of reflective practice.

RENEWAL AS A STRATEGY FOR THE FUTURE

We began this chapter discussing three different frames for thinking about teacher growth and development: in-service, professional development, and renewal. We noted in Figure 15–1, for example, that within the in-service frame teaching is viewed as a job. With job as the metaphor, the development of job-related skills through training and practice becomes an important process of supervision. In a sense, teaching is a job and such skills are important. But teaching is also a profession.

The professional development frame views teaching as a profession within which the development of professional expertise through problem solving and inquiry are considered to be the main focus of supervision. Teachers assume much more responsibility for what happens in staff development as they work closely with their colleague teachers and their colleague supervisors.

Teaching, however, is not only more than a job but more than a profession, at least as defined in its technical sense. For example, much of teaching is a personal extension of the teacher. The act of teaching itself is moral, thus values and beliefs loom large in deciding what to do and in determining what happened and in assigning worth. The caring ethic as represented by deep commitment to service is yet another unique characteristic of teaching. Together, these characteristics define teaching as a vocation. Though one may join a profession, one is called to a vocation. In referring to the work of Dwayne Huebner, Bolin points out that "if we look at teaching as a vocation rather than as a profession we must attend to the meaning and valuemaking of the teacher. Activity of this kind involves . . . re-evaluation."[22] She continues: "renewal is full of meaning that suggests ways to think about teacher renewal. . . . There is a spiritual dimension to the term, especially in its first two levels of meaning: to do over again, revise; make new, or as new again."[23] Renewal and vocation go hand in hand. The idea of vocation is consistent with an emphasis on professional authority and moral authority as motivators for teachers and supervisors, a theme discussed in Chapter 3. When professional authority and moral authority become the focus, the in-

---

[22]Bolin, "Reassessment and Renewal in Teaching," op. cit., p. 12.
[23]Ibid., p. 13.

service frame for teacher growth and development plays a minor role and the professional-development frame moves to a position of support for teacher renewal. As we move away from in-service and toward professional development and renewal, teacher development changes from something someone does to teachers or for teachers to something that happens to teachers as a result of what they do.

CHAPTER 16

SUPERVISION AND SUMMATIVE EVALUATIONS

EVERY community is made up of individual personalities. Those individuals have their own talents, hang-ups, dreams, idiosyncrasies—all of which both enrich the community as well as place a collective strain on it. There is a need to keep alive the sense of community identity, a sense of what distinguishes that community from other communities, a sense of something special that holds people together. Sometimes that sense of identity derives from the central purpose that the community was founded to serve; other communities are bound together by their ethnic, religious, racial, or cultural traditions; other communities are made up of people who choose a certain lifestyle or recreational interest. In most communities there are certain requirements for initial membership and other requirements for maintaining membership. Sometimes these requirements are formalized through admission procedures and initiation rites, and through periodic ritual restatements of commitment to the community (renewal of marriage vows, celebrations of anniversaries, annual awards ceremonies, the publication of annual reports, tenure review, annual corporate retreats, etc.). Sometimes membership comes from simply remaining in the community long enough to be accepted. Most communities, however, need rituals by which they can assert their identity, maintain their identity, and protect their identity.

A school as a community of learners brings together youngsters, families, and other adults. Though belonging to a variety of other communities, these people form a community with a mission to perpetuate and renew the life of the larger civic community by exploring ways to carry the culture and the polity forward in the next generation. One of the mechanisms or rituals by which this community reasserts its identity as a learning community is through periodic evaluation. Through evaluations the community agrees to assess what progress they are making in their mission as a community. For students, these evaluations take the form of tests, oral and written quizzes, final exams, portfolios, projects, and competitions. For teachers, they take a variety of forms.

Formal teacher evaluations have traditionally been sources of tension, alienation, and conflict. Some of that is inescapable, and perhaps even healthy (when it involves arguments about what constitutes an authentic expression of the mission of the school community). Much of the discomfort concerning evaluation can be eliminated, however, if it is treated as a community exercise in self-governance, as a way for the school community to maintain and strengthen its identity as an entity committed to learning, rather than as a mechanism of bureaucratic control exercised over subordinates. One significant way to make the evaluation process a community exercise is to require that all members be evaluated, including supervisors, administrators, and evaluators.

In the previous chapters we have been emphasizing supervision as a process for promoting teacher growth and enhanced student learning. Within the distinction between formative and summative evaluation, we have been emphasizing formative evaluation, that is, that kind of interaction with teachers that develops information, points of view, questions, and inquiries into alternatives, all of which teachers can use as part of an ongoing reflection on and within practice.

In this chapter we turn to summative evaluation. This kind of evaluation involves coming to a conclusion or making a judgment about the quality of the teacher's performance. This kind of evaluation rates the teacher's performance as meeting, exceeding, or falling below some standard of teaching competence or some level of acceptable teaching performance. Often summative evaluations are tied to a formal personnel decision, such as a decision whether to grant a teacher tenure, whether to promote a teacher to a higher position or rank, or whether to renew a tenured teacher's contract. A summative evaluation may be used to rate a tenured teacher according to a scale, which may or may not affect the teacher's salary or "rif number." Formative evaluations *assume* membership in the learning community; summative evaluations invite a more structured reflection on the demands and meanings of membership in a learning community with a specific mission. Summative evaluation employs clear standards of membership; the basic characteristics of the community are identified in and safeguarded through summative evaluation. Formative evaluations are ways to enliven and enrich that identity, although both forms of evaluations can serve that purpose.

Supervisors are excluded from some summative evaluations that are considered the responsibility of administrators. Sometimes administrators are also supervisors, as in the case of principals or assistant principals. In that instance they have to decide whether a particular involvement in summative evaluation requires them to wear an administrative hat or a supervisory hat. Sometimes personnel who are not administrators but who engage in supervision of teachers for formative purposes are asked to participate in a summative evaluation of a teacher.

Whether a supervisor acts in an administrative capacity or is functioning in a purely supervisory capacity, there should be very clear, formally described distinctions between supervision for formative evaluation, supervision for summative evaluation, and supervision for administrative evaluation and decision. The process of supervision for promoting teacher growth and enhanced student learning should be clearly distinguished from the process of supervision for personnel decisions; where possible, separate personnel should perform them. Where that is not possible, teachers should know beforehand what the differences among the various processes are, and which one is being used at that time. Leaving such distinctions fuzzy and indefinite engenders widespread lack of trust among teachers and undermines the formative potential of formative supervision. When the supervisory process is carried on as though the various types of evaluation are one and the same, then the supervisory episode is perceived as threatening and adversarial.

CLARIFYING THE DISTINCTION

Teachers and administrators in the school should know the difference between formative and summative supervision. Summative evaluations differ according to purpose. Each format should have a structured series of steps, with mutual responsibilities clearly spelled out. Depending on the kind of personnel decisions to be made, the structure of the evaluation may vary. The following hypothetical examples from Sunlight School show how different summative evaluations might be structured.

I. The process of summative evaluation for nontenured teachers at Sunlight School

   A. Six months prior to the tenure decision, the nontenured teacher will be provided an oral and written evaluation of his or her teaching performance. This evaluation will be structured according to the evaluative criteria presented to the beginning teacher within the first month of his or her teaching duties.

   B. Prior to the summative evaluation report, the beginning teacher's classes will have been visited at least six times a semester. Each visit will be followed by an extensive discussion of the teacher's performance. Suggested improvements will be noted. At least two people will have participated in those class visits in order to ensure at least two voices in the gathering of observational data.

   C. At least three people, one of whom will be the principal or someone else designated by the superintendent, will discuss the class observation data and follow-up discussions, and the three will prepare the summative evaluation report and attach their names to it.

    D. The criteria for evaluating beginning teachers will have been decided by the tenured teaching faculty.

    E. If the evaluation is unfavorable, the teacher will have one month to show why the evaluation is incorrect, or why he or she should be granted tenure despite the evaluation.

    F. During the months following an unfavorable evaluation, the beginning teacher will participate in a series of discussions with administrators and teachers chosen for this task to determine whether to stay in teaching as a career, consider what steps may be required to do so, or consider looking into some other career.

II. The process of summative evaluation of a tenured teacher recommended for termination of contract at Sunlight School

    A. Termination of a tenured teacher's contract shall be justified for the following reasons only: legal or moral turpitude; clear and repeated violations of school policies; repeated demonstration of incompetence as a teacher, after repeated warnings about the need to improve performance; clear and repeated neglect of duties as a professional member of the staff. All these are considered indications that the teacher has opted out of membership in the school community and, as such, require the community to verify whether such options are indeed being exercised. If they are, then membership should cease. In the case of evidence of a serious crime, the teacher will be suspended until a legal disposition of the matter is reached.

    B. The teacher must be notified by the appropriate administrator of a serious deficiency in his or her performance and of the need to correct that deficiency as soon as it is perceived, or if the teacher has been rated as probationary on the periodic evaluation.

    C. If the teacher believes the complaint is incorrect or unjustified, both the teacher and the administrator may ask others to verify the presence of the deficiency.

    D. If the complaint is not verified, then the teacher is not required to take any action. If the complaint is verified, the teacher must take steps to correct the deficiency within a specified time frame. The teacher is listed, in this case, as "on probation," and an account of the matter is entered into that teacher's personnel file.

    E. If, after the specified time, it appears that the teacher has not corrected the deficiency, at least two other professionals on the staff must verify that the deficiency has not been corrected.

    F. If the deficiency is verified, then the teacher may be notified that his or her contract will not be renewed. Notification of nonrenewal must be made before February 1 of the present contract year. If the case warrants, however, the contract may be terminated immediately.[1]

---

[1]For a more detailed treatment of approaches to dealing with incompetent teachers, see Edwin M. Bridges, *The Incompetent Teacher.* London: Falmer Press, 1986; Jim Sweeney and Dick Manatt, "A

Notice the difference between the two evaluation procedures. In comparison with nontenured teachers, tenured teachers have more opportunities to turn the situation around; there are more opportunities to engage colleagues in making additional evaluations to prevent unfair treatment. Notice the difference between these procedures and the following procedures, which might be employed in what is considered a more normal evaluation experience.

III. The process of periodic evaluation of tenured teachers at Sunlight School

   A. Every 3 (or 5) years each tenured teacher will undergo an in-depth evaluation. This evaluation is an opportunity for the teacher to demonstrate how he or she has maintained or grown in commitment to the mission of this community of learners. It is an opportunity for the community, acting through persons delegated for that purpose, to assess the contribution each teacher is making to the life of the school.

   B. Upon receiving tenure, each teacher is required to present a 3-year growth plan. This plan will include all or some of the following: efforts to improve in areas noted as needing improvement in the prior evaluation; efforts to develop one's knowledge base through university courses, staff-development opportunities in the district and in the region, or other avenues of study; efforts to expand one's repertory of teaching strategies, and to improve diagnostic abilities to assist students with difficulties; efforts to network with other teachers in the school, in the system, or in the region for professional development purposes; cultural enrichment; and so on. Every teacher will maintain a portfolio that contains evidence of systematic progress on their growth plan.

   C. At the beginning of the year in which the in-depth evaluation is to take place, an administrator or senior teacher will be assigned to work with the teacher involved. That person (the evaluator) will review with the teacher what progress has been made on the growth plan and together they will prepare a report to be included with the in-depth report for review by the principal. That person will also prepare a plan with the teacher, outlining how the in-depth evaluation will take place during that year.

   D. At the opening meeting the teacher will choose one of the five in-depth evaluation formats chosen by the faculty and spelled out in the faculty contract, or, with approval of the principal, some other format that appears suited to the teacher's particular needs and that satisfies the general purposes for these in-depth evaluations.

   E. At the opening meeting the teacher will review with the evaluator the format of the final report of the in-depth evaluation, especially the criteria for arriving at each of the four general ratings (superior, satisfac-

Team Approach to Supervising the Marginal Teacher, *Educational Leadership,* vol. 41, no. 7 (April 1984), pp. 25–27.

tory, less than satisfactory, and probationary). Those ratings have consequences for the type of growth plan to be submitted at the end of the year. Those receiving superior ratings will undergo the next in-depth evaluation in 5 years and are free to devise their growth plans in ways that serve both the needs of the school and the needs of their own professional growth. Those receiving satisfactory ratings will undergo the next in-depth evaluation in 3 years and may devise a growth plan in ways that serve the needs of the school and their own professional growth. Those receiving a less than satisfactory rating must submit a growth plan that is targeted at improving in those areas that caused the unsatisfactory rating and will undergo their next in-depth evaluation in 3 years. Those who are rated as probationary will be required to undergo the procedures called for by that evaluation process beginning with the next semester.

F. During the initial meeting the evaluator will arrange to hold five lengthy sessions with the teacher during the in-depth evaluation year. They will be followed by a concluding meeting for a review of the evaluation report prior to its submission to the principal. The format for those five sessions will be shaped by the evaluation format chosen by the teacher.

G. If, in the course of those sessions, disagreements arise over what the evaluator perceives to be a problem, each is free to request other members of the faculty to enter the discussion, and even to observe classes. If serious disagreements ensue from the outset, the principal and a faculty member chosen by the teacher may be called in to arbitrate the dispute.

H. The final report submitted to the principal will contain the following items:

1. An assessment of the results of the growth plan for the previous period. There should be some evidence of how involvement in that plan has influenced the teacher's classes.

2. An assessment of the teacher's present performance according to the evaluation format employed during the year. That assessment should contain, but not be limited to, the following: some assessment of the teacher's understanding of the material being taught in class (Is the teacher reflecting current understandings and trends in the field? Is that understanding of the material related to the schoolwide goals?); an assessment of the teacher's responsiveness to the students in the class(es) (Can the teacher talk about the strengths and weakness of each student in the class and how instruction is, at least occasionally, individualized to respond to individual students? Are performance assessments of students fair, challenging, and true tests of the material being taught?); an assessment of the teacher's strengths and how they relate to student learning; an assessment of areas that both evaluator and teacher agree need further work, and how improvements in these areas will strengthen student learning.

3. The evaluator's overall rating of the teacher, listing the reasons for the rating.
4. Additional comments by teacher or evaluator.
5. The teacher's growth plan for the period before the next in-depth evaluation.

I. The evaluation report will be submitted no later than May 1 to the principal, who will review these reports with each teacher during the month of May.

This example illustrates how, in some of the more enlightened schools, periodic summative evaluation is carried on. The system is different from that used for the untenured teacher, and from that for tenured teachers on probation. The tenured teacher participates much more in a professional evaluation process; there are more options; the evaluator and teacher can shape the evaluation to the circumstances of the teacher; there are checks and balances built into the process to protect the teacher.

Supervisors can work in either the formative or the summative process without losing trust with the faculty, as long as the evaluation systems are kept carefully distinct. Figure 16–1 provides an overview of these distinctions. Participa-

FIGURE 16-1   Types of evaluation.

TYPE	Administrative Evaluation	Supervisory Summative Evaluation	Supervisory Formative Evaluation
PURPOSE	• Tenure decisions • Probation decisions • Dismissal decisions	• Periodic, in-depth reflection • Membership renewal • Reappropriation of mission • Assessment of growth	• Ongoing reflective growth
PROCESS	• Legally correct • Highly structured • Highly directive • Either-or criteria • Either-or judgments	• Structured alternatives • Collegial • Checks and balances • Multifaceted	Action research: • Pursuit of growth targets • Staff development workshops • Clinical supervision • Peer coaching • School renewal projects • Networking with regional groups
PRODUCT	Decisions Negative Positive Dismissal Retention	Summative Evaluation Negative Positive Administrative New growth evaluation plan + Formative evaluation	• Reflective practice • Invention • Integration of classroom activities with schoolwide goals • New materials, strategies • New courses

tion in the summative evaluation system will probably cost the supervisor some trust, at least initially, in establishing a formative supervisory relationship with a teacher. During the 3- or 5-year interim period between summative evaluations, teachers will remember the rating that the supervisor gave, but even more important, they will remember that the supervisor has the *power* to give a summative rating. What teachers sometimes forget is that they have voted for such a system and have had a hand in designing it. Unless a teacher receives a superior rating, the tendency is to resent the supervisor who gave the lower rating. The resentment may be diminished if the system is perceived as being as fair and evenhanded as possible.[2]

PROBLEMS WITH SUMMATIVE EVALUATIONS OF TEACHERS

Supervisors need to be aware that there are several unsupportable assumptions about summative evaluation of teachers. Precipitous action based on these assumptions can lead to legitimate grievances against supervisors. Consider the following examples.

Assumption 1. There is a clear set of criteria or standards understood and accepted by all with which a teacher's performance can be evaluated.

Rebuttal. There is no conclusive and incontrovertible research that any specific teacher behavior or any set of teacher behaviors causes learning to take place in any specific student. What evidence there is points to relatively weak correlations between some sets of teacher behaviors and some increase in aggregate scores on tests of basic competency. In these cases there is evidence that teachers teach directly to the test and ignore what is not on the test.[3] This leads to clear distortions in student learnings, as other legitimate learning outcomes are neglected.

Assumption 2. Sporadic, unannounced classroom visits, with no prior conversations and no subsequent discussion, are a legitimate and acceptable way to assess teacher performance.

Rebuttal. The visitor has no understanding of why the teacher is doing what he or she is doing. Until the final judgment, the teacher has no way of knowing what the visitor thinks about what is going on and has no way of changing his or her own behavior, assuming there is agreement that it is inappropriate. There is also the assumption that what the visitor sees is a fair sample of what the teacher tends to do in most classrooms, an assumption not supported by the research.[4]

---

[2]Milbrey Wallin McLaughlin and R. Scott Pfeifer, *Teacher Evaluation: Improvement, Accountability, and Effective Learning.* New York: Teachers College Press, 1988.

[3]See Michael Kirst, "Interview on Assessment Issues with Lorrie Shepard," *Educational Researcher,* vol. 20, no. 2, pp. 21–23, 27; Lorrie A. Shepard, "Why We Need Better Assessments," *Educational Leadership,* vol. 46, no. 7 (April 1989), pp. 4–9.

[4]Susan Stoldowsky, "Teacher Evaluation: The Limits of Looking," *Educational Researcher,* vol. 13, no. 9 (1984), pp. 11–19.

Assumption 3. Student achievement of course objectives is the only way to evaluate teacher performance.

Rebuttal. What is meant by "student achievement"? If it refers to mean aggregate scores on standardized tests, then what really is being measured and who determines what is measured? Even if these tests were accepted as legitimate measures of teachers' and school goals for student learning, a pretest of students' readiness levels would be necessary. Are baseline data available that allow for computation of gains or losses in mean test scores? Even when pre- and postintervention data are available, educators must deal with the mean scores of a group of students. What if the teacher is successful in teaching slower students and not as successful with brighter students, or vice versa? Does that count for nothing? What if the teacher is good at teaching creativity, collaboration, research skills, and artistic criticism, but the tests do not measure student achievement in those areas?

Suppose, on the other hand, that student achievement is evaluated in terms of grades. Suppose the grades range from A to F. Is a teacher rated on his or her ability to increase the number of A students in the class? What if F students improve from a very low F to a very high F? In other words, how much improvement in each student's performance counts for how much in the scale of teacher ratings? Teachers must work with the hands they are dealt; why should one teacher receive a low rating for less than spectacular student achievement when her students are two or three grade levels behind to start with? What if student average daily attendance is abysmal, so that there are rarely the same 12 (out of 27) students in class on any given day, and hence it is impossible to assume any continuity of classroom experience for most of the students? Clearly, evaluations must take many additional, contextual factors into account besides the student achievement of course objectives.

Assumption 4. Evaluation of teacher performance should deal only with observable classroom behaviors.

Rebuttal. This assumption is derived partially from clinical supervision, in which supervisors attempt to avoid subjective judgments by concentrating on observable behaviors, pointing out patterns in both teacher and student behaviors. One of the problems is that this observational posture assumes a separateness from content considerations; for example, it fails to consider whether the teacher was teaching his or her subject matter accurately. Counting the number of times the teacher gives positive or negative feedback, the number of times the teacher calls on the same student, the number of seconds of wait time after a question, the number of times the teacher uses visual displays does not indicate whether the teacher did a good job teaching quadratic equations or the causes of the First World War. Furthermore, the connection between observable teacher behaviors and student achievement on a variety of measures appears tenuous, according to some research evidence.[5]

[5]Michael Scriven, "Can Research-Based Teacher Evaluation Be Saved?" *Journal of Personnel Evaluation in Education,* vol. 4 (1990), pp. 19–32.

These four assumptions do not stand up under rigorous cross-examination. If a supervisor, acting on these assumptions, were to render a recommendation or a decision not to rehire a teacher or not to grant tenure, the supervisor would encounter legal and professional difficulty. Courts have established very clearly that teachers, even beginning teachers, must be given due process. The essence of due process is that teachers know beforehand the criteria or standards as well as the procedures by which they will be evaluated, and that these procedures and standards have in fact been followed. Beyond due process concerns, the very criteria and standards that a school or school system establishes for such evaluation can be challenged.

DUTIES-BASED TEACHER EVALUATION

Michael Scriven has proposed a different set of criteria for summative evaluations of teachers.[6] Claiming that the present criteria for summative evaluation of teachers are not ethically, scientifically, or legally supportable—due to lack of incontrovertible evidence of causality, observer bias, infrequent observations of classroom practice, and lack of other kinds of evidence besides classroom practice—Scriven offers "duties-based evaluation" as the answer.[7] By "duties" he means a list of teacher job specifications that answer the question What is a teacher hired to do? He distinguishes between primary duties (teaching students worthwhile knowledge to the extent of the students' abilities) and secondary duties (talking to parents, supervising corridors or playground, referring students to counselors, etc.). While secondary duties are ancillary to primary duties, they are nonetheless essential. Using duties as the basis for evaluating teachers enables those charged with the administration of the schools to report that teachers are performing the required duties. Figure 16–2 shows Scriven's extensive, detailed list of the teacher's professional duties.

Scriven proposes that multiple sources of evidence be gathered on each of these duties, using more than one evaluator (and more than two if there are discrepancies in the evidence). Over the course of over 5 years, many educators from the United States and Australia developed several drafts of the list, so there is a reasonable claim for the validity of the list, at least for those two countries. To date, however, this list of teacher duties for the purposes of summative evaluation has not been used frequently enough to measure its effectiveness. Nevertheless, the duties-based approach appears to have sufficient merit for school systems to attempt it as an alternative to the present evaluation systems, which Scriven rightly criticizes. A sample of his criticism indicates its persuasiveness. The first relates to the listing of multiple indicators of effective or competent

<hr>

[6]See Michael Scriven, "Evaluating Teachers as Professionals: The Duties-Based Approach," in James Popham (ed.), *Teacher Evaluation: Six Prescriptions for Success*. Alexandria, Va.: Association for Supervision and Curriculum Development, 1988, pp. 110–142.
[7]See Michael Scriven, "Can Research-Based Teacher Evaluation Be Saved?" *Journal of Personnel Evaluation in Education*, vol. 4, no. 1 (1990), pp. 19–32.

1. Knowledge of duties
The teacher is responsible for knowing all the duties for which he or she may be held accountable.

2. Knowledge of school and community
The teacher should understand the special characteristics of the school, its students, and the surrounding environment, in order to shape learning activities that respond to those characteristics.

3. Knowledge of subject matter
The teacher should have adequate and up-to-date knowledge of subjects he or she is hired to teach in order to represent the matter clearly and accurately to the students, as well as in across-the-curriculum subjects such as English, study skills, computer skills, etc.

4. Instruction design
The teacher should be able to develop a detailed course plan; select or create appropriate learning materials and aids; evaluate the impact of the curriculum on students; and respond to special groups of students such as the sensory-impaired, nonnative speakers, etc.

5. Gathering information about student learning
The teacher should be able to construct, administer, and grade a wide variety of student performance appraisals and tests. This includes understanding the relative merits of various testing protocols, and the correct use of various grading procedures.

6. Providing information about student learning
   a) to the student
   b) to the administration
   c) to parents, guardians, and other appropriate authorities

7. Classroom skills
   a) Communication skills
      Teachers should be able to present material clearly and efficiently and maintain student attention.
   b) Management skills
      Teachers should know how to control and direct conditions.

8. Personal characteristics
   a) Professional attitude
      The teacher should conduct himself or herself according to accepted standards of the teaching profession.

b) Professional development
The teacher should engage in self-evaluation and seek to improve in various areas that relate to increased student learning.

9. Service to the profession
The teacher should be knowledgeable about the profession, its history, its present problems, its standards of ethics, and work in service to the profession in one or more of a variety of activities.

FIGURE 16-2 The teacher's professional duties *(Source: Summarized from Michael Scriven, "Evaluating Teachers as Professionals: The Duties-Based Approach," in James Popham (ed.), Teacher Evaluation: Six Prescriptions for Success, Alexandria, Va.: Association for Supervision and Curriculum Development, 1988, pp. 129–134.)*

teaching (as many as 29 in one state evaluation system, as many as 52 in another) as though they made up some organically integrated set.

One cannot fail to be concerned, also, about the problem of combining multiple indicators. Very few of the (research) studies will support general claims about the extent or absence of interactions between the indicators studied, and in the absence of solid evidence on this point, it is not clear that scores on the indicators can be combined to give an additive indication of merit, in the way that is quite common, nor that one can recommend the adoption of one of these aspects of (teaching) style regardless of interactions with other aspects already in place.[8]

Another criticism concerns the use of indicators that have no justification in a teacher's list of duties.

One of the popular entries is the use of advance organizers, provided to the class verbally or in writing. . . . Research has allegedly shown that this activity "characterizes effective teaching." As many of us know from interviews or direct observation, many teachers rated as outstanding by peers, pupils, and principals do not normally use advance organizers, except possibly when visitor/evaluators are present. It's not their style, and they see it as wasting time. They know what they're after, and they jump straight in, letting what they do—and have the class do—speak for itself. Should they be penalized if the evaluator observes or discovers that they do not use this approach? For the duties-based approach, of course, the answer is no, because there is no duty to provide advance organizers, nor does doing so flow from any duty. . . . Does a good teacher become a better teacher by adding this to [his or her] teaching approach and give up the time it takes and the rigidity many teachers say it tends to encourage? Nobody knows, because correlational research doesn't address that question.[9]

[8]Ibid., p. 20.
[9]Ibid., p. 30.

EVALUATION FOR ACCOUNTABILITY AND SCHOOL IMPROVEMENT

Efforts to develop summative evaluation systems in several states seem to falter on some of the same unstable grounds that Scriven points out.[10] Pressured by state legislatures and state departments of education for greater accountability in their use of tax dollars, school systems have attempted to show that they are being accountable, and are working toward improving student learning, by devising teacher assessment systems. As one reads accounts of comments by administrators who use these systems of accountability, it is not difficult to perceive the subtext of the word "accountability," which is "Get rid of incompetent teachers." That message was heard, and many of these new evaluation systems initially focused on establishing defensible standards for doing just that. In many instances, one of the items highlighted in reports to the state was how many incompetent teachers had been identified and induced to resign under the new system.

Influenced by research on effective classrooms, these school systems enlisted the assistance of university-based consultants to help them generate evaluation items directly tied to this research. In the interests of fairness, many of these school systems also instituted ambitious staff-development programs for training in the very skills listed in the evaluation instrument. Teachers who wanted to avoid negative evaluations or whose evaluations pointed out deficiencies could avail themselves of these staff-development opportunities. Through these workshops both teachers and administrators learned a common vocabulary and absorbed a unified view of what constituted acceptable or effective teaching. Teachers felt protected, because they were learning how to get good evaluations. Administrators felt fulfilled because teachers were showing increased attention to "effective" teacher protocols. Because such evaluation schemes and staff-development schemes have been listed in the school renewal literature as comprising "school improvement," administrators could point to their systemwide effort at school improvement effort. Everyone agreed that teachers were the key to improved student learning, and improved student learning was what school improvement was all about. Accountability, effective learning, and school improvement were linked in a neat, logical formula.[11]

A DEEPER LOOK AT STUDENT LEARNING

While there is no doubt that all teachers can improve their effectiveness with students, and no doubt that students can and should be learning more and at a

---

[10]See the case studies reported and analyzed in Milbrey Wallin McLaughlin and R. Scott Pfeifer, *Teacher Evaluation: Improvement, Accountability, and Effective Learning.* New York: Teachers College Press, 1988; see also the theme issue, "Progress in Evaluating Teaching," *Educational Leadership,* vol. 44, no. 7 (April 1987); Penelope L. Peterson and Michelle A. Comeaux, "Evaluating the System: Teachers' Perspectives on Teacher Evaluation," *Educational Evaluation and Policy Analysis,* vol. 12, no. 1 (Spring 1990), pp. 3–24.

[11]McLaughlin and Pfeifer, op. cit., chap. 4.

deeper level of personal appropriation, are these newly devised teacher assessment instruments the primary factor in increased student learnings and improved teacher instructional effectiveness? Or, are there other factors, perhaps
equally as influential on student learnings within the school? As was indicated
in Chapter 7, family background factors have been shown to account for the
greatest variability in student school performance.[12] Looking within the school,
may one say that the teachers' classroom behavior is the single most important
in-school influence on student learning? The research is by no means conclusive
on this question. As studies of mastery learning indicate, students' time on task
seems to be clearly related to student learning as well as students' academic self-
concept or students' sense of self-efficacy. Other studies show that students'
sense of their future, their sense of controlling their own fate or destiny, also influences student learning.

Rather than focus on a one-to-one correspondence between teacher behaviors
and student learning, educators must look at a critical *intervening* variable—the
students' state of mind as they approach the learning task. How motivated are
students to learn the material? Even at the level of an extrinsic motivation of
wanting to get a good grade (regardless of whether the learning holds any personal significance to the student), is getting a good grade valued by this student?
Do students have a sense that getting a good grade, getting promoted, and getting the school diploma are meaningful? Is schooling connected to getting a job?
What kind of job is seen as possible in students' minds? Do students have a sense
that they control their own destiny, that by working hard, by obeying the rules,
they can get ahead in life? Or do they feel that their chances are in the hands of
others, or, worse, are a matter of luck and street smarts, not at all related to the
"stuff" that schools deal with? In other words, if students approach the learning
task with a sense that learning this material really doesn't matter, then whether
the teacher employs 29 or 52 effectiveness protocols, the chances of improved student performance are slim at best.

Besides the teachers' classroom efforts to motivate students to learn, to improve their academic sense of self-efficacy, to engender a sense that they have a
bright future if they apply themselves, the school as an *institutional environment*
must contribute to student motivation and academic self-concept.[13] Is the school
as a totality "user-friendly"? Is it a place where children are respected and cared
for, a place made bright and colorful by the adult community, a place where student performances are on display, where pride and self-esteem are carefully nurtured? Does the whole school environment express a concern that the curriculum be related to students' experiences; that it be seen to have practical

[12]See James S. Coleman et al., *Equality of Educational Opportunity*. Washington D.C.: U.S. Office of
Education, National Center for Educational Statistics, 1966; Christopher Jencks et al., *Inequality: A
Reassessment of the Effects of Family and Schooling in America*. New York: Basic Books, 1972.

[13]See A. S. Bryk and M. E. Driscoll, *An Empirical Investigation of the School as Community*. Chicago:
University of Chicago, Department of Education, 1988; Thomas B. Gregory and Gerald R. Smith,
High Schools as Communities: The Small School Reconsidered. Bloomington, Ind.: Phi Delta Kappa
Educational Foundation, 1987.

applications not only to the world of work but also to the world of family and neighborhood; that learning be seen as involving self-expression, building teamwork, engendering pride in the achievement of student projects; that the curriculum offer quality learning experiences that students will cherish?

Or is the school not user-friendly? Do students get the feeling that their interests and desires do not count in the school environment, that the adults see them as untrustworthy, as the adversary to be controlled, coerced, intimidated, and badgered into learning? Do students perceive the school as a place that demands uniformity, passive conformity, automatic obedience, suppression of spontaneity; as a place of constant correction and punishments or threats of punishment such as grades, demerits, detention, and teachers' sarcastic and humiliating remarks in front of their friends; a place where hall monitors scowl at them, security guards check them into and out of school; a place where the school bell is the enemy, demanding them to get to class, wolf down their food, interrupt an interesting or funny conversation?

Figure 16–3 presents a larger picture of other variables in the school, besides instructional factors, that affect student learning. As shown, the learning environment is an important factor that affects student learning. Teachers do not have complete, or even the major, influence over the learning environment. The general student-adult interaction throughout the school building and grounds communicates a positive or a negative feeling to students. Peer expectations and peer subculture affect the learning environment. School learning may not only not be valued within the peer culture, it may be seen as a kind of "selling out" to the authorities, an act of disloyalty to the group's cohesive resistance to the school authorities. When questions of accountability are raised, they should include the question: What is the school administration doing to create a positive learning environment throughout the school? Without a positive institutional learning environment, an individual teacher cannot be held exclusively accountable for the lack of progress of his or her students.

The same may be said for the influence of the curriculum. There are obvious technical questions about how well the curriculum is put together, its scope and sequence, the authentic relationship of tests and grades to the learning implied in the curriculum. Beyond the technical concerns, there are questions of perceived connections to reality and perceived relevance to students. This does not mean that the curriculum should be watered down to simplistic elements of teen music or video game culture. Rather, learning Shakespeare must have some connection to understanding oneself and one's world. Learning how to read a map of a state or a country can be an exercise in memorizing nonsense or it can be a very exciting journey, enabling students to see connections between rivers and mountains and highways and population and industrial centers. Is the curriculum

FIGURE 16-3   A conceptual model on student outcomes (Source: Joseph Murphy and Phillip Hallinger, "Equity as Access to Learning: Curricular and Instructional Treatment Differences," Journal of Curriculum Studies, vol. 21, no. 3 (1989), p. 132.)

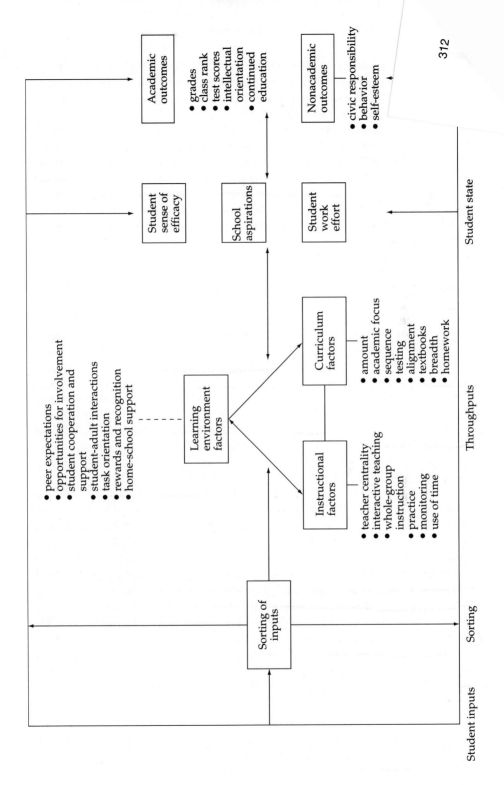

312

viewed as a list of things to be memorized, a collection of right answers, an approved anthology of what others have deemed to be important information? If so, then teachers who use effectiveness protocols may have little success in improving students' academic outcomes.

Any form of teacher assessment that is tied to the rhetoric of accountability is unbalanced, and indeed unfair, if it is not integrated with school assessment. If it is possible to say that the whole school, as a total institution, has done its best to create an environment conducive to student learning, then looking at how teachers capitalize on that or fail to capitalize on that makes eminent professional sense. By the same token, when the institutional framework of the school is inimical to student learning, blaming teachers for inadequate levels of student learning misses the mark.

ASSESSMENT FOR AUTHENTIC STUDENT LEARNING

Mounting evidence indicates that teacher assessment based on lists of classroom effectiveness protocols, when tied to student outcomes on tests, leads teachers to teach to the test. However, although test scores on basic skills rise as a result of these teaching methods, scores *decline* in other academic outcome areas such as writing essays, analytical reading, solving mathematics problems, reasoning in science.[14] This evidence leads to further questions about the wisdom of creating assessment instruments based on effectiveness protocols of teaching. Besides questions raised by Scriven about the research base from which these protocols are derived, and about the logic and validity of combining various protocols as though they were organically related, there are other questions prompted by reflections on the nature of learning itself.

Despite their protestations to the contrary, proponents of teaching effectiveness and teacher assessments based thereon impart a fundamentally passive role to the learner. The learner is to absorb what the teacher is teaching. Through drill and seat exercises, the student acquires sufficient familiarity with the material and with the way the tests solicit information about the material to score well on tests about that material. Defining learning as this kind of ability to absorb instructional material and score well on tests that elicit that absorption is to reduce learning to a model of passive intake and repetition of intake on exams. Teaching then becomes reduced to generating these kinds of student outcomes on examinations.

When students really learn something, they take it inside themselves and relate it to a network of other learnings in a framework of meaning and personal significance; they understand those connections; they are able subsequently to

---

[14]See Linda Darling-Hammond and Arthur E. Wise, "Beyond Standardization: State Standards and School Improvement," *Elementary School Journal*, vol. 85 (1985), pp. 315–335; see also Brian Rowan, "Commitment and Control: Alternative Strategies for the Organizational Design of Schools," in Courtney B. Cazden (ed.), *Review of Research in Education*, vol. 16. Washington D.C.: American Educational Research Association, 1990, pp. 353–389.

retrieve that learning and use it to interpret new material, reconfigure new information, analyze and name new problems, and express a new series of relationships. This kind of learning is not a guaranteed outcome of what a teacher does. The *student* does the learning. Rather than simply respond passively to a stimulus, the student has to internalize the material, look at it, fiddle with it, go back and ask the teacher something about it, come back and fiddle some more. Gradually the student understands how the material works, how it applies, what it means, how it is connected to other things or situations or people. The student does this work. Learning is active, it is constructive, it involves the whole person of the learner—body, intellect, imagination, feelings, memory, present view of the world.

What the teacher does is to try to bring the student to the activity of learning. The teacher cajoles, persuades, entices, threatens, encourages, supports, stimulates, invites, teases, explains, tells interesting stories, describes, demonstrates, suggests, nudges. The most important questions to ask about a teacher's work with students are: Does the teacher bring the student to the activity of learning? Does the teacher get the student to engage the material actively? Does the teacher have the degree of versatility, patience, creativity, persistence, and clarity in using a wide variety of strategies necessary to engender in the student a curiosity about and interest in the material under study? In evaluating teaching, educators must look at student activity and ask: Are students engaged? Is the process of leading them to the material caring, respectful, accepting of their readiness? Is the teacher's activity also challenging, demanding, relentless, so that the students stay with the material? Is the teacher's facilitating activity intelligent, that is, does it encourage students to make connections with larger patterns of meaning? Does the teacher's activity lead student learning toward those larger learning goals of the school's mission statement?

Consistent with our claim that the institutional support of a positive learning environment is critical to student learning, the process of teacher assessment should also include questions such as the following: What kind of home environment are these youngsters coming from? What is their sense of self? What is their sense of efficacy? Are they willing to work, to dig into the material to learn something valuable? What do they aspire to? How do they connect this learning activity with what they consider to be real in their lives, in their futures? Is this classroom reflective of a larger institutional environment that encourages initiative, pride, self-esteem, community, caring about their world? Do youngsters arrive in this classroom with little or no sense that the work expected of them has any intrinsic meaning or value to them? The answers to these questions should provide the person performing the summative evaluation of a teacher with some perception of the chances for success in that teaching/learning endeavor. If youngsters begin that endeavor with no feeling of support from the institutional environment and with feelings of alienation and conflict toward that environment, then that should be noted at the beginning of the teacher's assessment. Administrators, in the process of reviewing such assessments, should take note of the grade the institution receives for promoting a learning environment.

If assessment is to be linked to student learning and to school improvement, then the teacher assessment must include an assessment of the students' state as they approach the learning activity, as noted in Figure 16–3. The evaluator should try to discover whether and in what direction that state is influenced primarily by the teacher or primarily by the institutional environment. When both the institutional environment and the teacher's activities simultaneously and conjointly communicate positive support for students' motivation, sense of efficacy, and connectedness to real life, the evaluator should note how the interface works to increase student learning. When the institutional environment and teacher efforts are at odds, teachers and evaluators should discuss what needs to be done.

SUMMARY

In this chapter we explored the controversial topic of teacher evaluation. From the start we situated teacher evaluation within the context of the school as a community of learners. Summative evaluation relates to decisions about membership in that community and to ways the community can honor outstanding contributions. Summative evaluations can be used to make various personnel decisions. In cases of possible termination of teacher contracts, these evaluations lead to administrative processes. We also looked at examples of summative evaluations for periodic assessment of tenured teachers. These examples provided maps of the terrain of summative evaluation. We then considered what might legitimately constitute standards for summative teacher evaluations. Michael Scriven offers one approach, which seems to avoid the pitfalls of many systems in use in the schools. We suggested that student learnings are as much influenced by institutional supports for a positive learning environment as they are by teachers' activities. Assessment of teachers should not be carried on independently from institutional assessment. Furthermore, a deeper look at what is meant by student learning provided a different base for constructing a different set of questions to ask in a system of summative teacher evaluation.

Because summative evaluation relates to the members of a community deciding whom to admit, whom to retain, and whom to honor for enhancing that community, the process often is hindered by adversarial and legal considerations. Ideally, summative evaluation should be used to identify and celebrate extraordinary contributions to the learning community.

FOUR

A LOOK TO THE FUTURE

CHAPTER 17

SUPERVISION AND THE RENEWAL OF SCHOOLS

Supervisors would not, in the minds of teachers, superintendents, policy-makers, and critics, be the ones expected to start a revolution in schools. They are traditionally seen as those who oversee the appropriate implementation of new policies or the following of standard operating procedures. In the discussions over restructuring schools, the focus has been on the state legislature and state department of education to legislate major changes, or on the teachers at the school site who will participate in site-based change efforts. In either case, supervisors are not considered as major sources for change. In the state-initiated teacher assessment programs, supervisors have been called in as players in implementing those initiatives, but they have had little to say in forming the policies.

If supervisors are to play a significant part in the renewal of schools, they will have to move beyond their traditional roles of working within the given environment to exercising leadership in the transformation of that environment. The process of supervision, whether exercised by a department chair, an assistant principal, a principal, or a district supervisor, has to be seen as requiring more than seeing that the job is done according to standard criteria. The supervisory process has to be seen as an intellectual process of "reimagining" the learning situation, of reimagining the learning environment of the classroom and of the school. The reimagining, of course, will be done with teachers and administrators as they work together on problems of practice. The supervisor needs to come to that task with a moral commitment to move the activity of teachers, students,

317

and administrators beyond a technical rendition and acceptance of services to the activity of a community that is bound together by common values and meanings.

Those who engage in supervision have a unique perspective to bring to the job of school renewal. Supervising brings the supervisor into contact with many teachers, with many classrooms, with many different groups of students whose varied approaches to the demands of learning may be strikingly different. The supervisor's view is larger than the individual teacher's view. It is larger because the supervisor sees many teachers, all of whom exhibit different talents and who express their approaches to the design of learning activities differently. It is larger because the supervisor moves back and forth between different institutional levels of administration and policy and therefore has a better sense of the whole school than any individual teacher.

Moreover, the supervisor is closer to the realities of the classroom and of student engagement with or resistance to the learning tasks than are school administrators who do not exercise supervisory responsibilities. The supervisor can speak as an advocate for students and for teachers in discussions with administrators about making the school environment more "user-friendly." The supervisor, in short, is the one person whose work is involved with all levels of the school, or at least with most of them.

Because of these contacts with a variety of people in the school, the supervisor is in a unique position to articulate a new vision of teaching and learning, to bring a super-vision to the discussions with various school personnel. One might say that the supervisor is potentially the primary reflective practitioner in the school; besides reflecting with individual teachers, and with groups of teachers (in departmental level or grade level meetings), the supervisor reflects with administrators and district personnel about staff-development programs, curriculum redesign, and resource allocation in administrative staff meetings. The supervisor is in an ideal position to be a carrier of ideas, a conduit of new thinking, a mapmaker who can help teachers and administrators reconceptualize the terrain of their work.

People who supervise usually have two or three additional responsibilities. Sometimes supervision is considered the least important task in the supervisor's job description. Yet, were the supervisor to reconceptualize supervisory work as a central activity for school renewal and make supervision the centerpiece of his or her work, it might enable a better integration of the other tasks. More specifically, how might that role be worked out in practice?

INTELLECTUAL AND MORAL DIMENSIONS OF SUPERVISORY LEADERSHIP

First, supervisors would need to see the leadership possibilities in the supervisory process, see it as involved in the *educational* mission of the school, rather than as a bureaucratic activity fulfilling bureaucratic demands for control and record keeping. Supervisors would need to appreciate the intellectual dimension of their work. As professionals who have studied the complexities of teaching and learning and human motivation and curriculum design, they should be conversing with other educational professionals about how to make the schools work better for youngsters. Besides being diagnosticians of instructional performances, they should be diagnosticians of curriculum units, of student readiness for learning, of the learning environment within the school, and, perhaps most important, they must be diagnosticians of the community, sensing when it is sick and what might restore its health. That is intellectual work. Supervisors are perhaps better positioned than most to reimagine how the parts might work together more effectively.

Supervisors also need to appreciate the moral foundation of their authority as supervisors. That authority derives from the shared values held by the community. When the school is not a community but simply a legally constituted organization that provides services to clients—much the way a hospital does to patients or an automotive shop does to car owners—then the authority of the supervisor remains predominantly at the legal and technical level. When a school is a community, youngsters are happy to go there in the morning; such cannot be said for hospital patients or car owners on their way to their respective institutions.

In the school as a learning community, supervisors' moral authority is based on the trust that youngsters and teachers place in them to care for them, to respect and honor the integrity of each of them, as they engage in the demanding pursuit of the mission of the school. As a community their common mission is to explore and understand their past and their present, understand their natural and human environment so they can preserve and enhance it through their intelligent labor, understand themselves and their mutual responsibilities to each other, and understand the difficult but fulfilling challenge of communal self-governance. Within that mission, teachers are committed to nurture the intellectual, social, and personal growth of every youngster. Within that mission supervisors are committed to support and enhance the teachers' work with the youngsters, and to facilitate and enhance those institutional supports for the community's task of learning. There is a moral expectation, then, for supervisors to maintain a super-vision of what the school is supposed to be; a moral expectation that they will remind teachers and students and administrators, gently, diplomatically, but firmly, of that vision; a moral expectation that they will work with members of the community to enhance the community's commitment to its mission. This implies an intrinsically moral leadership in school renewal.

A TRANSITION FROM BUREAUCRATIC TO ORGANIC MANAGEMENT

This view of supervisory leadership, however, typically assumes that it will be exercised within the present hierarchic, bureaucratic management of school systems. A more decentralized management of schools is already being tried in various cities and states in what has come to be known as restructuring, or site-based management and participatory decision making. Centralized bureaucratic management still provides the larger umbrella of authority, but where decisions involve the actual teaching-learning process, teachers have a greater say.

As it becomes more apparent that teaching is a complex technology exercised in rather fluid classroom contexts, it likewise becomes apparent that teachers should have the autonomy and authority to decide what is best to do in any given circumstance, rather than having to respond to bureaucratic policies and rules that assign a decontextualized uniformity and simplicity to teaching and learning. In other words, schools are moving toward more organic processes of management in order to enable those with the expertise to make those practical decisions needed to respond to the fluctuating and unpredictable situations in schooling. Organic management is beginning to replace some of the bureaucratic, hierarchic management. Instead of pervasive, centralized bureaucratic authority that controls the teaching-learning process through standardized operational procedures and uniform measures of input and output, small clusters of professional authority are emerging in schools where groups of professionals are deciding how best to promote learning.

Central office administration of school systems will continue, but probably with a reduced central office staff of supervisors and program directors. As more and more authority is transferred to local schools, more discretion over the allocation of resources will flow to the individual school. Various central office functions may remain, especially those that provide economies of scale. State departments of education, on the other hand, may remain rather sizable, and perhaps increase, as state legislatures increase their effort to improve education throughout each state.

Granting that most school systems have a long way to go in organic management at the school site, suppose for the moment that this way of managing schools were to become a major force in most school systems. In such redesigned schools, would there be any place for supervisors? The answer is that we really do not know. We can speculate, though, that supervision in these redesigned schools, if present at all, would be quite different from what it is today. Supervisors would probably function much more in a resource capacity, as facilitators of networking, as troubleshooters, as the ones who, after brainstorming and discussing among teachers, may be designated by the teachers to come up with a tentative redesign of a curriculum or a learning space or a series of comprehensive student performance assessments.

There is some evidence that even teachers who have had good experiences with site-based management find the time spent at planning and coordination meetings a heavy burden, one that distracts them from their teaching responsibilities. While they find the sharing of information about their work rewarding, they are less enthusiastic about having to spend so much time on administrative procedures. Supervisors may have some role in relieving teachers of these burdens.

Various staffing differentiations among teachers have been promoted, such as lead teacher or head teacher or mentor. Much of the work of these positions involves coaching and mentoring beginning teachers, running staff-development programs, working with probationary teachers. In other words, some teachers have been largely removed from classroom responsibilities to deal with instructional matters and professional growth matters. These teachers appear to be the ones who will do much of what supervisors used to do, except that they are not viewed as part of the administration—at least not yet.

Between the present, more traditional organization of schools and school systems and the future, redesigned school and school systems, there is much that those who exercise supervisory leadership can do. Precisely as schools struggle to make the transition, supervisory personnel can arbitrate the disagreements and misunderstandings that arise between administrators and teachers. As both groups grope toward redefining their respective authority within the school, supervisors can serve as brokers and mediators, bringing to the attention of both the overriding mission they are supposed to be pursuing, namely the education of youngsters. Supervisors could be the primary spokespersons for the community as it experiences the strains of realignment of roles and responsibilities.

There is also another crucial task for supervisors in these efforts at school reform, and it involves a greater attention to a significant segment of the community that has been overlooked during the national flurry over school reform, namely, the students. Most of the discussion about granting teachers greater autonomy over instructional matters seems to imply that that autonomy will be exercised in classrooms and schools as they are currently structured, without questioning whether such structures are obstacles to student learning.

Few people are asking whether the learning environments in schools as they are presently structured are stimulating, flexible, and supportive, or whether students learn what they do *in spite of* spaces and time schedules and curriculum units that *inhibit* their learning potential. Moreover, few are analyzing the passive position most students must assume in relationship to adults in schools. They are told what to do, when to do, how to do, and what they definitely should *not* do. They rarely encounter teachers who are interested in what they think, what they dream about, what they fear. Students encounter a massive effort of most adults in the school to get them to pay attention to their agenda, with little concern whether that agenda has even the remotest connection to the youngsters' experience of life.

Traditionally supervisors have the responsibility to work with teachers to improve their instruction, with the assumed goal, of course, of enhancing student learning. Both supervisors and teachers, in this traditional conception of supervision, rarely discuss the students' state of mind as they approach the learning task. It is as though by focusing on the clearer presentation of the subject matter, or the use of various media representations, or the dividing of the class into work groups, there will be some automatic increase in learning in students who have been generalized into a group mind. If teachers can just get the instruction right, the group mind, sitting there awaiting enlightenment, will absorb the new knowledge.

More detailed studies of learning, however, show it to be a much more complex and individualized process affected as much by the youngsters' emotional state—their self-image, their sense of efficacy and control over the future, their life history and the residue of affect attached to words and images—as it is by what appears to be a more absolute trait of intelligence. Learning, then, is a highly contextualized matter. The state of mind youngsters bring into the classroom or to learning activities assigned outside the classroom very much determines the quality of the learning. Hence both teachers and supervisors need to give much more attention to the frame of mind youngsters are in when they face a learning task, and attempt to deal with features of that frame of mind that inhibit readiness for engaging in the learning activity. Obviously, in settings of group instruction and group learning activities, complete awareness of each student's frame of mind in each hour of the school day is impossible. Insofar as they have some control over the learning environment, however, educators can remove from the environment those features that have a negative impact on the feelings and self-image of the student.

It is here that the supervisor may have a major role to play. If the supervisor sees the school as needing to be a *community* for it to maximize student growth and to maximize the potential of teachers to stimulate that growth, then the supervisor can make the promotion of community a centerpiece of his or her supervision. In a school environment that promotes community, youngsters are more likely to feel cared for and respected. In a learning community environment they are more likely to be invited to explore the subject matter *with* the teacher, rather than experience academic work as something indifferently pressed upon them with warnings about the dire consequences of failing to do the assignment. In a learning community, students' questions are more likely to be given a sensitive hearing and an honest answer. In a learning community, knowledge will more likely be seen as a precious heritage of the community, rather than as property to be accumulated by individuals in a competition for scarce rewards. In other words, the environment of a learning community will affect the state of mind students bring to the learning tasks. Within the context of a learning community, supervisors can indeed work with teachers in exploring better ways to engage the students in this or that unit of learning, but the focus on the teaching protocol will also include attentiveness to the students' frame of mind.

The first wave of school reform focused on mechanisms of control: bureaucratic mandates for more courses, longer school days and years, more rigorous tests, and enforcement of nonpromotion policies. The second wave of school reform emphasized increasing the commitment of teachers to improving their instruction: By stressing their professional expertise, teachers were to be given greater autonomy and authority over decisions affecting the teaching-learning process. But few have talked about the need to increase *students'* commitment to the learning task. To be sure, there are stories in the literature about principals who constantly exhort students to improve their grades, to stay focused on their academic tasks. But these exhortations are simply part of the external control apparatus, linked with grades, class ranks, promotion, and graduation criteria. Nothing there about the intrinsic worth of learning something well; nothing about the connections between what they are learning and understanding themselves and their world; nothing about the awesome collective responsibility they have to understand their world, since they will be running it in the future; nothing there about the excitement of exploring the world with others, of coming into contact with the soaring of the human spirit in the humanities and the sciences; in short, no super-vision of learning, no super-vision of a learning community.

The various attempts at school renewal will fall short of their goal unless there is greater attention to nurturing a positive frame of mind among learners. Supervisors and teachers working together can begin to transform the learning environment into a more user-friendly environment, into an environment that communicates caring and respect for each student, into an environment supportive of a community of learners. That remains a primary intellectual and moral challenge of supervisory leadership. That is what all these chapters have centered around: attention to climate and culture, motivation and platform, curriculum and assessment, clinical supervision, reflective practice, staff development.

These concerns all affect how the learning community manages its affairs in the pursuit of its super-vision of schooling. If supervision is not to be left on the sidelines passively watching the spectacle of school reform, but, rather, to play a significant part in school renewal, then it must take up the intellectual and moral challenge of promoting this super-vision of what the school can become—an authentic community of learners.

INDEX

INDEX